The Melancholy of Race

RACE AND AMERICAN CULTURE
Arnold Rampersad and Shelley Fisher Fishkin
General Editors

THE MELANCHOLY OF RACE

Anne Anlin Cheng

OXFORD
UNIVERSITY PRESS

2000

OXFORD
UNIVERSITY PRESS

Oxford   New York
Athens   Auckland   Bangkok   Bogota   Bombay
Buenos Aires   Calcutta   Cape Town   Dar es Salaam
Delhi   Florence   Hong Kong   Istanbul   Karachi
Kuala Lumpur   Madras   Madrid   Melbourne
Mexico City   Nairobi   Paris   Shanghai   Singapore
Taipei   Tokyo   Toronto

and associated companies in
Berlin   Ibadan

Published by Oxford University Press, Inc.
198 Madison Avenue, New York, New York 10016

Oxford is a registered trademark of Oxford University Press

Library of Congress Cataloging-in-Publication Data
Cheng, Anne Anlin.
The melancholy of race / Anne Anlin Cheng.
p. cm. — (Race and American culture)
ISBN 0-19-513403-6
1. United States—Race relations—Psychological aspects.   2. National characteristics,
American.   3. Melancholy in literature.   4. Melancholy in art.   5. Minorities in
literature.   6. Minorities in art.   7. American literature—Asian American authors—
History and criticism.   8. American literature—Afro-American authors—
History and criticism.   9. Asian American arts—Psychological aspects.
10. American arts—Psychological aspects.   I. Title.   II. Series.
E184.A1 C4455 2001
305.8'00973—dc21   00-026833

1 3 5 7 9 8 6 4 2

Printed in the United States of America
on acid-free paper

to Stephen and Mei-Yin Cheng
for their courage

Grieving is a pattern that is cut
and fitted around my mind.
     —*Elektra*, Sophocles
        translated by Anne Carson

Grievances are a form of impatience.
Griefs are a form of patience.
     —Robert Frost

PREFACE

In the 1930s, social psychologists Kenneth and Mamie Clark conducted a series of experiments—the by now famous "doll tests"—designed to study how African American children perceive racial difference, if at all. In interview after interview, when given the choice, the majority of the African American children, including three-year-olds, found the brown dolls to be "bad" and preferred instead to play with the "good," white dolls. Several of the children went on to identify the white dolls as the ones "most like themselves." The kids not only displayed an awareness of racial difference but also appeared to have processed the symbolic values of that difference: that white dolls connote "whiteness" and that whiteness connotes security and probity. In Kenneth Clark's words, what was most difficult for the adults to witness was in fact the depth of these children's understanding:

> We were really disturbed by our findings, and we sat on them for a number of years. . . . Some of these children . . . were reduced to crying when presented with the dolls and asked to identify with them. They looked at me as if I were the devil for putting them in this predicament. Let me tell you, it was a traumatic experience for me as well.[1]

Clark's consternation at the moral and political implications of his findings pales by comparison with the polemics that followed this research. As many readers will recognize, this experiment was the key but explosive evidence in the landmark case to desegregate America, *Brown v. Board of Education* (1954).

In 1970, Toni Morrison will revisit this drama in her novel *The Bluest Eye*, which tells the story of a black girl living in segregated America in the late thirties who prayed every night for God to make her brown eyes blue and whose mother reserved her tenderness for the blond, blue-eyed children she was hired to tend. And in 1975, in a different ethnic tradition, Maxine Hong Kingston will describe in her contemporary novel *The*

Woman Warrior a scene in which her child narrator stands in a deserted school bathroom physically abusing another Asian American child who reminds her of herself. Thus more than twenty years after Dr. Clark testified that "this type of [racial] wound stays raw for a life time,"[2] it would seem that the "wound" endures, not only in the individual psyche but in the American national psyche as well, inherited across time and even across racial groups.

Yet the status of that "wound"—along with *Brown*'s legal and socio-psychological implications—remains contested and ambivalent to this day. What the *Brown* legacy shares with these two literary instances is not mere thematics but a profound quandary over the construction of social meaning and its subjective impact at the site of racial injury. And behind that quandary lies a broader question: What kind of a social claim can the psyche make at all?

We are a nation at ease with grievance but not with grief. It is reassuring (and requires less patience, as Frost says) to believe in the efficacy of grievance in redressing grief. Yet if grievance is understood to be the social and legal articulation of grief, then it has also been incapable of addressing those aspects of grief that speak in a different language—a language that may seem inchoate because it is not fully reconcilable to the vocabulary of social formulation or ideology but that nonetheless cuts a formative pattern. This study is interested in uncovering these interior patterns of grief and how they both constrain and are constrained by subjectivity.

How a racially impugned person *processes* the experience of denigration exposes a continuous interaction between sociality and privacy, history and presence, politics and ontology. These intersecting spheres hold debilitating and productive implications for the study of race. On the one hand, anyone who has been confronted by racism face to face understands the complicated, vexing web of feelings that ensues: shock mixed with expectation, anger with shame, and yet again shame for feeling shame. This book is intent on examining the intricacy and the afterlife of these contradictions. Though a difficult topic and thus rarely discussed, the social and subjective formations of the so-called racialized or minority subject are intimately tied to the psychical experience of grief. This psychical experience is not separate from the realms of society or law but is the very place where the law and society are processed. Even as racism actualizes itself through legal and social sanctions, it is *animated* through imaginative procedures. On the other hand, that psychical experience cannot be reduced to a mere replication or a fully compliant repository for social injunction. We need to take on the task of acknowledging racial grief in a theoretically and socially responsible way. A sustained focus on the intangible wounds that form the fissures underneath visible phenomena of discrimination should be taking place *in addition to*, not in the place of, the work of advocacy.

This book grows out of this need to find an intellectually rigorous vocabulary to talk about racial grief, not as merely a symptom but as an analytical paradigm responsive to the material *and* imaginative realities of racial dynamics. I begin by turning to Freud's formulation of melancholia, and I use his insights into grief as a springboard from which to construct a model of what I call "racial melancholia." I then take this theoretical paradigm as a critical basis for unpacking the fragility and bravado that haunt American national integrity. Specifically, I am interested in how racial melancholia tracks a dynamic of rejection and internalization that may help us comprehend two particular aspects of American racial culture: first, dominant, white culture's rejection of yet attachment to the racial other and, second, the ramifications that such paradox holds for the racial other, who has been placed in a suspended position. I will suggest that racial melancholia is both the technology and the nightmare of the American Dream.

This study contends that racial melancholia affects both dominant white culture and racial others; indeed, racial melancholia describes the dynamics that constitute their mutual definition through exclusion. The terms thus denote a complex process of racial rejection and desire on the parts of whites and nonwhites that expresses itself in abject and manic forms. On the one side, white American identity and its authority is secured through the melancholic introjection of racial others that it can neither fully relinquish nor accommodate and whose ghostly presence nonetheless guarantees its centrality. On the other side, the racial other (the so-called melancholic object) also suffers from racial melancholia whereby his or her racial identity is imaginatively reinforced through the introjection of a lost, never- possible perfection, an inarticulable loss that comes to inform the individual's sense of his or her own subjectivity. Already we see that these two "sides" are in fact implicated by one another.

This study explores the consequences of this insight for studies of raced subjects. The model of melancholic incorporation, far from prescribing or reifying the conditions of the racial other, reveals an intricate world of psychical negotiation that unsettles the simplistic division between power and powerlessness. I argue that these seemingly discouraging recognitions into the dynamics of racialization may in fact provide the seed for revising political thinking in ways that may finally be more powerful than denying or sentimentalizing affective history. The model of melancholia can help us comprehend grief and loss on the part of the aggrieved, not just as a symptom but also as a dynamic process with both coercive and transformative potentials for political imagination. In this project, racial melancholia serves not as a description of the feeling of a group of people but as a theoretical model of identity that provides a critical framework for analyzing the constitutive role that grief plays in racial/ethnic subject-formation.

This is by no means an exhaustive or definitive book on race relations. Rather, I ask questions that I believe we need to consider, and I raise certain lines of inquiry that have been foreclosed out of either political expediency or fear. This project is also a personal effort to clarify some of the more contradictory psychical dynamics informing my own immigrant experience. Coming to America at age twelve, I had many lessons to learn beyond the linguistic one, including finding my own relation to the terms "American" and then, later, "Asian American." Immigrating when I was almost an adult protected me from certain experiences of social exclusion (since the immigrant has the comfort of imagining she cannot be excluded from that to which she never belonged), but such consolation is already an act of psychical management. It is the foreigner within me who most eagerly needs to understand the web of American racial dynamics and their particular articulations of aspiration and rejection, assimilation and expulsion.

CONTENTS

The Melancholy of Race

THE MELANCHOLY OF RACE

Quantifying Grief

How does an individual go from being a subject of grief to being a subject of grievance? What political and psychical gains or losses transpire in the process?

This transformation from grief to grievance, from suffering injury to speaking out against that injury, has always provoked profound questions about the meaning of hurt and its impact. Although it may seem that the existence of racial injury in this country is hardly debatable, it is precisely at moments when racial injury is most publicly pronounced that its substance and tangibility come most stringently into question. The struggle to translate racial grief into social claims, for instance, formed a central drama in the desegregation of the nation. Arguably the most momentous Supreme Court ruling in United States history, *Brown v. Board of Education*[1] (1954) overturned the Court's 1896 decision in *Plessy v. Ferguson*, which upheld Jim Crow laws through the chimera of "separate but equal" public accommodations and institutions for blacks and whites. It was the moment when American apartheid gave way. In his effort to challenge *Plessy v. Ferguson* and to argue that "separate is inherently unequal" even if the facilities are materially equal, NAACP lawyer Thurgood Marshall enlisted the help of social psychologists Kenneth and Mamie Clark, whose work focused on the detrimental effects of racism on children of color.

The use of psychological evidence had been introduced into the courts by the turn of the century, but Marshall's use of it was a gamble.[2] As Marshall warned Clark, whatever psychological evidence they gathered had "to *prove* damage."[3] The social psychologists assembled by Kenneth Clark to write the document entitled "The Effect of Segregation and the Consequences of Desegregation—A Social Science Statement," which served as

an appendix to Marshall's oral argument, struggled through painstaking revisions, haunted by several problems, not the least of which were the very
definition of the term "damage," the quantification of grief, and the translation of so-called scientific data into social meaning.[4] Indeed, in court, the
appellees' brief asserted that the "Finding of Fact" on the part of the appellants
presented no fact at all but "broad and general conclusions" that could not
prove "actual personal harm" or the deprivation of quantifiable benefits.[5]

actual
vs.
imagined
harm

   Yet in an astounding response, the Supreme Court turned away from the
sole authority of constitutional history (finding the history of the debates
surrounding the Fourteenth Amendment "inconclusive" and insufficient to
the question at hand) and drew instead from the very evidence that had
seemed eccentric. Chief Justice Earl Warren specifically cited the "authority" of the social psychologists and the "Social Science Statement" as a de-
cisive factor in the ruling to overturn *Plessy v. Ferguson*, concurring with
Marshall's argument that "separate is inherently unequal." The opinion of
the Court reads:

> Our decision . . . *cannot turn on merely a comparison of . . . tangible factors*
> in the Negro and white schools involved in each of these cases. We must
> look instead to the *effect* of segregation itself on public education. . . .

> *Does segregation of children in public schools solely on the basis of race,*
> *even though the physical facilities and other "tangible" factors may be*
> *equal, deprive the children of minority groups of equal educational op-*
> *portunities? We believe that it does.* . . .

> To separate [minority children] from others of similar age and qualifica-
> tions solely because of their race generates a feeling of inferiority as to
> their status in the community that may *affect their hearts and minds* in a
> way unlikely ever to be undone.[6]

This decision is momentous for many reasons, but one of those reasons must
be the expansion in the notion of justice to accommodate the "intangible"
effects of racism. The original *Brown* ruling then may be said to be an unprecedented judgment about the necessity of examining the invisible but
tenacious aspect of racism—of allowing racial grief to have its say even if it
cannot definitively speak in the language of material grievance.

   This receptivity proved to have lasting legal and philosophical ramifications—both positive and threatening—for segregationists and liberals alike.
This attention to the "hearts and minds" of raced subjects has taken on many
contradictory nuances in the years since. Almost a decade after the pivotal
decision in *Brown v. Board*, the same evidence resurfaces in another class
action suit—this time, on behalf of white southern segregationists. In 1963
in Savannah, Georgia, a suit (*Stell v. Savannah-Chatham County Board of*

Education) was filed by African American parents against the Chatham County Board of Education for conducting "biracial" education; that is, the county had integrated black and white children in the schools but not in the classrooms. A group of white parents joined the defense as supporting intervenors and, in a surprising move, cited the social psychology evidence from the *Brown* case as an argument *for* segregation, contending that segregation will grant black children the opportunity to develop a stronger, "healthier," more independent black identity.[7] These "intervenors" (that is, a third party, not named in a case, that offers evidence on the grounds that its interests are involved) brought in further psychological evidence contending that "major differences exist in the learning ability patterns of white and Negro children," hence the benefit of separate education for both black and white children.[8] This line of argument advanced by the white segregationists aimed to transform psychical damage as the result of social injury into a notion of inherent disability. The initially liberating concept of psychical injury from the *Brown* case has suddenly taken on the unsavory look of racist weapon. Within this new context, the last clause of Chief Justice Warren's statement about racist effects (as "unlikely ever to be undone") started to resound with different aftereffects. In short, we were witnessing the beginnings of the slip from *recognizing* to *naturalizing* injury.[9]

In this brief history we see all the urgencies and complications surrounding formulations of racial injury. The debate continues today. In Austin Sarat's words, *Brown* was "at once a turning point and a source of resistance, a point of pride and an object of vilification"(5). The legacy of *Brown* in the fields of law, sociology, psychology, and advocacy continues to change as the case gets narrated and renarrated in these disciplines.[10] Contemporary scholars in race studies have come to join researchers in social science and psychology to challenge the scientific legitimacy of Clark's methods and to critique, at times stridently, his conclusions (for example, James Alsbrook, H. S. Ashmore, Leon Jones, Judith Porter and Robert Washington, Gloria Powell-Hopson, and Austen Sarat). Others have emphasized the resiliency of minority group members in the face of discrimination (Harriette McAdoo). African Americans in the seventies, for example, were encouraged to internalize the Black Is Beautiful credo and to fight actively against discrimination rather than to permit the degradation of the self. While this urge to reclaim racial beauty has always seemed to say more about the keenness of the hurt than a cure, it is even more disturbing to find certain leftist, antiassimilation advocates today speaking from a position that eerily echoes racist enunciations: the rhetoric of solidarity speaking in the rhetoric of isolation.[11]

An equal amount of work has reiterated both Clark's original line of investigation and his findings. Sociologists and psychologists over the years have continued to expand and conduct versions of the Clark doll test, suggesting that the question of psychical injury remains a pressing one.[12] As recently as August 1999, the *Atlantic Monthly* published the work of social psychologist Claude M. Steele, who, in researching the relationship between the self-perception of black college students and their "inferior" academic performance, was anxious not to repeat the damage hypothesis even as he asserted that material factors such as socioeconomic differences are not the only or even primary culprits. Steele refines the idea of psychological impact: what he calls the "stereotype threat" that haunts African American students and inevitably accompanies and hinders their performances.[13]

Racial ideals continue to drive those most oppressed by it. Even market researchers have become invested in this question of racial preference. In 1995 the *Boston Herald* featured an article on the toy giant Mattel, who spent millions of dollars in market research and new product development only to find, as the article muses, what Kenneth Clark could have told them nearly fifty years ago: that African American (and other ethnic) children, given the chance, would rather play with a blond, blue-eyed Barbie than dolls that "look more like themselves."[14] In African American communities, skin lightening cream has enjoyed a long and profitable history. (One of the first black millionaires in America, A'leila Walker, was heiress to a fortune made in black hair straighteners and skin lightening cream.)[15] In 1996 Linda Brown, for whom the celebrated *Brown* case was named, filed another suit against the same Topeka school system her parents filed against over forty years before.[16] In a sense, the drama of *Brown v. Board* and those dolls has been repeatedly reenacted in the last four decades across America in courtrooms, in classrooms, in boardrooms, and in homes.

My intention here is not to privilege the Clark experiment as correct or to prove white preference but to direct attention to the facts that racial preference and its inverse have persisted as an interpretive and ideologically invested question. Moreover, we hardly know how to confront the psychical imprints of racial grief except through either neglect or sentimentalization. Part of the problem has to do with how we understand social healing and the tendency to rely on exclusively material or quantifiable terms to articulate that injury. The vocabulary of grievance (and its implied logic of comparability and compensation) that constitutes so much of American political discourse has ironically deflected attention away from a serious look at the more immaterial, unquantifiable repository of public and private grief that has gone into the making of the so-called minority subject and that sustains the notion of "one nation."

The prospect of integrating a history of fierce difference, social injustice, and psychical injury into one nation has proven to be one of the more unyielding tasks of social progress. Our first lesson must be to not mistake an attention to the psychical for essentialization. Both essentializing and denying the deep psychological impact of discrimination are equally troubling.

There are still deep-seated, intangible, psychical complications for people living within a ruling episteme that privileges that which they can never be. This does *not* at all mean that the minority subject does not develop other relations to that injunctive ideal which can be self-affirming or sustaining but rather that a painful negotiation must be undertaken, at some point if not continually, with the demands of that social ideality, the reality of that always-insisted-on difference. Beneath the reductionist, threatening diagnosis of "inferiority complex" or "white preference" there runs a fraught network of ongoing psychical negotiation instigated and institutionalized by racism. The connection between subjectivity and social damage needs to be formulated in terms more complicated than either resigning colored people to the irrevocability of "self-hatred" or denying racism's profound, lasting effects.

If one traditional method of restitution has been the conversion of the disenfranchised person from being subjected to grief to being a subject speaking grievance, what are the advantages and disadvantages of that transformation? What can political agency mean for someone operating in a symbolic, cultural economy that has already preassigned them as a deficit? The contemporary American attachment to progress and healing, eagerly anticipating a colorblind society, sidesteps the important examination of racialization: How is a racial identity secured? How does it continue to generate its seduction for both the dominant and the marginalized? And what are the repercussions, both historical and personal, of that ongoing history? While much critical energy has been directed toward deconstructing categories such as gender and race, less attention has been given to the ways in which individuals and communities remain invested in maintaining such categories, even when such identities prove to be prohibitive or debilitating. The rhetoric of progress or cure can produce its own blind spots. As Christopher Lasch puts it, "[a] denial of the past, superficially progressive and optimistic, proves on closer analysis to embody the despair of a society that cannot face the future."[17] And when it comes to the future of the race question, to borrow Faulkner's words, the past is not dead; it is not even past. Rather than prescribing how we as a nation might go about "getting over" that history, it is useful to ask what it means, for social, political, and subjective beings *to grieve*.

Melancholic Formations

In 1917, Freud wrote an essay, "Mourning and Melancholia," which proposes two different kinds of grief.[18] According to Freud, "mourning" is a healthy response to loss; it is finite in character and accepts substitution (that is, the lost object can be relinquished and eventually replaced). Mourning is healthy because, Freud tells us, "we rest assured that after a lapse of time, it will be overcome" (*MM*, 240). "Melancholia," on the other hand, is pathological; it is interminable in nature and refuses substitution (that is, the melancholic cannot "get over" loss.)[19] The melancholic is, one might say, psychically stuck. As Freud puts it, "[i]n grief [mourning] the world becomes poor and empty; in melancholia it is the ego itself." Melancholia thus denotes a condition of endless self-impoverishment.

Curiously, however, this impoverishment is also nurturing. In fact, Freud describes melancholia as a kind of consumption:

> An object-choice, an attachment of the libido to a particular person, had at one time existed; then, owing to a real slight or disappointment coming from this loved person, the object-relationship was shattered. The result was not the normal one of a withdrawal of the libido from this object and a displacement of it on to a new one, but something different. . . . [T]he free libido . . . was withdrawn into the ego . . . to establish an *identification* of the ego with the abandoned object. *Thus the shadow of the object fell upon the ego. . . .*
>
> The ego wishes to incorporate this object into itself, and the method by which it would do so, in this oral or cannibalistic stage, is by *devouring* it. (*MM*, 248–250; my emphasis)

The melancholic eats the lost object—feeds on it, as it were.

This apparently abnormal way of digesting loss seems to occupy an inversely primary role in psychical formation, for Freud tells us that melancholia affords us the rare chance of viewing "the constitution of the human ego" (*MM*, 247). Freudian melancholia designates a chain of loss, denial, and incorporation through which the ego is born. As other readers of Freud have pointed out, it is unclear in Freud's essay whether there could have been an ego prior to melancholia, since the ego comes into being as a psychical object, as a perceptual object, only after the "shadow of the object" has fallen upon it.[20] By taking in the other-made-ghostly, the melancholic subject fortifies him- or herself and grows rich in impoverishment. The history of the ego is thus the history of its losses. More accurately, melancholia alludes not to loss per se but to the entangled relationship with loss. We might then say that melancholia does not simply denote a *condition* of grief but is, rather, a *legislation* of grief.

Moreover, there are drawbacks to this "dining" and self-constituting experience. The "swallowing" does not go down easily. As the libido turns back on the ego, so do the feelings of guilt, rage, and punishment (Freudian melancholia is anything but mild!) originally attached to the initial object of loss and disappointment. The "shadow of the object" that falls on the ego carries with it a reproach. Since the melancholic subject experiences resentment and denigration for the lost object with which he or she is identifying, the melancholic ends up administering to his or her own self-denigration. Implicit in the essay is the profound ambivalence that continues to be generated around the "swallowed" object. The melancholic's relationship to the object is now no longer just love or nostalgia but also profound resentment. The melancholic is not melancholic because he or she has lost something but because he or she has introjected that which he or she now reviles. Thus the melancholic is stuck in more ways than just temporally; he or she is stuck—almost choking on— the hateful and loved thing he or she just devoured. Freud writes, that melancholics' "complaints are really 'plaint' in the old sense of the word. They are not ashamed and do not hide themselves, since everything derogatory that they say about themselves is at bottom said about someone else" (*MM*, 248).[21] Although Freud is right in pointing out that the source of the plaint is against the object, if we were to follow his logic that the thing-within is now the ego, then we would also have to see that the plaint can no longer properly belong to either subject or object since the two are now intrinsically (con)fused.

At this moment *loss* becomes *exclusion* in the melancholic landscape. What Freud does not address in this essay but what must be a consequence of this psychical drama is the multiple layers of denial and exclusion that the melancholic must exercise in order to maintain this elaborate structure of loss-but-not-loss. First, the melancholic must deny loss as loss in order to sustain the fiction of possession. Second, the melancholic would have to make sure that the "object" never returns, for such a return would surely jeopardize the cannibalistic project that, one might note, is a form of possession more intimate than any material relationship could produce. Thus although it may seem reasonable to imagine that the griever may wish for the return of the loved one, once this digestive process has occurred, the ego may in fact not want or cannot afford such homecoming. As Thomas Mann once put it,

> the calling back of the dead, or the desirability of calling them back, was a ticklish matter after all. At bottom, and boldly confessed, the desire does not exist; it is a *misapprehension* precisely as impossible as the thing itself, as we should soon see if nature once let it happen. What we call mourning for our dead is perhaps not so much grief at not being able to call them back as it is grief at not being able to want to do so.[22]

Mann's account of grief's dilemma is really elucidating the melancholic ambivalence toward the object. At the heart of loss there is now an active exclusion and denial of the object. In a sense, exclusion, rather than loss, is the real stake of melancholic retention. Indeed, Freud's text itself may be considered quite melancholic in *its* ruthless exclusion of the object. For the ego is not the only ghostly presence in this essay. That is, the melancholic ego is a haunted ego, at once made ghostly and embodied in its ghostliness, but the "object" is also ghostly—not only because its image has been introjected or incorporated within the melancholic psyche but also because Freud is finally not that interested in what happens to the object or *its* potential for subjectivity.[23]

Thus the melancholic ego as formed and fortified by a spectral drama, whereby the subject sustains itself through the ghostly emptiness of a lost other. Several aspects of this psychical drama are relevant to this study's interest in American racial dynamics. First, it is this peculiar and uneasy dynamic of retaining a denigrated but sustaining loss that resonates most acutely against the mechanisms of the racial imaginary as they have been fashioned in this country. While psychoanalytic readings of melancholia have been mostly theorized in relation to gender formation,[24] melancholia also presents a particularly apt paradigm for elucidating the activity and components of racialization. Racialization in America may be said to operate through the institutional process of producing a dominant, standard, white national ideal, which is sustained by the exclusion-yet-retention of racialized others. The national topography of centrality and marginality legitimizes itself by retroactively positing the racial other as always Other and lost to the heart of the nation. Legal exclusion naturalizes the more complicated "loss" of the unassimilable racial other.

Second, Freud's notion of this uncomfortable swallowing and its implications for how loss is processed and then secured as exclusion lend provocative insights into the nature of the racial other seen as "the foreigner within" America. In a sense, the racial other is in fact quite "assimilated" into—or, more accurately, most uneasily digested by—American nationality. The history of American national idealism has always been caught in this melancholic bind between incorporation and rejection. If one of the ideals that sustained the American nation since its beginning has been its unique proposition that "all men are created equal," then one of America's ongoing national mortifications must be its history of acting otherwise. While all nations have their repressed histories and traumatic atrocities, American melancholia is particularly acute because America is *founded* on the very ideals of freedom and liberty whose betrayals have been repeatedly covered over. Even as the economic, material, and philosophical advances of the nation are built on a series of legalized exclusions (of African Americans, Jewish Americans, Chinese Americans, Japanese Americans, and so on) and the labor provided by those excluded, it is also a history busily disavowing those repudiations. In his essay "The Two Declarations of American Independence," Michael Rogin suggests that this paradox erupts on the very surface of the Declaration of Independence:

> The Declaration of Independence, demanding freedom from enslavement to England for a new nation built on slavery, is the core product of that

mésalliance in political theory. . . . [The Declaration] bequeathed a Janus-faced legacy to the new nation—the logic on the one hand that the equality to which white men were naturally born could be extended to women and slaves, and the foundation on the other of white freedom on black servitude.[25]

Melancholia thus describes both an American ideological dilemma and its constitutional practices.

Rogin further posits in *Blackface, White Noise* that "racial exclusions, be it chattel slavery, the expropriation of Indian and Mexicans, or the repressive use and exclusion of Chinese and Mexican American labor, were the conditions of American freedom rather than exceptions to it."[26] It is at those moments when America is most shamefaced and traumatized by its betrayal of its own democratic ideology (the genocide of Native Americans, slavery, segregation, immigration discrimination) that it most virulently—and *melancholically*—espouses human value and brotherhood. In his *Notes on the State of Virginia*, Thomas Jefferson, for example, meditates on his discomfort about the apparent discrepancy between the Declaration of Independence and the colonial practice of slavery only to console himself by reassuring himself and his readers that the inhumanity of blacks exempted them from considerations such as human rights, freedom, and equality. Blacks were seen as lost to moral and human concerns. Through this consolation of philosophy (which exemplifies his melancholic relationship to blackness), Jefferson disentangles the new republic from the ideological burdens of slavery and at the same time reconciles slavery to the ideology of the new nation. Precisely because the American history of exclusion, imperialism, and colonization runs so antithetical to the equally and particularly American narrative of liberty and individualism, cultural memory in America poses a continuously vexing problem: How does the nation "go on" while remembering those transgressions? How does it *sustain* the remnants of denigration and disgust created in the name of progress and the formation of an American identity?

Dominant white identity in America operates melancholically—as an elaborate identificatory system based on psychical and social consumption-and-denial. This diligent system of melancholic retention appears in different guises. Both racist and white liberal discourses participate in this dynamic, albeit out of different motivations. The racists need to develop elaborate ideologies in order to accommodate their actions with official American ideals,[27] while white liberals need to keep burying the racial others in order to memorialize them. Those who do not see the racial problem or those who call themselves nonideological are the most melancholic of all because in today's political climate, as Toni Morrison exclaims in *Playing in the Dark*, "it requires hard work *not* to see."[28] Both violent vilification and the indifference to vilification express, rather than invalidate, the melancholic dynamic. Indeed, melancholia offers a powerful critical tool precisely because it theoretically *accounts* for the guilt and the denial of guilt, the blending of shame and omnipotence in the racist imaginary.

Like melancholia, racism is hardly ever a clear rejection of the other. While racism is mostly thought of as a kind of violent rejection, racist institutions in fact often do not want to fully expel the racial other; instead, they wish to maintain that other within existing structures. With phenomena such as segregation and colonialism, the racial question is an issue of *place* (the literalization of Freudian melancholic suspension) rather than of full relinquishment. Segregation and colonialism are internally fraught institutions not because they have eliminated the other but because they need the very thing they hate or fear. (This is why trauma, so often associated with discussions of racial denigration, in focusing on a structure of crisis on the part of the victim, misses the violators' own dynamic process at stake in such denigration. Melancholia gets more potently at the notion of constitutive loss that expresses itself in both violent and muted ways, producing confirmation as well as crisis, knowledge as well as aporia.)

American values tend to acquire their sharpest outline *through*, not in spite of, the nexus of investment and anxiety provoked by slavery and other institutions of discrimination. As Eric Lott and Michael Rogin have so well demonstrated in their works on blackface minstrelsy, the dominant culture's relation to the raced other displays an entangled network of repulsion and sympathy, fear and desire, repudiation and identification. As Paul Gilroy observes in *The Black Atlantic*, "the consciousness of European settlers and those of the Africans they enslaved, the "Indians" they slaughtered, and the Asians they indentured were not, even in the situations of most extreme brutality, sealed off hermetically from one another."[29] It is this imbricated but denied relationship that forms the basis of white racial melancholia.

Racial melancholia plays itself out not only in national formation but also in one of its expressions: the formation of canonical literature. By citing African American presence as the formative but denied ghost in the heart of American literature, Toni Morrison has essentially identified the national literary canon as a melancholic corpus. In *Playing in the Dark*, Morrison calls for "an examination and reinterpretation of the American canon, the founding nineteenth-century works, for the 'unspeakable things unspoken'; for the ways in which the presence of Afro-Americans has shaped the choices, the language, the structure, and the meaning of so much American literature."[30] The canon is a melancholic corpus because of what it excludes but cannot forget—what Morrison calls "the ghost in the machine." Other critics have observed that social categories that exemplify conditions of marginality have in fact been long central to the making of the "mainstream" insofar as they serve to define and delimit that recognized "center."[31] Gilroy suggests that the "cultural history of blacks in the modern world has a great bearing on ideas of what the West was and is today" (45). And in talking about the psychodynamics of black-white relations, Frantz Fanon writes that "the black man is rooted at the core of a universe from which he must be extricated."[32]

American literature and nationhood contain other suspended, racialized "ghosts" as well. Rogin points out that critics from D. H. Lawrence to Richard Slotkin have contended that "American literature . . . established its national identity in the struggle between Indians and whites."[33] In her study of early American novel of the Federalist period, Julia Stern suggests that the very founding of the American republic already embodies such a complex relation to "other" raced bodies, pointing out that early American fiction registers the elaborate cost of the Framers' vision:

> Such literature suggests that the foundation of the republic is in fact a crypt, that the nation's noncitizens—women, the poor, Native Americans, African Americans, and aliens—lie socially dead and inadequately buried, the casualties of post-Revolutionary political foreclosure.[34]

Realizing the full extent of Morrison's ghostly allegory, Stern spells out the structure of loss, grief, and entombment on which the origins of the American dream were built:

> These invisible Americans, prematurely interred beneath the great national edifice whose erection they actually enable, provide an unquiet platform for the construction of republican privilege, disturbing the Federalist monolith in powerful ways.[35]

Stern places racialization in the dead center of the American founding, arguing that race constitutes a distinctive locus of exclusion for American nationality.

The disparity between Enlightenment ideal and social practices is only an active expression of the fundamental tension in the democratic ideal that still haunts us today. In tracing another American frontier, David Palumbo-Liu argues, in *Asian/American: Historical Crossings of a Racial Frontier*, that in the last century and a half American citizenship has been legally, economically, and culturally *defined* over and against the simultaneous exclusion and the unseen racialization of the Asian immigrant.[36] Race has always and continues to constitute an unresolved issue in the evolution of American democracy.

But how does recognizing this melancholic dilemma underlying dominant power *help* those who have been buried and then resuscitated only as serviceable ghosts? It is one thing to unveil authority's internal contradictions and debts; it is another to imagine that this critique addresses suffer-

ing on the part of those who have supposedly been interred. Indeed, melancholic suspension rather than interment may be a more fruitful and perhaps
more accurate description for the status of the racial other in this system of
consumption and denial. Let us ask the question that Freud does not ask:
What is the subjectivity of the melancholic object? Is it also melancholic,
and what will we uncover when we resuscitate it? In other words, what
implications do insights into the melancholic origins of American racial-
national identity hold for the study of the racialized subjects?

Melancholic Responses

It may appear tremendously difficult to talk about the "melancholia" of
racialized peoples, especially since it seems to reinscribe a whole history of
affliction or run the risk of naturalizing that pain. In *Beyond Ethnicity*,
Werner Sollors talks about "Indian melancholy," referring *not* to how Native Americans process their history of genocide but to how dominant
American culture romanticizes and naturalizes "the cult of the vanishing
Indians."[37] The rhetoric of the "melancholic Indian and his fate" serves to
legitimize the future of the white conqueror. In the African American tradition, Richard Wright notes that the African American community embodies a "tradition of bitterness . . . so complex . . . as to assume such a tight,
organic form that most white people would think upon examining it that
most Negroes had embedded in their flesh and bones some peculiar propensity towards lamenting and complaining."[38] Talking about racial grief thus
also runs the risk of repeating a tool of containment historically exercised
by authority. The worry is of course that such a focus on injury might be
naturalized and used against the plaintiffs, as was the case with *Stell v.
Savannah-Chatham Board of Education*. The path connecting injury to pity
and then to contempt can be very brief.[39] In short, it can be damaging to
say how damaging racism has been.

   Yet it is surely equally harmful *not* to talk about this history of sorrow.
The ontological and psychical status of a social subject who has been made
into an "object," a "loss," an "invisibility," or a "phantom" has never been
fully explored, since the implications of such a study are on the one hand
inconvenient to a racist culture and on the other potentially threatening to
the project of advocacy—or at least advocacy as it is traditionally conceived.[40] The quick jump from psychical injury to inherent disability (as
exemplified by *Stell*) provides an example of the kind of imprecise thinking
surrounding perceptions of the relationship between psychical response and
social influence. The historical use of psychology in racial analyses has suffered from a series of elisions: (1) the tendency to confuse psychological
analysis with prescription; (2) the assumption that "damage" (in the form

of having internalized harmful dominant ideals) amounts to the same thing as having no agency or, conversely, the presumption that having agency or "a strong ego" makes one impermeable to such invasions; (3) the neglect of authority's melancholic attachments; and, finally, (4) the failure to address the psychodynamics of psychological vulnerability and their *intrinsic* relations to identificatory and subject formations—formations that are as unstable as they are historical, as multifaceted as they are coercive.

What is needed is a serious effort at rethinking the term "agency" in relation to forms of racial grief, to broaden the term beyond the assumption of a pure sovereign subject to other manifestations, forms, tonalities, and gradations of governance. When it comes to facing discrimination, we need to understand subjective agency as a convoluted, ongoing, generative, and at times self-contradicting negotiation with pain. To reduce the issue of psychical injury to a simplistic and prescriptive pronouncement of black self-hatred is to miss a fundamental insight revealed by Clark's work and the works of those after him: that the psychology being dramatized by those children in the doll tests reveals the results, not the cause, of social relations. At the very least, Clark's lifelong work shows that social relations *live* at the heart of psychical dynamics and that the complexity of those dynamics bespeaks a wide range of complicated, conflictual, interlocking emotions: desire and doubt, affirmation and rejection, projection and identification, management and dysfunction. This debate, which has in essence lasted over fifty years and shows no signs of resolution, is really a debate about the assignment of social meaning to psychical processes. And restricting the terms of this debate is the stubborn antipathy between advocacy and more complex signs of cultural desire and unease.[41]

One place where such complex signs come into play and where such complexity gets theorized is literature. My purpose here is not to locate in literary works the "truth" of colored people's self-hatred or to diagnose symptoms of racial injury in literary texts. Rather, my intention is to discern how these cultural texts (free from certain immediate political-legal protocols but nonetheless speaking to those demands) tease out the complex social etiology behind the phenomenon of racial grief. In Ralph Ellison's *Invisible Man*, a text whose treatise on black invisibility might be seen as a forerunner to Morrison's "ghost in the machine," Ellison gives us an enigmatic picture of a racist encounter. In the opening sequence, after telling us that he is invisible "because [white] people refuse to see [him]," the narrator runs into a violent confrontation:

> One night I accidentally bumped into a man . . . he looked insolently out of his blue eyes and cursed me . . . I yelled, "Apologize! Apologize!" But he continued to curse and struggle, and I butted him again and again until he went down heavily. . . . I kicked him profusely . . . when it oc-

curred to me that the man had not *seen* me, actually; that he, as far as he knew, was walking in the midst of a walking nightmare . . . a man almost killed by a phantom.[42]

I call this scene enigmatic because the description opens up a range of questions about the difference between perception and projection, between action and reaction. To begin with, from the narrator's perspective, we see the white man's "insolence" as anger from having to confront what he presumably did not want to see. The white man's curse, upon being bumped, expresses an active wish to deny the invisible object now demanding a competing presence. What the narrator thinks troubles the white man is the "bumping"—that *point of contact with invisibility*—that has in fact historically ensured the white man's ability to see and to not see.[43] This white man both sees and does not see the black man in that alley. In describing a white store owner who had difficulties seeing a little black girl right under his nose trying to buy candy from him in *The Bluest Eye*, Toni Morrison depicts a similar moment of seeing/not-seeing. She describes the man as having been "blunted by a permanent awareness of loss."[44] In this subtly turned phrase, Morrison has located the precise and peculiar nature of "loss" in white racial melancholia: teetering between the known and the unknown, the seen and the deliberately unseen, the racial other constitutes an oversight that is consciously made unconscious—naturalized over time as absence, as complementary negative space. It is precisely the slippery distance between loss and exclusion that racial myopia effects. Part of the central dilemma of dominant racial melancholia—since its authority is constituted, sustained, and made productive by this system of the suspended other—is that it does not really want the lost other to return (or demand its right of way).

At the same time, when we enter Ellison's scene more fully, we have to ask: Is the white man the only one suffering from not-seeing in this scenario? The writing is ambiguous. Who is the invisible one? If the narrator bumps into the white man, is not the white man the one who is invisible to the black man? The narrator bumps into what *he* did not see and then accuses the other of blindness. If we do not take the narrator's account at its surface value, it is conceivable that the white man cursed the black man for his clumsiness rather than for racist reasons (that masculinist rather than racial confrontation may be at stake) and that the narrator's interpretation of "insolence" may be itself a melancholic response to the (historically) incendiary sign of "blue eyes" and his own self-denigration and wounded pride. That invisibility is rarely a one-way street is one of its most insidious effects. In this confrontation, there is potential mutual invisibility and mutual projection. Indeed, the racial moment is born out of this dynamic locking of the two men in mutual projection. In a response that is both macho and hysterical, the narrator demonstrates that he is trapped, not by having been seen as invisible *but by suspecting himself to be so. This* is racial melancholia for the raced subject: the internalization of discipline and rejection—*and* the installation of a scripted context of perception. The invisible man's racial radar, at once his perspicacity and his paranoia, is justified. For the invisible man is both a melancholic object and a melancholic subject, both the one lost and the one losing.

This internalization, far from denoting a condition of surrender, embodies a web of negotiation that expresses agency as well as abjection. In Toni Morrison's *The Bluest Eye*, we find another (feminine) confrontation with the sign of blue eyes and a similar response of self-denigration and pride. Morrison's child narrator describes how every Christmas she would receive the "loving gift" of a "big, blue-eyed Baby Doll":

> I had only one desire: to dismember it. . . . But the dismembering of dolls was not the true horror. The truly horrifying thing was the transference of the same impulses to little white girls. . . . What made people look at them, and say, "Awwwww," but not for me? The eye slide of black women as they approached them on the street, and the possessive gentleness of their touch as they handled them.

> If I pinched them, their eyes—unlike the crazed glint of the baby doll's eyes—would fold in pain, and their cry would not be the sound of an ice box, but a fascinating cry of pain. When I learned how repulsive this disinterested violence was . . . my shame floundered about for refuge. The best hiding place was love. Thus the conversion from pristine sadism to fabricated hatred, to fraudulent love. It was a small step to Shirley Temple. I learned, much later to worship her.[45]

For a child coming to racial discrimination, affective formation and distinction (how one tells the difference between love and hate) become so entangled and twisted that love and hate both come to be "fabricated" and "fraudulent." We are witnessing the loss of affective discrimination in the face of racial discrimination. The social lesson of racial minoritization reinforces itself through the imaginative loss of a never-possible perfection, whose loss the little girl must come to identify as a rejection of herself.

The internal processes of this lesson on the part of the child, however, embodies a critique as well. For underneath the pop-psychological insight of an "inferiority complex" lies a nexus of intertwining affects and libidinal dynamics—a web of self-affirmation, self-denigration, projection, desire, identification, and hostility. To claim that racial difference on the part of the racialized subject provokes self-shame that leads to compensatory white preference drastically foreshortens the complex process of *coming to* racialization/socialization. The pedagogy of discrimination is painfully installed in multiple stages. White preference is not a phenomenon that simply gets handed down from society to black women and then to black girls; instead it travel a tortuous, melancholic path of alienation, resistance, aggression, and then, finally, the domestication of that aggression as "love." Here the cultural lesson and the racial lesson coincide: that is, Is not the conversion of the grief of being black into the enjoyment of whiteness a very *cultural* lesson of mastering personal displeasure as social pleasure?

In spite of the collusion between acculturation and racialization, *The Bluest Eye* tracks, rather than naturalizes, the etiology of white preference. Morrison shows us that shame does not come from the child's own blackness per se (the debased value placed on her blackness made the child angry, as it should, revealing in fact quite a sense of self-possession) but rather from the social message that there is no place for such anger and grief, which must go into hiding. The little girl must internalize not only the white ideal but also the ideal of black womanhood as a longing after the white ideal. That is, what is hard to swallow is not just Shirley Temple, a competition for attention, but precisely the "eye-slide" of black mothers.

This profound internalization of ideality, in its history and practice, can gesture, surprisingly, to shades of resistance as well as acquiescence: "It was a small step to Shirley Temple. I learned much later to worship her, just as I learned to delight in cleanliness, knowing, as I learned, that the change was adjustment without improvement."[46] Is the concluding claim a statement about the self's continued inability to assume fully that white ideal, a reminder of the "fraudulence" that in fact conditions this adulation, an acknowledgement of the self-harming that such "preference" engenders, or even a larger allusion to the idea of African American social progress itself? The answer must be all of the above, or, at least, the statement's ambiguity informs us that, for the object of discrimination, it is impossible to disentangle these competing interests.

When a few years later Maxine Hong Kingston writes what comes to be widely acknowledged as the preeminent Asian American feminist text, *The Woman Warrior*, she stages an unforgettable scene in which the Asian American girl child narrator can be found standing in a school bathroom acting out what Morrison's narrator, Claudia, fantasizes about: pinching, pulling the hair, and otherwise abusing another girl child—except this time the other is not a white girl but someone who looks like herself. The violence that Claudia initially feels toward "little white girls," which she then turns inward, in *The Bluest Eye*, has reached a delirious re-enactment in the Kingston encounter, where the object of rage is the fantasmatic likeness of oneself. This Kingston scene of collapsed intersubjective and intrasubjective conflict in the school bathroom (which I investigate more fully in chapter 3) is most certainly having a conversation with the *Brown* legacy, Morrison's text, and the historical problem of self-denigration instituted by the pedagogy of racism. Indeed, both Morrison's and Kingston's texts remind us that

Kenneth Clark's experiment in those dusty classrooms over fifty years ago does not give us information about the psyche of black children per se; rather, it gave us a dramatization of an *education* of black children. Morrison and Kingston highlight the insight that the education of racism is an education of desire, a pedagogy that tethers the psychical inextricably to the social. Political domination is reproduced at the level of personal experience.

Kingston's choice of the bathroom (as a classic site of gender differentiation) further dramatizes what was left unsaid in the *Brown* doll test and implicit in the Morrison text: the configuration of gender valuation in the face of a pressing-but-exclusive racial ideal. While gender was not an element of analysis in the original Clark experiment, the receptions of the dolls by the adults themselves hint at the presence of a fair amount of gender discomfort. Descriptions of the experiment, both contemporary to the case and after, invariably alluded to gender in the form of jokes about dolls. In Richard Kluger's definitive account, *A Simple Justice*, he repeatedly made the point that the adult male lawyers on both sides of the litigation felt uncomfortable dealing with dolls. (Indeed, Kluger offers a small humorous moment in describing Clark's initial meeting with the NAACP lawyers, who found it "weird" and disturbing to find a grown man with a suitcase full of dolls. They were visibly relieved and put at ease once they received the verbal reassurance that the dolls were "for business" rather than "pleasure."[47] These men were willing to read the racial but not the gender signs to which the children were subjected.) But in the Morrison and Kingston renditions, reading race is a prerequisite to reading femininity. That is, both Claudia and Kingston's girl narrator show how femininity (what it means to be a girl) comes to acquire its social and aesthetic values under the signs of racial difference. As Elizabeth Abel reveals in her essay "Bathroom Doors and Drinking Fountains," the visual imaginary that supports Jim Crow laws, clustering around the bathroom and drinking fountains, offers a startling proposition that "race [in this case, black and white] not sex is the dyad that founds the symbolic register."[48] This insight not only disturbs the usual psychoanalytic prioritization of gender identification over racial identification but also reminds us that the American racial symbolic register is in fact not dyadic but multiple.

We continue to witness connections (even conversations) between Asian American and African American literary meditations on psychical, racial, and gender injury. Asian American critical anxiety over Kingston's supposedly damaging representation of the community (and especially of Asian American masculinity) is not so different from African American discomfort over Kenneth Clark's findings. Even as we recognize how deeply uncomfortable it is to talk about the ways the racialized minority is as bound to racial melancholia as the dominant subject, we must also see how urgent it is that we start to look at the historical, cultural, and crossracial consequences of racial wounding and to situate these effects as crucial, formative elements of individual, national, and cultural identities. Only then can we begin to go on to analyze how racialized people as complex psychical beings deal with the objecthood thrust upon them, which to a great extent constitutes how they negotiate sociality and nationality. Within the reductive notion of "internalization" lies a world of relations that is as much about surviving grief as embodying it.

The Morphology of Ghostliness

When we turn to the long history of grief and the equally protracted history of physically and emotionally managing that grief on the part of the marginalized, racialized people, we see that there has always been an interaction between *melancholy* in the vernacular sense of affect, as "sadness" or the "blues," and *melancholia* in the sense of a structural, identificatory formation predicated on—while being an active negotiation of—the loss of self as legitimacy. Indeed, racial melancholia as I am defining it has always existed for raced subjects both as a *sign* of rejection and as a psychic *strategy* in response to that rejection.

Black cultural forms have hosted and even cultivated dynamic rapport with the presence of death and suffering.[49] W. E. B. Du Bois has written of "sorrow songs," folksongs sung by the slaves, not just as expressions of sadness but as a profound spiritual wrestling with meaning and freedom in a world of immense sorrow: "they tell of death and suffering and unvoiced longing toward a truer world, of misty wanderings and hidden ways . . . they grope toward some unseen power and sigh for rest in the End."[50] In *The Black Atlantic*, Paul Gilroy points out that, for the powerless, the association of death with freedom is not one of mere morbidity. On the contrary, he argues that the slaves' intimate relationship to death signals not merely a reaction to probable threat but also a *choice*. Referring to the work of Frederick Douglass, Gilroy proposes that "the slave actively prefers the possibility of death to the continuing condition of inhumanity on which plantation slavery depends" (63). Gilroy does not see this turn toward death as a giving up or empty victory; he sees it as an active act of will in a situation devoid of will. Since slavery depends on the slave being alive, the threat of suicide in this context bespeaks an unlawful act of rebellion and self-assertion. This turn toward death thus "points to the value of seeing the consciousness of the slave as involving an extended act of mourning" (63). In *Scenes of Subjection*, Saidiya Hartman further lays out the affective and psychical intricacies of these sorrow songs:

> [S]uch indulgence in song reflected neither an embrace of slavery nor a unity of feeling but . . . was a veiled articulation of the extreme and para-

doxical conditions of slavery. . . . My task is to . . . give full weight to the opacity of these texts wrought by toil, terror, and sorrow . . . [to emphasize] the significance of the opacity as precisely that which . . . troubles distinctions between joy and sorrow, toil and leisure.[51]

Hartman argues that, owing to the brutality of slavery, the "distinctions between joy and sorrow, toil and leisure" no longer provide productive measures of analysis. By implication, under such extreme conditions, survival and the management of grief exceed our vernacular understanding of agency, of what it means to take control of oneself and one's surroundings.

In exploring racialized minorities' melancholic responses to dominant racial melancholia, this study agrees with Gilroy's and Hartman's insights that the internalization of dominant oppression may not signal pure conformity or defeat but rather point to new ways of thinking about what agency means for one stripped of it. As Gilroy and Hartman have demonstrated, the sorrow songs confound the simple assignment of emotions (such as sadness or resignation); they indeed confound singular meaning altogether. Similarly, in *The Bluest Eye*, Morrison demonstrates that one of the consequences of an education in racism is the loss of affective discrimination. In the context of unimaginable, persistent racial grief, we must begin to acknowledge the complex nexus of psychical negotiations being engaged and develop a political vocabulary accordingly.

Today we need to confront the inheritance of that historical principle of negativity—not only within the African American community but also with respect to other marginalized, racialized peoples. The racialization of Asian Americans and African Americans are two distinct but related processes. This study focuses on the latter because so much of historical and contemporary racial discourse is modeled on that category and because African American studies constitutes the most established discipline in the field of race studies. As the most enduring and visible racial category in America, African American identity formation and cultural manifestations provide an important basis from which to track the process of racializing America.

I also concentrate on Asian American formation probably because of my own "tribal" allegiance and because I want to understand some things about my own relation to this category. But there are other reasons as well. As both *the* targeted, racialized group in United States immigration policy and yet the least "colored" group in racial debates, Asian Americans offer a charged site where American nationhood invests much of its contradictions, desires, and anxieties. While Asian American history (especially, though by no means exclusively, in California) carries a tremendous reservoir of denigration and abuse, that history occupies a less pronounced place in American consciousness than does African American suffering.[52] This has to do with several facts: the lack of Asian American political mass in contrast to

African Americans; the specific history of racism directed against Asian immigrants and Asian labor (that is, the different history of economic competition with the white labor class); the difference between immigrant and slave relations to American nationality; and the strange status of "Asians" in American conceptions of race, which is predominantly understood as black and white. Racism against Asians and Asian Americans has been heavily filtered through the nineteenth-century European inheritance of Orientalism and its publicity, as well as through an elision in the black-and-white dyad that dominate American racial discourse. In their enormously popular treatise *America in Black and White: One Nation, Indivisible* (1997), Stephen and Abigail Thernstrom, for example, specifically dismiss Asian Americans as a racialized group in America.[53] Quoting Gunnar Myrdal, who on the eve of World War II compared Asian Americans with African Americans in their status as an "unassimilable caste," the Thernstroms go on to claim that Myrdal's pronouncement is no longer true, since Asian Americans have acquired spectacular economic and social mobility in recent decades. The authors write, "it is hard to find anyone who cares much what [Asian Americans'] 'race' is." One might wonder whether the Thernstroms considered the racialization of Asian Americans in American immigration and legal history or if they paid attention to daily news. Furthermore, the disavowal of racism against Asian Americans because of their supposed economic and social success misses the point that economic competition often fuels the very energy behind racism, as well as intensifying conflict with other minority groups.

With black and white as the dominant racial categories, historical memory tends to overlook the fierce contestation over the shades, as it were, in between—conflicts that involve not just ideological differences but economic and social privileges. Indeed, the formulation of the government's sovereign power to exclude is historically tied to the definitions of aliens and citizens.[54] Well before *Brown*, there was a series of key rulings in school segregation, in addition to the well-known *Plessy v. Ferguson*, that involved the problem of racializing Asians in this country. In 1929, Chinese immigrant descendants in the Mississippi Delta, having for some time socialized with and even married blacks, nonetheless came into fierce protest around the issue of where the Chinese should be slotted in the Jim Crow school system, culminating in *Gong Lum v. Rice*.[55] (In that case, the Chinese appellants claimed that since they were clearly not black, they should be considered closer to being white.) During the *Brown* litigations, the constitutionality of racialization-as-segregation in the form of Japanese internment (*Korematsu v. U.S.*) was relegitimized on the grounds that "national security" was at stake.[56] (In Arthur Dong's documentary about traveling Asian American performers in the forties and fifties, there were poignant testimonies of Asian American performers who, after traveling long distances, could not find a bathroom, since "black" and "white" were the only options proffered.) The question of the racialization of Asian Americans is in some ways more apparently melancholic than that of African Americans in American history in the sense that the history of virulent racism directed against Asians and Asian Americans has been at once consistently upheld and denied. Shuttling between "black" and "white"—the Scylla and Charybdis between which all American immigrants have had to "pass"—Asian Americans occupy a truly ghostly position in the story of American racialization.

The formation of modern America in the early twentieth century is deeply and particularly attached to the fantasm of the "East." In her seminal work *Immigrant Acts*, Lisa Lowe has proposed that "Asia"—both within and outside of America—has always been a complex site on which the manifold anxieties of the American nation-state have been figured.

> History and materially, Chinese, Japanese, Korean, Asian Indians, and Filipino immigrants have played absolutely crucial roles in the building and sustaining of America; and at certain times, these immigrants have been fundamental to the construction of the nation as a simulacrum of inclusiveness. Yet the project of imagining the nation as homogenous requires the orientalist construction of cultures and geographies from which Asian immigrants come as fundamentally "foreign" origins antipathetic to the modern American society that "discovers," "welcomes," and "domesticates" them.[57]

An analysis of the racialization of Asian Americans, in addition to African Americans, thus remains crucial to understanding the project of nation-making in the United States. In the background of—and at times *as* the foil to—the black civil rights struggles gripping this country, Asian Americans have come to occupy a curious place in the American racial imaginary, embodying both delight and repugnance.[58] I am thinking, for example, of the notion of the "model minority," the figure who has not only assimilated but also euphorically sings the praises of the American way. (I discuss a particularly extravagant version of this in Rodgers and Hammerstein's *Flower Drum Song* in chapter 2). The very history of Asian immigration (itself far from homogenous) has often been solicited to inflect, on the part of the Asian immigrant, a manic relation to the American Dream. This strain of Asian euphoria in America in turns serves to contain the history of Asian abjection, as well as to discipline other racialized groups in America. Thus, from African American to Asian American, narratives of sorrow and joy alike encode the yearning and mourning associated with the histories of dispersal and the remembrance of unspoken losses.

An understanding of melancholia as experienced by the raced subject must extend beyond a superficial or merely affective description of sadness to a deep sense of how that sadness—as a kind of ambulatory despair or manic euphoria—conditions life for the disenfranchised and, indeed, constitutes their identity and shapes their subjectivity. From the theater of Rodgers and Hammerstein to that of David Henry Hwang, from the novel of Maxine Hong Kingston to that of Ralph Ellison, from the experimental work of Theresa Hak Kyung Cha to that of Anna Deavere Smith, the rest of this study builds on and explores the manifestations and vicissitudes of racial melancholia for Asian American and African American subjects. When we begin to exhume, as Morrison proposes, the buried body in the heart of the American literature, we see that the nature of the "presence" uncovered is overlaid with political, intellectual, psychological, and ethical significations. The crypt reveals not *an* object, nor a whole subject prior to defilement, but the morphology of ghostliness itself. This study will demonstrate that comprehending this morphology will alter some of our most basic assumptions about a series of terms, such as *citizenship, assimilation, fantasy, trauma,* and *performance.*

Race and Psychoanalysis

To see racial identity as a melancholic formation is to apprehend that identity's instability and its indebtedness to the dis-identity it is also claiming. If race and ethnic studies grew out of the civil rights movement and remains affiliated with political activism, to question the grounds of identity can be seen as either a luxury, or worse, irresponsible. Yet, as I have argued in this chapter, to maintain a series of binary views that bar identity from dis-identity, injury from strength, and politics from aesthetics is to limit with detrimental consequences our understanding of racial grief as the result of (and as an agent in shaping) a complex interaction between sociality and psycho dynamics. The next generation of race scholars has to address the fundamental paradox at the heart of minority discourse: how to proceed once we acknowledge, as we must, that "identity" is the very ground upon which both progress and discrimination are made. What may be uneasy for some to entertain is the possibility that the future of ethnic studies may take a form very different from its original inception. New lines of inquiry may even appear antagonistic to (even as they are indebted to) the political activism that founded ethnic studies. The tension between politicized scholarship and scholarship that is political has long plagued the more established discipline of African American studies. In 1987, Barbara Christian and Henry Louis Gates could be found debating in *Critical Inquiry* the ability and inability of "high" critical theory to address racialized subjects and literary products. More than a decade later, a similar debate can be found—this time on the front page of the Arts and Leisure section of the *New York Times* between Henry Louis Gates and Manning Marable.[59]

I am always troubled by this divide between "theory" and "politics." On the one hand, I understand that theorization is often taken to be an indulgence, because its practice may produce ambiguities and instabilities that seem antithetical to the demands of political necessity. This is especially true for psychoanalytic modes of inquiry; as Max Weber writes in the first pages of *Economy and Society*, "You cannot call up the subjective dimension and keep it in place." (This is also why Sau-ling Cynthia Wong's characterization of the double impulses of "extravagance" versus "necessity" in the production and critical practices of Asian American literature so powerfully encapsulates the fundamental double bind between political exigency and private imagination at the heart of any ethnic-racial work of art.) Hence I see my study as finally an intellectual project and, as such, not a political manual. On the other hand, I am convinced that the work of interrogating and unlocking the complexities of racial dynamics, realized in both institutionalized and psychical processes, must finally *inform* the direction of long-term political reimagining. What would it mean *not* to look at the subjective dimension of race for fear of its unwieldiness?

I suggest that it is often precisely at the most unmanageable instances of political mediation that we begin to understand the impact of racial allegiance and repudiation. It is when we press against the most intense points of political discomfort that we see what it really means to adopt a political stance. This study does not claim to have a *solution* to "the race question"; instead, it investigates the assumptions underlying the very notion of a solution. We do not know yet what it means for politics to accommodate a concept of identity based on constitutive loss or for politics to explore the psychic and social anchoring points that keep us chained to the oppressive, wounding memories of love and hate that condition the mutual enmeshment of the "dominant" and the "disempowered." To refuse to contemplate these aspects of racial dynamics, however, has not been productive either, as is evidenced by the ongoing national drama of racial repudiation and reprisal.

What has been missing in much of the critical analysis of race relations and representations has been a willingness to confront the psychic implications of the haunting negativity that has not only been attached to but has also helped to constitute the very category of "the racialized." The truth is that race studies still turns with more comfort to sociology, anthropology, and history rather than literature or philosophy. This discomfort has everything to do with an abiding attachment to the notion that we have to talk about racial subjects as "real" subjects. This tendency is not hard to understand, since dehumanization has long been the tool of discrimination. The problem, however, is that in trying to compensate for that history, we often sacrifice discussions of all the immaterial, pressing, unquantifiable elements that go into the making of "reality" and end up with a very narrow definition of what constitutes "material" history. Similarly, this attachment gets reproduced at the level of methodology, where "material analysis" comes to take precedence and legitimacy over other, supposedly more ephemeral or quietist analytical tools. This study argues that we have to reconceptualize not only the subject and object of race studies but also the methodology.

In trying to nuance the notion of identity, some critics have turned to a discourse of multiplicity and hybridity. While both concepts contribute to complicating assumptions of subjective integrity, their evocations have also led to another form of nomination whereby identity becomes multiple and serialized without addressing the fundamental processes of identification. Lisa Lowe's important essay, entitled "Heterogeneity, Hybridity, Multiplicity: Asian American Difference,"[60] highlights both the urgency and the limitation of positing heterogeneity and hybridity as safeguards against essentialism in the formations of racial and disciplinary categories. Echoing Gayatri Spivak's notion of a "strategic essentialism," Lowe writes:

> I argue for the Asian American necessity—politically, intellectually, and personally—to organize, resist, and theorize *as Asian Americans*, but at the same time I inscribe this necessity within a discussion of the risks of a cultural politics that relies upon the construction of sameness and the exclusion of difference. (68; my emphasis)

But how does this balancing act really work? The idea, while lucid on a political level, is less so on a subjective level. It cannot address the complexity of identification as a psychical process. In short, beyond the strategic issue lies the psychical issue: What are the conditions and expenses for supporting such double consciousness?

I cannot but wonder if an illusory opposition has been established between hybridity and essentialism, as though the former cures the latter; as though differences of class, gender, and nationality eliminate essentialist positions when clearly those different positions are themselves each effecting their own brands of allegiances, each demanding "an" identity. When we turn to Lowe's analysis of Maxine Hong Kingston's novel *The Woman Warrior*, we see the kind of question that remains to be explored:

> [T]he making of Asian American culture may be a much "messier" process than unmediated vertical transmission from one generation to another, including practices that are partly inherited and partly modified, *as well as partly invented* . . .

> [Kingston] asks: "Chinese-Americans, when you try to understand what things in you are Chinese, how do you separate what is peculair to childhood, to poverty, insanities, one family . . . from what is Chinese? What is Chinese tradition and what is the movies?" (65; my emphasis)

Lowe reminds us that "Chinatown" and "Chinese American culture" are themselves the very emblems "of shifting demographics, languages, and populations"(65). I want to focus attention, however, on that part of Asian American culture that Lowe calls "partly invented." To arrive at that "partly invented" seems to involve a different set of inquiries than a question of negotiating either strategic self-positioning or false homogenization and has much more to do with the problematics surrounding self-identification, the desire for such fiction, and the longing for the alibi of a genealogy not always available.

In the Kingston passage to which Lowe alludes, the narrator addresses the entanglement between private and public desires and, by extension, between personal and public self-representations. In the line "What is Chinese tradition; what is the movies?" Kingston questions precisely the possibility of maintaining a lucid, delineated identity when subjectivity as a discrete realm has been fundamentally compromised. We are viscerally reminded that the deconstruction (as "in taking apart") of the "composition of differences" (i.e., "class, gender, national diversities"), while crucial, remains insufficient to understanding how the process of identification is itself always already generating difference and sameness. The psyche has its own systems of heterogeneity, and we ought to ask: What are the ontological conditions under which "identify" can takes place? We are so often afraid in academia to talk about ontology, for fear of essentialism, universalism, or intellectual quietism. Yet sometimes the stringent fear of essentialism or essentialist labels prevents certain categories from being discussed, categories that, for all their inherent instability, nevertheless operate in powerful, fantasmatic ways.

A key term to mediate the relation between sociality and ontology must be *fantasy*, the very stuff of the"partly invented."[61] In a way, we can read the Kingston narrator's dilemma as a metaquestion about our methodology: how do we separate ontic and familial "selves" (an assumption and a preoccupation inherited from psychoanalysis) from the subject positions invented by society, culture, and politics? In fact, the very inability to tell the difference informs us that social and psychical cathexes work in collaboration. Social forms of compulsion and oppression may have their hold precisely because they mime or invoke ontic modes of identification.

If one of the sealing elements of American democracy—as well as that which threatens to undo it—is the process of racialization, then the nature of racial fantasy and of racial melancholia must surely alter how we conceive of ethics and politics. It is along these lines that psychoanalysis could illuminate the race question: not insofar as it elucidates private desires and psychology, but because psychoanalysis understands those private desires to be enmeshed in social relations. My use of psychoanalysis, to the purists, will most likely appear idiosyncratic. I do not deploy psychoanalysis as a diagnostic tool or as a prescription for universal psychological or familial development. I agree with Hortense Spillers who considers the Freudian Oedipal drama of the nuclear family to be an insufficient model for addressing those "occupied or captive persons and communities in which the rites and rights of gender function have been exploded historically."[62] I do, however, find in psychoanalytic thinking a powerful vocabulary for addressing that component of racial identification that is imaginatively supported, at once brash and elegiac.

There are currently several models for formulating psychoanalysis as a politically viable tool.[63] One approach comes from uncovering the socio-historical roots of psychoanalysis, whether it be an analysis of the development of psychoanalysis itself as a cultural history beginning in anti-Semitic Austria (Sander L. Gilman), a reading of class dynamics inhering in the psychoanalytic treatment (Jane Gallop on Dora), or a contextualization of Freud's work within the inheritances of nineteenth century imperialism and the colonial imagination (Mary Ann Doane). Yet another strategy is to subvert the terms within psychoanalysis by feminists interested in retrieving psychoanalysis as a productive tool (Jane Gallop on Jacques Lacan, Luce Irigaray and the school of *l'écriture feminine*, Spiller on incest, Tate on the Oedipal drama.)

These forms of intervention through psychoanalysis, however, still do not answer why we turn to psychoanalysis at all. One can reveal the social constituents or internal contradictions or hidden ideological suppositions of psychoanalysis itself, but why do we turn to that paradigm at all? This book hopes to begin a conversation about not why we *can* use psychoanalysis but why we *already do*. That is, as shown from *Brown* to Ellison and Morrison, the politics of race has always spoken in the language of psychology. The lesson of psychoanalysis speaks above all to the possibility that *intrasubjectivity exists as a form of intersubjectivity* and that *intersubjectivity often speaks in the voice of intrasubjectivity*: a mutually supportive system.[64] A progressive politics that does not recognize the place of subjective complicity can only be shortsighted.

Far from inscribing essentialism, psychoanalytic thinking recognizes essentialism as but a *guise* of subjectivity. The psychoanalytic subject is universal only insofar as it posits every subjective being as *historical* beings, embedded in time, family, and sociality. In her introduction to *Supposing the Subject*, Joan Copjec warns against the shortsightedness of seeing history as antithetical to the purviews of psychoanalysis.[65] She points out that history conceived linearly is truly ahistorical, while the psychoanalytic perspective teaches us to be attentive to the disjunctive and retroactive hauntedness of history—and, I might add, of the haunted of that history within the subject.[66] We should not conflate a haunted history with nonspecificity; on the contrary, haunted history alerts us to *context*. And it is from within this attention to contexts that we might be able to begin to reenvision a politics attuned to the reality of grief in all its material and immaterial evidence.

By looking at racial formation under the rubric of melancholia, this investigation generates a series of critical terms to address the repercussions of loss, fantasy, and mourning in American racial history. The goal is to forge a vocabulary with which to talk about subjective states vis-à-vis a racial geography beyond the immediate demands of advocacy. It is my hope that this study of racial melancholia will resist the closure of categories that we imagine to be vital to political conduct. If we are willing to listen, the history of disarticulated grief is still speaking through the living, and the future of social transformation depends on how open we are to facing the intricacies and paradoxes of that grief and the passions that it bequeaths.

BEAUTY AND IDEAL CITIZENSHIP

Inventing Asian America in Rodgers and Hammerstein's
Flower Drum Song (*1961*)

Overture

No genre is more familiar with, or more sympathetic to, the expression of pathological euphoria than the musical, and no musical more attached to the pathological euphoria of being "Asian American"[1] than Rodgers and Hammerstein's musical film extravaganza *Flower Drum Song* (1961). Directed by the Hollywood veteran Henry Koster and produced by the master of visual spectacles Ross Hunter, *Flower Drum Song* is a work that everyone who has seen it remembers. It is astounding how many people of various backgrounds and both genders can and do immediately launch into their renditions of "I Enjoy Being a Girl" whenever *Flower Drum Song* is mentioned. The very mention of this movie elicits response—song even—which is then usually followed by a gentle shake of the head or a roll of the eyes. What is this pleasure of identification and its immediate renunciation? Why is embarrassed irony used to counter the seduction of that tune? One might say that *Flower Drum Song* itself, as a public memory, symptomatically exhibits a form of excessive euphoria—an involuntary delight that finds itself slightly unseemly.

In 1957, San Francisco writer C. Y. Lee wrote the best-selling novel *Flower Drum Song*, which detailed love and life in Chinatown in the fifties.[2] Something of this story about an insular Chinese community invited avid public attention: shortly after the novel's publication, Broadway came knocking. Edward G. Robinson took a striking fancy to the novel and insisted on playing the father lead himself. Joseph Fields, the Broadway producer, quickly purchased the rights and was soon eagerly approached by Richard Rodgers and Oscar Hammerstein, who offered to develop the project. The musical, opening two years later in 1959, was directed by Gene Kelly. And two years later, Universal Pictures released the film version, made by Koster and Hunter.

So in 1961 *Flower Drum Song* burst into song and dance on the wide screen. Its appearance, however, remains extraordinary both in the history of Hollywood and in the history of imagining racial assimilation in the service of a national ideal. The first and arguably only Hollywood production to employ a full cast of actors of Asian descent (the original Broadway version used some white actors in "yellow face"), *Flower Drum Song* introduced Asians in America, as theme and body, into CinemaScope. Phenomenal for its time, and perhaps still for ours, the usually cinematically unseen bodies of Asians in America, suddenly enjoyed a unprecedented centrality on the wide screen. *Flower Drum Song* is noteworthy in other respects as well. Of Rodgers and Hammerstein's three "Orientalist" musicals, only *Flower Drum Song* is specifically preoccupied with the Asian presence *in* the United States. Unlike *South Pacific* (1958) and *The King and I* (1956), *Flower Drum Song* takes place within the domestic borders of America, and of these it is the one most obsessed with remarking that boundary. Set in San Francisco's Chinatown, the Hollywood version of *Flower Drum Song* is wholly preoccupied (at the multiple levels of plot, theme, music, and the visual) with the specific and anxious transformation of *Asians* into *Asian Americans*, from *aliens* to *citizens*.

This tale of citizenship is told through a story about beauty. The plot is simple. Framed by a clash between romantic and marital customs of East and West, the movie tells the story of the erotic choice faced by young Wang-Ta (James Shigeta) between two "Oriental beauties": Linda Low, a flashily Westernized nightclub singer (played by Nancy Kwan), and Mei Li, a subtle Eastern beauty (played by Miyoshi Umeki). Concurrently, we also find a subplot about immigration, focused on the successful rite of passage into American citizenship via naturalization of Wang Ta's aunt, Madame Liang (Juanita Hall). Read as a morality play about the intimate relationship between erotic and national choice, between beauty and racial imagination, *Flower Drum Song* offers us an American comedy of amatory and social integration by performing love, song, and nationhood with insistent jubilance.

But the very appearance of this movie, its determined elation, and its basic plot raise two central questions. First, what does it mean in 1961 to celebrate American nationhood vis-à-vis a community that, from a legal and historical perspective, has been all but excluded from U.S. citizenship, at least right up to the mid–twentieth century, the time of this production? Second, how does Hollywood in 1961 make palatable, even desirable, those bodies normally not allowed in the field of vision, much less idealized?

Arriving in California as early as the 1820s and initially regarded as welcomed labor, Chinese workers subsequently became competition for the white labor force made up largely of European immigrants. A series of treaties was signed to exclude the Chinese from naturalization, land ownership, and other rights. While the Naturalization Act of 1790 provided for citizenship by naturalization for "any free white person of good, moral character who had resided in this country for at least two years" and the Naturalization Act of 1870 extended this privilege to aliens of African birth and persons of African descent, nothing was said about allowing naturalization to individuals neither white nor black.[3] Meanwhile, restrictions on Asian immigration tightened, culminating in an act of national denial: in 1882, the Chinese Exclusion Act barred entry of laborers for ten years; the exclusion was then extended indefinitely in 1904; then the Immigration Act of 1924, also known as the National Origins Act, prohibited entry into the United States for permanent residence to all persons whose national origin sprang from within what was labeled the Asia-Pacific Triangle, constituting the first and only act of legalized immigration discrimination based on race in the United States. This 1924 law stayed in place until World War II when, out of embarrassment because of the United States' alliance with China and the Philippines against Japan, the government repealed the Chinese Exclusion Act in 1943. Not until 1952 did the McCarren-Walter Act abolish the restrictions on the Asia-Pacific Triangle and race-based exclusions from naturalization, making the character Madame Liang in the novel *Flower Drum Song* (1957) the first generation of Asians to be legally recognized by the nation as American citizens. The McCarran-Walter Act preserved a system of racial quotas, which were not completely revoked until the Hart-Callar Act, which took full effect in 1968. Starting in 1965, with the repeal of laws that had sharply restricted immigration from Asia since the 1920s, the number of Americans of Asian descent rose from one million in the mid-sixties to nine million in the mid-nineties.[4] Hence, *Flower Drum Song* the novel and its subsequent theatrical incarnations (Broadway in 1959 and Hollywood in 1961) are sandwiched between these significant reformations (of 1952 and 1968) in U.S. immigration policy and are at the cusp of a great demographic change. The progression from the novel to its theatrical disseminations registers both the birth of these new American citizens and the nation's response to them.

Out of this history of begrudging national acceptance comes *Flower Drum Song*, singing its affirmation of the place of the Chinese in the American melting pot. The intricate conjunctions and disjunctions between body and sign, at this pivotal point of immigration, citizenship, and demographic transformations, renders this nationally released movie a particularly powerful site where the Chinese in America comes to be figured. This gala confirmation of the place of the Chinese in the American narrative through the marital plot of familial and comic unification is even more peculiar when we consider the gender history that accompanied the history of racialization instituted by the immigration policies just briefly outlined. In the years between 1850 and the 1950s, as a result of the immigration laws restricting female immigration, there arose what came to be called "bachelor societies" in the Chinatowns of New York and San Francisco.[5] The original novel by C. Y. Lee, for instance, was much more bittersweet, even tragic, in its recounting of life and love in San Francisco Chinatown in the fifties. It addresses the problems of immigrant cultural formation, generational transmission of cultural mores, and sexuality in a confined community newly coming to grips with radically changing demographics.

Produced in the wake of the repeal of the Chinese Exclusion Act, the Rodgers and Hammerstein movie version in contrast clearly aims to promote assimilation and reflect a new, positive image of Chinatown, and the Chinese, across America. Similarly, in focusing on erotic and marital rites in Chinatown, the movie seeks to resexualize (that is to say, heterosexualize) the face of Chinatown. But the face of this new national and gendered American citizen grows more and more perplexing under examination. A morality play about national identity, *Flower Drum Song* offers multiple narratives (diegetic, visual, choreographic, musical) that tell very different stories about that identity. The love choice in the movie presents itself as a choice between opposing images of female beauty, each of which is in turn symbolically and lyrically linked to standards of legality and nationhood. The movie thus codifies a national narrative about immigration, aimed to create a new face of citizenship that is in fact unsightly for the audience and for the self. (As the song goes, "Love, look away . . . from me.")

It is perhaps not so surprising that this supposedly new positive image of Asians in America would turn out to have its negative counterface. In *Romance and the "Yellow Peril": Race, Sex, and Discursive Strategies in Hollywood Fiction*,[6] Gina Marchetti gives us a comprehensive account of how Hollywood filmmakers deploy Asia and Asians, whether they be insidiously evil or naively innocent, as screens against which nationalist fantasies of interracial rape, lynching, tragic love, and model marriage are projected and played out. It is almost a truism today to point out the constitutive ways in which Orientalism has been enlisted to secure Occidentalism. Indeed, the Asian presence in the history of Hollywood cinema has mostly been thought of as a dismal parade of stereotypes. It is generally believed that "Asian American cinema" did not exist as such until the late 1980s when it was launched by the groundbreaking works of Wayne Wang in films such as *Chan Is Missing* (1982) and *Dim Sum* (1985). Yet this perception of the birth of Asian American cinema out of a history of unbearable discrimination and visual denigration, while accurate enough on some level, elides the more intricate effects of that history, as well as contemporary Asian American filmmakers' complex engagement with that history.[7] What is missing from such an overview are the historical complexities involved within the enactment of (and contact with) those images, both for the dominant culture and for those being stereotyped.

Out of that dark history, the brilliant colors of *Flower Drum Song* flicker, refusing to lie flat. The disregard for ethnic differences aside (and there was a profound disregard), *Flower Drum Song* still astonishes simply because it fills the stage with Asian-looking bodies. This visual investment should not be underestimated. I propose that this visual impact complicates, rather than confirms, the Orientalist fantasy that this movie is supposed to offer. For the "real" Asian bodies solicited to "play themselves," far from granting substance to the fiction, heighten the instability underlying such efforts of delineation. It is difficult, not to mention shortsighted, to dismiss this piece of mass culture as yet another mere Orientalist fantasy to emerge out of Hollywood, precisely because of the questions it raises about racial embodiment and disembodiment, about presence and projection.

As this chapter will demonstrate, while the Rodgers and Hammerstein production of *Flower Drum Song* "whitewashes" the more historically and racially negative aspects of Lee's novel, the resulting product still evinces traces of that dark history. The inevitable staining attests not only to the irreducible, historic denigration structuring the heart of this particular imagined community but also highlights the musical's generic and inherent affinity for the abject lurking underneath forms of cultural mania.[8] This affinity, furthermore, complicates the binarism separating the truth of subjection and the pleasures of performance.

Flower Drum Song troubles the history of gendering and citizenship-making through its conflicted recruitment of feminine beauty in the service of creating an image of the ideal citizen, making femininity at once the very sign and excess of the *ideal national subject*. While this movie attempts to delineate a visage of citizenship—an ideal, gendered American identity—through the ideology of beauty and the morality of a culturally "healthy" erotic choice, it is equally enthralled by the face of degradation. The female subject made to confront such ideality, in all her acts of approximation, however, may still exude an affect and a presence that exceed that ideality and its humiliations. This chapter is an effort to find a vocabulary to talk about that affect and presence.

In this film about Asian Americans played by Asian Americans, the stereotype—along with its accompanying vocabulary of beauty/unsightliness—produces an extravagance about and a specularization of the racial self that reveals fraught negotiations between notions of social and national alienation and familiarity: a negotiation of distance and approximation that I will suggest is the very movement of beauty and of the racial imaginary. For the denigrated racialized subject, self-representation must finally be much more complicated than either denying or assenting to stereotypes. In other words, in *Flower Drum Song*, the question of the stereotype does not expose the difference between East and West; rather, it *announces* the active engagement between the ideological constructions of the two, which in turn articulates a profound anxiety about one's own racial difference and national position. And the expression of that apprehensive negotiation declares itself in both manic and depressed forms. In the end, as I will contend, exuberant theatrical extravagance offers neither the denial nor the containment of that anxiety, as one might expect; instead, it is the very *mode* of that anxiety on which a peculiar form of melancholic national identity—what will be called "Asian Americanness"—gets born.

Disciplining the Stereotype: Law and Disorder

The Chinese remain the world's most erratic top gymnasts, and today, like many a Ming vase, their routines looked lovely but had cracks in several places.

—*New York Times* (on the 1996 Summer Olympics)

Flower Drum Song's "bad" (that is, Orientalist, politically incorrect) representations highlight a set of unresolved complexities that still plague our moral certitude about stereotypes today. I do not mean to suggest only that Asian stereotypes continue to operate; they of course do in various manifestations. It is always easy to identify grotesque, racist images, such as a recent cover of the *National Review* where, in response to the Asian campaign donation controversy, we are treated to the faces of the Clintons morphing into "Asians" with buck teeth, slanted eyes, Mao suits, and coolie hats.[9] The issue, however, gets stickier when we encounter more elaborate fields of representation, whereby representation itself comes to be highlighted as a *constitutive* apparatus of identity, constructing what Homi Bhabha calls "regimes of truth,"[10] or when that representation foregrounds itself as the very *technology* of embodiment. I am thinking, for example, of Anna Deavere Smith's mimetic theater, where the lines between caricature, stereotype, and political representation become far more difficult to distinguish, or of Philip Kan Gotanda's much celebrated play *Yankee Dawg You Die*, which builds its central conflict around the equivocal difference between *assenting to* and *using* a stereotype. It is clear that we do not yet have a vocabulary, beyond the moralistic one, in which to examine the space in between: the ambiguous middle area in the continuum between egregious *stereotypes* on the one end and the strategic deployment of *types* (tropes by which we recognize ourselves) on the other end.

Whose truth is being constituted in these systems of representation, these "regimes of truth"? What about their afterlife? Once in circulation, what happens to these truths and on whom do they continue to act? What is the fetish object's relationship to the fetishistic imagination?[11] Where do we as contemporary viewers locate the "truth," for example, when we enter *Flower Drum Song* and see "authentic" Asian actors singing a celebration of their own "Chop Suey-ness" while denoting the falseness of the stereotype? In a well-known scene, the character Madame Liang, played by Juanita Hall, receives her citizenship certificate (from a certain Professor Cheng) and a musical celebration ensues (figure 1).[12] This party may be considered a communal celebration, since Madame Liang would be one of the first new generations of Asian immigrants to receive citizenship, in essence one of the first new "Asian Americans." To praise Madame Liang as a new sign of mutual American and Asian integration, Madame Liang and the entire party sing the song "Chop Suey," which the characters themselves inform us is a purely American fiction of Asian cuisine—that is, none of the characters on that stage imagines that he/she is celebrating "chop suey" and their own cultural status as "the real thing." Furthermore, everyone in the world of this movie seems to be aware that what *sells* Chinatown is not "real Chinese food" but chop suey. This is a peculiarly self-conscious performance of the stereotype as stereotype. How do we read this layered, self-conscious, and staged solicitation of the stereotype? While we can simplify the issue at hand by saying that Rodgers and Hammerstein, and theatrical circumstances, forced such a stereotype onto the actors, this cannot account for why the number itself gets introduced *as a stereotype* and the breach between meanings consequently opened up for those singing. Beyond the apparent irony, there are some truths being sung here: the truth that the "real" America is constituted by a fantasy of ethnicities, what these Asian American performers denote when they meticulously place Chinatown in the heart of America: "Grant Avenue, San Francisco, California, U.S.A." By situating and performing this exoticized, overly produced other-world as the recursive, constitutive negative space of American nationalism, in a sense, these "foreigners" are acting out the essence of Americanness.[13]

At the same time, the "essence" of these "foreigners" is also being transformed. That is, born out of Rogers and Hammerstein's most dramatic efforts, the *mise en scène* of the *mise en scène* is already registering the anticipation that "the people" of Chinatown (already culturally misrecognized and legally unrecognized by the larger American national narrative) may enact their "authentically" ethnic narrative precisely through the solicitation and the acting out of the very signs of their misrecognition. Beyond assenting to the practical and limited conditions of theatrical employment for Asian Americans in the fifties, the cast of *Flower Drum Song* reminds us that Chinatown is itself already a construction of American Orientalism in both its most abjecting and most idealizing forms. Chinatown as a geographic formation, after all, grew out of economic and racial segregation, and its subsequent revival is founded on the economy of tourism, an excursion through the specularization of "Oriental style." In other words, it is sufficient to note not just that Rodgers and Hammerstein enlist Oriental decorations on the set and in the score but also that Chinatown as an American

Figure 1. *Madame Liang (Juanita Hall) in "Chop Suey." Courtesy of the Museum of Modern Art, New York*

concept *is*, to a large extent, Oriental decoration—*is*, as we all know, it-self a *mise en scène* of Victorian buildings made over with Orientalized facades. And the people in it remain to this day relentlessly engaged with the intimate, productive, disabling, profoundly complicated effects of public self-representation.

"Chinatown" as a tenacious exercise in and engagement with Asian stereotypes can be seen not only in its architecture but also in its self-presentation to the public and to the nation. In the same year that *Flower Drum Song* was released by Universal Pictures, the Chinese Chamber of Commerce published a publicity booklet, "San Francisco Chinatown on Parade: In Picture and Story," which undertook to explain everything from "Oriental manners" to "Oriental beauty."[14] Chinatown as a business and a community fostered economic opportunities by profiting from and encouraging certain racial stereotypes that were clearly crippling in other ways. Included in this booklet is an essay by C. Y. Lee, author of the novel *Flower Drum Song*, who expressed gratitude to Rodgers and Hammerstein and Universal International for making his story a popular household name in America. But Lee's delight with the newfound, mainstream interest in his book is not without a tinge of disenchantment. There is an odd moment of repressed anxiety, when Lee volunteers (and then immediately dismisses) a quote from journalist Walter Winchell, who had wondered whether *Flower Drum Song* was a story about "some pansy and a bongo player."[15] Anyone who has seen the play understands that the "bongo player" refers to Mei Li, the female star, in her leading song "One Hundred Million Miracles," while her partner the "pansy" could refer only to her father (who coperforms that song) or her love interest, played by James Shigeta. The journalist's barely disguised homophobia and racism clearly provoke anxiety on Lee's part about the tenuous condition of Asian American masculinity in American cultural perception—a concern that is to provide the backbone of David Henry Hwang's play *M. Butterfly* some thirty years later on Broadway.

Thus even as Lee, the spokesperson for Chinatown in this pamphlet, celebrates mainstream America's open endorsement of *Flower Drum Song*, he is not unaware of the darker timbres of that reception. What turns out to be most interesting about this booklet is the evidence of a "community" that is trying to imagine itself into being *precisely* through an act of self-representation that is fashioned on a continual, difficult, and intimate engagement and disengagement with previously existing images about it, stereotypical or otherwise. When approaching a text such as Rodgers and Hammerstein's version of *Flower Drum Song*, it is crucial to examine it not just as a "white" cultural product but within the context of its layered exchange with and initial address to the community from which it came. Consequently, a reader needs to bypass image analysis on the level of moral judgment and instead work toward an analysis of the ways in which the evocations of stereotypes in this movie provoke deeper and more vexing problems surrounding the cultural signification of the object of fetish, the racial-ethnic subjects. Clearly a representation not constructed by Asian Americans, *Flower Drum Song* the movie can nonetheless teach us about the complexities behind the seeming luxury of "self-representation."

Such nuances are, of course, not recognized on the diegetic level, which blithely constructs itself on a series of traditional dramatic conflicts: age versus youth, past versus future, family versus desire, etherealness versus sensuality, poetry versus "Fan Tan Fanny"—the very stuff of musical melodrama. These simple binaries are here marshaled under the overarching conflict of "East" versus "West." But almost immediately, complications trouble these simplistic thematic oppositions, for we of course never leave the West. The movie begins by reminding us of our domestic location, when stowaways Mei Li and her father, landing in Chinatown, discover that no one speaks or reads Chinese. Right away, Chinatown as a community is made to embody within its borders a transnational conflict, and a confusing one at that, since we have here two Chinese characters breaking not just into America but into Chinatown. Later we see, within the racial figure of Nancy Kwan, a fantasmatic interracial threat, making a profound statement about Chinatown *as* a cultural and ethnic predicament in

America, a predicament of boundary. But for now, we note that the very *mise en scène* of the American musical in Chinatown confounds the politics of reading "East" and "West." Not only do Rodgers and Hammerstein tack on "Oriental" motifs to a "regular" American musical—after all, where else could one come home, not to a Dear John letter, but to find "in the icebox" a farewell "can . . . of Moo Goo Gai Pan"?—but more provocatively, their deployment of stereotypes evokes a fundamental problem of authenticity in ethnic representation.

Even in the politically unlikely theater of Rodgers and Hammerstein, we are beginning to see an uneasy confluence of race as sign and body, suggesting that prior to our heightened contemporary consciousness about the stereotype, the stereotype was already foregrounding itself as a problem about "truth." The appearance of the stereotype as symptom and as performance always already *marks* a disturbance in its supposed fixity. And the problem of truth (and authentic representation) boomerangs back to whiteness itself. Homi Bhabha has deconstructed the ideology of "fixity" assumed by the stereotype in its construction of otherness. He points out that persistent presence of the stereotype reveals instead an expression of instability:

> a form of knowledge and identification that vacillates between what is always "in place," already known, and something that must anxiously be repeated . . . as if the essential duplicity of the Asiatic or the bestial sexual license of the African that needs no proof, can never really, in discourse, be proved.[16]

In other words, the stereotype's promise of a fixed image exposes an anxiety about the verifiability or tangibility of such fixed truth.

In addition to the anxiety of fixity, we should be attentive to how the *very deployment of the stereotype already traces the impossibility of its desires.* For the work of management cannot operate without coming into intimate contact with that which it seeks to separate, contain, and fix. Even in a simplistic image such as the cover of the *National Review* briefly mentioned earlier we can see that in the stereotype there is a constant encounter, if not literal collusion, with the other, offering us a series of vertiginous paradoxes. The faces of America (symbolized by the First Couple) "pass" into the faces of Asia. The intended disgust comes not from the fixity of the stereotype but from the dissolution of boundary effected by the stereotype. More than rehearsing grotesque racial stereotypes, the cartoon caricature presents the real horror of an identificatory assimilation that has taken place *on the white body.* The complication that renders this clichéd racist image provocative is that we get to witness the *collision* between the stereotype as the other and the usually unarticulated anxiety of the white self to remain unaffected by its use of the stereotype. The introduction of the racial stereotype must therefore always bring into question the unquestionable realness supposedly untouched by the stereotype, the "original real," what the stereotype supposedly cannot speak to: whiteness itself.

So the question of what is Chinese in this movie also cannot escape its double: what is American. Not surprisingly, this Orientalist movie's central conflict between Eastern and Western ways reveals a profound preoccupation with Americanism, its definition and its limitations. By Americanism, I mean the work, the ideologies, the memories that go into constructing the idea of America. In 1959, white domestic America was struggling to emerge from McCarthyism, barely processing the philosophical and practical implications of *Brown v. Board of Education*, and reeling from traumatic challenges such as the Montgomery bus boycott. On the international front, America in 1959 is perhaps not so far away from memories of World War II and the more recent end of the Korean War (1953). (Certainly the presence of Asian war brides, of so-called Oriental femininity, in America further troubles the boundaries of American integrity.) The tectonic plates of "what is American" were shifting in profound and radical ways. Hollywood, as the last haven of preserved dreams, worked overtime to produce its Technicolor reassurances. And *Flower Drum Song* insistently harks to the 1960s ideas of the aesthetic making of cultural America. Choreographically, for example, the movie offers a jubilant exhibition of American dance styles, from square dancing to jazz, from the cha-cha to the cakewalk (figure 1). Such insistent celebration, in a changing ethnic enclave of America in the fifties (and in light of those styles' own ethnic origins), can only announce an anxiety over the very idea of "an" American style. Contemporary reviewers of the movie and the Broadway play noted the show's lack of stylistic innovation,[17] but its absence of stylistic innovation is linked to its fundamental desire for thematic and formal conservation.

Choreographically recording the history of American dance and music, *Flower Drum Song* articulates a deep longing for that history, for that "style." And where better to enact that yearning than the newly opened Chinatown as a potential hotbed of freshly assimilating citizens? Equally concordant, in "Chop Suey," a lyrical homage to and recipe for American diversity, the ingredients do not include anything "Asian": "Hula hoops and nuclear war, Doctor Salk and Zsa Zsa Gabor,"[18] as though the imagination for American pluralism in 1961 cannot include anything that might have originated in Asia, as though *diversity is being sung here to withstand the threat posed by the very people singing it.*

Flower Drum Song's ambivalence toward the fulfillment of what we today call American diversity finds its fullest expression in theatricality itself. As Ralph Ellison once wrote, "When American life is most American it is apt to be most theatrical." Pointing to the Boston Tea Party and the rebelling colonists' donning of Native American masks as an originary moment in

American founding, Ellison tells us that the tradition of masking, especially the adopting of racial masks to both veil and authenticate whiteness, has played a persistent role in the process of Americanization. Quoting from Yeats, Ellison makes a direct link between theatricality and discipline:

> "There is a relation between discipline and the theatrical sense. If we cannot imagine ourselves as different from what we are and assume the second self, we cannot impose a discipline upon ourselves. . . . Active virtue, as distinct from the passive acceptance of a current code, is the wearing of a mask. It is the condition of an arduous full life."[19]

Indeed, the "arduous" chore of authenticating Americanness must have been further fortified when, two centuries later, white Americans no longer need to assume that racial mask, especially when the racial other can be made to perform the tasks of both the masking and the discipline. In short, why discipline the other when the other can be made to discipline her/himself?

Here in Madame Liang's number, "Chop Suey," extravagance becomes the very *mode* of national exclusion: the enactment of the multicultural desire needs to maintain its extravagance—a pronounced distinction between performer and the performed—in order to save the lyrics being rendered from the miscegenation taking place on the visual level (that is, the "Asian" bodies performing and occupying the history of "American" song and dance). *You can sing it but you can't be it.* Thus by calling these moments *pathological euphoria* I do not mean to repathologize the Asian American figure; instead I am alluding to the solicitation of euphoria (and here the euphoria of being a hyphenated subject, the "Asian-American") as a means of alleviating the pains of exclusion.

Madame Liang's exclusion from the ideology she is singing is doubly poignant when we consider the central role that music has historically played in orchestrating the dream of the melting pot in the popular imagination. Werner Sollors has observed that musical metaphors—symphony, harmony, orchestra—have long played central roles in symbolizing the melting pot.[20] Citing songwriters from Stephen Foster to George Gershwin, from E. P. Christy to Irving Berlin, Michael Rogin has proposed that music in America has served as an instrument, not just a symbol, of such diversity.[21] It is little wonder then that the musical is a genre particularly taken to the formulation of the melting pot. The musical as a genre has thus long sung out with fervor the American dream of harmonizing ethnic and religious differences that are much harder to reconcile in social reality.[22] But at the edge of the musical's celebration of intermixing, the discordant note of racial difference (and the potential threat of miscegenation) has always introduced a tragic key, or at least lent a desperately insistent tone, to the radiance of its songs.

Flower Drum Song's fundamental ambivalence about the transformation of the alien body into a domestic body shows up in characterization as contradictions, so that the very bodies embodying the realization of domesticated otherness are also made to bear, paradoxically, the imperfection of that transmutation. In the opening sequence, we find two main characters, the young woman Mei Li and her father, stowed away on a boat that docks in San Francisco. When Mei Li offers to sing a "traditional Chinese song" (that Rodgers and Hammerstein creation "A Hundred Million Miracles") on the streets of San Francisco for money, the father worries about the propriety of such performance and warns, "It is unlucky to start in a new country by breaking the law." The irony that this man is anxious about breaking civic law when he has already flagrantly broken the larger law of immigration highlights a deeper double bind within "naturalization": to survive, the stranger who has violated the law must also represent law, as an ideal citizen. When he enters San Francisco's Golden Gate, the father simultaneously becomes both the illegal alien *and* the model minority.[23]

Indeed, illegality furnishes the very solution to this national morality play. Initially the very picture of Chinese health and beauty, praised for possessing not only "a figure like a Ming vase" but also "good teeth," Mei Li turns out to be, concurrently, an agent of transgression and disorder. In the finale, after despair and frustration, Mei Li finally lights upon a solution to free herself from the bonds of an arranged marriage. On the threshold of that undesired marriage ceremony, she turns away from the minister and announces to her newfound American friends: "I must confess . . . my back is wet!" She declares her own abject status with barely suppressed joy. In other words, only by exposing herself as an object of prohibition can she claim the particularly American dream of the liberty to marry for love. Only by assenting to illegality can she hope to acquire "free" love and make herself worthy of the ideal privileges granted to citizens of the United States. Her public confession and self-indictment ironically anticipates the naturalization process, where one acquires citizenship through a rhetoric of rebirth predicated on self-renunciation ("Do you swear to give up . . ."). In addition, we recall that Mei Li lifted her "wetback" idea from a Western B movie she saw on television the night before, echoing a tradition of Western border crossing. When Mei Li turns around to denounce herself, she simultaneously assents to three interpellative calls: American law, public/communal judgment, and American cinema.[24]

Mei Li's borrowing of the term "wetback" may be even more uncanny than it first appears. The term "wetback," understood mostly as referring to illegal Mexican aliens, also has an entangled history with illegal Chinese aliens. The disparaging label (*mojado*) has been used since the 1920s to designate unsanctioned immigrants who crossed the Rio Grande from Mexico in order to enter the United States without legal inspection,[25] but it was in the interest of excluding Chinese illegal entry that the first efforts were made to establish "border control." The 1882 Chinese Exclusion Law was passed, for example, to prevent the illegal trafficking in Chinese, not Mexicans. In a sense, in the eyes of immigration authorities, the Chinese were the first "wetbacks." Media manipulation of the term increased in the 1940s and 1950s as part of the political struggles over U.S. immigration and labor policies, which not only targeted Mexican immigration but also raised the central concern of the so-called Chinese Question.

This movie suggests that to assume a national identity always partially involves the remembrance of one's original status as alien, other, illegitimate. This national identity may be said to be actively melancholic in that it is an identity that is legislated through loss. With the Asian American and the immigrant figure such as Mei Li, we have a doubly melancholic figure: her loss to and exclusion from the nation into which she steals is not only remembered but celebrated as remembrance and the very cachet of membership in American nationhood. Since nationhood designates a modern community that subordinates traditional, "organic" ties such as ethnic communities under national allegiances, it can never be reduced to purely symbolic bonds; that is, a nation can confer citizenship at will, but how does it solicit faith in that contract? National identity thus very often constitutes itself through the resistance to threats, and it just as often stages those threats. This is why transgression is the adventure of civilization, why the defense of the law often requires the violation of law. Hence the jubilant acquisition of ideal citizenship instantiates both the demand of and the transgression against law, the pathological euphoria undergirding American citizenship.

The images of Asians and Asian Americans in this movie both instantiate and threaten the idea of ideal citizenship; the healthy, lawful female body comes to embody disorder and malady. Mei Li's deft and timely verbal plagiarism reminds us that the popular cultural narrative of America has always already included sites of transgression that are detours through which one arrives at the "home-ness" of America.[26] The immigrants who finally attain this national ideal, especially those who enjoy the memory/narrative of attainment as part and parcel of their new national identity, are those initially branded as prohibited by law. While the movie celebrates on one level the elective nature of immigrant citizens (that is, Madame Liang, one of the first generations of Asian immigrants to become a U.S. citizen and who apparently *chooses* the American way, unlike her old-fashioned brother-in-law) it also underscores the transgressive, even unnatural, nature of that adoption.[27] For Mei Li—an *improper* subject, the illegal alien—to become proper, she must learn to own (and own up to) her impropriety: as that which exceeds appropriate and appropriable boundaries *and* as that which cannot be fully owned by the self, since that "self" is already hegemonically defined as unauthorized. Consequently, Mei Li's loveliness must have its "cracks." The perfect "good Chinese girl," Mei Li is after all also the consummate thief in the movie, stealing everything from a bowl of rice to movie lines to citizenship.

Beauty and Narcissism

There is a song, a white song . . . who can tell me what beauty is?
—Frantz Fanon

Flower Drum Song's implicit beauty contest, like its real-world versions, stages a competition as much of racial and national ideologies as of beauty. The claim that notions of female beauty turn on racial standards, however, is simultaneously assumed, noted, and undertheorized.[28] What is beauty in the racial imaginary? Turning to the overly aestheticized figure of Nancy Kwan, the "other beauty" in this love competition, I take up here the question of beauty: its song, seduction, and excess in relation to the racial imaginary. Like most visual transactions, film is a medium inflected by specular politics and narcissism. Its built-in look-at-me-ness produces a structural politics of the gaze: who is watching whom; who is performing for whom. So it is not surprising that this Ross Hunter production of ethnic spectacle would be obsessed with the question of beauty: what constitutes to-be-looked-at-ness and what constitutes unseemliness. Wang Ta's erotic choice between the sexy Linda Low and the ethereal Mei Li is thematized as an aesthetic dilemma, which in turn implicates moral and racial standards.

In the history of Hollywood, beauty is very specifically linked to whiteness (and its various synecdoches: blondness, certain bodily features such as long legs, large, wide-set eyes, and so on). As Richard Dyer points out, "the codes of glamour lighting in Hollywood were developed in relation to white women, to endow them with a glow and a radiance that corresponds to the transcendental rhetoric of popular Christianity."[29] Whiteness, Dyer reminds us, *is* indeed a color, and *the* predominant color of cinematic beauty.

For years, yellow face remained a Hollywood tradition; Caucasians from Marlon Brando to Katharine Hepburn have played Asians on screen.[30] In spite of the elisions of ethnic differences, *Flower Drum Song* was and is still astounding in its insistent display of the Asian body. It remains the first and only major Hollywood production to have this claim.[31] How, then, did Hollywood in 1961 make palatable those bodies normally not allowed in the field of vision? How do we consider as visually gratifying those bodies usually framed as abject?[32] Right away, we can think of two answers: one can either remake that alien body over as much as possible in the image of whiteness or one can make that alien body so exotic and other that it can be admired as such. Here we have the two poles of beauty: beauty as norm/standard and beauty as exoticism. Although one can easily see the figurations of Linda Low and Mei Li as representing the two alternatives, I want to propose in what follows that the already culturally coded figure of Nancy Kwan playing Linda Low embodies a fantasmatic promise of *substitutive* whiteness and exoticism, thereby disturbing the security of that binarism even as it offers the complacent pleasure of having it both ways—a double promise that raises a set of questions about *distance* and *approximation* in the topography of racial imagination. Elaine Scarry has pointed out that beauty performs a kind of "radical decentering" by "unselfing" the spectator.[33] I would add that this radical decentering is not a moment of unselfing but a double movement of unselfing *and* selfing. That is, I argue, the prospect of beauty solicits and *enacts* in the viewer (even when the view is the self) the desire that is a form of identification and alienation already at work in the racial imaginary. A negotiating agent between the familiar and the exotic, beauty (whether it is about witnessing it or having it) interiorizes for the subject of the gaze a topography of distance, and as such, it enacts a synchronous process of identification and estrangement, which remains central to, yet always destabilizing, the notion of racial difference.

A material girl with all her bourgeois and economic sensibilities, Linda Low played by Nancy Kwan is coded by the movie, both visually and verbally, as "white." How much the actress and the character can assent to or be contained by that coding remains to be examined, but I will begin by looking at what is at stake in this curious "whitening" in the first place.[34] Diegetically categorized as the quintessential "L.L.D." ("long-legged dame"), Kwan's body is continually glamorized as a Western body.[35] In the movie's most famous scene, we find Linda Low in front of a three-way mirror entranced by her own visuality (figure 2). In the "I Enjoy Being a Girl" number, Linda/Nancy serenades herself in a tribute to her own beauty and femininity.[36] The most obvious things to notice are how insistently white the room is, how white the furnishings and the towel that covers her body are (not enough to hide those long legs of course), and how at ease she is in Western fashion. (In this literally white setting, Linda proceeds to put on a fashion show worthy of a salon in Paris, the preeminent stage of the European ideal of beauty and femininity). Indeed, the only time in the movie that Linda gives a bad performance, the only time she fails to be "a success in her gender," is when she puts on a Chinese dress. At Wang Ta's college graduation party, Linda crashes the soirée with a fake brother in tow, in a preemptive effort to introduce herself as Wang Ta's fiancee to his father, the old patriarch Wang Chi Yang (Benson Fong). Dressed for the first time in the traditional *chi-pao*, Linda tries to "act" Chinese, with miserable results. When her overeager perfume fills the night air and Mei Li the innocent asks,

Figure 2. *Linda Low (Nancy Kwan) in "I Enjoy Being a Girl." Courtesy of the Wisconsin Center for Film and Theater Research*

"Sweet incense! Do you wear it to keep away the evil spirits?" the actress in Linda cannot resist the opening and quips, "Oh, no . . . to attract them" (figure 3)! That is, even the tightly stitched *chi-pao* cannot prevent the Mae West in her from coming out.

Much to the consternation of everyone around her, including herself, the "real" Linda keeps resurfacing. Just seconds after this initial faux pas Linda commits her second blunder when, asked by the younger brother if she knows the song "You Be the Rock," she once again answers the call of Hollywood and launches into song and dance. An incurable performer, Linda must always respond to the call of exhibition. She continually exposes her worst shortcomings by displaying herself, foreshadowing her later and more fatal exposure in a strip act (figure 4). The problem with Linda Low is thus her Americanness: her irrepressible energy, her independence (living alone and needing the alibi of a pseudoguardian), her economic desires, her affinity for rock-and-roll, her love of being seen.

The plot tells us that for Wang Ta, the respectable Chinese boy, to marry Linda Low would indeed be to lower himself, to taint the "purity" of his Chinese background. According to Wang Chi Yang, the patriarch of the Wang family, Chinese purity can be preserved only through marriage with a "real Chinese girl from China." The threat represented by Linda Low the working girl, who is all too American and "white," turns out to be the threat of interracial relation itself. Insofar as the vocabulary of racial purity, tied

Figure 3. *Linda Low (Nancy Kwan) crashes house party at the Wangs' and meets her competition Mei Li (Miyoshi Umeki). Courtesy of the Museum of Modern Art, New York*

to prohibition against miscegenation and historically directed against African Americans, has played a significant role in American thinking about segregation and race relations through the nineteenth and twentieth centuries,[37] this movie effects a curious displacement, whereby Chinese masculine insistence on racial purity is allied with white masculine insistence on racial purity. This alliance, however, has its limits; it in fact serves to annul the potential threats of Chinese masculinity, since the preservation of Chinese racial purity would also sequester the Chinese away from the white world literally just outside of Chinatown. Thus, even as the movie diegetically sees "old Chinese ways" as old-fashioned and a hindrance to successful American assimilation, it also privileges those ways in order to redraw the boundary of Chinatown — limits that are threatened not by Mei Li who breaks into Chinatown but by assimilating characters like Madame Liang and Linda Low who do not understand the division between the world within Chinatown and the world without.[38] Thus the reification of Chinese patriarchal ideals serves to close off yet again the borders of Chinatown. Just as Mei Li's entry into America is marked by stealth, so is that white world's entry into Asian America marked as transgression, for the one white character/actor who appears in this movie is a thief who holds up Wang Chi

Figure 4. *Linda Low (Nancy Kwan) in the strip tease "Fan Tan Fanny."
Courtesy of the Wisconsin Center for Film and Theater Research*

Yang, the old Chinese patriarch, in front of a bank. The boundary separating America and Asian America is once again underscored, where the only crossing imaginable is one of theft and transgression.[39] This small incident also highlights the movie's underlying enmity between white and Chinese masculinities, in spite of their seeming alliance at the level of patriarchal value.

In the end, social order is restored and community confirmed by two "appropriate" marriages: the westernized nightclub owner Sammy Wong (Jack Soo), who speaks in perfect 1950s hipster slang, marries the equally westernized Linda Low, while Wang Ta, in order to marry Mei Li, must announce his willingness to lose his citizenship. (As Wang Ta cries to the assembly upon hearing Mei Li's confession about being a "wetback": "I don't care if they send me back to the old country!") All's well that ends well when partners of "equivalent" citizenship and legal status unite. The double wedding ratified by the Chinese Family Association dispels the threat of any kind of miscegenation. For Wang Chi Yang, the old Chinese patriarch, the "interracial" threat turns out not to be the other, but the self-as-other: the assimilated Chinese woman. In other words, interracial threat can finally never be fully entertained in the movie, except as a fantasmatic threat within intraracial relations: that is, except as the psychical threat of assimilation.

We have entered a precarious landscape where, even though we never leave the intraracial stage of Chinatown, we can feel the anxious vibrations of the "outside" world pressing up against the boundary of this set. While the marriage plot across ethnic and religious lines often symbolizes a celebratory form of Americanization, African Americans and Asian Americans are of course legally and symbolically excluded from that plot. Insofar as the language of miscegenation is tied in to a specific fear about African Americans,[40] Asian Americans, as neither black nor white, constitute a complicated category within the general American fear of miscegenation. With Asian Americans, the anxiety about miscegenation is just as strong but expresses itself in more veiled ways. One of those ways, as seen here in *Flower Drum Song*, speaks in the language of authentic immigrant, racial purity. (The presence of Asian war brides in America after World War II in the forties and after the Korean War in the fifties must have heightened the apprehension around the figure of the Asian woman and the dissemination of Asianness in America.) The tension between the American assimilative national ideal on the one hand and ethnic purity on the other creates mutually supportive exclusions, so that it becomes possible for us to see a reenactment of interracial anxiety on an essentially intraracial stage. Thus on the cusp of great legal immigration and citizenship reform in the United States for Asian Americans, we find underneath *Flower Drum Song*'s exuberant celebration a nostalgia for the Oriental exclusionist politics of the California labor and progressive movements.

Although we are to understand that, in this race for beauty, both Linda and Mei Li are beautiful in their own ways, according to different cultures and different values,[41] the movie tacitly asks an aesthetic-moral question: Which beauty bears a sustained gaze and which tarnishes over time? The diegesis gives us one answer: the plot educates Wang Ta, and perhaps the larger American audience, to appreciate Mei Li's brand of beauty, to learn to prefer "a figure like a Ming vase" over the "long-legged dame," just as Wang Ta himself had to slowly learn the truth of his final words to Mei Li, "You Are Beautiful to *Me*." The plot tells us that Linda's kind of overexposed beauty will pass into unseemliness, literally the obscene body in a strip act at the climax of the movie (a repeat performance of "Fan Tan Fanny"). I want to suggest, however, that the movie as a specular and narcissistic medium makes a very different choice. And it is *that* choice (who seduces the movie) that holds complicated implications for racial and cinematic representation.

The camera is in love with Linda Low. To understand this cinematic affection for Linda Low, we have to first unravel the publicity package that comes with Nancy Kwan, the actress. This movie's "white" makeover of this biracial actress might not be so peculiar were it not for the place she occupies in public memory. This is, after all, the very woman who, just a year before, in *The World of Suzie Wong*, had made a name for herself as Pure Asian Beauty itself and who to this day can be seen on television infomercials in the early morning hours still trading on that reputation as the spokesperson for Pearl Cream, hawking the "secret to eternal Oriental beauty."[42] The original trailer of *Flower Drum Song* released by Universal Pictures in fact drew on that memory of Kwan as representatively "Oriental," billing Nancy Kwan as "the star of *Suzie Wong.*" (It is of course revealing that the woman representing the "essence of the Orient" who would redeem Western degeneracy—William Holden's alcoholic character—would also be the representative prostitute.) Kwan therefore brings to *Flower Drum Song* a fully recognizable cultural signification as Asian femininity with all its idealization and denigration before even stepping into Linda Low's shoes.

Yet, while it was as Suzie that Kwan made the breakthrough move in her Hollywood career, the cultural (indeed, racial) signification she bears is anything but stable. After *The World of Suzie Wong* (1960) and *Flower Drum Song* (1961), Kwan played an Italian circus performer in *The Main Attraction* (U.K., 1962), an English Tahitian in *Tamahine* (U.K., 1963), and two English sisters in *The Wild Affair* (U.K., 1965). The public appetite for the "Oriental Lotus Blossom" reveals itself to be a fascination for not just exotic otherness but its ability to continually transform itself into *other* othernesses. In a series of publicity shots released to *This Week* magazine on September 4, 1960, at the height of her success, we see Kwan in a succession of costumes and roles: as a "Western gal," a "beatnik," an "Indian beauty," an "Eskimo," a "Spanish lady," and a "Parisian." Her "beauty" then is a beauty not only of racial mélange but also of racial *changeability*: it gives the sense that you are always getting something other than what you see. Hence in *Flower Drum Song*, whether it be Linda dressed up in a *chi-pao* or Linda stripped down in a nightclub, we get a peculiar sense of the "threat" posed by Linda as the body that can be resignified: the body beneath the dress *can* be in fact another kind of body. In the heart of beauty and ideality, we find perversion and changeability. Assimilation as a cultural ideal demands a tasteful makeover on the part of the unassimilable, racial other, but if the latter shows itself to be infinitely transformable, then that body will exceed the bounds of taste and normalcy. (This is perhaps why Linda's literal and moral unveiling in the end was so mortifying for the diegetic audience: they finally got to see what they feared, suspected, and desired all along, Linda's inappropriate combination of protrusive "whiteness" *and* "Asianness" in "Fan Tan Fanny," a truly obscene revelation in this world.)

The irony and sadness for Kwan as an actress is, of course, that while the public fascination for her turns very much on her fantasmatic "mixedness," the same public nonetheless never could in fact accept that multiplicity in practice. So while the same article and photospread in *This Week* magazine proclaimed that Kwan "can do anything any other eight girls can do," Kwan never could successfully escape being typecast as "the beauty from the Orient" and hence never became the kind of Hollywood star the media predicted she would become.

The complication surrounding Kwan's body as a cinematic, racial sign produces provocative effects on the notions of nationhood and citizenship that are being constructed in *Flower Drum Song*. The movie's most spectacular and most self-referential scene, turning on Kwan's performance of "I Enjoy Being a Girl," lays out an ideological system: the standard of beauty conditions the standard of femininity, which in turn conditions the standard of nationhood. What the "strictly female female" wants above all is the "home of the brave and free male." Not only is Linda singing the dream of American idealism but she is also enacting it by participating in the long tradition of, to borrow Michael Rogin's words, "making America by making music." It is easy to see Linda in this scene as merely assenting to the dual calls of gender and nationalism: a scene of perfect Althusserian interpellation. After all, Linda tells us, "I'm happy to know that the whistle's meant for me."[43] This scene also highlights something that Althusser does not talk about, which is how pleasure secures interpellation. Indeed, the scene suggests that ideology comes in the forms of pleasure and drama. What we enjoy is revealed to be part of the law; indeed, *how* we enjoy may be law itself.

It seems theoretically facile, however, to dismiss that pleasure as a side effect or technology of interpellation. There is a compelling sense of enjoyment and plenitude in this scene that makes it hard to read that pleasure as solely a pathological effect. Yes, Linda Low exhibits the euphoria of subjection. Yes, she has internalized the mirror of idealized whiteness as well as femininity. And yes, she reads like a classic case study of the Freudian beautiful woman who is pathologically narcissistic. But the movie medium, the dynamics of spectatorship, and Kwan's irreducible, extradiegetic Asian presence (as corporeality and as a famous namesake) on the screen, however white she is coded within the film, demand further thinking about how we understand pleasure, narcissism, and agency in relation to law.

The internalization of hegemonic mirroring or interpellation may be inevitable—one may always have to answer the call—but a consideration of the (racial, gender-based, historical) contingencies attached to the "answerer" profoundly changes the question of agency or compliance. According to Freud, the beautiful woman is pathologically and excessively narcissistic, unable to relinquish her primary infantile narcissism. In his essay "On Narcissism," Freud tells us that

> Women, especially if they grow up with good looks, develop a certain self-contentment which compensates them for the social restrictions that we imposed upon them in their choice of object. Strictly speaking, it is only themselves that such women love with an intensity comparable to that of a man's love for them. . . . The importance of this type of women for the erotic life of mankind is to be rated very high.[44]

Freud then claims that beautiful women hold profound fascination for men, because men find erotic incentives in being ignored, just as they find fascinating the indifference of the "child," "cats," and "large beasts of prey" (89). In other words, what is terrible (and wonderful) for Freud about female narcissism turns out to be the fact that such women do not *see* men. Freud goes on in the same paragraph to say, as if he has in his mind's eye some young woman in a Vermeer painting, "It is as if we envied [beautiful women] their power of retaining a blissful state of mind" (89).

Yet if Linda Low is pathologically narcissistic, she is also euphorically self-sufficient, a patient who enjoys her symptoms for all the world to see. Making props out of those symptoms, she performs gender for us: a brand-new hairdo, a frilly dress, a pound and a half of cream upon the face. To perform something is to denaturalize and alienate it, and here to alienate something is to enjoy it. Halfway through the number in front of the mirrors, Linda sits down and begins to watch with pleasure her reflections perform all on their own. Pleasure is to be found in the very specularization of the self. The three-way mirror acts as a literalization of what is going on specularly in that scene: not just *how I see myself* or *how others see me* but *how I see others seeing me*. This virtual third point of view turns this scene of mediation/interpellation into a scene also of multiplication, plenitude, and potential agency. Linda Low's body fractured into several images seems much less a fragmented body than a multiple and infinitely reproducible body.

So what differentiates multiplicity from fragmentation, a body occupying several places from a body in pieces? That is, is this a body of impoverishment or a body of production? In speaking of ego formation and the "mirror stage," Jacques Lacan offers a link between the fragmented body and the whole body. He proposes that the ego comes into existence at the moment when the infant subject first apprehends the image of its body within a reflective surface, and that this ego is itself a mental refraction of that image.[45] Ego formation for him is thus predicated upon an idealized wholeness: *le corps morcélé* is transfigured into a "spatially bounded totality," a promise of self-control and containment. In *Black Skin, White Masks*, Frantz Fanon reads the mirror stage as a racial parable. Speaking about black male subjectivity, Fanon calls the white-black relationship "narcissistic," suggesting that if the ideal racial/social mirror reflects the image of idealized whiteness, then "blackness" can only become an abhorrent, even obscene, visual image. He writes that, seeing himself through the white gaze, "[m]y body was given back to me sprawled out, distorted, recolored, clad in mourning in that white winter day."[46] The black body mourns for the totality/ideal bodily ego it has been told it has forever lost *and* never had, for the black body *is* formed by deformation. For the black man, this enforced identification can lead only to self-objectification and violent fragmentation:

> I took myself far from my own presence, far indeed, and made myself an
> object. . . . What else could it be for me but an amputation, an excision,
> a hemorrhage that spattered my whole body with black blood? (112)

Although Fanon is talking specifically about black male subjectivity—indeed, he has little time for women of color[47]—I would like to rethink his
insight into the logic of "minority ego" in relation to idealized whiteness
and ask, If the mirrors in Linda Low's room are social mirrors of idealized
whiteness, could we not very well imagine for this Asian American character that the result would be one of fragmentation, inapproximation, and self-
abhorrence? Linda's potential incommensurability in front of the racial mirror
is all the more pronounced when one recalls her Hollywood predecessor:
Marilyn herself in front of *her* three-way mirror in *How to Marry a Million-
aire* (1953). In that scene, there is never a question of Marilyn Monroe's
fullest assumption of the (racialized) image she projects, for she *is* image: the
very prototype of the idea of beauty, the essence of Warholian repetition.

So how does Kwan compete against Monroe in reflection? One answer is
that Linda Low's identification with idealized whiteness has been facilitated,
the potential self-abhorrence covered over, by gender identification. In short,
Kwan can persuade the audience of the sixties into accepting her as a substitute precisely through the fantasy of a female beauty that can erase
racial disparity, through the sincerity of her insistence, "I enjoy being a girl."
Another answer is performance itself. That is, in all the ways that an Asian
American actress and character may not measure up to the racial and/or
gender standards encoded in a history of Hollywood images, the act of
denaturalization paradoxically brings closer those impossible standards,
making them accessible, enjoyable, *wearable*. A third answer has to do with
the ideology of aesthetics and its mediation of race and gender. The woman
in front of the mirror is an image that has enjoyed a long cultural presence;
think of the stepmother of *Snow White*. Psychoanalytically speaking, mirror encounters have not usually been pleasant for female subjects; as Kaja
Silverman sums it up,

> the normative female subject is simultaneously coerced into an identifi-
> cation with anatomical and discursive inadequacy, and exhorted over
> and over again to aspire to the ideal of "the exceptional woman," the
> woman whose extravagant physical beauty miraculously erases all
> marks of castration.[48]

With Linda, we have precisely the fulfillment of that impossibility: a woman
whose extravagant physical beauty promises to erase all signs of castration
and all signs of racial difference. Perfection, after all, promises completion:
the lack of lack. As the script also tells us, in one of its most memorable lines:
"The most important thing for a woman to be is a success in her gender."

And Linda's feminine achievement can only be considered all the more successful for its warranty against racial lack. "A filly who is ready for the race," indeed.

If it is beauty's task to banish the specters of castration and race, then beauty offers an coercive identity predicated on an equally compulsive reminder of the haunting conditions of lack. For beauty as the fulfillment of a promise—a promise of fullness itself—is always most pronounced when its nominee proves to be less than sufficient to the nomination. (Suppose we were to revisit that dressing room twenty years later to find the same woman executing the same device. One may very well imagine another classic Hollywood plot where that lissomeness over time, still slender and now hardily maintained, may have acquired a harsher edge in the service of "landing a guy," whereby the joy of being a girl must now be considered in light of a last chance, shadowed by shades of nostalgia and taking on the more injunctive, burdensome flavor of a feminine weapon.) So beauty poses a consideration that always offers the opportunity for recognizing failure. The proposition that the Asian woman can be (or is always) even more feminine than the American woman embodies a teleological inscription of lack: the "strictly female female" does not have to worry about her racial lack because it guarantees the fullness of her femininity, of her castration.

Thus the mastery and assumption of female beauty by a nonwhite woman must also announce her remoteness from the norm of beauty, which is white female beauty. Indeed, beauty continuously provokes the negotiation of the distance between ideal and self: a negotiation of commensurability that paradoxically both announces itself (since that announcement is its own reward) and denies its own operations. Beauty promises an identity of wholeness and commensurability that is conditioned by incommensurability. Its logic not only echoes but expedites the logic of racial ideals: a demand for approximation that enunciates the simultaneity of desire and impossibility. The reason, therefore, that this beauty scene appears so jubilantly devoid of the threats of inapproximation and rejection is *not* because there are not any but because Kwan performs the protocols of beauty under the tautological assumption that such mechanisms have indeed already *worked*. Clearly the performance of an identity is most credible and all the more gratifying when accompanied by one's faith in oneself as already *being* what that performance/mirror promises—the sincerity of a performance being the true seduction of performance for any performer. That is, the whistle is always, and can only be, meant for her.

Only through the mark of beauty (that is, the claim that she is a "real beauty") can this biracial woman in Hollywood play out an ideal of authenticity. This entitlement, however, has dual effects: it reminds us of the possible negativity that it is working hard to cover over (such as racial difference), but it also produces an excess beyond its own disciplinary function.

The character's effusive joy in her own *presence* and the contagious plenitude it exudes suggests we need to think about this scene in terms beyond
"pure" wish-fulfillment (that is, the fantasy that feminine beauty could erase
the harsh consequences of difference or subjection). For if aesthetics denotes
a nostalgia for presence and the fetish bespeaks an impoverishment of
presence,[49] then beauty's relationship to the fetish—and *this* beauty's
reltionship to herself *as* the fetish—is more complicated than mere capitu-
lation. We are reminded, first, that the fetish, as a form of substitution, is
always insufficient to and yet in excess of the longing it carries; and second,
that within the context of racial projection and the problem of the over-
materialization of Asian female bodies, a fetishistic nostalgia for presence
(especially "self-presence") can take on a different valence. That is, the
nostalgia for presence both reveals the nature of that presence to be a per-
formance-effect *and* serves as a peculiar form of self-materialization—the
former delimiting the sentimentality that the latter might have solicited.

Kwan has gone from playing the "Asian prostitute with the golden heart"
to playing the American working girl who is simply after the gold, but far
more provocative than her character's materialism is her relationship to her
own materiality. The narcissism of racial ideology here, unlike for Fanon,
produces not self-abhorrence but self-pleasure—a pleasure, furthermore,
that those watching her very often want to claim for themselves, *even for
the brief duration of singing her song.* Part of the pleasure Linda enjoys is therefore her megalomaniac capacity for substitution. In this scene, she occupies,
not alternately but concurrently, the positions of object/subject, performer/
performance, Western/Eastern beauty. Kwan stands as the double cinematic
choice: as the beauty to be seen *and* as the beauty that *sees.* Certainly we can
read Linda's enjoyment as disguised or naturalized subjection, and it is to a
large extent, but what do we do with her multiple assumption of gazes?
Imagine Freud's horror at this woman who not only sees men seeing her
but also sees *as* a man. As we watch Linda watch and relish herself, is not
"the problem of Linda" the very possibility that whenever she proclaims "I
enjoy [a guy] . . . who'll enjoy being a guy having a girl like me," we hear
the echo of another possibility, that she might in fact be saying "I enjoy *being*
the guy who enjoys having (or being) a girl like me"? (Can we not easily
imagine an alternative mirror relationship, not between Linda and herself,
but between her and the gay man watching her performance? [figure 5])[50]

Singularly nonsingular, her figure becomes not gender-restricted at all,
in spite of, or rather precisely because of, her insistence on the signs of femininity. Hers is a transmutable body that *can be* the other, that can assume
numerous points of view, that can make the idealizing image perform for
her in turn. The image being mirrored and thus mimed is therefore not ideality but *alterity* itself. There is a joy (and cheekiness) in her performance,
in the number and in the scene (in watching it, remembering it), which

Figure 5. *Nancy Kwan performing "I Enjoy Being a Girl" under the gaze of producer Ross Hunter (in high chair). Courtesy of the Academy of Motion Picture Arts and Sciences*

would be disingenuous to dismiss as interpellative production. This is after all a performance that exceeds its own boundaries, cannibalizing even the audience. To relish that figure on the screen *is* to be Linda herself. Yes, interpellated, subjected, mediated, but something in the subject produced here exceeds that subjection, and that excess is the pleasure and source of self-identification: *I enjoy being.* The celebration may be less about "being a girl" than about transforming the abject state of being a (racialized) girl into celebrated materiality.

Femininity for Linda Low then operates as both heterosexual, symbolic norm and generative, imaginative matrix. Do these truths compete, and if so, how? Judith Butler distinguishes "performativity"—defined as the reiteration of norms that precede, constrain, and exceed the performer—from "performance," with its traditional assumptions of agency and will. Butler writes:

> Performativity is thus not a singular "act," for it is always a reiteration of a norm or a set of norms . . . this act is not primarily theatrical . . . its apparent theatricality is produced to the extent that its historicity remains dissimulated (and, conversely, its theatricality gains a certain inevitability given the impossibility of a full disclosure of its historic-

ity). . . . Indeed, could it be that the production of the subject as origina-
tor of his/her effects is precisely a consequence of this dissimulated
citationality?[51]

We mistake performativity for performance, Butler argues, because the
former's efficacy depends on the dissimulation of its own historical alibi (that
is, the history of reiteration and citationality). The performative only appears
original/natural to the extent that an illusion of agency may be maintained.
Seen in this light, Linda Low may think she is performing cultural codes at
her will, but those codes are in fact performing her. Her claim to being a
"strictly female female" acquires its ratification from the citationality and
reiteration of a history of gender codes.

Yet both the complex of ambivalent racial codes affixed to her figure and
what we have been noting about her uncontainable joy, the way it exceeds
even its subject to cannibalize the gaze, raise a question left over from
Butler's account: can performance ever disturb performativity? Or does
that question retreat into an atavistic idea of agency that a concept like
performativity wants to qualify? Surely there must be a play between the
two poles, moments when performance outstrips performative constraints
and vice versa? That is, for Butler, each reiteration is of course an approximation that is retroactively smoothed over, but the question is, Does the
smoothing over always work? Linda's performance of the performance of
gender, with its dangerously unruly assumptions of the various positions
and gazes of desire, renders inadequate the notion that she is merely laboring under cultural performativity and suggests that her performance, however hegemonically dictated, exceeds the boundaries of what that dictation
would consider a *proper* joy.

My location of this potentially subversive moment of improper and
inappropriable joy, to be clear, is quite specific to and confined within the
frames of this performance. If we were to step outside of the frame and consider Nancy Kwan as an actor in Hollywood performing on the set and not
contained within the solipsistic circularity of herself and the three-way
mirror (again, figure 5) but rather under the intent observation of Ross
Hunter and the crew, we would have to acknowledge the lack of agency for
an actor under contractual injunction to performance. Linda might be en-
joying the view of herself, but what Kwan the performer (with her voice
dubbed over) saw was not herself but the watchful eyes of the camera and
her producer. The unsettling effect of the "I Enjoy Being a Girl" number and
its peculiar agency is thus visible only when framed by the performance as
performance. This, however, does not detract from the persuasion of her
infectious "joy," for it is precisely the slippage, the accidental eruption, between performance and performativity that can create some other effect

beyond the equally binding lexicon of performance and performativity. In other words, the critic cannot impute subversive intentions on the part of Nancy Kwan (that would be a facile assumption of agency), but some kind of agency has irresistibly emerged in the unpredictable dynamics between an individual's performance and the performativity that scripts her. The world of theatrical performance *is* the dynamic struggle between performance and performativity.

Is it possible to escape performativity? I am not sure there is a single answer to this question. It is, however, clear at least that we need a more nuanced sense of agency that goes beyond volunteerism or a positivism blind to performative constraints. We need to imagine a form of agency that recognizes *competition* between performance and performativity, between historicity and reenactment. Only then can we understand the coexistence of coercion and agency in any act of cultural performance. Only then can we see the performances of citizenship and nationalism as a continuous navigation between a scripting history and individual response.

When we encounter a performance piece like *Flower Drum Song*, which works overtime to cite (choreographically, musically, thematically) various other American theatrical performances—in fact, *Flower Drum Song* achieves its status as an *American* performance precisely by exposing its reliance on the performativity of "Americanism" continually renewing itself on the stage of Chinatown—we suddenly realize that performativity's relationship to agency (or lack thereof) becomes far more complicated than traditional history would like us to believe. The singers of "Chop Suey," even as they are excluded by the very lyrics they are performing are of course also *performing* it. On that stage, the *performativity* of Americanism through the iterative citations of "hula hoops and nuclear war" is at once supported by and in tension with the *performance* by Asian bodies. Furthermore, the movie's Orientalist spectacles distract us from its Americanist stereotypes (stereotypes about what is American and what is American nationalism), which not only animate racist stereotypes but also find their very *form* through those racist constructs of the "others." That is, this very veil—the hiding of America-making in the heart of racist constructions—continues to confer on American nationalism its manifest vivacity.

We so often think of stereotypes as about the minority that sometimes we fail to see that the norm is of course itself a stereotype: a stereotype that has been legitimated, a performative expression par excellence. The performance within *Flower Drum Song* reveals Americanism to be a performative phenomenon, whose *historicity* has been disguised in order to stage its originality and history. More than a mere parade of Orientalist stereotypes, this movie gives us stereotypes of Americanism whose performative efficacy is at once reproduced and disturbed by the racialized bodies solicited to articulate its desires.

Epilogue: The Geography of Melancholia

> It must strike us that after all the melancholic does not behave in quite
> the same way as a person who is crushed by remorse and self-reproach in
> a normal fashion. . . . One might emphasize the presence in [her] of an
> almost opposite trait of insistent communicativeness which finds
> satisfaction in self-exposure.
>
> —Sigmund Freud, "Mourning and Melancholia"

Before we leave the stage of *Flower Drum Song*, there is another beauty
in the running to consider, a third choice: the often present but consistently marginalized figure of Helen Chao (Reiko Sato). Why did Wang Ta
(and the diegesis) not choose Helen, whose name connotes not only beauty
but the classic *chosen* beauty? While Mei Li is, as they say, "fresh off the
boat" and Linda is so assimilated that she poses a fantasmatic threat of miscegenation, Helen would seem to offer a logical compromise, the perfect
choice. The seamstress who seamlessly weaves together her Chinese heritage and American style, Helen seems to embody "good" assimilation and
is the only character who achieves "true" cultural mixing. Yet she is the
classic odd woman out, the "right girl" whose "just rightness" no one
chooses.

Within the world of this movie, the "right combination" is perhaps not
so sexy or so desirable. Although the character of Helen enjoys consistent
screen presence (she appears in several scenes throughout the movie), neither Wang Ta nor the audience ever imagine her as a possible contender
in this race for love. Neither did the filmmakers, apparently, since Reito
Sato did not receive star billing in the opening credits along with Kwan,
Umeki, Hall, Shigeta, and Fong, even though she clearly had one of the
"big numbers." Only the audience gets a glimpse of her star potential when
she performs her unexpected big number, a dream sequence. In the dream
sequence (itself a musical euphemism for a diegetic black hole, where we
do not know what is really taking place but suspect a one-night stand with
a drunken Wang Ta), Helen reveals her inner longings and her body in
"Love, Look Away" (figure 6). Singing that song of self-denial and unre-
quited love, Helen runs after a wedding gown on a faceless mannequin and
miraculously, through the magic of editing, assumes that costume, only
to have it ripped away from her by a team of grotesque, faceless male danc-
ers in black with Chinese opera masks. The choreography alternates between the dreamy and the nightmarish, containment and extension, bal-
let and jazz.

The number signals to the audience for the first time that Helen *is* a
player, and it is in that dream sequence with its not-so-subtle rape fantasy
that we see her sexuality. Helen reveals herself to be a possible contender at

Figure 6. *Helen Chao (Reiko Sato) in "Love, Look Away." Courtesy of Museum of Modern Art, New York*

the moment when she exhibits the "other side," the sexy potential under the prim seamstress. She might be the right choice insofar as, in the reality of everyday life, she might represent the package that would allow the chooser to have the hidden "Bad Girl"—that is, would allow the chooser to have Linda Low masked as Mei Li. Yet in this case, as the model of successful compromise, Helen turns out to be *not* enough, *not* the real thing: neither the sex goddess nor the innocent girl, neither authentically West nor authentically East. The potential plenitude of biculturalism promised by Helen becomes an evacuation of authenticity, revealing authenticity as finally but another form of investment in "types."

In this national and cultural parable, accommodation without transgression is failure and thus not of interest. In other words, Helen has not failed enough. Helen is the category celebrated as culturally desirable throughout the movie but is in the end undesirable, because this is a world that is finally not very interested in witnessing the fulfillment of racial integration. This is another reason why the authenticity and authority of Chinese patriarchy represented by both Wang Chi Yang and the Three Family Association have to be maintained in order to restabilize the borders of Chinatown, threatened by the repeal of the Chinese Exclusionary Act. Helen has not only been rejected as an erotic choice but has been abjected as the potentially privileged signifier of that which "the discriminating man" (and the *discriminating* American culture in this movie) both dreads and wishes he desires: the extinction of difference itself, the potential of being "everything mixed in," like the celebrated chop suey itself. If Helen succeeds, then the determinants of identity, which have operated throughout the movie as types, would be defeated. She poses the threat of entropy feared at the heart of all organization and differentiation: the woman who signifies that proclaimed, desired state where everyone is the same, that absence of the pain of differentiation that must then be made *present* and *painful*. Her traumatic dance consequently lays out this impossible geography of American biculturalism. In a choreographic journey from East to West, Helen, besieged by men in Chinese opera masks, makes her way across a stage marked with ocean waves into the haven of Wang Ta's extended arms, proffered from a platform . . . only to have Wang Ta drop her back down a slide into an ocean of fog. Her choreography continually allegorizes a crisis of passage. Between the threat of masked Chinese masculinity and the rescue of "new" Asian America represented by Wang Ta, there is neither bridge nor path. And the prospect of America the Beautiful (even in Chinese, *Mei Guo*) provides no harbor.

If Linda offers the obscene body and Mei Li the proper (even properly marred) body, then Helen represents the morbid body—the body whose desires we are to turn from as though they were sickly, the body that gets thrown down the chute in its own dreams.[52] And this perhaps suggests that the vision of "balancing two worlds" must remain a social ideal (a dream sequence, if you will) and not become a social reality. Although in many ways she is the image of the ideal new citizen, Helen's beauty and the cultural harmony it promises cannot be looked at, cannot remain in representation. And that, finally, is the problem with Helen. She is *impossible*. The inexplicability of her nonchosenness must be its own explanation: that is, it is not that she was not chosen but that she was never even a choice. Exclusion is her a priori condition.

Love, look away. Love, look away from me. If the comic idiom is usually quite confident in its ability to dissolve romantic melancholia through the magic of love, it is much less stalwart in the face of a racial melancholia generated by the prospect of a new national subject. Helen's marital ineligibility reflects her social and national ineligibility. Near the core of desire that this movie is trying to work out, Helen stands as the secret abjection of the racial assimilation that the diegesis claims to celebrate. Lost forever in exile and endlessly mourning, Helen embodies both the longing for and the relinquishment of communal desire: "I have wished before. I will wish no more." In the perverse logic of denial, to command love to look away is of course also a demand to be looked upon by love, just as this number is itself the moment in which Helen performatively insists on our attention.

Insofar as love throughout the movie has been aligned with the racial imaginary and national choice, the loveless Helen *is* the figure of racial melancholia—the figure of refusal who announces herself through renunciation and who consoles us with the beauty of aversion: *"Love, look away. . . . Love, let us say we're through. No good are you for me, No good am I for you."*

A FABLE OF EXQUISITE CORPSES

*Maxine Hong Kingston, Assimilation,
and the Hypochondriacal Response*

Hypochondria: Gr. *hupokhondria*, pl. of *hupokhondrion*,
abdomen (held to be the seat of melancholia)
—*American Heritage Dictionary*

Rodgers and Hammerstein's dream world teaches the racially melancholic female body to enjoy the lessons of its own rejection. At the same time, as already seen, the effects produced by the various performances of that renunciation often exceed and disrupt the meaning of the intended castigation. This history that we are tracing gives us much more than a record of unresolved briefs, but also a revelation of transformative potentials within grief. The project of examining this cultural and psychical history of renunciation may ultimately lead us, not toward the ambition of "resolved grief," as envisioned by Freud, but rather toward redefining a profoundly different notion of mourning altogether.

Turning away from the theatrical imagining of an Asia America on the stage of Rodgers and Hammerstein in the early sixties to "real," contemporary Asian America, we encounter hypochondria in one of the most well-known representative texts of Asian American literature, Maxine Hong Kingston's *The Woman Warrior: Memoirs of a Girlhood Among Ghosts* (1979). One aspect of this much-read text that remains unexamined or even mentioned is the problem of self-aversion and nostalgia in its racial self-representation. The narrator's nostalgia for yet allergy to her own racialized body reveals hypochondria to be a form of melancholic self-allergy. That is, melancholia is linked to hypochondria, not only etymologically but symptomatically. Indeed, we can think of the Freudian melancholic as someone hypochondriacally aware of and allergic to the abjection lodged within.

Offering us with one of the most passionate, self-conscious, and sustained ethnic autobiographies about cultural unease, *The Woman Warrior* in fact gives us a protagonist who enjoys an unironic, even rapturous, identification with hypochondria. In the middle of the novel, the narrator as a child falls into a "mysterious illness" for a year and a half, characterized by an inability to speak for which the doctors can find no cause. For the narrator, this lapse spells pure rapture:

> I spent the next eighteen months in bed with a mysterious illness. There was no pain, no symptom, though the middle line in my left palm broke in two. . . . I lived like the Victorian recluses I read about. It was the best year and a half of my life.[1]

This child will grow up to become a vigilant diagnostician of signs of health and illness. As an adult, she announces to her mother that she can no longer go home to Stockton's Chinatown for health reasons:

> When I'm away from here [Chinatown] . . . I don't get sick. I don't go the hospital every holiday. I don't get pneumonia, no dark spots on my x-rays. My chest doesn't hurt when I breathe. . . . And I don't get headaches at 3:00. . . .
>
> I've found some places in this country that are ghost-free . . . where I don't catch colds or use my hospitalization insurance. Here I am sick so often, I can barely work. (108)

Illness and the prospect of illness slowly emerge as bound to the personal history of racial, familial, and gender discrimination being detailed in the text. According to the narrator, to be with her mother and in Chinatown (literally, this narrator's biological and geographical origins) is to suffer debilitating illness; to be elsewhere is to enjoy perfect health. The assertion of absolute health *through* an active and repetitive negation of illness also suggests an attachment to a pathological imagination. Furthermore, this imagination preoccupied with threatening debility transforms familial and racial-ethnic relations into somatic susceptibility.[2] In the landscape of this geographic allergy, the dream of a culturally healthy body defines itself through displacement, through the renunciation of ethnicized and maternal origins, through escape and subsequent assimilation into the space of the other, a "ghost-free" country.

We have to wonder whether the idealized "ghost-free" country is in fact possible in this confession. As Sau-ling Cynthia Wong points out in her essay "The Politics of Mobility," while mobility in canonical American literature has long been associated with visions of independence and freedom, for the immigrant, and Asian Americans in particular, mobility rarely bears positive connotations. As Wong puts it, mobility in Asian American literature metaphorizes "psychological nomadism."[3] For Kingston's narrator, most at home when she is not at home, has surely fashioned for herself a subjective map that guarantees perpetual unease. If one cannot go home again, then the Kingston passage quoted here reminds us that there is often the other half of that prescription: *and yet one always has to*. Here the traditional American ethos of health and progress as a departure from home takes on a particularly ethnicized cast. In Kingston's text, bodily and geographic hypochondria converge, and the sources of dread trace back to maternal and ethnic origins, which are themselves decentered within the nation. The "dark spots" on the x-ray of this psyche mark the place of the mother (a psychically ambivalent source) and Chinatown (a historically abjected space in the nation). This body dreads the very contamination from which it comes and finds home in homelessness.

Hypochondria—as a dread of invasive contagion that materializes on the body, making the self the very source of that contagion—emerges with particular insistence in this text. The language of hypochondria has much to contribute to discussions of the fundamental dilemmas of the racialized subject within the national project of assimilation. In Asian American literature, where assimilation foregrounds itself as a repetitive trauma, we find frequent manifestations of hypochondria as metaphor and condition. In David Wong Louie's *Pangs of Love* (1992), the character Edna, upon being set up by her Caucasian American professor with a Chinese rather than Chinese American man, tells us that she "blushed, acquiesced, and went to [her] room and was sick for a week" (209). Edna finds the professor's facile elision of the difference between what is Asian and what is Asian American so psychically painful as to sicken her physically. In Jessica Hagedorn's *Dogeaters* (1990), a tale set in postcolonial Manila, mysterious illnesses strike various characters and are almost always linked to the problem of cultural integration: Baby Alarcon, the "assimilated" product of Americanized Philippine culture, develops undiagnosable, "nonspecific fungus" symptoms, while Narcisa's husband becomes the "first white man" to be stricken with *bangunggot*, a local illness that is as much lore as disease—an illness said to claim men and attributed by the local doctor to "a figment of overwrought Filipino imagination" (14). In Hisaye Yamamoto's collection of short stories *Seventeen Syllables and Other Stories* (1988), hypochondriacal responses make repeat appearances: most notably, Esther Kuroiwa's complicated reactions in "Wiltshire Boulevard" after witnessing an incident of Asian discrimination on a public bus (she feels something "insidiously sickening . . . nothing solid she could come to grips with, nothing solid she could sink her teeth into"); and Miss Sasagawara's famously mysterious hypochondriacal hospital run in "The Legend of Miss Sasagawara."[4]

While I cannot do justice here to the varied nuances within this confluence of texts, I can begin to note the theme of hypochondria persists in Asian American literature and how it coalesces around the prospects of assimilation—and, specifically, assimilation for a racially different body. Hypochondria is often staged in the texts just cited (and in *The Woman Warrior* in an especially concentrated way) as a response to racism, not only from others but also from the self: an illness close to, and of, home. How do we understand this disturbing affinity between familial-ethnic origin and the anticipation of illness? The fact that the racialized body is made to bear, indeed somatize, the fear of contamination is not surprising, nor is the proposition that hypochondria can surface at the site of racism for the racist subject. What remains unexplored, however, is the connection between hypochondria and racism *on the part of the racialized*. That is, it is not unexpected to hear that racist persons might find the racial other sickening or for the discriminated to find such racism revolting in turn, but when the source of that sickness gets located *within* the discriminated, then we are dealing with an unsettling, interlocking network of collapsed identification, repudiation, and projection. This chapter is an effort to try to tease out the strands of this entangled dynamic.

I should make it clear from the outset that I am not interested in a vernacular understanding of hypochondria as an imaginary illness or in suggesting that Kingston's narrator is "making up" her illness whenever she is at home in Chinatown. Instead I am interested in the subjective and cultural values that the narrator herself attaches to those symptoms and in the psychical pressures that are being revealed and that play out a larger dilemma of negotiating the transitions from childhood to adulthood, from ethnic enclave to mainstream America, from infirmity to vitality. This chapter also by no means offers a medical diagnosis of a group of people or of Kingston. The medical-psychological study of "racial groups" as such has always seemed to me highly problematic, revealing the limits and generality of psychological theories and mental health practices as they exist today.[5] Nor does this chapter venture to provide a comprehensive treatise of the relationship between hypochondria and melancholia, which would have to take into account several, simultaneous perspectives: medical, philosophical, psychological, and literary, among others.[6] The more limited goal of this chapter is to meditate on the role that the discourse of hypochondria might play within the confines of racial melancholia as I have outlined it. I read hypochondria as a parable for the narrator's psychical activities in the face of assimilation, activities that help to organize the self's response to intrasubjective threats in a racist and sexist world.

I analyze the notion of "Asian American hypochondria" as a persistent linguistic and imaginative paradigm structuring self-representations in Asian American literature. I will argue that hypochondria on the part of the assimilating-but-racially-differentiated subject offers a metaphor for social perception. *Hypochondria is a way of perceiving the world and one's body with respect to social relations.* The task before us is to unveil the drama of hypochondria as it plays out anxieties about the prospect of assimilation for Asian American subjects, caught between the assimilationist model (whereby minority cultures are expected to adopt mainstream values or behavioral patterns) and the pluralist model (whereby ethnic minority cultures are expected to value and maintain their culture of difference).

If in the classic hypochondriac, we see a person endlessly preoccupied with his or her body's signification, its legitimacy, and the origins of its failure, then the assimilating racial-ethnic body can also be said to be hypochondriacal in that it is, too, a body continuously plagued by questions of its own authenticity and etiology. Within the national imagination, Asian Americans in particular suffer a "phantom illness": because they occupy an unstable position in the ethnic-racial spectrum, their projected place in America is ghostly. (Consider, for example, the easy colloquial confusion between the terms "Asian" and "Asian American," whereas a similar elision between "African" and "African American" is much less acceptable or even likely.) Because of their immigrant and diasporic histories, Asian Americans are at once physically distanced from yet inextricably assigned to their cultural "roots." Their relation to America proper is of course equally disconnected.

Indeed, Asian American assimilation highlights the fact that assimilation for the racially marked body brings a whole different set of problems. Assimilation tenders a promise of ethnic intermixing that draws itself short of the color line. As Michael Rogin has argued, American usage of ethnicity as something that can comfortably straddle this double bind (as something assimilable and yet distinct) in fact elides and excludes the inassimilable fact of race. After all, the standard of assimilation, "Americanness," denotes whiteness.[7] (This is one reason why European "ethnicities" operate on a very different register within this economy, and why the use of the term "ethnicity" often disguises the underlying issue, which is race.) Because of the built-in impediment of racial difference, the prospect of assimilation for the "Asian" is fraught with potential failure, shame, and humiliation, not to mention the threatening indictments of self-denial and self-beratement. Reading Kingston provides an opportunity to further understand the ways in which racial exclusion within a melancholic structure expresses itself and, specifically here, why it speaks in the language of hypochondria.

Part I: The Apprehensive Sociable Body

Self-love and the love of others are both modes towards increasing self-
valuation and encouraging political resistance in one's community.

—Cornel West

A strong egoism is a protection against disease, but in the last resort we
must begin to love in order that we may not fall ill, and must fall ill if,
in consequence of frustration, we cannot love.

—Sigmund Freud

While racial and social integration offer the preeminent American social
myths, assimilation remains one of the deepest sources of anxiety in the
American psyche. That is, while integration promises a socionational
dream, assimilation as its cultural corollary catches all the material and
immaterial anxieties inadmissible to that promise. Today Asian Americans
present one of the most charged contemporary focuses for the mainstream
culture's idealization and fear of assimilation.[8] To be the objects of that
national ambivalence means having ambivalent responses of one's own. In
the mainstream media, Kingston's particular brand of haunted racial identity is most often overlooked in favor of an alternative narrative: the narrative of ethnic euphoria. For example, recently on the occasion of the Fourth
of July, *Newsweek* selected Asian American writer Bette Bao Lord as the
spokesperson for American multiculturalism:

> I do not believe that the loss of one's native culture is the price one must
> pay for becoming an American. On the contrary, I feel doubly blessed. I
> can choose from two rich cultures those parts that suit my mood or the
> occasion best. And unbelievable as it may seem, shoes tinted red, white
> and blue go dandy with them all.[9]

Here we have an extreme version of cultural agency: you can be anything that
you want to be. Putting aside for a moment the question of what price retail
therapy might exact to alleviate racial anxiety, let us take a closer look at this
euphoric vision of cultural crossdressing, the ease with which Lord can claim
for herself a racial body that would look good in just about anything.

Lord's racial crossdressing partakes of the tradition of the melting pot.
But, as already shown in chapter 2, while imaginary intermixing across
ethnic, religious, or economic lines has been long celebrated by the myth of
the melting pot and the rhetoric of assimilation, racial crossing and miscegenation have in fact been scrupulously excluded from those imaginings.
It is clear from Lord's writing that being the object of historical national
unease—of suffering irreducible difference in the face of injunctive assimilation—is here expressing itself not as nihilism but in the guise of opti-

mism. (This is what I called the pathological euphoria of hyphenated subjects in the previous chapter, whereby the euphoria of double identity often
conceals the pain of dividedness.)[10] We can hear, lurking underneath the
stylistic ease of Lord's assimilation machine, the shuttles spinning overtime
to weave a seamless match between difference and hegemony, race and
culture, nativity and nationalism, compulsion and voluntarism. In Lord's
passage, racial difference has been defused as a cultural (even aesthetic)
difference, which is imagined to be easily surmountable. To be a "good"
American here means learning how to mitigate, and indeed erase, the "bad
taste" of racial difference. The insistent health of Lord's American proclamation works, perhaps too hard, to deny that there is any racial difference
that could make us ill. (Finally, her vision hardly offers an escape from the
curse of difference, for what could be in worse "taste" than "shoes tinted red,
white, and blue"?)

But I do not wish to dismiss Lord's response to racial difference as either
merely politically incorrect or shortsighted. Implicit in Lord's optimistic
message is its dysphoric counterpart: the fear that such a notion of social
integration may in fact be "unbelievable" and differences irreducibly incompatible. The abhorrence of a self in "bad taste," as suggested by what we
might call Lord's "racial drag," is not so far from the insistently sanitized
version of health of Kingston's narrator and equally hints at the presence
of a hypochondria about the self. Lord's fantasy of the melting pot raises
questions about the conditions of such pleasure and unstated disgust. Before condemning the symptom, it is appropriate to unpack what work its
management is doing and to develop a fuller sense of the conflictual demands
of social survival, cultural allegiance, and political exigency. What is the
offense that is being so joyfully averted? What would it mean to reside within
inassimilable difference and incommensurability, to experience one's ontology as constantly at odds with the available cultural dressing? *That* is of
course the very condition of pain that this euphoric vision is fending off. The
racial drag act that Lord performs highlights as false the assumption that
we can refuse to negotiate difference. It also underscores the bad faith of
thinking that we do not always perform some version of such adaptation as
social beings, especially those who are made uneasy in their sociality because of racial difference.

The Lord quotation, placed alongside Kingston's words, reveals the inadequacy of a two-dimensional response to assimilation that resorts either
to the sentimentalization/approval or the denial/disapproval of racial difference. We are in fact speaking about two sets of inadequate binarisms:
assimilation as either a culturally or politically "good" or "bad" activity and
assimilation as either the sign of choice or the sign of coercion. The drag
metaphor elicited by the Lord passage reminds us that the realization of
agency in drag (be it racial or gender) is borne out of a maneuver between

opposites: that is, in drag, one is neither "just acting like" nor "really being" but some complicated combination of the two.[11] Similarly, the faculty of agency in assimilation—the *work* that it takes to negotiate one's ego relation to a dominant (and at times rejecting) culture—demands a conceptualization beyond that of pure will or the utter loss of will.

Returning to Kingston's proclamation of (personal and perhaps cultural) health, we have to reread that insistent pronouncement with an ear toward its self-sabotage. Her ability to claim health is *articulable* specifically under and only through the shadows of bodily malaise and displacement (physically putting herself *elsewhere*). Indeed, cultural health may not speak except *as* illness. In his essay "Of Sickness in General," Michel Serres draws an inverse relation between illness and speech:

> It might have been first believed that health was only the silence of the medical sciences, all astir from speaking of pathology. The normal does not say much, if anything at all . . . the normal, like many of our concepts, is a crest, an optimum concept: maximum force and minimum discourse. We speak only of shadows.[12]

The normal does not say much; it is only heard through and in pathology. By extension health/cultural norm, does not need speaking, or if it does, it does so at the site of racial pathology. What speaks in the Kingston passage *is* the mis-speaking body, the hypochondriacal body itself. The body that insists "I don't get sick. . . . I don't go to the hospital. . . . I don't get pneumonia, no dark spots on my x-rays. . . . I don't get headaches. . . . .I don't catch colds . . ." is becoming increasingly indebted to illness for its definition. This definition of health is entangled with awarenesses of illness. This wishful incantation fulfills itself only through an endless haunting, by the fantasy of an exquisitely incorruptible body.

Like the hypochondriac, the assimilating racial-ethnic body is trained to be preoccupied with its own legitimacy and authenticity. It is in the *breakdown* of the binary between "the real" and "the fake" that the phenomenon of "Asian American hypochondria" is most arresting. For in the context of assimilation and racial difference, the symptom of hypochondria is most revealing not in the mundane sense of imagined or unreal injury but in its sincerity—in its profound confusion between health and pathology, wholeness and disability.[13] Cultural assimilation may thus be said to be a form of haunting, whereby the dream of the socially immaculate body simultaneously introjects itself and provokes a host of hypochondriacal responses. The double malady of melancholia for the racial-ethnic subject *is* the condition of having to incorporate and encrypt both an impossible ideal and a denigrated self. More than any other identificatory disorders, racial melancholia speaks of a dream of perfection.[14] And it is this dream that provides the fodder for hypochondriacal anxieties.

In the framework of a racism turned against the self, hypochondria *as a mode of perception* opens up new ways of approaching the textual forma-tions of the ethnic ego as precisely that which has been delicately config-ured at the edge between racial imagination and materiality, marking a profound conflation between realness and fantasy. The place of hypochon-dria as the site of subjective negotiations on the part of the racialized per-son is thus finally not that surprising, for racial signification has always come into its fullest play precisely at the intersection between materiality and fantasy, between history and memory. At these intersections, the ra-cial body acquires its most prominent outlines—and requires its greatest camouflage.

The Print on the Skin

In a liberal discourse where the language of subversion is often privileged and too easily located, it is profoundly difficult for us today—queasily so— to think about the ways in which a minority/ethnic subject might patholo-gize herself. But prior to the language of subversion, we need to recognize the complicated language of complicity. The socially pathologized body does not merely mirror the social projection of illness; it has some forms of imag-ined relations to that reflection. Accordingly, it is important to work through the connection between a demonized notion of internalization in social dis-course and the psychoanalytic insight that internalization may be a funda-mental process of ego formation.

Scenes in *The Woman Warrior* repeatedly circle around the theme of in-ternalization. Indeed, the narrator's most manifest bout of hypochondria-cal suffering is intimately related to an episode of intrasubjective and intersubjective confusion. The onset of the narrator's year and a half of idyl-lic seclusion in fact follows a traumatic encounter at school,[15] a painful and protracted scene of torture where the narrator physically and verbally abuses another child in the school bathroom. Cornering a quiet Asian American classmate there, the narrator repeatedly shouts the command "Talk, Talk, Talk!" at her captive (176). In between physical attacks on the other girl, the narrator repeatedly demands that the girl speak and give her name:

> She wore black bangs. . . . I thought I could put my thumb on her nose and push it bonelessly in, indent her face . . . work her face around like a dough. . . . I hated her weak neck. . . . I wished I was able to see what my neck looked like from the backs and sides. . . . I grew my hair long to hide it in case it was a flower-stem neck. . . .
>
> I reached up and took the fatty part of her cheek, not dough, but meat, between my thumb and finger. . . . "Say your name. Go ahead. Say

it." . . . She tried to shake her head, but I had a hold of her face. . . . Her skin seemed to stretch . . . I reached up . . . and took a strand of hair. I pulled it. . . . I squeezed . . . I pulled. . . . (176–7)

This scene acts out Toni Morrison's dramatic etiology of love and hate in the racialized child in *The Bluest Eye*. Morrison's novel explores the nuances of feminine, black self-rejection. Here, by restaging the confrontation between two Asian American girls, Kingston makes explicit that self-rejection on the part of the Asian American girl. For the Kingston narrator, the disgust provoked by the other girl bespeaks an anxiety about a racial body that is also her own. What the narrator dreads in both the other girl and in herself is that ineluctable compliance of the visible: the roundness of the face, the black bangs, the shape of the nose, the fragility of the neck— what the narrator sees as the girl's vulnerability to Asian female stereotypes. It would be easy enough to suggest that a counterlesson of self-love ought to cure this narrator, but *in the face of racism*, how is that to be achieved? Furthermore, there is a deeper, more chronic illness of how-to-love-the-self on the part of the subject who is *constituted* by debilitating difference. Looking at the mindscape of Kingston's narrator, teetering between dreams of perfection and disability, we have to face the double bind that fetters the racially and ethnically denigrated subject: How is one to love oneself and the other when the very movement toward love is conditioned by the anticipation of denial and failure?

To the narrator who herself has been haunted by her own inability to become "American feminine," the other girl's physiognomy spells a painful deterrent to successful assimilation. In enjoining the anonymous girl to assume an autobiographical position (to account for her name, history, and position), the narrator is also reproducing her own traumatic experiences. In fact, being asked to account for herself has been a recurring trauma for her: repeated moments when she is enjoined to account for herself, whether it be in the schoolroom or in a taxicab as an adult. So not only does the narrator, throughout this protracted scene, obsessively meditate on the other girl's bodily details in terms that duplicate her own fears about her own bodily, racial appearance but she also, just a few pages earlier, suffers from a similar incident of abject interrogation by a teacher in her school:

It was when I found out I had to talk that school became a misery. . . . "Louder," said the teacher, who scared the voice away again. The teacher who had already told me every day how to read "I" and "here" put me in the lower corner under the stairs again. (166–7)

It is no accident that the two words that render her aphasic are "I" and "here": being and presence. The teacher fails to interpellate the narrator into a language that would *place* her.[16] Being a "bad student" and essentially a "bad subject" provokes shame, another technology of interpellation. Critics have pointed out all too often the coercions effected by interpellation, how terrible it is to be *placed*. Yet the shame in this scene highlights the way that interpellation might work precisely via its failure, via placelessness. That is, as harrowing as it may be to be interpellated, it may be all the more horrifying and humiliating to answer the call only to find you are not the one for whom the call was meant.[17] (Imagine Linda Low's consternation in *Flower Drum Song* if the whistle were not meant for her!)

The narrator suffers the trauma not of being a victim but of being the aggressor. The juxtaposition of these two scenes (the narrator in the bathroom with the other little girl and earlier in the classroom with her teacher) not only plays out the autobiographical coercion but also acts out the internalization of that coercion and its subsequent epistemological aporia. Who is "I" when the "I" can never place herself? And how would that voice lacking a model come to articulation? Surely what is most disarming about the bathroom incident is that the aggression is being performed by someone repeating her own trauma in the form of persecution. This bathroom trauma thus offers the profound and disturbing suggestion that the denigrated body comes to voice, and the pleasure of that voice, only by assuming the voice of authority.

Since the act of torturing the silent other is the closest that the narrator-as-child comes to being what she associates with "Americanness," assimilation for the narrator reveals itself to be not the adaptation of behavior or customs per se but the repetition of a violence (against an other that is also the self) that she has already experienced. This peculiar form of imitation enacts a vicious, hypochondriacal circle of identification and disidentification: the subject manages the fear of her own bodily "failures" by asserting an identification with power and health, an identification whose fundamental incommensurability has made the subject abject in the first place. Dramatizing a simultaneous staging and collapse of the differences between "the torturer" and "the tortured," the bathroom scene signals a moment of disidentification predicated on identification. The meeting of the *ontic* (how I come to a sense of my being) with the *racial* (how society labels my being) gives this scene its haunting, vertiginous effects. Through the other girl, the narrator is able to fend off *and* anticipate the sickening effects of racial abjection.

We are clearly in the realm of the imaginary. This hypochondriacal moment bears more affinity to a Kleinian model of object relations (with its underpinning interplay of projection, introjection, expulsion, reintrojection of "bad" objects) than a Freudian model of ego formation. Melanie Klein will spell out more explicitly what remains implicit in Freud's picture of (melancholic) ego formation: the double dynamic of projection and introjection necessary to ego formation. But the conceptual origin of object relations, like other branches of psychoanalysis, elides the role that this dynamic plays in the racial imaginary, even as it is looking at that connection eye to eye. I am thinking of Klein's formative essay "Infantile Anxiety Situations Reflected in a Work of Art and in the Creative Impulse," in which race makes not one but two guest appearances. Klein begins this essay by introducing an interpretation of a Ravel opera that forms the basis of her theory of infantile anxiety. In the libretto, a boy is left alone in a room, where he proceeds to destroy the furniture. The plot takes on a surreal turn when the furniture comes to life and attacks the boy in return. The story serves as a parable for Klein's thesis about projective anxiety. She describes the ways that the objects in a little boy's room retaliate against him: "The clock has a dreadful stomach ache and begins to strike the hours like mad. The teapot leans over the cup, and they begin to talk Chinese."[18] Thus "talking in Chinese" signals the same ominous threat of maddening disorder as the idea of inanimate furniture coming to vengeful life. In the same essay, in her classic case study of the painter Ruth Kjar, Klein describes the painter's art as psychically repairing the root of infantile anxiety (the girl's fear of a retaliating mother). Klein tells us that "it is instructive to consider what sort of pictures Ruth Kjar has painted since her first attempt, when she filled the empty space on the wall with the life sized figure of a naked negress" (93). Klein indeed goes on to do just that—interpret Kjar's subsequent paintings as her effort to work through issues of her sexuality and relationship to her mother. Meanwhile, Klein completely bypasses that extraordinary *first* painting and all its projective-introjective racial implications. If we were to read aesthetic production as an extension of self-knowing, as Klein here suggests, then surely it is significant that this white woman is working through her own issues via the projection of a life-sized "naked negress."

I cannot do justice to these fascinating elisions in Klein here, but it is clear that the constitution of the self often speaks through the racial projection of an other, that the racial imaginary may inform, not just act as a result of, ego-formation. As evidenced by the Klein case study, the racial other is already the (unexamined) *stuff* and *imago* feeding the theorization of object relations. Kingston's drama of racial-ethnic hypochondria, I would suggest, attempts precisely to theorize, in this bathroom scene, the constitutive racial element *at work* in the interplay of projection and introjection. The subject caught in this projection-introjection dynamic is also the subject for whom intersubjectivity presents something of a crisis. Freud in fact often describes the project of intersubjectivity—of learning to move toward and love another—as a kind of hypochondriacal dilemma. In his essay "On Narcissism" (1914), Freud writes "A strong egoism is a protection against falling ill, but in the last resort we must begin to love in order not to fall ill, and we are bound to fall ill if, in consequence of frustration (*Versagung*), we are unable to love."[19] Although Freud's love advice is essentially a call for a movement outward (for the ego to direct its energy outward, toward intersubjectivity), it also articulates Freud's characteristic fear of contact with others. So this therapeutic formula indicates a series of double binds: while a strong ego might protect against disease, we nevertheless must pass beyond the boundary of our ego in order *not* to fall ill; yet again, the potential for frustration as a result of that reaching out will surely make us ill. (Not only may one fall ill or fail at love presumably because of unreturned love, but the effect of such rejection might be so devastating that one would fail to love henceforth and cannot love at all.) Hence an impossible and melancholic situation has been set up where the ego can neither remain *in* or *out* without suffering.

Furthermore, this aphoristic recommendation for a healthy love life presumes that there *are* conditions under which the possibility for attachment may itself be foreclosed (and "we are *unable* to love"). The specter of failure not only attends the outcome of love but also inhibits the very motion toward love. Missing from the English translation of "*Versagung*" as "frustration" is the German denotation that refers to denial, disavowal, or renunciation and implies a condition of denying oneself as well as being denied. Hence "in consequence of *Versagung*" can refer to the absence of an external object capable of satisfying the instinct (such as not having that love returned) or it can refer to a refusal on the part of the agent. Since *Versagung* takes its etymological root from *sagen* (to say) and literally means a kind of naysaying or mis-saying,[20] hypochondria in this Freudian account might in fact denote a mis-saying against the self. So we trip over yet another potential stumbling block on Freud's road to love: the paradox presented by those subjects who speak against themselves even as they are about to achieve their desires, subjects who fall ill at the very prospect of acquiring cure.

There is a chicken-and-egg quality to this dilemma between the inability to give or accept love and the hypochondriacal anticipation of loss. For Freud, this sickening dynamic forms the foundation of the ego-economy, suggesting that the subjective dilemma is also an intersubjective one. I am particularly interested in this no-win game, in what the aspiration toward love thwarted by the hypochondriacal anticipation of loss has to tell us about the intricacies of assimilatory desires and their relation to sociability. Freud's advice has in fact outlined a kind of intrasubjective hypochondria, where the subject is in essence *hypochondriacal about the self* in the face of intersubjective engagement.

As the process by which a minority group or individual adopts the customs and attitudes of the prevailing culture, assimilation is meant to cover over sites of cultural breaks, gaps, and incommensurability. In contrast, hypochondria would seem to impose a logic whereby that which is (or might be) broken, disordered, or incompatible gets continually exposed. Yet a counterintuitive connection between assimilation and hypochondria can reveal, on the parts of racial-ethnic subjects, the crisis of a sociability *conditioned* by the anticipation of its own failure. It is a crisis that gets played out *on and against* the body in a drama of hypochondria. In the heart of every assimilative gesture lies the haunting anxiety of social failure. Rather than positing a causal relationship (that the anxieties surrounding the prospect of assimilation lead to hypochondriacal reactions), I want to suggest that hypochondria is the *form* of assimilation: an intersubjective movement outward that may result in, but is in fact already conditioned by, the anticipation of some kind of intrasubjective failure. Assimilation and hypochondria share similar logics and can be experienced as indistinguishable, and precisely in their interchangeability we can begin to unravel some of the most stubborn assumptions underlying the notions of racial health and cultural healing.

Kingstonean hypochondria emerges as a persistent mode of processing interpersonal negotiations: a dread of invasive contagion that materializes on the self. This scenario of hypochondriacal acting-out of the racially abjected body finds its perfect distillation in one specific detail in the bathroom scene: "I reached up and took the fatty part of her cheek . . . meat between my thumb and finger. . . . I gave her face a squeeze. . . . When I let go, the pink rushed back into my white thumbprint on her skin" (176–7). At the point of physical contact, we see an implosion of the confrontation between notions of an ontic self and the racialized self. The *blood tainting the white thumbprint of the self left on the skin of the other* dramatizes the tautology of contagion: a fear of contamination that contaminates. It is as though, in this intraracial exchange, an interracial conflict is nonetheless taking place. Abusing the other girl allows for a self-identification with whiteness/American pedagogical authority ("the white thumbprint of the self"), which serves to mask even as it exposes a racial identification (by "blood") between the girls. For Kingston's narrator, the act of assuming the position of authority simultaneously projects a sick self outside and installs it within, in a coincidence of desire and denigration—literally, a malady of otherness. Hypochondriacal anticipation thus continually supports the reflexive paths of this version of "cultural assimilation," a dynamic of frustration and denial always at once projected onto another and assumed by the self: *Versagung.*

The Becoming Body

Instead of adopting the traditional thinking about assimilation as a kind of self-loss, an evacuation of the subject (the notion that to assimilate means to lose aspects of oneself),[21] I would like to examine how assimilation effects the inverse: occupation, subject-ion, embodiment. Assimilation in fact de-

notes a form of internalization so intense as to be almost a bodily incorporation of another. We need to scrutinize this "incorporation," not because
it interferes with some notion of a real or an authentic self but because it
augments a psychical condition of susceptibility. As much as the narrator
repeatedly reminds us that she wishes to mime idealized bodies (whether it
be trying to "turn [her]self American feminine" (111) or inventing "an
American-feminine speaking personality" (171) or imitating the heroism of
the Woman Warrior), they do not actually constitute the most powerful sites
of identification. The bodies that come to hold the narrator's most passionate, psychical investments—the bodies that she *lives*—are often the least
idealized bodies. We recall that, in addition to all the idealized, impeccable
ego-ideals, the narration also features a host of weakened, sad, or diseased
bodies (the much-cited suicidal No-Name aunt whose body stuffed up the
family well, the weakened and paranoid aunt Moon Orchid, the retarded boy
in the neighborhood, the silent girl from the bathroom scene, the narrator's
own sickly body). Being susceptible means one is open to both idealized *and*
dreaded identifications. The question of assimilation is therefore not limited
to the assumption of dominant cultural ideals but extends to a range of other
identifications.

If we recall that racial melancholia perversely and continually evokes
dreams of impossible perfection (think of Helen's longing-filled dream sequence in *Flower Drum Song*), then we can begin to understand the narrator's passionate disgust for *and* endless absorption in "freakish" figures.
Her paradoxical reactions of identification and disidentification with figures
like the retarded boy, who the narrator was sure was meant to be her
"match," expose the specter of racial melancholia: an obsession with the
norm (imagined to be perfection), accompanied by an exquisite sensitivity
for any deviation from that norm. That sensitivity, so well honed over time,
takes on somatic manifestations: "Indeed I was getting stranger every day.
I affected a limp. And, of course, the mysterious disease I had might have
been dormant and contagious" (190). Here we see hypochondria's paradoxical reasoning at its keenest: the assumption of the mask of infirmity as a form
of protection. The narrator is at once suffering from the fearful injunction
against things "freakish" and a willful absorption in that prospect—dread,
defiance, and desire circling one another.

This preoccupation with perfection and its obverse lends an insight into
two related fundamental activities of assimilation: comparison and mimicry. When it comes to examining mimicry in relation to assimilation, the
question of mimetic "failure" or "success" often arises, but such a question
deflects the focus away from what is really at stake psychically for the assimilating person: that is, what that logic of mimicry *does* for him/her sub-
jectively. In "Of Mimicry and Man: The Ambivalence of Colonial Discourse,"
Homi Bhabha proposes the thesis that colonial mimicry is an injunction for

the colonized to assimilate to colonial standards but that the injunction is in effect an impossible one since the colonized, by virtue of their racial difference, will always fail in their mimicry, fail in "measuring up." Indeed, in *The Woman Warrior* we often see the impossibility of choosing between a master language and a language "of one's own." If "speaking English" constitutes a kind of "faking" for Kingston's narrator, "speaking Chinese" does not seem any more real: "You can't trust your voice to the Chinese, either" (169). The narrator's prolific, self-descriptive metaphors of division (her split tongue, her cracked voice) suggest an autobiographical cleavage that plays out what Bhabha calls the "colonial discourse of mimicry." For Bhabha sees mimicry as a disciplinary device, one that is nonetheless doomed to fail. He explains that "colonial mimicry is the desire for a reformed, recognizable Other, as *a subject of a difference that is almost the same, but not quite.*"[22] So: American but not American, Asian but not Asian—the Asian American subject must be disguised, mimed, as *almost* the same but not quite.

Although Bhabha's argument aims to highlight ambivalence on the part of authority (its divided desires for compliance and failure on the part of the colonized it is "educating"), Kingston's text compels us to extend the inquiry to ask, How is that ambivalence parodied, modified, or even reproduced on the part of the racial other? In a sense, the narrator's persistent, hypochondriacal identification with invalidism and its inverse functions as a mode of protection *against* a national sociability that was meant to exclude her in the first place. Her convoluted paths toward a dream of health signify a paradox in the heart of assimilatory management: a desire for sociability that reveals a crisis of sociability.

While assimilation would be most readily recognized as the emulation of an ideal other ego, what this understanding hides from view are the ways in which assimilation effects the incorporation and internalization of a "failed" bodily ego. This propensity to take in bodies both good and bad, I want to suggest, has everything to do with a subject caught in the logic of assimilation. *It is not that assimilation prevents one from being real but that it renders impossible the experience of being secure within such a fiction.* It fosters an endless propensity for comparison. For those living in a racial imaginary that continually sees them as not normal, not healthy, and incommensurate, hypervigilance begins to condition subjective formation. By the term "racial imaginary" I mean an American public repertoire of racial images and conceptions that renders the notion of a racially healthy body at once highly desirable and problematic. The social injunction to measure up to mainstream racial and gender ideals creates for the racialized subject in America a paradoxical consciousness of desire and incommensurability.[23] By incommensurability I do not mean the failure to achieve mainstream social ideals; in fact, minorities often do achieve such goals. Instead, I am referring to the psychical condition of *measurement and approximation* that continues to haunt the racialized subject even, or especially, when she/he attains those ideals. (Indeed, it may be argued that it is the "high achievers"—those who are invested in these ideals—who are most prone to this psychical condition of vigilant comparison and anxiety.)[24]

I wish to concentrate on that moment, as described by Freud, when the subject denies her/himself at the very moment of achievement—the subject who, while doing everything she/he can to obtain "love and company," refuses them. The curious agency inhering in acts of assimilation then may reside much less in any successful assumption of otherness (acting like the other) than in the active provocation of the self into some kind of competition. If one is emerging from a condition of "dormant contagion," then the most successful prospect of social integration may be just to be in the game at all: the point is not even to become the ideal other, but to be *able to act* against the paralysis of alienation, in the interest of becoming *comparable* with that ideality.

We cannot help hear an echo of Frantz Fanon's proclamation that the raced subject (specifically "the Negro") *is* comparison. According to Fanon, the black man, heeding the call of assimilation ("blanchir ou disparaître"), endeavors to assume mainstream culture but on his way to the metropolis finds his "true" face to be ineluctably black, not white.[25] This lesson of failure has been rephrased by Homi Bhabha as the inherent failure of colonial mimicry and by David Lloyd as the "residue of difference."[26] However, in the context of a nation founded (at least rhetorically) on pluralism, the play, meaning, and value of such "residue" vary widely. Theorizing assimilation in an Asian American context requires some adjustments from the postcolonial framework. In the postcolonial context, the paradox of assimilation is that the subject immersed in the acts of comparison finds that he/she cannot compare; the failure then reconfirms the stigmatism attached to the minoritized individual. In the contemporary Asian American context, the assimilating subject often finds him/herself vying for even *the opportunity of* such a comparison. The assimilating subject, having chosen the American Dream, finds that she/he cannot do anything but compare her/himself against the ideal norm; furthermore, such comparison, however painful or debilitating, can come perversely to open up a position of contestation that can be preferable to invisibility.

Because the narrating subject in *The Woman Warrior* is engaged in this simultaneous combat of consent and refusal in relation to dominant culture, negative traces remain that cannot be metabolized by the drive of the ethnic *Bildung*, in spite of all the critical positivism surrounding the text's ethnic and feminist representations. This speaking subject never escapes this psychical world of comparison. Near the end of the text, the narrator speaks from the vantage point of being grown-up, worldly, and assimilated into mainstream American life: "Now colors are gentler and fewer; smells are antiseptic" (205). In other words, at her "healthiest" she is still smelling the hospital. (Do we not hear a mournful strain in this celebration?) Indeed, the supposedly nonmelancholic world—the world of the "ghost-free country"—recreates a probing and deadly form of anaesthetization:

> I had to leave home in order to see the world logically, logic the new way of seeing. . . . I enjoy simplicity. Concrete pours out of my mouth to cover forests with freeways and sidewalks. Give me plastic, periodic tables, t.v. dinners with vegetables no more complex than peas mixed with diced carrots. Shine floodlights into dark corners: no ghosts. (204)

No ghosts: pure salvation. Yet, metaphorically and perhaps psychically, the narrator is back in the ward.

Again we are witnessing a careful delineation and maintenance of her subjective boundaries *through* the very denial of shadows that clearly threaten the integrity of those boundaries.[27] For the assimilating but racially different subject, the rejecting dominant cultural ideals has transformed into an internal hypochondriacal police, the superego of assimilative desires. For the narrator, this internal hypochondriacal police rarely relaxes its guard.[28] In my view, the most profound problem posed by assimilation is not political in the conventional sense but is in the added burden of comparative injunction imposed on already fraught processes of intersubjective negotiation.

Bruised Ecstasy

Assimilation as a coping mechanism (with all its hypochondriacal stagings) has all the signs of its own undoing. Indeed, the coping itself often resembles a rehearsal of trauma. When we look at the narrator as an adult, presumably a successfully assimilated adult ("I've found some places in this country that are ghost-free"), we find her still rehearsing old wounds:

> I [kept] learn[ing] new grievances. . . . "Did you roll an egg on *my* face like that when *I* was born?" "Did you have a full-month party for *me*?" "Did you turn on all the lights?" "Did you send *my* picture to Grandmother?" "Why not? Because I am a girl? Is that why not?" "Why didn't you teach me English?" "You like having me beaten up at school, don't you?" (46)

I pursue the role of the mother in this drama of grievance in the next section; for now I want to stress how the narrator continues to look for reasons to legitimate her potential inability to assimilate, both within her family and in the social world at large. The point here is not to claim that the narrator is making up stories about how her family treats her but rather that she is clearly invested in rehearsing a historical origin, true or not, for the difficulties she has in "fitting in." This search for explanation—this taking on of the role of the investigator/self-diagnostician—in turn cauterizes the pain of social adversities.

Traditionally taken to imply an illness without cause or reality, hypochondria here not only embodies the form of a crisis of sociability, as I have been discussing, but also denotes an effort at negotiating such a loss by constantly seeking and staging the question of origin. This staging of renunciation, trauma, and pain turns out to be an integral and even productive psychical element of assimilation. There is a certain pleasure of subjection at work in assimilation, too, for what is desired is precisely the *eligibility* for subjection—even the eligibility of failure. For the one whose very status within the nation has been and continues to be attenuated (more tenuous than African Americans), to vie for the opportunity for comparison *is* to participate in the American Dream.

The Woman Warrior suggests that assimilation, with its hypochondriacal staging, does not protect a subject from social demands as one might imagine it would (the way Jane Austen's Mr. Woodhouse might find relief from social obligations through his hypochondria). On the contrary, it allows this subject to live with tremendous, conflictual social demands, even as it keeps those demands alive. Insofar as assimilation displays a pattern of mastering, a "binding," that works through anticipating and repeating a failed or painful experience of social entry and contact, it is also *the* form of cultural interpellation available to the racialized, immigrant minority: not a smooth process of seamless interpellation but a process that constantly rubs the subject up against the limits of "proper" subjecthood. In a curious reversal, we can say that assimilation functions as a protection against the *trauma* of incommensurability by restaging the *drama* of incommensurability. In short, the unfolding drama of assimilation stages social trauma in order to contain it: a hypochondriacal logic, the anticipation of illness in order to domesticate it.

Part II: Transgenerational Writing

> I cannot believe in Western sincerity because it is invisible, but in feudal times we believed that sincerity resides in our entrails, and if we needed to show our sincerity, we had to cut our bellies and take out our *visible* sincerity.
>
> —Yukio Mishima

> The dead—who, having suffered repression by their family or society, cannot enjoy, even in death, a state of authenticity.
>
> —Nicolas Abraham

This narrative's anxious preoccupation with the questions of legitimacy and authenticity renders the critical dispute over this novel's cultural authenticity all the more perplexing. The critical debate over the place of the text in Asian American letters duplicates the narrator's own struggle over the question of her place within an Asian American culture. I need not rehearse the much-publicized debate between Frank Chin and Maxine Hong Kingston over the issue of her "authenticity," except to note that a complex of accompanying issues (from gender and cultural competition to the political anxieties of racial representation) has been brilliantly laid out by Sau-ling Cynthia Wong in her seminal essay "Autobiography as Guided Chinatown Tour?"[29] For my purpose, which is to explore the injunction of authenticity and its relationship to social hypochondria, it is sufficient to note that detractors and admirers of Kingston alike form their opinions on the grounds of cultural legitimacy: the former criticize her for false representations; the latter praise her fiction for its imagination. The former refuses to see the fictionalization fundamental to any representation, while the latter revolves around the freedom of self-representation without questioning the deeper and more troubling relationships that fantasy and desire come to have with what is being stereotyped. Both sides have simply assigned different values to the notion of fantasy without examining the internal structure of fantasy on which any identity is built.[30] These judgments of Kingston's textual cultural authenticity are all the more ironic when we consider the fact that this "book of grievance" and of grief is itself intensely *enacting* a quest for cultural origin and authenticity. It is the *origin of loss*, which the narrator can never really know and must keep staging, that renders the question of memory and authenticity so profoundly spectral in this text and in the field of ethnic literature at large.

In *The Woman Warrior*, racial origin itself has become a traumatic inheritance, where "origin" exists as transmitted memory, where history is thrown into crisis by a delay in its registration as a result of immigration. In a footnote in their essay "The Lost Object—Me: Notes on Endocryptic Identification" (1975), Nicolas Abraham and Maria Torok suggest an intimate connection between spectral inheritance and subjective formation:

> Should a child have parents with "secrets," parents whose speech is not exactly complementary to their unstated repressions, the child will receive from them a gap in the unconscious, an unknown, unrecognized knowledge—a *nescience*—subjected to a form of "repression" before the fact. . . . .This unknown phantom can return . . . its effect can persist through several generations and determine the fate of an entire family.[31]

The passage first implies that traumatic *effects* can be transmitted even if (or precisely because) the traumatic *event* itself has not. Second, prohibition and repression ("secrets") can be as productive ("a *nescience*") as they are limiting. Third, such "secret transmission" may contribute to the formation of an "unconscious."

The story of the No Name Aunt, for instance, at first glance seems to offer a case-study dramatization of such a formative "rift" and subsequent "nescience." On the occasion of the narrator's entrance into puberty, the mother tells the narrator the story of the No Name Aunt who drowned herself in the family well after giving birth to an illegitimate child. The narrator's mother warns: "Now that you have started to menstruate, what happened to her could happen to you. Don't humiliate us. You wouldn't like to be forgotten as if you had never been born" (5). This injunction effects sexual difference on the one hand and erases it on the other. After all, she has been warned not to be like the aunt *only because she has the potential of being exactly like the aunt*. (What happened to her could happen to you; don't assume the sexuality you are on the verge of entering.) The maternal message places the child in an impossible position. On the occasion of becoming a woman, the narrator is told what it means to be a woman and also how *not* to be a woman. "You must not tell what I am about to tell you" (3): the child, just by listening, has already been drawn into a contract and is already at fault—a double bind that works much like Derrida's favored example of the sign "Do not read this."[32] For Derrida the impossibility of this injunction (to hear it is to transgress it; to obey it one has to be already guilty) tells us about how law works. For us, this "reading act" enacts an aspect of the cultural transmission taking place between the narrator and her mother. What binds the daughter is the ambivalence of maternal transmissions. The moment the narrator hears and is exiled from the story of the No Name Aunt, she is conscripted into a relation with the aunt as the same and not the same.

The No Name Aunt, however, does not, strictly speaking, constitute a "rift" or "phantom" in Abraham and Torok's sense of the words, because the function of this metadiegesis is, after all, not repression but its opposite. The maternal, injunctive, narrative foreclosure surrounding the figure of the aunt has the exact opposite function of sending the narrator into sustained ruminations on sexual difference as well as her own relations to prohibited familial lore. The narrator "outs" the aunt, so to speak: "I am telling on her" (16). We can actually see this moment as the text acting as its own therapist, catering to a psychoanalytic mode of confession by staging both the burial and the unearthing of a "family secret." The novel is, after all, a story *constructed* to be just such a confession, with all its revelatory and transgressive impact.

But this "outing" does not really reveal a secret. The No Name Aunt has been named only through very name of exclusion ("No Name"), reminding us that to *name* something does not at all guarantee its symbolic reassertion, especially when it has been named by its very unnameability. In other words, if an identity is *founded* on prohibition, denial, marginalization, or loss, then the simple act of naming cannot recuperate that loss, except as a *representation of* recuperation. (This should offer us a parable for thinking about identity politics.) Indeed, for all the naming in the narration, the text also retains several figures and identities that it fails to name or unearth. It is as if the ghosts cited in the text are merely mundane manifestations of a deeper morbid disturbance. Sometimes I suspect that all the ghosts named in the narrative have been thrown in our path to prevent us from detecting the unnamed phantoms at work in this profoundly haunted narrative. That deeper disturbance, I suggest, has to do with a submerged history of immigration being documented in this text.

Abraham and Torok call the melancholic identification with a lost love or unknowable inheritance an "endocryptic identification," to stress the cryptic and crypt-like quality of that identification:

> This mechanism consists of exchanging one's own identity for fantasmatic identification with the "life"—beyond the grave—of an object of love, lost as a result of some metapsychological traumatism. . . . The melancholic complaints translate a fantasy—the imaginary suffering of the endocryptic object—a fantasy that only serves to mask the real suffering, this one unavowed, caused by a wound the subject does not know how to heal. (142)

Endocryptic identification would thus seem to be a melancholic tool in a rather classic Freudian sense: a substitution and preservation of loss without having to acknowledge that loss as loss. And one may be tempted to call the narrator's identification with the aunt an endocryptic identification. But I want to suggest that this endocryptic identification (this melancholic incorporation) in the text can be a ruse. That is, there is *another* loss being buried here and another fantasmatic identification being established: not the loss of the dead aunt that is being flaunted by the narrator but a loss that is truly inarticulable between mother and daughter—a loss that extends beyond inevitable, expected parent-child losses to whole cultural, national, and historical losses that the mother has herself endured, is herself barely processing, and has in fact passed on to the daughter.

In *The Acoustic Mirror*, Kaja Silverman points out that in the Oedipal drama, female subjectivity formed in response to a positive Oedipus complex is always already melancholic.[33] According to Silverman, the Oedipal drama exacts a double price from female subject: to separate from the mother as an originary object of desire under the threat of castration, while suffering tremendous cultural pressures to identify with the mother. What Silverman stresses is the double bind inherent in female subjectivity as traditionally and psychoanalytically conceived: the mother is simultaneously rejected/degraded and internalized—hence her melancholic shadow on the daughter. But what happens when that gender melancholia gets compounded with the racial melancholia of having relinquished—

or never having had direct access to—an originary cultural identification that is simultaneously degraded by one's current culture at large and required as the very definition for the self?

The Woman Warrior dramatizes the mother–daughter relationship as a map for the convoluted and covered-over crossidentifications. For example, the story of the suicidal aunt that begins this text and that the narrator presents as a site of female identification over and against the mother's prohibition in facts entails much more of an identification with, not against, the mother. The mourner whom the story never names as such and the mourner whom the daughter/narrator is herself mourning is the mother, Brave Orchid. Indeed, is not Brave Orchid, by name as well as by deed, the true Woman Warrior in the book? Seen in this light, even the novel's subtitle ("Memoirs of a Girlhood among Ghosts") produces a confusion between narrator and mother. In short, the *hidden* endocryptic identification being structured and safeguarded by the text is the daughter psychically living the life of the mother and reliving her mother. *The mother is the mourner in the text, and the daughter the melancholic repeater of her grief.*

This double, transgenerational writing would account for those moments in the narrative where the reader cannot distinguish between what the narrator is contributing herself and what are the mother's words. This doubleness is most evident in the "Shaman" chapter. Appropriately a story about ghosts, this chapter is itself saturated with nostalgic longing for the mother as the embodiment of pragmatism and materiality: a doctor, a scientist, a ghostbuster. This chapter introduces the mother as an invincible woman who can exorcise even ghosts. Yet the mother's subsequent losses through the process of immigration must have been tremendous, traumatic, and spectral. She lost a family, a village, her profession (going from being a highly respected, even fabled midwife to laundry woman) and social positions. These losses were never articulated on the mother's part. This "Shaman" chapter devoted to the mother ends not with an account of the mother's subsequent immigration experience but with the narrator's own experience growing up in Chinatown, as though the latter has substituted for the former.

The shift from the silence of the mother's immigrant experience to the daughter's plaints symptomatizes the substitution that has been assumed by the narrator. The narrator tells us: "Whenever my parents said 'home,' they suspended America. They suspended enjoyment" (99). It is because the mother's relationship to America is still one of psychical inadmissibility that the daughter experiences America as a projected place of rest that is always displaced. If the mother is the immigrant and the daughter the "new" Asian American subject, then the latter's access to her mother's origins can be only at best a form of melancholic, endocryptic fantasy—hence the fraught relationship between daughter and mother and hence the daughter's very definition of a "ghost-free" country as a plaint directly *against* the mother in a way that is also a proclamation of the impossibility of ever leaving the mother.

Caught between competing national and familial narratives, the daughter as an Asian American citizen supposedly enjoys a social commensurability that the mother as the immigrant never quite possesses but which the daughter of course never really feels precisely because she is her mother's daughter. The unasked but glaring question in the text is what happened to the mother; what were her losses? We need to turn to the possibility that the immigrant trauma of the mother (surely not even fully registered by the mother herself)[34] has been passed down to the daughter *as* inherited trauma, trauma without an origin. In other words, we must hear beyond the narrator's obsessive tales of her own grievance to an echo or rehearsal of the mother's grievance.

The plaint is being filed: not on behalf of the mother, but *as* the mother in a kind of endocryptic repetition. The daughter is a melancholic echo of the mother. To speak against the mother is also to be the mother. Indeed, the narrator often talks about the mother's speech as if it has been introjected into the narrator's own body. The mother's words are described, for example, as moving like "a curtain flapped loose inside my brain" (91)—except the narrator does not choose to use a simile. The mother's words do not enter *like* a curtain, but *flap* (that is, already installed) inside. Similarly, the narrator collapses temporal frameworks in telling the monkey brain story (where the narrator is listening to a tale of how the Chinese eat monkey brains and suddenly she is also at the dinner table recoiling from the mother's injunction to "Eat! Eat!"), creating a fantasmatic collision between different narrative and temporal contexts. In *Articulate Silences*, King-Kok Cheung shrewdly points out that readers often tend to collapse the time lines in Kingston's text, confusing the consciousness and statements made by the narrator as a child versus the narrator as an adult looking back—what Cheung calls "the author's mature conviction."[35] The difference is crucial to Cheung's argument that the text chronicles a "progression from a silent child to a word warrior" (88). For me, the "double" time line has more to do with the narrator's ongoing ventriloquy of the mother than with being a sign of chronological perspective—the collapse, rather than success, of distance. The mature perspective of the narrator alone cannot address the very peculiar kinds of temporal telescoping that happen, especially when the narration is talking about the mother. "Talk story" *is* the *mise en scène* of maternal transmission.

I suggest that this contextual conflation, what Victor Burgin describes as the "intertextual mutual imbrication of anecdotes,"[36] conditions the very possibility of cultural perception. The mother, in trying to assimilate the child into a Chinese culture that the latter does not know, is in fact *creating* that very culture. The internalization of cultural origins as subjective or ontological origins indicates a path to theorize the act of hearing a story, how a story enters us, structures us. In other words, these narrative acts play out a transmission of fantasy, a transmission that *is* fantasy. The mother infuses her tales into the narrator's psychical and daily landscape: this is what we mean when we say a story "speaks to something inside us."

While this may look like an overdetermined parable for maternal invasions as such, we should still recognize the force of this invasion and the cultural implications in this particular case.[37] The child not only internalizes but also *racializes* this maternal introjection. She processes the call of the mother as a call of Chinese origin and culture. This explains the text's continual conflations of the spaces of the mother and of racial-ethnic identities. It is both appropriate and ironic that this mother who facilitates births (a professional midwife) and seduces ghosts would have a daughter perpetually haunted by questions of origin. The narrator's hypochondriacal fear of invasion, contagion, and her own vulnerably porous body is also precisely how she in fact establishes a connection with her mother.

Hypochondria here effects and enables a profound, albeit "twisted," connection with the mother.[38] In his essay "The Common Neurotic State" (1917), Freud offers an insight into a link between hypochondria and traumatic memory. He gives the startlingly clear proposition that hypochondria is a symptom, a coating—even a *memory*—of an "original, real" pain. He argues that hypochondria is the memory-trace of a missing original trauma: "[there was] at one time a real [pain] and it was then a direct sexual toxic symptom . . . which plays the part of the grain of sand which a mollusk coats with layers of mother-of-pearl."[39] If hypochondria acts as a memory of some lost "real" pain, then hypochondria is the very *manifestation* of the absence of origin. The narrator's hypochondriacal tendencies articulate a defense against the lack of origin; after all, being unimaginably healthy elsewhere saves you from feeling sick everywhere. (It also means you are never very far from your mother even as you are proclaiming otherwise.)

Origin, both material and cultural, occupies this peculiar status in the text: at once a dream and a nightmare. Near the end of the novel, the narrator carefully stages a story about the abduction and rape of Han princess and poetess Ts'ai Yen by the "barbarians" (non-Hans) and her eventual ransom back to the Hans "so that her father could have Han descendants" (109). The narrator posits a redemptive moment by referring to the creation of a song, the song that Ts'ai Yen sang to barbarian flute music during her captivity: "a high note . . . found and held . . . an icicle in the desert" (208). This moment of crystallization, emblematic of cultural birth through the processes of migration and translation, ends the book:

> She brought her songs back from the savage lands, and one of the three that has been passed down to us is "Eighteen Stanzas for a Barbarian Reed Pipe," a song that the Chinese sing to their own instruments. It translated well. (109)

This moment of lyrical birth is predicated upon a bloody history of Chinese ethnic warfare and unification, itself a tale of violent national formation based on ethnic domination, annihilation, and trafficking in women. This tale tells us that there is no such a thing as "pure" culture; culture is in fact often borne out of acts of violent translation. Cultural formation, the crystallization of that "Chinese" song, grows out of a turbulent, heterogenous crossbreeding.

Most readers have taken the statement "it translated well" to be unironic—indeed, redemptive. Yet what does the narrator mean that the song "translated well" in a text so burdened with the prices of cultural translation? This redemptive gesture seems unconvincing when we remember that, after all the desperate efforts to piece together her history, the narrator is then thrown into what must have been total epistemological confusion when her mother told her that she has been misinterpreting all along: "You can't . . . tell real from false . . . That's what Chinese [do]: we like to say the opposite" (202–3). The source of meaning, the mother, has just rescinded itself. Thus I do not believe in the final claim that this song or story can translate well. Whether my skeptical take on this epiphany can be proven true or not, it seems pertinent to ask why the narrator needs this moment of recuperation, so out of character with the tone of the narrative. It is as though the narrator's suspicion of such a vision can only express itself as desire (again that hypochondriacal logic): the desire for a cultural legibility and sense that the autobiography suspects it can never affix. Where could such an affirmation come from, except as yet another hypochondriacal expression in the face of threatening incommensurability/untranslatability? For hypochondria is not merely the staging of illness but also the paradoxical staging of health in fear and anticipation of the haunting prospect of illness. The hypochondriacal fantasy of "translating well," as in the fantasy of a perfectly healthy body, staves off the nagging fear that a poor "translation" would mean the loss of the mother, for this story of the barbarian reed, too, is inherited from the mother. As long as the narrator narrates in anxiety or in longing, she need not relinquish the mother, who is in fact already being left behind as the narrator replaces her voice with her own: a movement of love and a movement of loss.

Nothing displays the sign of exile more glaringly than the nostalgia for "roots." The acquisition of "roots" that "translate well" becomes urgent when Asians in the diaspora and their subsequent generations seek to construct a political agenda in which ideal rootedness is imagined to be a prerequisite for cultural integrity. The narrator uses the tale of Ts'ai Yen to refigure the cartography of dispersal and exile. But the tale supplies a metastatement on the narrator's desires, for the creation of national culture, revealed by Ts'ai Yen's story, is always already itself a response to loss and exile. The Princess found consolation for her captivity in a song she heard in the desert, and she eventually brought that song home to China. The memory that the song consecrates is thus not Chinese nationalism or culture per se but an importation of the nomads, an indelible souvenir of her passage.

What the narrator shares with the character Ts'ai Yen is not original Chinese culture or the promise of China as secure homeland but rather the condition of exile and the necessity of journey. Whatever "hope" this story might offer, it cannot be the promise of having recovered a hermetically sealed and culturally absolute tradition. Instead, the story provides the means of figuring the inescapable and legitimate values of transmutation, hybridity, and intermixture. More than family grievances or stories, the phantom of immigration and the condition of diaspora pass from mother to daughter. And the very notion of origin is itself embedded within heterogeneous, historical, and multisubjective "coatings," an origin of illness and an illness of origin.

Part III: Morbid Community, Ritual Grief

> Since language acts and makes up for absence by representing, by *giving figurative shape* to presence, it can only be *comprehended* or *shared* in a community of empty mouths.
> —Nicolas Abraham and Maria Torok

Rather than reading Kingston's text as representing an Asian American community, in this section I examines Kingston's novel as a meditation on the possibilities of such a community. Specifically, I am concerned with what Kingston's private grief and its hypochondriacal expression might teach us about the advantages and disadvantages of forming a collective communal identity united not by ethnic homogeneity but by racial grievance.[40]

The perversely intimate connection between hypochondria and community is not new to literary imagination, nor is the fascination that hypochondria holds for writers (from Montaigne to Mann to Kafka to Austen). Kingston's bedridden narrator herself reminds us of that long tradition: "I lived like the Victorian recluses I read about" (182). This Asian American child's longing to belong in the company of European literary ancestors echoes a very American longing for legitimacy vis-à-vis its European origins. Of course those European origins have their own allergies about such longings directed at them. The notion that hypochondria (as a fear of racial contamination) might discipline the white, national body of "Englishness" is not difficult to grasp. George Cheyne has long established an inextricable link between hypochondria and the English spirit in his classic treatise on melancholia, *The English Malady* (1621).[41] Indeed, hypochondria and hypochondriacs have made their presences acutely felt in the nineteenth-century novel and have come, especially in the Victorian novel, to signal the very sensibility that authenticates national character.

"'Here was a family of helpless Invalids whom I might essentially serve"![42] With this exclamation by Miss Diana Parker, for example, begins the action of Jane Austen's unfinished novel *Sanditon*, set in a seaside retreat of the same name, a new community developed by the hypochondriacal Mr. Parker, whose social and business worlds center around an unremitting preoccupation with Health and the prospect of a place whose very air and breezes might cure every disorder imaginable to the civilized, from a badly turned ankle to rheumatism to gout. The socially respected propensity for a healthy dose of hypochondria, however, begins to wane when intimations of a racial body appear on the horizon. The family in question— the much-desired visitors to Sanditon, whose arrival promises the fulfillment of the Parkers' mission of cure—includes a certain Miss Lambe, "a young Westindian of large fortune" who is a "half-mulatto" of "delicate health," "as Wealth & a Hot Climate are apt to make us" (419,409).[43] Since the manuscript ends before Miss Lambe arrives in person, it is not clear how Mr. Parker or Sanditon can cure Miss Lambe of the racial delicacy that surely accounts as much for her condition of melancholia as her large fortune qualifies her in this marriage plot.

As much as the Parkers share Miss Lambe's hypochondriacal sensibility and expect to benefit economically from her needs, their regard is not a little tempered by a hypochondriacal response of their own. Consternation develops around Miss Lambe's arrival, for the anticipation of her arrival initiates a case of mistaken identity, whereby the Parkers expect yet another family to be guests at Sanditon—"a Lady from Camberwell"—who turns out to be Mrs. Griffith, guardian of Miss Lambe. Thus the family arriving from Camberwell reveals itself to be the same as the family from the West Indies. And the mistake is ardently refuted:

> "It was very strange!—very remarkable!—very extraordinary" but [the Parkers] were all agreed in determ[in]ing it to be *impossible* that there should not be two Families; such a totally distinct set of people as were concerned in the reports of each made that matter quite certain. There *must* be two Families.—Impossible to be otherwise. "Impossible" & "Impossible," was repeated over & over again with great fervor. (419)

Apparently the merging of such "distinct set[s] of people" defies the imagination. What is clearly impossible, and to be resisted, is the very evidence
of miscegenation from which Miss Lambe suffers and which she is made to
represent, however "diluted" her entitlement to that condition. If for the very
British Diana Parker and her siblings, invalidism serves as a mode of sociability, an endless source of conversation, rumination, and connection, then
for Miss Lambe we have to speculate a different relation where invalidism
serves as the corporeal sign of her spectrality in this (racially) scrupulous
company.

At the same time, Miss Lambe is ironically most "British" herself in her
own hypochondria, that is, in having the exquisitely good taste of being
delicate about her own (racially ambiguous) body. While marking her embodied ghostliness (we might say her vagrant presence), Miss Lambe's delicate constitution must also make its claim on that civility and national identity that would have readily renounced her. Hypochondria on Miss Lambe's
part constitutes at once an exclusion by and a claim on civility. What is troubling, as is beginning to be suggested by Miss Lambe and more glaringly
insistent when we come to contemporary American ethnic literature, is the
adoption of the hypochondriacal discourse on the part of the one who has
traditionally been the object of such an anxiety. That is, while we can read
the hypochondriacal Miss Lambe as an ironized echo of, and encroachment
against, insular British society, it is more vexing to encounter such an appetite for hypochondria in a text such as *The Woman Warrior* with its fairly
explicit investment in ethnic and gender politics. I have been analyzing
hypochondria in Kingston's text as an expression of assimilatory anxiety, but
what finally are the implications of Kingston savoring, almost embodying,
hypochondria for the political project of Asian American representation? If
the project is designed to "heal" the racial wounds that called for such a
project in the first place, how does Kingston's text contribute to or redefine
that agenda?

Communal anxieties—whether they be about ethnic, literary, or gender
allegiances—have always been drawn to Kingston's body of work. On the
one hand, when the novel was first published, we see mainstream responses
such as those of *Publishers Weekly*, which effusively proclaims "Rarely does
East meet West with such charming results as occur in *The Woman Warrior* . . . myths as rich and varied as Chinese brocade . . . in a prose that often achieves the delicacy and precision of porcelain,"[44] or of Jane Kramer
of the *New York Times Book Review*, who pronounces *The Woman Warrior* as "undoubtedly as Chinese as *A Portrait of the Artist* is Irish."[45] *The
Woman Warrior* has also been relentlessly acclaimed for its exposure and
rejection of the patriarchal structure so rooted in the Asian kinship system.
Paul Gray in *Time* magazine calls the book a "triumphant journey of the

female imagination through a desolation of spirit"; Diane Johnson in *New York Review of Books* claims that "Kingston reaches to the universal qualities of the female condition and female anger."[46] Academic readers have reproduced these lines of argument in more sophisticated versions.[47] In short, much of the negativity in the text has been normalized by readers in search of a more well-rounded, more inspiring tale of "successful mourning."

This text's reception within the Asian American community, on the other hand, has been more than ambivalent, generating everything from adoration to an ongoing debate about its authenticity and thus its value.[48] At the heart of the "authenticity" debate lies a deeper problem relating to the formation of a community and the issue of racial mourning. It is precisely Kingston's negotiation between grief and grievance that has divided the "Asian American" community as such. For a large segment of Kingston's "own" community, she has been grieving too publicly, too loudly, and in a way that is too unseemly. This problem of "proper" grievance raises provocative questions about acts of resuscitation and notions of cultural health. If social health defines itself through racial pathology, then what could a redemptive political vocabulary do, or not do?

Before we approach the prospect of "cure," we might do well to first analyze the assumptions of health. In a fascinating treatise connecting the work of mourning to nation-building entitled *Stranded Objects: Mourning, Memory, and Film in Postwar Germany*, Eric L. Santner offers a study of postwar efforts in Germany to work through the legacies of fascism and the Holocaust. Santner's insights into the role that mourning plays in the reconstitution of a guilty community sheds light on a pattern of bereavement on the part of dominant American culture: "white guilt" and "white indifference" may be considered as two sides of the same coin, deployed in the service of trying to reconcile the nation's internal betrayal of proclaimed national ideology. But while Santner retains a fundamental attachment to the notion of "working through" and hence a privileging of the ideal of a national "health," American racial politics—especially from the perspective of the "objects" of that guilty history—demands an alternative formulation whereby the desired goal may not be to "work through" or "get over" something but rather to negotiate between mourning and melancholia in a more complicated, even continuous way.

Are the assimilatory desires expressed by Kingston for a "ghost-free" country an act of racial mourning or melancholia? Indeed, for the racialized communities, what forms can and do racial mourning take? We can say that assimilation is a self-cure trying to be a remedy for the suffering racial body, but as already discussed, such a "cure" remains dubious so long as health and pathology remain tethered to race and so long as assimilation reinforces the logic of incorporation that in turn repeats and prolongs the susceptibility of the already susceptible racialized body. Thus to remain caught up in the critical swing of adulation versus denigration is to miss Kingston's solicitation of that very polarity as a crucial constitution of community and of American nation formation.

The larger question that is important to explore is What does it mean, in a world haunted by racial melancholia and the difference between desirable and undesirable social bodies, to assimilate, and what does it mean not to? How does one master the world at large on the one hand and sustain difference as identity on the other? What kind of mourning enables social survival and what kind disables communal relations? If we come to understand assimilation as a continual act of coping, of psychical management in the face of threatening incommensurability, then there is much more work to be done in terms of rethinking the conditions of that survival and the judgments surrounding it. Furthermore, the specific dynamic of that psychical management may radically alter our conceptualization of what it means for the suffering racial body to heal.

Given that a vocabulary of grief and grievance has gone into the making and erasure of the racialized subject, and given that hypochondria gives us a theoretical model in which the body takes on cultural meanings and bears constant vigil over inflections of normality and infirmity, then assimilation can be seen as something of a parallel register for racial mourning and the social relations it is meant to engender—and perhaps finally endangers. The question of how to "get over" the racial issue has profound implications for the future of social relations in America. American idealization of health, cure, and mourning (i.e., "getting over" something, or "moving on") is itself symptomatic of the culture's attachment to coercive normality. I would like to pursue this connection between assimilation and cultural health. If cultural assimilation is commonly thought of as a process of "taking on" or "taking in" a foreign characteristic, then it may be useful to investigate its correlation to psychoanalytic conceptualizations of incorporation and psychic health.

Historically speaking, "incorporation" is most often associated with the term "introjection"; both terms are central to a psychoanalytic conception of mourning and its vicissitudes. As psychical responses to loss, both incorporation and introjection negotiate that loss by subsuming it. The former denotes a "process whereby the subject, more or less on the level of phantasy, has an object penetrate his body and keeps it 'inside' his body. . . . [It] provides the corporal model for introjection and identification."[49] There has been a consistent sense, from Freud on, that incorporation and introjection operate in similar ways: both impede the relinquishment and growth necessary for mourning. In their recent work on mourning, Nicolas Abraham and Maria Torok, however, offer a new definition of introjection that distinguishes—even opposes—introjection from incorporation. In the first volume of *The Shell and the Kernel*[50] Abraham and Torok propose introjection as a vital, psychical process for mental development, suggesting that introjection, far from being pathological, may in fact be vital to psychical development, even survival:

> Most of the characteristics falsely attributed to introjection in fact apply to the fantasmatic mechanisms of incorporation [which] implies a loss occurred before the desires concerning the object might have been freed. The loss acts as a prohibition and . . . constitutes an insurmountable obstacle to introjection. The prohibited object is settled in the ego in order to compensate for the lost pleasure and the failed introjection. (113)

Thus, for Abraham and Torok, introjection is a healthy version of incorporation. This new emphasis on introjection resembles more closely a Freudian notion of "successful mourning" or of "working out" and denotes a necessary, developmental process, indicating a vital, psychical assimilation of trauma into a network of mental association, which saves individuals from instability, disturbance, and devastation.

Abraham and Torok's reworking of introjection offers powerful insights into how we might theorize cultural assimilation at the intersection of loss and adjustment.[51] What if we were to think about cultural assimilation as akin to introjection, a vital part of social development? Abraham and Torok's theoretical differentiation between introjection and incorporation, however, reveals an investment in distinguishing healthy and unhealthy forms of "taking in." Juxtaposed to the contexts of race, assimilation, and racial grief, *that* investment itself becomes a site for inquiry. What deserves further consideration is the very likely possibility that "unhealthy" forms of grief (something closer to melancholia) may also be an integral part of mourning and necessary to development. I am therefore less interested in lauding assimilation than in teasing out the intricate *relationship between grief and survival that assimilation stages.*

The hypochondriacal body in *The Woman Warrior*, for instance, not only grieves for the lack of a socially idealized body but also plays out the management of that grief as a constant negotiation between loss and recollection. Rather than staying with the apparent analogy or accept introjection as the psychoanalytic truth of cultural assimilation, the interesting task is to create a dialogue between these two concepts. As we begin to unpack some of the deeper assumptions underlying both our notions of social assimilation and our ideas about psychical growth and health, we also recognize more and more that we do not yet have an adequate vocabulary to talk about issues such as the different *forms* of taking in, whether traumas can ever be successfully "introjected" or assimilated, how mimicry and commensurability play into standards of value, and so forth.

For Abraham and Torok, introjection/psychical assimilation is an instinct that saves us from trauma, instability, devastation, and war and protects us from "the illness of mourning" (that is, melancholia).[52] It is easy to see how this definition can acquire a "New Age" tone. For example, Nicolas Rand, the translator of *The Shell and the Kernel* to the English-speaking audience, in his introduction calls introjection "the myriad of ways of being in touch with ourselves, of enhancing our contact with ourselves, of adjusting to interior and exterior changes in the psychological, emotional, relational, political, or professional landscape" (13). While I want to follow Rand in his expansion of Abraham and Torok's work into the social and the political arenas, I believe that his positivistic interpretation of Abraham and Torok elides some of the more provocative complications implied by the notion of "good introjection." A closer look at the concept will reveal a dilemma in the distinction between healthy introjection and pathological incorporation and help to unpack some of the difficulties in talking about the ethnic and gender mourning that is taking place in *The Woman Warrior*.

Significantly, in making that link between Abraham and Torok's psychoanalytic theories to social issues, Rand draws on a literary example. Rand alludes to Maupassant's short story "At Sea" about two brothers lost at sea. The younger brother severely injured his arm in an accident but refused to have the arm cut off even when it became infected with gangrene. Eventually, according to Rand's synopsis, the younger brother was finally "talked into" amputating that arm. The story of the younger brother finally cutting off his pestilential arm illustrates, for Rand, a lesson in learning how to handle traumatic loss: a literalization of successful introjection.

But when we turn to the story itself, a very different picture of personal and communal grief emerges. Rand's schematic interpretation does not account for the peculiarly persistent ways in which the arm is held onto, ritualized, fetishized, and even canonized throughout the story. The most curious aspect of the story is the way in which everyone lingers lovingly over the amputated arm. Javel, Jr., is not the only one who cannot relinquish his amputated arm. First, the other sailors on board (significantly, a "trawling smack" designed to "ransack and plunder the depths"—a salvaging machine)[53] also find the arm fascinating. "His comrades also examined it and handed it from one to the other, feeling it, turning it over, and sniffing at it," and then they helped the injured man to "pack it in salt, in barrels" (6). Second, once on land, an entire crowd, including young Javel's family and friends, "[f]ollowed the funeral of the detached arm," which, placed in an especially built small coffin, receives a proper burial with the blessing of the holy church.

The very fact that the renunciation of the arm requires meticulous ritualization hints that something more complicated is going on than a parable of healthy renunciation. Or rather, that there is no such a thing as "just" letting go. Unlike Rand's reading, there is nothing in the Maupassant story itself that suggests young Javel's process of grief is in any way discontinuous: he never has a "change of heart," nor is he in fact "talked into" burying the arm. Rather, from the salting of the arm to its burial, the story presents a continuous process, a process of ritualized hanging on: a retention celebrated by an entire community; indeed, a retention that unites the community. (Indeed, before the invention of antibiotics, a synonym for gangrene was "mortification"; we might say that the younger brother's embrace of his gangrenous, mortified arm literalizes an embrace of the morbid.) More than anything else, the story tells of young Javel's success in *not* abandoning his arm. Even the form of the short story declines closure, for it is a story without an end. It never returns to the framing story that introduces the tale. The telling of the story is itself contaminated by the refusal of finitude that the story finally emblematizes.

Is the relinquishment of the arm, in all its rituals, an act of mourning or of melancholia? The act clearly encompasses both impulses. The final mourning is in fact *enabled* by the young man's melancholia. I have suggested already that even Freud could not prevent his descriptions of pathology and melancholia from seeping back into the "healthy" work of mourning. Here the story generates a further possibility: What if melancholia is a necessary, perhaps even continuous, stage of mourning? This would seem more plausible than the peculiar finitude, the perversely murderous relinquishment, of Freud's vision of successful mourning. Indeed, this story demonstrates precisely that there is no such a thing as a "clean cut." The final, highly ritualized renunciation of that arm bespeaks loving care and attention: "salted it like the fish caught at sea and stored it in a container." The story shows above all the *ongoing exchange* between hanging on and giving up. To keep the arm is to learn to let it go; to bury the arm is to be able to *not* lose it again. Successful mourning/introjection, if it takes place at all in this story, takes place *as* the maintenance of loss and retrieval. The psychical cauterization of the traumatic bodily amputation is only possible through re-membrance and jubilant public recollection.

If progress at times connotes forgetting, "At Sea" suggests an alternative where there is progress only through raw, insistent remembrance. The communal reassimilation of young Javel (his getting embraced back into the fold of this seaside community) is made possible through the ritualized repetition of his loss. That is, what prevents young Javel from being an object at worst of horror and at best of extreme peculiarity is the fact that everyone else is participating in the enjoyment of his loss, literalized by the communal absorption of the severed arm itself. Only through a communal intimacy and involvement with Javel's morbidity can his trauma be socially digested. Social mourning, which is not far from socialized morbidity, repeats the figure of loss in order to simultaneously commemorate and exorcise that loss: that is the very logic of melancholia.

Rand's application of Abraham and Torok in his reading of the Maupassant story elucidates both the contribution and limitation of the differentiation between introjection and incorporation. Freud's attachment to the division between healthy relinquishment and unhealthy retention in grief was too binaristic, an argument that was in danger of collapsing in on itself even in that 1917 essay. Abraham and Torok attempt to renuance the division by stressing that certain forms of incorporation and retention are vital to psychical development, which they rename "introjection." But in a way they have merely reproduced Freud's binarism at the level of healthy introjection versus unhealthy incorporation; once again, in the heart of this analysis of grief, there is an investment in establishing some liminal difference in healing and pathology. This investment, while possibly structural to the therapeutic responsibility of psychoanalysis, is less productive when it comes to analyses of socioracial grief, because memory, loss, retention, and rejection in socioracial dynamics, involving several communities of heterogenous histories, revolve around "un-curable," persistent ties, allegiances, and interests.[54]

The inadequacy of a conceptual attachment to the difference between health and pathology when it comes to discussions of grief can be seen in America's national dialogue as well. Because the opposition between health and pathology melds into the opposition between racial normality and difference, an investment in health continues to exercise difference and discrimination while still fostering a false sense of availability of a social or cultural "cure." The application of a medical oppositional model of health versus pathology to discussions of racial grief is also problematic since that model has historically been a tool of racial discrimination. (I am thinking, for example, of the late-eighteenth-century use of the medical model of health and pathology to differentiate between the races—a paradigm that founded racial difference itself.)[55] Thus, the relabeling of a historically sickened body as a newly privileged healthy social body may alleviate the immediate symptoms, but it can hardly speak to the conditions of the problem or the history and logic of its generation. As long as the notion of cultural health still dictates normality, then there will always remain a supplementary position of "the unhealthy" waiting to be filled by the next object of marginalization.

The Maupassant story offers an alternative perspective to questions of communal grief. The story not only complicates the psychoanalytic project of trying to distinguish incorporation from introjection, or melancholia from mourning, but also tells us something about how a community might be constituted and imagined through a kind of *enlivening morbidity*. When it comes to national mourning and nation-making, melancholic retention (the figuring of the injured/injurious "minority" through either denigration or fetishistic attachment) can often provide the very form of national integration. When it comes to "ethnic" communal mourning and community-making, the restaging of the self as an object of morbidity duplicates the very preconditions of that community's grief—a repetition that, while disabling, is also highly seductive as a strange stand-in for a community jeopardized by diluted and disappearing origins. When it comes to racial mourning about and for the self, melancholia (the hanging-on to a self synecdochized as a "pestilential arm") provides the form of grievance necessary for grieving—and communal assimilation of that melancholia the perverse embodiment of progress and moving on.

Returning to the world of *The Woman Warrior*, we see that "community" is a liminal concept, that is, a concept *about* boundary. In the opening pages, in one of the few direct addresses made by the narrative, the narrator simultaneously calls into being and renders impossible the notion of an imagined community:

> Chinese-Americans, when you try to understand what things in you are
> Chinese, how do you separate what is peculiar to childhood, to poverty,
> to insanities, one family, your mother who marked your growing with
> stories, from what is Chinese? What is Chinese tradition and what is the
> movies? (5–6)[56]

Being an "other" does not mean that one has lost a retrievable origin. Rather, it means that one has lost relative cultural discretion itself, whereby what can be affirmed is not culture (real or original) per se but rather its promiscuity, its impossible margins: the inadequacy of ethnic categories, fantasies contaminated with public and private ones,[57] the complicity and the resistance between ontology and ready-made cultural contexts. Earlier I asked how assimilation (with all its implied introjective logic) contributes to the collective fantasy of community and nationhood. It is clear that the notions of a discrete, physical body and of private grief are simply not possible, if they ever were, and especially not for immigrant and postimmigrant subjects. If anything, the "source" of grief is precisely the inability to maintain the fiction of one's distinction, the fiction of having or being "one's own."

One of the most engrossing aspects of *The Woman Warrior* for me is the way it calls forth and mobilizes an ethnic community—not at all through cultural claims (as almost all readings of Kingston's text posit, hence the endless and finally unproductive debates about its authenticity)—but rather through its insistent, continual engagement with the frictions inhering in the formation of such a community: the text's acknowledged confusion between states of healing and illness, its record of melancholic retention as the thing that creates and renders problematic the idea of a discrete racial-ethnic community within a national project. Kingston's succinct, anguished, almost performative call to her racial-ethnic community evokes all the inherent antagonisms residing in the notion of "one's own" community and reminds us how cultural claims are almost always contaminated by alterity. A unified, whole, discrete community of "Chinese Americans" is above all else an imagined one (in Benedict Anderson's sense of the word).[58]

Moreover, Kingston's call-to-community reminds us that assimilation is not only an American but also an international question. It reminds us that the assimilationist dilemma, just like the "Asian American question," must be seen not only in the American nationalist context, but also as part of a pan-Asian diaspora. The story of the Woman Warrior, the Fa Mu Lan myth, is told as much for its negation as for its promise:

> What fighting and killing I have seen have not been glorious but slum grubby. I fought the most during junior high school and always cried. Fights are confusing as to who has won. The corpses I've seen had been rolled and dumped, sad little dirty bodies covered with a police khaki blanket. . . . [A]t the news of a body, I would find a way to get out; I had to learn about dying. . . . Once there was an Asian man stabbed next door, words on cloth pinned on to his corpse. When the police came round asking questions, my father said, "No read Japanese, Japanese words. Me Chinese." (51–2)

This vision of Chinatown hardly fulfills the dreams of American democracy. At the same time, the Chinese socialist counterpart that the narrator projects onto the fable (Fa Mu Lan's mission to free the villagers from economic oppression and tyranny) also finally presents a failed vision: "It is confusing that my family was not the poor to be championed. They were executed like the barons in the stories, when they were not barons. It is confusing that birds tricked us" (51o). The "birds" refer to Fa Mu Lan's spiritual guides in the fable.[59] Thus, the narrator implies she has been misled by the Fa Mu Lan story as much as the Chinese were misled by Maoist ideals. The narrative takes apart the ideal of Fa Mu Lan as a fable for both female heroism and political revolution. Instead of a wish fulfillment, the tale of the Woman Warrior gives the narrator an identification *through* difference, disappointment, and failure.

The story of Fa Mu Lan comes to represent not an exemplary model but *a hypochondriacal mirror of its own ideals.* The conceit of heroic female combat on the one hand is reduced to schoolyard skirmishes, and on the other hand is expanded to encompass contemporary socioethnic friction, the nightmarish landscape of bruised souls and mutilated lives that is Chinatown's historical past. The anonymous, clearly racialized but ethnically ambiguous corpses strewn on the street inscribe the history of anti-Japanese and anti-Asian sentiments in the United States—sentiments that have structured not only American experiences but also interethnic relations within Chinatown.[60] The other fable examined critically here through the ghostly landscape is of course that great American fable of integration and China-town's problematic history in that progressive narrative—as well as China-town's capacities for speaking to and for the Chinese diaspora at large.[61] The narrator's "failed" assumption of the Woman Warrior story exposes not only the failed promises of American integration but also any nostalgic appeal to a "motherland" or to a notion of inter-national relations. Caught between fantasmatic nostalgia for the former and ambivalent desires for the latter, the "Chinese-American"[62] community that the text imagines and addresses is at once unified by the very call of the text and made ghostly, "a street full of dead corpses."

The ethnic and gender mourning taking place in Kingston's hypochon-driacal text demand that we rethink the relationship between mourning and melancholia, between introjection and incorporation. The point is not to invoke psychoanalytic processes as the truth of cultural assimilation or to denounce the inattention of psychoanalysis to sociohistorical phenomena. On the contrary, the pairing of the two spheres of discourse highlights the complicity between the configuration of cultural demands and the con-ceptualization of psychical operations, leading to productive complications that surround *relational* notions of health, of psychoanalytic and social commensurability, and of what it really means to live *as* someone, to live with someone inside you. What is *political* about this highly and frequently politicized text finally cannot be the expected and often-cited feminist-ethnic *Bildung* built into the narrative.[63] That *Bildung* is, in fact, constantly jeopardized. Rather, its politics derive from its dark negotiations with the negativity attached to the demands of "the political" and from the uneasy ways these demands rub up against private and ontological desires.

In the fable of psychoanalytic mourning, the exquisite corpse is the lost/dead object held inside in immaculate suspension. In the fable of assimila-tion, the exquisite corpse is the sick self, living on in delicious failure as a perversion of the ideal other. The assimilated body, like the hypochondria-cal body, is a porous one. Open and susceptible, the racial-ethnic body, deli-cately poised at the edge between racial imagination and material history, is the hypochondriacal body par excellence: the corpse that lives on, the body that resists mere materiality and dreams of company in the impoverishment of sociality.

FANTASY'S REPULSION AND INVESTMENT

David Henry Hwang and Ralph Ellison

Race and Fantasy in Modern America

Is there any *getting over* race?

The answer would seem to be negative in light of what I have been examining so far. Even in contemporary vernacular culture, we observe the increased frequency with which the "race card" is displayed. As the O. J. Simpson trial and its accompanying rhetoric suggest, racial rivalry is hardly over. Indeed, it has acquired the peculiar status of a game where what constitutes a winning hand has become identical with the handicap. Reappearing with the vagrancy of a Joker, the race card brings with it a host of haunting questions about the value and perception of race and racial matters in America. What does it mean that the deep wound of race in this country has come to be euphemized as a card, a metaphor that acknowledges the rhetoric as such yet simultaneously materializes race into a finite object that can be dealt out, withheld, or trumped? Why the singularity of *a* card? Who gets to play? And what would constitute a "full deck"?

Holding a "full deck" may imply some idealized version of multisubjectivity (that is, the potential to play the race card, the gender card, the immigrant card, and so forth), but it also implies a state of mental health and completion that renders such playing unnecessary in the first place. One would "play" a card only because one is already *outside* the larger game, for to play a card is to exercise the value of one's disadvantage, the liability that is asset. The paradox doubles: the one who plays with a full deck not only need not play at all but indeed has no such "card" to play. Only those playing with *less* than a full deck need apply.

Not only is liability transmuted to asset and reformed yet again as liability, but the vocabulary of the card also reveals a conceptualization of health and pathology that underlies our very perceptions of race and its abnormali-

ties. Figuring the minority can be treacherous. We understand why repara-
tive and redemptive tendencies underlie much of the intellectual and material interests in "the minority." Yet, as the "race card" rhetoric makes clear,
there is more than a little irony, if not downright counterproductivity, in
the effort to relabel as healthy a condition that has been diagnosed, *and
kept*, as sickly and aberrant. In my preceding investigation of Maxine Hong
Kingston's *The Woman Warrior* I noted how "getting over" the patholo-
gies of her childhood and origin means, in a sense, never getting over those
memories, so that health and idealization turn out to be nothing more than
continual escape and nothing less than the denial and pathologization of
what one is.

More than a haunting concept in America, the minority subject presents a haunted subject. Denigration has conditioned its formation *and* resuscitation. Not merely the object of white melancholia, the minority is
also a melancholic subject, precisely because he or she has been enjoined
to renounce him/herself. In the landscape of racial melancholia, the boundary between subject and object, the loser and the thing lost, poses a constant problem. Even Freud's idea of a *proper* mourning begins to suffer from
melancholic contamination. In order for proper mourning to take place,
one would have to be already, somehow, "over it." For Freud, mourning
entails, curiously enough, a forgetting: "profound mourning . . . does not
recall the dead one."[1] Upon a closer look, the kind of healthy "letting go"
Freud delineates goes beyond mere forgetting to complete eradication. The
successful work of mourning does not just forget; it reinstates the death
sentence:

> Just as the work of grief, by declaring the object dead and offering the
> ego the benefit of continuing to live, impels the ego to give up the object,
> so each single conflict of ambivalence, by *disparaging* the object, *denigrat-
> ing* it, even as it were, by *slaying it*, loosens the fixation of the libido to it.
> (my emphasis, *MM*, 244)

Mourning implies the second killing off of the lost object. The denigration
and murder of the beloved object fortifies the ego. Not only do we note that
"health" here means re-killing an object already lost, but we have to ask also
how different is this in aim from the melancholic who hangs onto the lost
object as part of the ego in order to live and who often ends up, according
to Freud, denigrating and blaming the self? Both the melancholic and the
mourner are intense survivors: the cannibalistic melancholic murderously
assimilates the other's identity, thereby saving and fulfilling the self (even
if self-denigration is part of that fulfillment), while the mourner simply kills
off the object in order to save the self. Furthermore, it is clear that, for
Freud, what distinguishes one form of grief from the other (on the "nor-

mality scale") is purely theoretical. Freud writes that it is only because we know less about melancholia that it seems pathological to us. The good mourner turns out to be none other than an ultra-sophisticated, and more lethal, melancholic.[2] Thus the double bind of mourning turns out to be melancholia itself.

The confusion over the boundaries of "proper" mourning (the ironies of finding a "healthy" way to "lose" some injured person or impaired history) underlies a basic problem of American political thinking. In *States of Injury: Power and Freedom in Late Modernity*, Wendy Brown demonstrates the ways in which injury has become the limiting basis for political identity in contemporary life. She argues, not against the reality of injury, but against a discourse of liberty that elides precisely a true attention to suffering:

> Ideals of freedom ordinarily emerge to vanquish their imagined immediate enemies, but in this move they frequently recycle and reinstate rather than transform the terms of domination that generated them. Consider . . . blacks who imagine a world without whites, feminists who conjure a world without either men or without sex. . . . Such images of freedom perform mirror reversals of suffering without transforming the *organization of the activity through which the suffering is produced* and without addressing the *subject constitution that domination effects*, that is, the constitution of the social categories.[3]

Brown goes on to suggest that the state encourages the formation of political identities founded on injury and is in fact invested in maintaining that injured status. To put it in the terms of my project, Brown has located the melancholia of liberal discourse. For contemporary political discourse, political health (as in freedom or liberty) is paradoxically defined through and relies on injury and illness. One way to begin to examine the "organization of the activity through which the suffering is produced" is to study, not only how that organization is produced by the state, but also how it is reproduced by the subject as psychodynamic interactions.

Another, simultaneous, procedure must be to tease out the full implications of the melancholic constitution that affects both the subjects of domination and the subject of injury. (When Hurston writes "I feel most colored when I am thrown against a sharp white background," she refers not only to the constitution of blackness, but of whiteness as well, each defining the other's pathology.[4] Or, as Nella Larsen's narrator in *Passing* knows all too well, race is the company that you keep.) A conventional formulation of "liberty" cannot afford to account for the possibility that we may not be able to retrieve an unmarked, unscathed subject under the dirty bandage of racism. Liberal discourse has thus for the most parts studiously avoided confronting either the subjective implications of domination or its accompanying network of fantasy.

One site of such failure is the "cure" for stereotypes. Most often understood as ontologically negating and politically suspicious, fantasy and the activity of fantasizing seem a prerogative of the "dominant" culture, while fantasy on the part of the racialized is rarely, if ever, theorized. We are all too painfully familiar with popular racial fantasies that circulate within our public sphere, but rather than identifying those stereotypes yet again or simply denying those clearly troublesome images ("we aren't like that!"), it seems more fruitful and important to go on to the more complex question of how raced subjects participate in melancholic racialization. To propose that the minority may have been profoundly affected by racial fantasies is not to lock him/her back into the stereotypes but to perform the more important task of unraveling the deeper identificatory operations—and seductions—produced by those projections. The "truth" of "Asian Americanness" or "African Americanness" has always been and will continue to be a site of contestation for both those raced subjects as well as for whites. To remain complacent with the assumption that racial fantasies are hegemonic impositions on minorities denies complexity on the part of the latter's subjective landscapes. We have all heard the wisdom that women and other minorities have internalized dominant cultural demands, but we do not yet really know what that means, nor do we know how to confront the *desire* implied in this insight.

The elision of a more complex understanding of fantasy and desire also fuels an ongoing blind spot in the political thinking about assimilation versus cultural authenticity. The notion that cultural assimilation always requires certain acts of personal relinquishment and even disguise is a common one, easily and conventionally understood as the price of "fitting in." Think, for example, of the long literary alignment of "passing" with deception. Recall Homi Bhabha's formulation of the connection between assimilation and falsehood. He identifies "mimicry" as a colonial, disciplinary injunction and device, one that is nonetheless doomed to fail: "Colonial mimicry is the desire for a reformed, recognizable Other, as *a subject of a difference that is almost the same, but not quite.*"[5] By this account, the colonized finds him/herself in the position of melancholically echoing the master, incorporating both the master and his or her own denigration. What I have been calling the "internalization of the other" Bhabha attributes to authoritative injunction. Such injunction to mime the dominant can be seen from images such as the Indian servant dressed as the Englishman to the colonial institutionalization of language itself. We see here sophisticated versions of the "price of fitting in." To put it crudely, Bhabha has located the social injunction to assimilate and that injunction's built-in failure. The colonized's incomplete imitation in turn serves as a sign of assimilative failure, the failure of authenticity.

The concept of melancholic racialization, however, implies that assimilation may be more intimately linked to identity than a mere consequence of the dominant demand for sameness. To explore this proposition, this chapter turns to an unlikely pair: David Henry Hwang's drama *M. Butterfly* and Ralph Ellison's novel *Invisible Man*. Their juxtaposition yields an unexpected and revealing conversation about the conjunction of fantasy, assimilation, and dissimulation across time, political climates, and racial difference. Consider these images: a Chinese man dresses as a Japanese woman for over ten years; a white French diplomat wears the full "white face" of a Japanese geisha; in another vertiginous moment, some forty years earlier, an anonymous black man plunges through the streets of Harlem, finding himself impersonating a mysterious, hyperracialized, zoot-suited ghost of a man called Rinehart. These series of spliced-together images track the serpentine path between race and fantasy on the parts of "whites," "Asians," and "blacks." If it seems curious that a white man is making himself over in the image of Asian femininity, then it is no less perplexing to see a black man assuming the trappings of "blackness" or an Asian man donning the mask of "Asianness."[6]

In their figurations of men-in-disguise, *M. Butterfly* and *Invisible Man* provide two powerful textual instances where we might begin to work through the proposition that fantasy and melancholic incorporation are constitutive of and fundamental to the formation of any racialized body.[7] Indeed, both texts very self-consciously theorize about the conjunction between racial and masculinist fantasy *and* that conjunction's implication for liberal politics.[8] This chapter will propose that the play explicitly about fantasy will forsake that exploration to secure its political agenda, while the novel about "social reality" ends up offering the more radical exploration of the infusion of fantasy and desire into its formulation of political resistance.

FIRST STAGED IN WASHINGTON, D.C., IN 1988 AND THEN ON Broadway, David Henry Hwang's award-winning drama bills itself as an exposé of the complicity among racial, sexual, and political fantasies. By confronting the element of racial fantasy in this "true tale" of gender misidentification, Hwang attempts to address the persistent desexualization of Asian and Asian American men in Western cultures. As if in anticipation of film critic Richard Fung's 1991 essay "Looking for My Penis," which argues within the context of gay male pornography that Asian and Asian American manhood is always exoticized, feminized, and hence made invisible,[9] Hwang stages a tale of sexual masquerade that is intended to place Asian (and by his proposed extension, Asian American) manhood on center stage.

I will be looking more closely at what is in fact being put on display in Hwang's drama, but I should note here that Hwang's critical focus on Asian masculinity's invisibility in American theater culls at least part of its force from the other long history of invisible racialized masculinity in America: African American masculinity.[10] As Morris Dickstein muses in his 1999 essay "Ralph Ellison, Race, and American Culture," *Invisible Man* with its Marcus Garvey foreshadowing the Black Panthers, its thirties Marxism anticipating postsixties Marxism, and its midcentury conceptions of American diversity has remained remarkably germane at the end of this century as we debate multiculturalism and pluralism.[11] But there is another aspect of *Invisible Man* that speaks to us today: its exploration of fantasy in the racial-sexual dynamics of multiculturalism. Ellison's treatment of racial-sexual fantasy as both coercion and finally revision provides a potent lesson for contemporary progressive dialogue on race and sexuality—as well as a provocative lens through which to reexamine Hwang's Asian American racial-sexual politics of some forty years later.

Although in the American racial imaginary perceptions of African American manhood would appear to be the exact opposite of the cultural perceptions of Asian American manhood (the former having been hypersexualized, the latter desexualized), Ralph Ellison in *Invisible Man* dramatizes the point that African American masculinity, though animalized in certain contexts, is also often feminized and made invisible. From the narrator's "macho" yet "hysterical" retaliation in the novel's prologue against a white man on the street to the climatic hallucination of castration, *Invisible Man* draws one of the most indelible maps of the tortuous paths between racial fantasy, invisibility, and male sexual anxiety. As Danny Kim's perspicacious analysis of Ellison posits, *Invisible Man* can be seen as a direct response to Ellison's "experience of [masculine] humiliation." Working through analyses of Ellison's essays and early drafts of *Invisible Man*, Kim argues that Ellison "quickly came to believe that one of his primary responsibilities as a writer was to project a more virile image of African American aesthetic agency."[12] Kim goes on to demonstrate that *Invisible Man* analyzes white male racial psychology in terms that are astute yet homophobic. Although Kim does not see *Invisible Man* as finally offering a template for African American manhood in answer to white male racist psychology, his essay does raise the fascinating question of what kind of African American masculinity does Ellison's novel leave us. I will propose that the outcome of Ellison's masculinist agenda will turn out to be inextricably bound to his racial critique.

More explicit in its exposition of white racist male psychology, *M. Butterfly* is also a criticism of white racist homoerotic desires that is itself, as critics have contended, homophobic and misogynist (Gabrielle Cody, David Eng, Suzanne Kehde, Colleen Lye, James Moy, Karen Shimakawa, Robert Skloot). This oxymoron in itself should signal to us that racial-sexual fantasies are far from being the sole domain of white desire. What I wish to contribute to the existing treatises on these texts' racial-sexual intersections is a close analysis of the part played by fantasy in the reflexive economy of racial-sexual projections and internalization. Once we introduce the pres-

ence of fantasy on the part of not just the white racist but also on the part of
the racialized, and once we uncover fantasy's more intimate (even constitutive) function in the very act of self-identification, the racialized manhood
that is being reasserted by both texts takes on quite different tones.

Part I: Dissimulation and Its Open Secrets

Let us enter a scenario that immediately renders inadequate the understanding of fantasy as something unreal: a man falls in love, has sexual relations,
and produces a child with a woman only to discover over twenty years later
that the woman is a man. Fantasy and wish-fulfillment alone do not seem
sufficient to explain away the extent of the profound misrecognition in this
tale. Yet almost all discussions about this tale continue to surround the question of "reality" and thus continue to reaffirm the distinction between reality and fantasy. Many explanations (such as the various "real stories" published since the story broke) have been offered to decode the mysteries of this
real-life story. I will discuss some of those accounts later, but one well-known
interpretation comes from Broadway: David Henry Hwang's M. Butterfly.[13]
By way of commenting on the status of Asian American men in America
(as he describes his intention in his afterword), Hwang presents his version
of this tale of East–West intrigue and offers racial fantasies as the answer to
the puzzle of sexual confusion in this story of a French diplomat who after
ten years discovers that his Chinese mistress is not only a spy but also a man.
Positing a direct link from racial to sexual to political faith, M. Butterfly has
become a classic text on how racial fantasies can facilitate sexual fantasies.

Central to much critical attention has been the play's exposure of the
consistent emasculation of the Asian male in white society.[14] The proposition of the play goes as follows: the man-in-disguise-as-woman, Song Liling,
deploys the very racial, cultural, and gender stereotypes in which the target, Gallimard, believes in order to seduce and manipulate him. Song, the
play's political critic, explains to us that the "Perfect Woman" connotes the
passivity of the "China doll," which, in turn, connotes the feminized Asian
male. As these infamous and much-quoted lines state, Song attributes the
success of his sexual disguise to the power of Asian stereotypes:

> SONG: . . . because when [Gallimard] finally met his fantasy woman,
> he wanted more than anything to believe that she was, in fact,
> a woman. And . . . I am an Oriental. And being an Oriental, I
> could never be completely a man. (83)

Song can so thoroughly convince Gallimard that he is a woman because he
is Asian and thus already emasculated. According to the political critique
offered by M. Butterfly, then, the persistent cultural emasculation of the

Asian male (and, as the playwright asserts, by implication, the Asian American male in American society) elucidates how such a case of sexual misidentification can occur. Indeed, this criticism has been thematized by the play itself.

But is this account of collapsed gender and racial fantasy sufficient to the racial and sexual enigma unleashed by the play itself? The play presents complications surrounding, not just confirmations of, the common notion of fantasy as desire, substitution, and fulfillment. To begin with, at the level of critical desire, if the play means to denounce the equation of Asianness with passivity and femininity, then the end of the play hardly changes that. As critics have pointed out, the play's fundamental racial, gender, and sexual assumptions occlude nonstereotypical Asianness (Moy), complex female sexuality (Cody, Lye, Skloot, Shimakawa), and homosexuality (Eng). These critics demonstrate that a critique of racial assumptions does not necessarily extend to a critique of gender assumptions; in fact, playwright Hwang may be said to have built his racial critique on the very traditional ground of heterosexist presumptions. As David Eng so well explicates in his essay "In the Shadow of a Diva," the critical focus on the play's racism and sexism has ironically foreclosed a serious look at the issue of homosexuality in this drama of love between two men. Eng offers a crucial reading that I will return to later, but once we have, as suggested by Eng, uncovered the "real" homosexual story at the heart of this plot and urged Gallimard the gay man to emerge "unhindered" and "unhinged,"[15] we still will not have fully grasped the fantasm evoked by Hwang's dramatic rendition.

By the fantasm provoked by the play, I mean the ways within the play in which desire and fantasy do not necessarily align themselves on the same side, thereby producing a series of *contradictory motivations that conform to neither a heterosexual compulsion nor a homosexual reality*. After the fanfare of the various unveilings effected both internally within the play and externally by critics, we are left with unanswered questions concerning the lovers' subjective processing of these layers of truths, such as To what extent were they in control of the fantasy that they were living out? And to what extent were they *satisfied* by the ruse, whatever the political and sexual end of the deception was? There remains something about the extent and elaborateness of the deception on the parts of both parties that seem in excess of its apparent payoff. A series of unresolved questions circle around the difficult and complicit relationships between reality and fantasy, between knowing and unknowingness, even after Hwang or other critics have explained the sexual and racial fantasies at work. That is to say, even when we accept Gallimard's story as a simple fulfillment of a homosexual and homophobic fantasy (that is, the gay man who wants it both ways by hiding behind a socially sanctioned heterosexual "beard" while still secretly having the male lover; what Eng calls the "ultimate fantasy in which the gay Asian male literalizes the desired qualities of an effeminized oriental sissy"), we still need to account for the very peculiar ways in which "fantasy" gets deployed within the play.

For example, the most recognizable "fantasy" in the play, the central conceit of Madame Butterfly, is not evoked to reflect unconscious desires or titillate conscious ones; instead, it is constantly *staged* by both lovers to generate a series of scenarios involving *reversible* positions of passivity and aggression, femininity and masculinity. This ambiguity renders the political terms of the play, sexual and colonial, unstable. The baffling use of fantasy in the play remains to be explored in fuller detail, but for now we note that there is hardly a stable sexuality "underneath" (whether it be straight-racist-and-blind or closeted-racist-and-self-deceptive) from which to issue a translatable fantasy. The "staginess" of this central conceit hints that the discovery of Gallimard's "true" sexuality as the final interpretative key elides the play's foray into the attachment to the unreal. What does it mean for a person living in reality to *choose* fantasy when Gallimard offers this statement, "I've finally learned to tell fantasy from reality. And, knowing the difference, I choose fantasy" (90)? The founding moment of a belief in reality also instantiates the rejection of that belief; the distinction between the real and the unreal is posed, only to be refused. More than a cynical criticism of reality, Gallimard's assertion verbalizes a nagging problem throughout the play, and that is the vexing *excess* of fantasy—that which choice, action, and knowledge do not satisfy. Beyond the "truth" of Gallimard's or Song's sexuality there remain the particular and peculiar ways that these two characters go about scripting the mythology of their affair.

If anything, the fantasy of "Madame Butterfly" has been solicited not to accomplish desire but to deconstruct it. Indeed, there are two particularly metatheatrical aspects to this play that have largely gone unnoticed and that deeply problematize, as much as misogyny and homophobia do, its critical agenda: on the one hand, Gallimard's repulsion for the very mythology that he enacts; on the other, Song's investment in the very fiction that he stages. In what follows I hope to demonstrate that the play presents an epistemological problem in the face of a fantasmatic construction—epistemological not on the level of whether a character is or is not "really" gay, but on the level of how we come to know desire at all. To replace the "truth" of heterosexuality in this play with the "truth" of homosexuality does not actually address the play's more troubling unraveling of the notion of truth itself— and of sexuality *as a truth*. This unraveling, I will argue, will turn out ultimately to be too threatening even for the play to support.

Gallimard's white racist fantasies do not fully do what they are supposed to, nor is his relationship to these fantasies one of facile enjoyment. Let us begin with Gallimard's curious distaste for the very myth that he pursues. If one were to read racial stereotyping as the sole cause of Gallimard's blind-

ness, then one would also have to assume that if he had been more politically, culturally, and certainly sexually savvy, he would not have been
duped by the deception. Yet can "knowing better" or "political correctness"
redirect or correct, as it were, one's desires and fantasies? Gallimard the
character seems at times, oddly enough, to in fact "know better." His supposed ability to be duped is betrayed in these moments of seeming self-
derision and awareness, his repeated and conscious restaging of himself as
a "player" within the cultural cliché of "Madame Butterfly." How do we account for the coexistence of fascination and contempt that Gallimard exhibits toward his self-assigned role?

> GALLIMARD: . . . Cio-Cio-San . . . is a feminine ideal. . . . [T]he man
> for whom she gives up everything, is— (*He pulls out a*
> *naval officer's cap . . . pops it on his head, and struts*
> *about*)—not very good-looking, not too bright, and
> pretty much a wimp. (5)

In parodying Pinkerton, Gallimard exposes the racial and cultural assumptions underlying the logic of that story. He has understood the "trade-off"
in this Pinkerton-Butterfly contract. If *he* gets the beautiful feminine ideal,
then *she* gets the badge (and economic support) of his whiteness. We can
attribute Gallimard's dissection of the bargain struck between Cio-Cio-San
and Pinkerton as part of his hindsight wisdom, since this story is being narrated *in medias res*, but in fact we come to discover that this insight into the
trade-off between a white man and an Asian woman *initiates* Gallimard's
relationship with Song Liling. The lovers, after all, meet at a *performance* of
"Madame Butterfly."

The first time Gallimard meets Song in person, he is intrigued by the
latter's political shrewdness and his refusal to fit into an Asian stereotype.
Song in turn gives him what is essentially a lesson in cultural politics. They
meet backstage after Song's theatrical performance of "Madame Butterfly":

> GALLIMARD: . . . You were utterly convincing . . .
>
> SONG: Convincing? As a Japanese woman? The Japanese used
> hundreds of our people for medical experiments during
> the war. . . . But I gather such irony is lost on you. . . .
> It's one of your favorite fantasies, isn't it? The submis-
> sive Oriental woman and the cruel white man. . . . What
> would you say if a blonde homecoming queen fell in love
> with a short Japanese business man. . . . I will never do
> Butterfly again, Monsieur Gallimard. If you wish to see
> some real theater, come to the Peking Opera sometime.
> Expand your mind.

GALLIMARD: So much for protecting her in my big Western arms.
              (17–8)

Song appears to be offering Gallimard anything but fantasies; instead, Song gives Gallimard a quick lesson on cultural authenticity. In this first meeting of soon-to-be lovers, the play's central conceit (the question of who is really a "Butterfly") has been deconstructed by the dissimulator himself. Gallimard, as well as the audience, have already been told that the image *can be* a lie. The lovers' first exchange circles around the topos of demythification. Gallimard's last statement (an aside to the audience) ironizes his own clichéd position as the powerful white man.

If Song has refused outright to play Butterfly and proceeded to mock Gallimard's white assumptions, then why do Gallimard and Song himself continue to script, even mobilize, their affair through that myth? How Gallimard tells his life story reveals not just hindsight but the very map of a subject-of-desire in the making. That is, the Butterfly story provides more than a hindsight wisdom; rather, it had *scripted* the dynamics of the affair. Instead of accepting Gallimard's sexual identity as a complete, already-constituted thing that could then be disguised, repressed, and un-covered as some real truth, we must understand that "normal" sexuality itself also assumes its form only as it travels over a long and tortuous path and establishes itself, but never firmly, except in stories we tell about our-selves. Gallimard's life story is not so much about sex as about how sexu-ality comes to be.

For there is never any "truth" or "sex secret" at the heart of this drama to be unveiled, even if most of its dramatic drive seems to zero in on the unveil-ing that takes place on stage. The "original secret" of this dramatic plot sup-posedly turns on whether "she" does or does not have a penis. So how could drama come from a fact that everyone in the audience already knows? Pre-sumably the audience feels that they are already "in the know," since they are not the ones fooled, and they are there merely to witness Gallimard's rude awakening. Yet every one of the three times I have seen the production on Broadway, the audience gasped when Song undressed and bared his penis. The physical reality of Song's manhood can neither be news to the audience nor finally that astounding. Nor do I believe prudery to be the explanation, for stranger still, since Song drops his pants in front of Gallimard, who faces downstage, what most of the audience sees is Song's back or side. Thus at the very moment of revelation, of asserting Asian manhood in its full visibility, the *mise en scène* throws a veil over the disclosure. This visual nonplay ren-ders the audience reaction even more puzzling. Moreover, the stage direction has retreated into the very mystery that is critically *not* supposed to be a mys-tery: whether the Asian man does have a penis after all.

When we venture outside of Hwang's production to the attention generated by the real story of Bernard Boursicot, we find a similar cultural attachment to the "curiosity" of the story. Two documents offer themselves
as the "real story" behind the real story: print journalist Joyce Waddler's
Liaison: The Real Story of the Affair That Inspired M. Butterfly and the television interview with Boursicot and singer Shi Pei Pu conducted by Barbara
Walters in her ABC exposé "'The Strangest Love Story of All'—The Real
M. Butterfly." These "real" stories betray how *un*interested the media is in
the real, for the "real" story of Boursicot (either as a simple homosexual story
or the story of a very stupid straight man) affords very little sustaining interest. The public prurience, I would offer, has much to do with the threat
and titillation posed, not by nudity or its convention, but by the proposition
precisely that fantasy might in fact play a fundamental and persuasive role
in our most basic, daily perceptions. Fantasy's function becomes most externalized, visible, and disturbing *when* it encounters the supposedly indis-
putable realities of race and gender.

Two details not present in Hwang's play that emerged from the Joyce
Waddler account based on interviews with principal characters demand our
rethinking of the nature of fantasy beyond that of falseness or as mere fodder for desire. First, Bernard Boursicot initially met and knew the Chinese
opera star Shi Pei Pu *as a man*. That is, Shi moved about in the world as a
man. It is only after they became friends that Shi confessed to Boursicot that
he was in fact a woman disguised as a man for familial and political reasons.
This claim adds another spin to the masquerade: we have not just a man
disguised as a woman, but a man disguised as a woman disguised as a man.
Second, unlike the sexually inexperienced Gallimard in Hwang's play,
Boursicot has already had several homosexual experiences before he arrived
in China and continued to have homosexual relations throughout his life,
as well as relations with women. Both details complicate the "gay-man-
hiding-behind-the-skirt" account. This is not to say that Boursicot did not
suffer from the social constraint against homosexuality in the form of internalized homophobia—indeed, that is clearly part of Boursicot's psychical makeup—but that does not fully explain why he needed the elaborate
ruse of the Chinese damsel in a *double* disguise to have had a homosexual
or heterosexual relationship. Some other elements of desire are at work in
this attraction.

In various diary entries and interviews, Bernard Boursicot offered a surprising claim in self-defense: that it was easy to believe in Shi Pei Pu because
how could one tell anyway in China with "everyone walking about in a Mao
suit," in "identical uniforms."[16] Far from making an argument about gender as masquerade à la Joan Riviere, Boursicot is here making a specific and
much more mundane claim about sexuality in China or, more precisely, the
lack of sexual differentiation in China. This notion of China and Asia in

general as places where the fundamental differentiation between the sexes can be enigmatic has a long history in the European and American imagination. In nineteenth-century America, from the early 1870s to the 1900s, when the "Chinese Question" dominated domestic politics, popular pictorial representations of Asians in America played up this indistinction between the sexes among the Chinese through desexualization and animalization: men with "pigtails" and "Celestial Ladies" with ape faces. As late as 1976, we find in the introduction to the new translated edition of Saikaku Ihara's *Comrade Loves of the Samurai* an apology for Asian homosexuality by Terrence Barrow, Ph.D.:

> The idea of homosexuality is traditionally much more acceptable to Orientals than to Westerners. One reason for this may be the lesser physical differentiation of the sexes in the Mongoloid race (Japanese women and men have relatively sparse hair, while women's breasts and buttocks are small compared to those of average Caucasian women).[17]

In other words, it is easy to mistake an Asian male behind for a female one, so how can Asian homosexuality really count as homosexuality under these circumstances? In short, in this view, Asian homosexuality is an accident, an understandable mistake.

The racist-homophobic element at work in the Waddler and Walters accounts of the Boursicot–Shi affair, unlike the more tailored critique of Asian male emasculation in Hwang's drama, expresses a broader, popular anxiety about the epistemology of the Asian body, its threat against the differentiation of the sexes so fundamental to civil humanity. At the same time, much illicit pleasure accompanies this anxiety, for the East has become not only the site of projected sexual misgivings, but also the site of escape from sexual constraints: How can one be accused of homosexuality when one cannot even tell the difference between the sexes? This combination of anxiety and preoccupation trained on the Asian body shows itself in the public scrutiny of Shi Pei Pu's body after his confession. Both men were interrogated, with detailed, repetitive inquiries about the physical aspects of their sexual interaction; several teams of medical personnel took turns examining Shi; medical reports and diagrams of Shi's genitals were published. There has not been a public investment in the scopophilic dissection of racialized genitals to this extent since the exploration of Sarah Bartmann.[18] Emasculation of the Asian man is but part of the equation; the erasure of sexual differentiation itself confers on the "East" its dizzying indistinction and the unspeakable pleasures therein.

In a sense, returning to Hwang's stage, the Manhattan audience of the late eighties is equally enthralled not by the question of "what's under the costume" but by the possibility inhering in the costume itself, the operations of turning display into concealment. The audience cannot want to know the secret (because it already does); it wants to see the *secret* itself. The moment that Song drops his pants is also the moment that the structure of fantasy gets revealed in all its force. What has been put on exhibition is not the materiality of Song's body but the materiality of him as fantasy. Only because the audience was occupying Gallimard's point of view could they be shocked at the revelation, though there has in fact been no revelation. The gasp reveals the spectators' complicity in the very disguise they are there to see dismantled. This willingness to maintain the "open secret" effects an inverse but identical version of the spectators' silent compliance in the face of the "emperor's new clothes."[19] Physical evidence offers no key to this drama, just as it offers no key to Gallimard's psychical drama.

The conviction that fantasy denotes the unreal and can be separated out from reality grows thinner by the minute. The un/veiling of the physical body puts the spotlight on the incontrovertible seduction of the unreal. We might relocate our investigation from the "fact" beneath the costume to the costume itself: the structure of fantasy being exhibited. The question of truth versus falsehood has become far less interesting than the more vexing question of how do the categories of real and the fictive get processed—or rather, how those categories come to accrue or forfeit their respective status and currency. It is within Gallimard's undertaking to integrate radically disjunctive experiences (that is, the gap between his instinctual and social desires, his own ambivalence in the face of the irreconcilable social and psychical polarities of heterosexuality and homosexuality) that we can begin to discern that aspect of fantasy that exceeds its definition as the unreal or its designation as the henchman of desire. Instead, we begin to distinguish fantasy as the underpinning for the limits of reality and illusion and, as a result, constitute the *possibility* of desire itself.

The composition of desire, proper or otherwise, has always posed a problem for Gallimard. Gallimard recounts how, as a young man, he suffered acute abjection in front of a pornographic tableau (10). We have to remember that the audience sees Gallimard's narration being acted out on stage as he narrates. Hence the pornographic tableau is a tableau within a tableau, and "sexual fantasy" is itself being thematized and put on display in this scenario. In that metadiegesis, Gallimard remains passive before images of available women and is impotent *within his own fantasy*. One apparent interpretation of Gallimard's impotence is his repressed homosexuality, but it is also clear that Gallimard is reminding himself, if not the audience, that fantasy in the sense of a wish-fulfillment dream cannot produce desire. So what is it about the Butterfly fantasy that works where standard pornography and social pressures fail?

The play and its characters tell us that the answer is the racist element of Butterfly. Critics tell us that it is the homosexual content of Song's rendition of Butterfly. But I would suggest that it is not the content but the structure of the Butterfly fantasy that seduces Gallimard. Race and sex are not the content *but the conditions* for mobilizing the work of fantasy in this play. "Taking advantage" of the Asian stereotype, for instance, does not fully enable Gallimard to become a "real man"; on the contrary, the Butterfly story allows him to also be the "woman"—that is, it grants him the unspeakable pleasures of "oriental indistinction" for himself. We can now delve into something that I briefly touched on before: the reversibility of the roles of masculinity and femininity—and of whiteness and Asianness—in this play. By exposing the difference between the sexes and races as based on power rather than biology or even distinct sexual desires, the Butterfly script that Gallimard and Song adopt alternatively grants Gallimard the chance to enter this story from several different positions. The story offers Gallimard multiple entries, so to speak.

Let us return to that pivotal first meeting. Song's message for Gallimard in that encounter about "Madame Butterfly" is above all a lesson in the structure of power. In deriding Western masculine stereotypes, Song offers a supposedly comical and impossible counteranalogy of a "blonde homecoming queen with the short fat Japanese businessman." Meant to expose the racial fantasies underneath sexual desire, this example instead stresses the other element of desire: power. One could indeed very well imagine Song's hypothetical scenario in light of the increasing American anxiety regarding Asian "buying power" in the eighties and nineties. That is, an American would more likely believe the scenario if the "short, fat Japanese businessman" were, say, the president of Mitsubishi. The point is that Song's version of the reversed myth is culturally believable if power and economic fantasies come to reinforce racial ones. Consequently, instead of demonstrating the fact of racial inequality, Song betrays its contingency.

One may say that Gallimard learns his lesson in humiliation so well that he repeats it as the master. It is almost as if Gallimard comes to the lesson of power through Song's intended deconstruction of power. Gallimard's coming-to-love parallels his coming-to-sadism:

GALLIMARD: . . . I began to wonder: had I, too, caught a butterfly
              who would writhe on a needle? I felt for the first time
              that rush of power. . . . Watching the secessions of her
              humiliations is like watching a child under torture.
              (32–3, 42)

Gallimard has not learned the truth of "Madame Butterfly" as fiction; he learned the truth of "Madame Butterfly" as narrativity. And if we take a closer look at Gallimard's relationship to the Butterfly fantasy, we will find him enacting not so much the content of the story as its narrativity: the fantasy *of being able to act* "the Pinkerton." Gallimard recognizes that Pinkerton, the "exploiting white man," was always already a *type*, a role, and that power never came from Pinkerton the man per se but from his cultural position, the colonial privilege of being "a Pinkerton." This is one reason why Gallimard takes on this role even though he also despises Pinkerton as "really a wimp" (5). Similarly, the one consistent pleasure Bernard Boursicot identifies in his twenty-year old relationship with Pei Pu was strangely enough not physical pleasure, but the pleasure of secrecy, of having this elaborate secret story. As Boursicot repeatedly declared in various contexts, he reveled in having "a love story of a dimension that no one at the embassy will ever know," "a beautiful story no one else has," "a monumental story" (Waddler, 50, 133, 174, 248). Boursicot liked and was turned on by both secrecy and its narrative structure. We might say he did not fall in love with a man in drag or a woman in drag but with drag itself. Pei Pu's charm owes less to his femininity or his masculinity than to the charade he enacts.

The tale of "Madame Butterfly" allows Gallimard to play out not only the white male position but, more crucially, his *identification with* the passive woman. Gallimard presents himself from the beginning of the play as something of a "manly" failure. Already a "racial" crossbreed and far from being the "great white man," Gallimard is shy and effeminate, and he has a gender-indeterminate first name, along with an emasculating wife. Critics have pointed out that Song's superfemininity allows Gallimard to compensate for his uncertain masculinity. Yet Gallimard's attraction to Song goes beyond mere compensation to replication. Mirror images of each other at times, they are both described as shy, passive, not wanting to undress, and so on. Indeed, Song-as-woman very much resembles Gallimard-as-man. Gallimard's mastery over Song also paradoxically bespeaks his identification with the latter: Gallimard's sadistic position derives its pleasure and potency precisely through identification. Gallimard enjoys the sadistic position because it ensures his own subject position: "I" get to do this to "her." Thus even while sadism promises mastery, it also denotes a mastery that is based on denial. His capacity for abjection suggests, however, that his pleasure in these moments of sadism, his fascination with the sadistic point of view, may be merely that it provides the best vantage point, the best seat in the house, from which to see the masochistic story unfold. I would go as far as to say that Gallimard experiences the subjection of Song, the victim who supposedly occupies the passive position, as a *pleasurable repetition of his own history.*[20] Every time Gallimard asserts, "she is a butterfly on a needle," she is a "child under torture," he is also actively recalling and warding off the experience of being himself the butterfly on the needle, the child under torture.

For Gallimard, the moment of desire, initially mediated through the fantasy of being the "big white man," coincides with an identification with the very opposite:

GALLIMARD: Did I not undress her because I knew, somewhere deep
              down, what I would find? Perhaps. . . . At the time, I
              only knew that I was seeing Pinkerton stalking towards
              his Butterfly, ready to reward her love with his lecherous
              hands. The image sickened me, pulled me to my knees,
              so I was crawling towards her like a worm. By the time I
              reached her, Pinkerton . . . had vanished from my heart.
              To be replaced by something new, something unnatural,
              that flew in the face of all I'd learned in the world—
              something very close to love. (60)

The enthralled Gallimard rejects the Butterfly story—or at least, he renounces
it insofar as he wishes to assume the other role in the story. Crawling toward
Song "like a worm," Gallimard plays the abjected Cio-Cio-San. This moment
of counter-internalization, of turning the self into the other, not coincidentally also marks a moment of intense hypochondriacal response, and I have
already discussed how hypochondria almost always signals a concomitant
moment of subjective incorporation and rejection.

Within the power structure of "Madame Butterfly," it is the reversibility
of the sadistic and masochistic positions that Gallimard comes to mime and
repeat. We have been given not the fiction of a desiring subject, but the desiring subject *as* fiction. What is at stake in this distinction? First, to assume
an integral desiring subject is to rehearse the old argument of self-invention
and to fail to accommodate the ambivalence and fissure *prior* to having a
speaking voice. Second, an alteration of the idea of agency in relation to
fantasy may open up different considerations for how we approach the notion of racial fantasy as a political critique.

Psychoanalysts Jean Laplanche and J.-B. Pontalis would tell us that
fantasy's fundamental activity is not to compensate desire but to narrativize
it. Their essay "Fantasy and the Origin of Sexuality"[21] distinguishes different levels of fantasies and attempts to turn analysis of fantasy away from
content to its structure and its function within the psyche. Pointing out that
Freud's initial discovery of "psychical reality" turns out to be a retreat to a
very conservative, binaristic notion of reality and fantasy (26),[22] Laplanche
and Pontalis open new grounds for resuscitating a notion of fantasy that
fundamentally disturbs the distinction between reality and psychical reality. Rather than presupposing a fully formed subject daydreaming, fully in
control of his/her fantasies/stories, Laplanche and Pontalis suggest instead
that we cannot tell the dreamer from the dreamed:

> [F]antasy is present at both extremities of the process of dreaming. On
> the one hand it is linked with the ultimate unconscious desire. . . . [b]ut
> fantasy is also present at the other extremity of the dream, in the sec-
> ondary elaboration which, Freud insists, is not part of the unconscious

work of the dream, but must be identified "with the work of our waking thought." The secondary elaboration is an *a posteriori* reworking which takes place in the successive transformations which we impose on the story of the dream.

[A]nd the two forms of fantasy (i.e., unconscious and conscious) which are found . . . seem, if not to link up, at least to communicate from within, as it were, to be symbolic of each other. [Fantasy is] that form of novelette, both stereotyped and infinitely variable, which the subject composes and relates to himself in a waking state. (20–1)

Laplanche and Pontalis will come to call this work of elaboration *une fantasmatique*, to emphasize the work of fantasy over the traditional notion of fantasy as unconscious content. Laplanche and Pontalis thus specifically connect this "secondary elaboration" to a fundamental activity of autobiography or identity-positioning: how we *narrate* our lives and selves. The fantasmatic negotiates the real and the unreal, the conscious and the unconscious, in such a way as to render possible the sense of one's life as a whole. It is the fantasmatic that allows for a sense and structure of identity to take hold. The fantasmatic enables identification.

Their work emphasizes fantasy, not as an activity of an already formed and stable subject, but rather as the *constitutive and contingent* staging of the subject in the unconscious:

In fantasy the subject does not pursue the object or its sign; he appears caught up himself in the sequence of images. He forms no representation of the desired object, but is himself represented as participating in the scene although, in the earliest forms of fantasy, he cannot be assigned any fixed place in it (hence, the danger, in treatment of interpretations that claim to do so). As a result, the subject, though always present in the fantasy, may be so in a desubjectivized form, that is to say, in the very syntax of the sequence in question. (26)

In this account, fantasy does not have a target, an object per se; instead, it is a mental process that works much like a tableau in which the "subject" finds himself in multiple positions. Fantasy in this sense denotes not the object but the *setting* of desire. The "self" exists only in and as display. This insight does not function as some kind of facile claim that there is no "real" self; rather, it focuses on the question of what authenticates realness, what makes reality real. The fantasmatic reveals both a process of agency and agencylessness, both "stereotyped" and "variable." This is the paradox in Laplanche and Pontalis's formulation: that the fantasmatic signifies a process of desubjectivation, a state of agencylessness, that nonetheless constitutes the subject's sense of integrity and hence his/her potential for agency—a process of scattering the "self" in order to constitute a stage for the "self."

Judith Butler will read in this notion of fantasmatic authentication an operation of exclusion: "we can understand the 'real' as a variable construct which is always and only determined in relation to its constitutive outside: fantasy, the unthinkable, the unreal. . . . [T]he fantasmatic, precisely as such a constitutive exclusion, becomes essential to the construction of the real."[23] In a sense, Butler has located the melancholic logic within the work of fantasy. Translating Butler's insights into a reading of *M. Butterfly*, David Eng alludes to Laplanche and Pontalis's notion of the fantasmatic. However, by interpreting Gallimard's ability to be duped as a response to the "fantasmatic constraint against homosexuality," Eng misses Gallimard's participation in the fantasmatic mobilization of desire itself, a participation that puts him in various positions in this fantasy. That is, the critic has mistaken fantasy (in the traditional sense of an illicit, disguised wish for the forbidden) for the fantasmatic,[24] insofar as the fantasmatic refers to a question of the constitution of desire, of subjectivity even, rather than the location of a preexisting desire.

It seems less interesting to ask what a character like Gallimard psychically excludes (since he is such a figure of repression) than to ask what he puts on display—and what that display does for him on at the level of securing ontological purchase. In the context of *M. Butterfly*, the fantasmatic should point us away from the content of his "lie" to the form of the lie itself. The task is not so much finding the real homosexual man beneath the disguise as understanding the *function* of that masquerade.

The figure of Song offers Gallimard more than the fantasy of the perfect woman (or even the perfect man-as-woman): the fantasmatic possibility of *being* that woman himself. "Madame Butterfly" does not work well as a fantasy in the normal sense of that word, since it is demythified, made mundane, and even ridiculed from the beginning by the lovers themselves. But it operates as a powerful, fantasmatic stage on which Gallimard acts out (rather than masters) his subjective, racial, and sexual uncertainties. In the drama of "Madame Butterfly" as played out by Gallimard and Song, Gallimard's racial and gender position as the dominant, white man does not remain stable. Song at one point tells Gallimard that he needs to see "real theater." Indeed, Gallimard comes to enact less the content of "Madame Butterfly" than the reality of its theatricalization.

This distinction between a vernacular definition of fantasy and the psychoanalytic notion of the fantasmatic holds provocative political implications. To mistake the fantasmatic for fantasy is miss a chance for reimagining the status of "objecthood" within (sexual and colonial) fantasies. That is, fantasy assumes there is a stable and inviolate subject doing the fantasizing. The fantasmatic, on the other hand, unclasps fantasy's securing of subject and object position and pinpoints the unstable interaction that goes into informing the making of the mythology of the "object" or the fetish.

Even Homi Bhabha, who has done some of the most important and thought-provoking work on colonial mimicry, elides the intricate relationship between mimesis and fantasy in favor of a more traditional understanding of fantasy's effects as ontologically negating. In "Of Mimicry and Man" the Freudian figure of fantasy comes to stand for the strawman of colonial identity:

> [T]he visibility of mimicry is always produced . . . at the cross-roads of *what is known and permissible and that which though known must be kept concealed.* . . . The desire of colonial mimicry . . . may not have an object, but it has strategic objectives which I shall call the *metonymy of presence* . . . the prodigious and strategic production of conflictual, *fantastic*, discriminatory "identity-effects" in the play of a presence that is elusive because it hides no essence, no "itself." (130–1, my emphasis)

In other words, the open secret of colonial identity *is* the fantasy of its own presence. Bhabha is talking about the representative effects of the discourse of authority.

Yet implicit to this argument is the assumption that there is something underneath or other than "fantastic, discriminatory identity-effects." How would we begin to talk about the other's own relationship to this mirror of "fantastic, discriminatory identity-effects"—especially since identity-effects do not belong with utter discreteness to either the voice of authority or the voice of the oppressed? Rather, the interaction between Gallimard and Song demonstrates that *such identity-effects might be the preconditions for subjectivity itself.* In addition, if identification, by its nature, experiences itself *beyond* representation, then the representative effects of identity that Bhabha mentions cannot really get us anywhere near the problem of the mirror-effect. We still need to ask: Is it possible to negotiate sites of identity-performance as neither disavowal nor fetishization? When does performance disavow; when does it fetishize? And does one imply the other? To put it crudely, does racial performance (like gender performance) necessarily skirt the edges of fetishization?

For Bhabha, there is no way of escaping the economy of the fetish, because underlying his idea of "identity-effects" is the assumption that those effects are finally discriminating and opposed to some "non-fantastic" presence. Identity-effects would always lead to fetishization, as Bhabha's article indeed goes on to say. In contrast, Laplanche and Pontalis's reworking of Freudian fantasy as the fantasmatic shifts the discussion away from identity to the very process of identification. That is, while fantasy as deployed by Bhabha is apparently negatively inflected (that is, as opposed to essence), Laplanche and Pontalis evoke a use of fantasy that escapes such reification and suggests that it is precisely the *originary* role that fantasy plays that allows Gallimard to play against, as well as into, the master discourse of identity, whether it be white racism or heterosexual compulsion. Hence Gallimard's subjectivity in this narrative manifests both agency and divestiture—a paradox that recognizes, not just reinscribes, identity-performance's necessarily double axis of disavowal and fetishization. What shocks the spectators of this drama may not be homosexuality or the ability it has to disguise itself but rather a more profound suggestion that sexuality has no object at all. What makes the Manhattan audiences gasp may largely reflect a response to the play's insistent assertion of fantasy as the very stuff that makes "self" and "self-story" possible, as well as a reflection of the audience's own investment in that structure. The audience gasped because, in spite of what they knew, they were for a moment placed in Gallimard's point of view.

When at the end of the play Gallimard symbolically takes on Song's identity by physically donning the geisha mask of the Butterfly, he is only literalizing the cross-identification and the subsequent incorporation that he has been enacting all along. Gallimard tells us that the assumption of Song's role is so powerful as to effect a physiognomic change: "[it] re-arranged the very lines on my face" (92). We have in front of us a profoundly melancholic scene, where Gallimard in this (dis)guise is mourning after a ghostly butterfly he has in fact come to *be*. All along he has been preparing for the "real" possibility of these transformations between man and woman, between whiteness and Asianness.

Thus racial fantasy, although obsessively thematized by the play, serves as something of a red herring. It operates as a double disguise: it seems to be the key to unraveling this amazing case of misidentification, when in fact it is itself generative of cross and multiple identities. The solution itself stands as a cipher. The exposure of Gallimard's "false" assumptions reveals acts of masking. What can be recovered from underneath the "false type" is not a hidden "true type" but the act of disguise that goes into creating a type at all. Gallimard leaves the audience with the melancholic closing image of his suicide while in the full facial makeup of geisha white. By this point, that white mask resonates as the haunting collision between the masks of whiteness and Asianness. As Kwame Anthony Appiah has wisely said elsewhere, "there is nothing in the world that can do all we ask race to do for us."[25] But of course we do ask, and it is precisely race's surplus value *as value* that masks its nonreferentiality. In *M. Butterfly*, rather than seeing racial difference as facilitating sexual dissimulation, it is the fantasm of that difference that enables a racial "presence" to come into being.

This moment when Gallimard dons his geisha makeup is melancholic, not because he is mourning a lost love, but because the scene dramatizes a condition of identificatory confusion fundamental to the melancholic experience. Melancholia, after all, designates a condition of identificatory disorder where subject and object become indistinguishable from one another. This disturbance or confusion between the griever and the thing lost-but-taken-in-as-the-self renders unstable even Freud's attempt to distinguish mourning from melancholia. Caught in this Moebius strip of recognition and denial, subjecthood slides into objecthood and vice versa. Melancholia may well mark the *limit* of the very notion of "object-relation": not the deprivation of the object but the impossibility of an object relation. Translate this insight into the cultural, political problem of "racist projection," and we start to discern the limitations of insisting on the pure distinction between subject and object, oppressor and the oppressed, agency and the agentless. The guise of the binary opposition prevents us from examining the *structure* of desire and need nurturing that power distinction.

The fact that the melancholic object is also a melancholic subject turns out to be what the play refuses to acknowledge. While *M. Butterfly* dramatizes the white man's slippage between melancholic subject and objecthood, it draws short of making a similar claim for the raced subject, precisely because of what it imagines are the limits of political protocol. The interpretation of the instability of race and gender in the landscape of fantasy implied by the figure of Gallimard must finally be denied by the play itself, when it comes to the character Song Liling, for the sake of its political critique. The central symptom of this refusal comes from the play's attempts to armor the figure of Song against its own drama of melancholic contagion—attempts that end up placing Song under erasure. As an exposé of sexual intrigue and racial fantasy, *M. Butterfly* begs the questions it never ventures: Aside from his "professional" objective, does Song have a personal investment in his disguise? And what would it mean for the political agenda of the play if he did? In short, what is Song's desire?

In the three moments of the play where we might have glimpses into Song's private fantasies and desires, we are greeted instead with silences and deferrals. The first moment is provoked through an observation made by Comrade Chin:

CHIN: You are wearing a dress! And every time I come here, you're wearing a dress. Is that because you're an actor? Or what?

SONG: It's a . . . disguise, Miss Chin. (48)

The unspeakable possibility residing in Comrade Chin's "Or what?" has been confirmed and silenced within Song's pause. The second incident comes from Gallimard's query:

GALLIMARD: Don't you, even a little bit, wish you were here with me?

SONG: I'm an artist, Rene. You were my greatest . . . acting challenge. (63)

One might imagine other options for that telling pause. The third moment comes from the trial:

JUDGE: Just answer my question: did he know you were a man?

Pause.

SONG: You know, your Honor, I never asked. (83)[26]

In this series of cryptic moments—moments of blanking-out and of dis-guise—Song's desire is not articulated. In all three brief instances, Song's answer comes in the form of ellipses and pauses, as though his desires can be pronounced only as unutterability itself. Significantly, the play can have Song only as either the object of Gallimard's desire or as the critic of that desire. It is as though to articulate Song's desire would render him less "cool" or jeopardize his position as a proper critic of Western male fantasies. The moment of self-revelation for Song is made possible only through relegat-ing that revelation to the realm of disguise. In other words, Song must not *want*. His performance must remain a performance in order to guarantee the authenticity of his critique.

In Rodgers and Hammerstein' *Flower Drum Song* (taking place early enough after World War II and the end of the Korean War in 1953 that the memory of war brides was still a living reality), the "strictly female female" dreaming of the "home of the brave and free male" has to be rejected for the sake of American national integrity and security. In *M. Butterfly*, the fig-ure of the "strictly female female" is resurrected only to be killed off again for the sake of a brand of liberal politics. *M. Butterfly* both unveils the ideal female female to be extreme impersonation and rejects the implications embodied in that insight. If the "strictly female female" turns out to be a man, he must not be a man with desires of an "authentic" female female. If this "woman warrior" challenging the soul of Western imperial desires unveils her armor to reveal a penis, the script must reenlist that penis to the duties of war, not desire.

When it comes to the conventional notion of cultural assimilation, im-personation and its essential falseness stands as a fundamental principle of protection against the threats of that very possibility. I want to suggest that the terms "unauthentic performance," "fantasy," and "assimilation" are not causal but structurally identical and mutually affective. Consequently, the traditional understanding of their political implications needs to be recast. The melancholic activities of racialization imply that assimilation may not only be a consequence of the dominant demand for sameness but also inti-mately related to identity itself. In melancholia, assimilation (acting like an internalized other) is a *fait accompli*, integral to ego formation for the domi-nant and the minority, except that with the latter such doubling is seen as something false (acting like someone you're *not*.) The notion of racial authen-ticity is thus finally a cultural judgement that itself disguises the *identificatory assimilation* already taken place in melancholic racialization: "I am constituted by an other who finally must, and must not, be me." *M. Butterfly* thus suggests that "passing" may share a profoundly similar logic with the activity of identity itself.

Near the end of the play Song seems to have forgotten the terms of his own game. We see him protest, startlingly and tellingly, "So—you [Gallimard] never really loved me? Only when I was playing a part?" (89). The blindness of that question reveals Song as having been seduced by his own *mise en scène*. The failure of Song's deception comes from his plunge into the reality of that deception. And that failure of authenticity has the very specific affect of creating a sense of "the real self": Song cries "I'm your butterfly . . . it was always me" (89). The seduction of authenticity turns out to promise nothing less than the possibility of a pure self: "it was always *me*."

In his introduction to Abraham and Torok's book *The Wolf Man's Magic Word*, Jacques Derrida meditates on the fantasy of incorporation in a vocabulary that holds interesting echoes for this discussion:

> The first hypothesis of *The Magic Word* . . . supposes a redefinition of the Self (the systems of *introjections*) and of the fantasy of *incorporation*. . . .
>
> The more the self keeps the foreign element as a foreigner inside itself, the more it excludes it. The self *mimes* introjection. But this mimicry with its redoubtable logic depends on clandestinity. Incorporation operates clandestinely with a prohibition it neither accepts nor transgresses.[27]

The "foreigner inside" lives as the "self." *M. Butterfly* demonstrates how the internalization of the other has profound subjective effects, how taking on a role can mean taking in an identity. We saw too how the activity of dissimulation stages subjectivity. To racially assimilate (in the senses of blending in *and* taking in) implies an act of private and subjective dissimulation.

What if colonial desire itself is melancholic and longs clandestinely to mime the "foreigner" inside? What if we recast the failure of mimicry (in Bhabha's terms) as instead an allowance for dissimulation? And what if dissimulation—the other that is me—provides the very structure of identification? The figure of Gallimard presents an inverse of the Bhabha paradigm: instead of the colonized trying and failing to mime colonial authority, colonial authority is itself counter-identifying with the other. The failure of the colonizer to be the same as but not quite (Gallimard's rendition of Butterfly/Cio-Cio-San) opens up the space of reinscription within the colonizer's subjectivity. The play also suggests that the colonized may have internalized the very fable that he debunks precisely because it is profoundly difficult to dislodge the very internalization that is productive of identity: "*I'm* your Butterfly . . . it was always *me*." (89; my emphasis). Thus both Song and Bhabha cling to an "original" identity, revealing that original identity to be in fact itself "fantastic, discriminatory identity effects." The fetish is not only a logic of projection and objectification; it is also the logic of identity itself.

The "pure self" that Song asserts is, after all, figured after the master. Song does not come to power or his political critique by acquiring some authentic Chinese male identity. On the contrary, he does so by donning an Armani suit and adopting the colonial voice:

> You think I could've pulled this off if I wasn't full of pride? . . . Arrogance. It took arrogance, really—to believe you can will . . . the destiny of another. (85)

One might say Song has learned not only learned how to be with a white man, but also how to *be* the white man. This suggests that, within stereotype's necessary repeat performance, the *other* identificatory position available for the one stereotyped is not another stereotype (that is, Song saying, "Don't mistake me for the Japanese"), but the role of the master. The difficult lesson of *M. Butterfly* is therefore not that fantasy exists, as the playwright himself asserts in his afterword, but the more politically distressing idea that fantasy may be the very way in which we come to know and love someone—to come to know and love ourselves.

Part II: Rine and Heart—Toward a Politics of Melancholia

Can there be a progressive politics that reecognizes, rather than denies, the raced subject's melancholic desires? At the risk of speaking like a true melancholic, perhaps minority discourse might prove to be most powerful when it resides *within* the consciousness of melancholia itself, when it can maintain a "negative capability" between neither dismissing nor sentimentalizing the minority's desires. I turn now to an earlier text that, under equally binding racial and gender pressures, nonetheless opens up visions of the political potentials of melancholic subjectivity.

While *M. Butterfly* gives us racial melancholia as a theorization of subjecthood and its unstable place in power structures on the part of the dominant subject, *Invisible Man* extends that theorization to a meditation on objecthood and its entangled, vexing relationship to loss and history. I read *Invisible Man* as a seminal text for theorizing invisibility *as* a trope for the melancholic incorporation of the self-as-loss. If the ideology of "American cultures" sustains itself via the repeated exclusion and staged reincorporation of excluded others, then one may begin to read "racialized America" (for both the minority and the dominant subject) as a fantasy built on absences. It is crucial to recognize that *melancholic identity is built on an incorporative confusion.* The benefit of linking a colloquial understanding of racial assimilation to a psychoanalytic notion of melancholic incorporation lies in how we learn to read cultural loss and foreclosures. By locating cultural and racial exclusion as a loss, Ellison's text offers a theorization of identity that recuperates that loss not as presence but as invisibility. Or, more specifically, Ellison revalues invisibility as a strategy to identify that absence without denying that absence's constitutive power for the formation of the racialized subject.

Invisible Man provides a sustained meditation on the question of *strategy*, specifically a question of "how to master the master's tongue." Ellison is not an accommodationist, as is evidenced by his satirization of Booker T. Washington throughout the novel; but neither is he a separatist. (This, after all, is a writer whose protagonist notices in the paint factory that it takes a drop of blackness to produce true whiteness.) Hence, throughout the novel, there is a persistent exploration of different versions of assimilation, accommodation, and internalization. Metaphors of mirroring, swallowing, and even gagging abound in *Invisible Man.* These images of "taking in" appear in many guises: the yes'em-to-death of the grandfather, the mad internalized cynicism of the vet, Trueblood as the fantasy of inbred narcissism, the incorporating politics of the Brotherhood. These "assimilative" fantasies are all mutually contaminating: each incident bespeaks a mutual counter-incorporation, where the white man and the black man mime each another, both trying to approximate the certitude of their identity through the other, supported by their fantasmatic staging of the other, although of course power comes to nuance the implications of such mimicry for both parties.

I am thinking, for example, of Mr. Norton, the white man who sees himself in the invisible man's face, and Dr. Bledsoe, the black man who thinks he has to "'act the nigger!'"[28] Such "mirroring" plays out on the level of sexuality also. Mr. Norton's secret dream of the forbidden possession of his "pure" white daughter collapsing into the dreams of young black boys finds its horrified and salacious fulfillment in the story of Trueblood. Norton's projection, however, can be said to be an invasion that has already infiltrated the fantasy that he consumes. We recall that Trueblood is also haunted by the dream of a "white lady" the night—indeed, the moment—he impregnates his daughter. His incest coincides exactly with his encounter with Time and History, symbolized by the grandfather clock out of which the "white lady" emerges and into which Trueblood is swallowed. White ideality as both threatening and incorporating history inscribes itself unto the relationship between black father and daughter.

The invisible man is not so different from Trueblood in that his sexuality is both served up for consumption and contaminated in its own desires. This is why individualism is such a difficult phenomenon in the text. Individuals often find themselves in a crowd, or worse, served up for consumption.[29] There is no gaze that is not always already a mirror of another gaze. Consider, for example, the narrator's high school graduation. Instead of finding an audience for his speech, the narrator finds himself in a spectacle of humiliation arranged for the enjoyment of the white audience. The blond dancer, as well as the staged blindfolded fight afterward, lets the white audience witness the "bestial" nature of the black boys. The description of the woman offers a curious mixture of inanimation and bestiality:

> The hair was yellow like that of a circus kewpie doll, the face heavily powdered and rouged, as though to form an abstract mask, the eyes hollow and smeared a cool blue, the color of a baboon's butt. (19)

The dancer's face and body mirror the very animalistic qualities that the men have attributed to the black students. Thus the black bodies of the students and the female body of the blond dancer occupy similarly debased positions in the scopic regime of white male visual desire. As Danny Kim points out, this moment marks white racist effeminization of black male bodies as well as expresses a white racist homoerotic interest in those displayed black bodies. This conscription of the black male body for white scopic pleasure-and-denigration exercises an even more insidious psychical violation, for it is the white fantasm of a "black male psyche," in addition to black male bodies, that is also being put on display. The white patrons of the "battle royal" wish to stage not just the stripped-down black male bodies but also their appetite. When the narrator reacts to her with desire and hatred, wanting "to caress and destroy her, to love and murder her" (19), he is only performing the inseparability of desire and shame that he is *supposed to* feel. What has been exposed in that moment is a reflection of the history of the representation of black male sexuality, a history that instills fear and shame in the black man before the white woman. The *mise en scène* at Battle Royal is set up to unveil the black desirous and murderous gaze, collapsed in the fantasy of excessive black male sexuality, as a confirming mirror for white male desire and aggression. What is significant here is not that the fantasy exists but that the fantasy needs to be staged and restaged, for the restaging provides the tableau in which the white audience can mediate and witness their own desires through the other. The spectacle offers that detour, that doubling. The blond's display exhibits the spectacle of the boys' arousal and shame, which in turn reflect the arousal of the white audience.

If the invisible man's response in front of the nude is nothing but assenting to a stereotype, then is there any escaping that position? If a subject position has been preconditioned by certain laws and prohibitions, then the mere exposure of these laws and prohibitions cannot suffice to restore that subject to a "wholeness" it never had. The "black gaze" is always already a historical construct. Hence the one character who manages to "fall outside history," Clifton, does so by acting out—rather than denying—that history. After recognizing that he has been duped by the Brotherhood, Clifton takes to the streets of New York, performing the Sambo doll. Rather than reading his action as a concession to stereotype, I see the character as dramatizing and exposing the role that had been assigned to him. In taking up the Sambo doll, he is acting out what the Brotherhood has made him. The idea of a healthy progressive history, in which events can be successfully mourned and left behind, echoes far too closely the kind of blind, corrective, historical logic that undersigns projects such as the Founder's dream ("the history of the race a saga of mounting triumphs"[134]) or the Brotherhood's idea of progressive history.[30]

How *can* one repair the wounds of invisibility? Description—the delineation of presence and absence—turns out to be both the problem and the critique of the problem, of invisibility. Beyond the standard reading of invisibility as a metaphor for exclusion (that the black man is invisible because white society refuses to see him), the text offers us invisibility as a critical strategy: a metaphysical, intellectual meditation that explores the power of abstraction, disembodiment, and illusion. As the inadmissible fantasm configuring (not just configured by) social visibilities, the narrator's invisibility not only is an effect of social reality but also affects it. As was dramatized in the discussion of *M. Butterfly*, melancholia operates reflexively. Ellison gives us a demonstration of how to approach that reflexivity as a strategy rather than an impediment:

> I am invisible. . . . Like the bodiless heads you see sometimes in circus sideshows, it is as though I have been surrounded by mirrors of hard, distorting glass. When they approach me they see only my surroundings, themselves, or figments of their imagination. (3)[31]

In that hall of mirrors, who distorts whom? As much as racial blindness makes the narrator invisible, his invisibility also reflects emptiness back on those gazers as well. If he has been assimilated only through his invisibility, then he also renders dissimilar and strange the status of *their* visibility.

Here we have the potential for a kind of subversive assimilation, a kind of mimetic *dis*simulation inherent in, though differently inflected by, Bhabha's "discourse of mimicry." The fantasm of the narrator's invisibility reflects the fantasm in the heart of mainstream society. While blackness has traditionally been seen as all too visible and readable, whiteness, accordingly to critic Richard Dyer, operates through invisibility:

> Trying to think about the representation of whiteness as an ethnic category . . . is difficult, partly because white power secures its dominance

by seeming not to be anything in particular. . . . This property of white-ness, to be everything and nothing, is the source of its representational power. (44–5)[32]

The narrator in the prologue (which is also the end) assumes this represen-tational power for blackness. He hides under the city, so deep in its belly that he becomes undetectable, standing as the literalization of the swallowed but denied lost object at the heart of white racial melancholia. The city's cen-tral light source, Monopolated Light & Power, begins to take notice of some source draining its energy, a source whose origin it cannot determine: the "lost object" is beginning to eat its way out.

Underground, the narrator is at once everywhere and nowhere. The character who embodies and prefigures this strategy of reflection and imi-tation—of vagrant presence and omnipresence—is of course the fantasmatic figure of Rinehart. Literally the real invisible man in the text, Rinehart never appears except as pure appearance: Rinehart the runner, Rine the gambler, Rine the briber, Rine the lover, pimp, and reverend. The figure of Rinehart is often seen as providing a diametrically opposed alternative to the rigid nationalism of Ras the Destroyer. More often than not, however, Rinehart is seen to represent as impossible an option as Ras. Nathan Scott, for ex-ample, sees Rinehart as a "wily rascal who deals with the intractibilities of social circumstances by simply mocking them in the cultivation of an ex-travagant histrionism."[33] However, as the figure who actually stages invis-ibility and extracts its mimetic potentials, Rinehart occupies a central place in this meditation on how to master the master's tongue. In fact, the appear-ance of Rinehart produces a ghostly evocation of the grandfather whose words (at the beginning of chapter 1) almost literally initiate the central narrative:

But my grandfather is the one. He was an odd old guy, my grandfather, and I am told I take after him. It was he who caused the trouble. On his death-bed he called my father to him and said, "Son, after I'm gone I want you to keep up the good fight. . . . I've never told you, but our life is a war and I have been a traitor all my born days, a spy in the enemy's country ever since I give up my gun back in the Reconstruction. Live with your head in the lion's mouth. I want you to overcome 'em with yeses, undermine 'em with grins, agree 'em to death and destruction, let 'em swoller you til they vomit or bust wide open."

But my folks were more alarmed over his last words than over his dy-ing. It was as though he had not died at all, his words caused so much anxiety. I was warned emphatically to forget what he had said.´. . . It had a tremendous effect upon me, however. . . . It became a constant puzzle. (16)

Indeed, the novel that follows may be read as a continuous effort to understand that puzzle. Initially the narrator mistakes the advice to be that of pure accommodation (hence his approval by most "lily-white men" of the beginning of the novel). It is not until he encounters the figure of Rinehart, friend to both the Law and the criminal, that the narrator begins to fathom the subversion embodied in the grandfather's words, "live with your head in the lion's mouth."

As the figure of a figure, Rinehart represents form without substance, yet his substancelessness provides him with pure potential. The narrator muses:

> Could [Rinehart] himself be both rind and heart? What is real anyway? . . . His world was possibility and he knew it. He was years ahead of me and I was a fool. . . . It was unbelievable, but perhaps only the unbelievable could be believed. Perhaps the truth was always a lie. (498)

We return to the issue of authenticity. When it comes to identity, the question goes beyond what is culturally real or racially genuine to the question of context. To try to locate Rinehart's "true" identity would be to miss the lesson of Rinehart: who you are depends on whom you are talking to, which community you are in, and who is watching your performance.[34] Embodying dissimulative potential, glaringly visible in his invisibility, Rinehart operates and structures a network of connections in Harlem from religion to prostitution to the law. A man defined by costumes and props, he is at once the ultimate "outsider" and "insider," making visible the contingency of such distinctions and perverting the lines of power—or at least exposing power as *positionality*. (Are we seeing a politicized strategization of the fantasmatic?) As a parable for plurality, as a continually resignifiable sign, Rinehart critiques the ideal of an uncompromising individuality.

In critiquing individualism, Rinehart also interrogates racial essence. Rinehart (like the narrator) is all too easily recognizable as "Rinehart" by his glasses, his hat, and even his shoes. As a type ("poppa-stopper," "daddy-o," the "stylin'" one), Rinehart seems more stylized than racialized. More to the point, he exposes the idea that racial*ization* is always a matter of style rather than essence—a performance of type that can be either self-stereotyping or self-identifying. As the narrator says, "I was recognized [as Rinehart] not by features, but by clothes, by uniform, by gait" (485). His disguise (the dark glasses that throw him into a sequence of "dreamy, distorted" events) literally calls forth Rinehart. To impersonate Rinehart is to *become* Rinehart: "Something was working on me, and profoundly . . . being mistaken for him . . . my entire body started to itch, as though I had just been removed from a plaster cast and was unused to the new freedom of movement . . . you could actually make yourself anew" (498–9).

Rinehart as an event of visual performance demonstrates first, that the act of identification is dependent on representation and thus draws our attention to the power dynamics inherent in spectatorship; second, that the act of representation involves simultaneously, on a deeper level, an act of disidentification. By assuming Rinehart's strategy (in fact, Rinehart *is* strategy), the narrator at once acquires an identity and loses his capacity for naming. There is a *cost* to every identificatory staging. Thus even as the narrator celebrates a rebirth through his disguise, he suffers from a kind of identificatory aphasia, repeatedly asking, "Who actually was who?" Becoming a re-sign-able sign exacts a price of its own. It is crucial to nuance this identificatory freedom as provisional, if not downright shattering. By impersonating Rinehart, the narrator arrives not at an identity but at the fantasm that is the mode of identification. To follow Rinehartism is to plunge into the very heart of racial melancholia:

> So I'd accept it, I'd explore it, rine and heart. I'd plunge into it with both feet and they'd gag. Oh, but wouldn't they gag. . . . Yes, and I'd let them swoller me until they vomited or burst wide open. Let them gag on what they refuse to see. (508)

These words are almost a word-for-word echo of the grandfather's words. Through Rinehart, the narrator begins to grasp the will of the grandfather: a strategy for negotiating American culture since the Reconstruction. "Gagging" literalizes the melancholic condition of race in America: as a culture, *America gags on what it refuses to see*, for "American culture" is continually confronted by ghosts it can neither emit nor swallow. Rinehart as a "Spiritual Technologist" recommends a remedy for that social malady: "Behold the Invisible" (495), suggesting that only by recognizing invisibility can we begin to understand the conditions of visibility. *Invisible Man* thus offers a series of metaphoric, and literal, enactments of racial melancholia and incorporation. More than illustrating symptoms, these enactments highlight the subversive potentials within fantasies of incorporation and offer a sustained meditation on what I call a politics of melancholia: a theorization of objecthood and its entangled relationship to loss and history.

When Toni Morrison speaks of the ghostly "African American presence" in American literature, she refers not to "real" African American presence but to the fantasm of African American presence.[35] The racialization and phantomization of African Americans exist *to condition* American presence. The always already ghostly presence of African Americans in American literature implies that the entire process of racialization, of conferring visibility (who is white, who is black; who is visible, who is not), must be considered as itself a wholly melancholic activity. The act of delineating absence *preconditions* presence. Race in America is thus "stuck" on a moebius strip of inclusion and exclusion: an identification predicated on disidentity. It is a fear of contamination that works itself out through contamination, a denial of a remembrance that refuses to be forgotten.

Invisible Man finally hints that the solution to that melancholic condition is not to recover a presence that never was, but to recognize the disembodiment that *is* both the master and the slave. Disembodiment, metaphorized by Rinehart, becomes literalized in the narrator's own epiphanic hallucination, the scene of castration. In that state of neither dreaming nor waking, he confronts the groups and the individuals he has encountered and their particular brands of incorporating histories and ideologies:

> I lay the prisoner of a group consisting of Jack and Emerson and Bledsoe and Norton and Ras and the school superintendent. . . . they were demanding that I return to them and were annoyed with my refusal.

> "No," I said. "I am through with all your illusions and lies . . ."

> But now they came forward with a knife . . . and I felt the bright red pain and they took the two bloody blobs and cast them over the bridge, and out of my anguish I saw them curve up and catch beneath the apex of the curving arch of the bridge, to hang there, dripping down through the sunlight into the dark red water.

> "Now you're free of illusions," Jack said, pointing to my seed wasting upon the air. "How does it feel to be free of one's illusions?"

> And now I answered, "Painful and empty. . . . But look . . . there's your universe, and that drip-drop upon the water you hear is all the history you've made, all you're going to make." (569–70)

Not coincidentally, one of the most hallucinatory passages of this novel is also one that refers most specifically to historical reality: lynching, castration, brutalization. The novel thus does not place hallucination in opposition to history; instead, hallucination provides the stage on which renegotiation with history can take place. The narrator's dismemberment—his scattered, castrated ego—becomes his *resistance* against group consolidations and signifying processes. His refusal to refuse his own pain—his bodily containment of that brutalization—turns the reflection back on the torturers; his answer to his torturers is to point out that by trying to recruit him as a mirror image of themselves and by dismembering him to do so, the various social organizations reflect the very loss that they instigate. If history enacts denigration, then history will be structured by that brutalization. Furthermore, this scene suggests that "to be free of illusions and lies" may be viscerally brutalizing and involve profound loss, but it may the only freedom in a relentlessly coercive world.

This is a difficult and terrifying vision of freedom, its cost almost unimaginable. In this tactical paradigm, the melancholic subject/master is exposed as *structurally* embodying its supposed inverse (objecthood and loss), while the melancholic object/ghost bears the burden of that invisibility.[36] The symbolic equation of testicles and seeds with illusions—or at least, the notion that black manhood may be the price of freedom from illusions—seems incredibly radical, especially in light of what has been seen as Ellison's agenda to "project a more virile image of African American aesthetic agency" (Kim).[37] bell hooks draws an explicit link between African American liberal rhetoric and masculinist agenda:

> The discourse of black resistance has almost always equated freedom with manhood, the economic and material domination of black men with castration, emasculation. Accepting these sexual metaphors forged a bond between oppressed black men and their white male oppressors. They share the patriarchal belief that revolutionary struggle was really about an erect phallus.[38]

Here, by equating the discourse of black resistance with castration, Ellison severs even the bond of manhood. In order to break what hooks calls the "bond between oppressed black men and their white male oppressors," Ellison makes a radical break with his own masculinist agenda.

Indeed, the persecuting oppression in this scene comes not only from white men but also from men such as Bledsoe (who has already been bled dry). Within the context of the specific historical forces inhering in the notion of "dismemberment," this moment of terrible and terrifying relinquishment is all the more powerful in its insistence on the priority of renouncing cultural illusions—especially illusions that make use of ideals such as manhood and community, illusions that are as coercive as they might have been seductive. Ellison's vision of corporeal and metaphysical detachment thus implies that freedom comes not from political or masculinist identities but specifically from identificatory renunciation ("painful and empty"), because the vocabulary of freedom has for so long been deployed by the rhetoric of enslavement, as illustrated by the rhetoric of the Brotherhood. "To be free of illusions" paradoxically and crucially means to be free of the ideologies of authenticity.

Like the white man he met on the street whose reality can be shaped only by his nightmares, the narrator, for the most part, prior to this scene, has had his perceptions shaped by the ideologies that he tried to assimilate, his "soul-sickness" (575). Throughout the body of the narrative, he has been searching for visibility, individualism, and communal identification. The only vision of individualism in this text, however, comes from the state of disappearance, of pain and emptiness—a shattered rather than reconstituted subject. This shattered subject and its abdication of the flesh resist, too, what Lee Edelman has called "the fictitious but inescapable 'truth' of the whole" in the racist imaginary[39]—that is, the totalizing logic of taking the synecdoche of the pigmented flesh as the flesh or the body itself. Here "internalization" (that is, the narrator's internalization of racist castration and emasculation) bespeaks much more than passive receptivity and indeed addresses a whole history of identificatory and gender assumptions underlying the racist imaginary. In this scene of castration and relinquishment, invisibility has been theorized as a condition of disembodiment and abstraction, as an escape from "illusions" *and* from the racist equating of race, personhood, and the flesh.[40] This hallucination refuses to repeat the white fetishization of the black male member, in the senses of both genitalia and of a member of a race. Ellison locates black resistance, not in uncompromising individualism or manhood, but in these intra-subjective negotiations that are experienced intersubjectively *and* violently.

This "resistance" is of course not without its price, nor is it a pragmatic prescription for action. After exploring various political positions and strategies and then undermining them, the resolution of *Invisible Man* remains far from certain. What is the "socially responsible role" that the narrator will play by the end of the novel? The narrative has offered us more questions than final affirmations or specific courses of action. The narrator informs us: "So it is now I denounce and defend . . . I condemn and affirm, say no and say yes, say yes and say no. . . . So I approach it through division" (580). Much critical dissatisfaction with Ellison's political statement comes from this conclusion. On the extreme end, critics have seen Ellison's exploration of stable political identity as a neglect of "Negro duty."[41] An ongoing argument provoked by this novel has always been the problem of its open-ended ending, its protagonist's lack of action. In a way he represents the classic figure of melancholy (melancholy, after all, has for two hundred years been closely associated with the inability to act decisively). However, by viewing the invisible man's response through the lens of melancholia as an active process of subjective negotiation with loss and dismemberment, I am valuing not the indecision but the *space of contemplation before action that his melancholic condition affords him*—a contemplation that enables a profound reimagining of the history of brutalization and self-brutalization haunting the African American man.

Contrary to its critics, such as Irving Howe, who accused Ellison's conclusion of being a "sudden, unprepared, and implausible assertion of unconditional freedom," I have argued that "freedom" in Ellison is anything but unconditional.[42] Many critics, supporters or otherwise, have read Ellison's critique of black nationalism as a choice for aesthetics over politics, but Ellison's aesthetic choice (even, a choice for hallucination) is not separate from but is the very mode of his political critique. Ellison's critique of black nationalism is directly linked to a broader interrogation of the fantasy of community, both subaltern and hegemonic. "Community" embodies its inverse: exclusion. *Invisible Man* consistently questions the very group ideologies that "create" and isolate African American communities in the first place. As the enclave that protects but also marginalizes, Harlem is not free from that "soul-sickness." The narrator tells us that he had been "as invisible to Mary (the nurturing 'mother' in the heart of Harlem) as [he] had been to the Brotherhood" (571). When he asks after Clifton's death—"Why did he choose to plunge into nothingness, into the void of faceless faces, of soundless voices, laying outside history?" (441)—he anticipates his own falling underground, significantly, on the edge *between* the margin of Harlem and the rest of the city. *Invisible Man* collapses the literal question of "where you stand" into the metaphoric and political one, thus exposing that question's positionality. The discourse of identity fosters division and disidentification as well (I am this; therefore I am not that). The Brotherhood provides a quintessential example of group ideology: its membership requires the forsaking of other identities. Furthermore, its recruitment works through the borrowing of other discourses of community, built on racial and gender alliances: "black brotherhood."

Ellison's "choice for art" directly addresses, rather than transcends, the political question of racial grief. The horrifying vision of that final hallucinatory confrontation hardly precludes anger or protest, nor does it deny victimization. Instead, it dramatizes the potential and the price of confronting history. To some, Ellison's underground ending will always look like a "cop-out" or a political retreat. Yet within the context of racial melancholia as condition, the choice of the underground presents a decision to remain on the border, to neither "move on" nor be wholly subject to history: "The mind that has conceived a plan of living must never lose sight of the chaos against which that pattern was conceived" (*Invisible Man*, 580). Ellison's political thesis has thus always seemed to me more radical and expansive than traditional left-wing identity politics would find comfortable. Ellison's text undermines the integrity of group ideology and of communal possibilities, whether hegemonic or subaltern. The political platform of *Invisible Man*, contrary to the appeal of the ethnically representative novel and its *Bildung*, relies not on identity—because the protagonist never arrives at one—but on the nonexistence of identity, on invisibility with its assimilative and dissimulative possibilities. Yet this place of political discomfort provides the most intense examination of what it means to adopt a political stance.

Words from the invisible man in the epilogue remain to haunt us: "you carry part of your sickness with you" (575). *You carry the foreigner inside.* This malady of doubleness, I argue, is the melancholy of race, a dis-ease of location, a persistent fantasy of identification that *cleaves* and *cleaves to* the marginalized and the master.

HISTORY IN/AGAINST THE FRAGMENT

Theresa Hak Kyung Cha

Part I: Lost Objects, Found Memories

Stranded Memory

Ralph Ellison's *Invisible Man* leaves us in shattered history. How does one go on to *record* fragmented history? To take up this question I turn to a *récit* written by the avant-garde artist Theresa Hak Kyung Cha; her autobiography's antidocumentary desires make it one of the most peculiar and powerful meditations on the questions of recording history, trauma, and the politics of memory.

I will begin with some brief biographical information because readers may not be familiar with Cha or her work and because biography presents a vexing issue not only for the critical reception of her work, but also for Cha as an artist. Artist, writer, and filmmaker, Cha crossed as many geographic borders as generic ones. Born in 1951 in Pusan at the tip of South Korea, where her family was on the run from Seoul, seeking refugee from the advancing armies of North Korea and China in the tumultuous years of the Korean War (1950–1953), Cha's early years consisted of a series of flights and dislocations.[1] Cha and her family finally immigrated to the United States in 1961, where Cha went on to study film at the University of California at Berkeley and then at the Centre d'Etudes Americaine du Cinema in Paris with Christian Metz, Theirry Kuntzel, and Jean-Louis Baudry. Cha worked in New York City in the late seventies and early eighties. She produced videos, films, performance pieces, works on paper, poetry, prose, and art objects such as handmade "books" whose haunting repetition of words literally bruised their pages.[2] In 1982 Tanam Press published Cha's only full-length prose text, *Dictée*, and shortly after that, Cha died at the age of thirty-one. Known mostly in its avant-garde film and theater forms, her art has been featured in one-person and group exhibitions domestically and internationally, culminating in a one-person show at the Whitney Art Museum in New York in 1992.[3] Today the main corpus of her art, films, videos, and writings can be found at the UC Berkeley Art Museum, where her family bequeathed her work.

Dictée is generally accepted as Cha's autobiography, although it is hard to pinpoint what it is exactly that makes this text an autobiography, since we are not offered a name or a consistent narrating voice. If anything, this text exhibits a great deal of resistance toward autobiography as a traditional genre where an author might appear to be retrieving or chronicling her life. *Dictée* does not feature a central narrating voice, nor does it offer chronological events. Instead it speaks through multiple, disembodied voices; borrowed citations that range from film scripts to epistolary exchanges; pieces of uncaptioned photographs scattered throughout the text. Pressed to describe its tonal quality, one would have to depict it as a cross between Samuel Beckett and Marguerite Duras: concision laced with lyricism.

Cha's "novel" has more in common with poetic experimental writing dating back to the 1970s (Charles Olson, Robert Duncan) than with the majority of ethnic autobiographies flourishing in the 1980's. (In a way, *that* aesthetic quality may be the most autobiographical aspect of the book, since Cha was an experimentalist.) Cha's written text borrows heavily from avant-garde film techniques such as jagged cuts, jump shots, and visual exposiiton— techniques that recall the experimental films of Maya Deren and other visionary filmmakers[4] and the movement in documentary films of which Trinh Minh-ha was the center. What remains more difficult to explain is this text's ambivalent relationship to autobiography as a genre: its insistence on, yet resistance to, modes of self-revelation, both personal and political. This problem of how to "read" the text in turn evokes two larger dilemmas: first, how to integrate the concerns of cultural studies with postmodern aesthetic practices; second, how to understand ethnic texts beyond their representative values.

The history of the reception, disappearance, and rediscovery of *Dictée* itself as a printed document also hints at these problems. When it first appeared in 1982, its narrative inaccessibility and its failure to present a recognizable model of ethnic identity generated it little critical attention in the nascent field of Asian American letters. What attention *Dictée* did receive came from postmodern and avant-garde critics, such as Michael Stephens, in *The Dramaturgy of Style*, and Stephen-Paul Martin, in *Open Form and the Feminine Imagination*—both, for the most part, glossed the enigmatic quality of Cha's writing as "female experimentation," with all the immediate connotations of experimentation as mystification, difficulty as incomprehensibility, and feminism as simply antimasculinist. *Dictée* soon fell out of print.

More than a decade after it fell out of print and became impossible to find in most bookstores except for the occasional copy in a handful of museum stores, *Dictée* is rapidly acquiring critical currency as one of the most recent pieces of ethnic autobiographical evidence to be "discovered" by researchers in Asian American, feminist, film, and postcolonial studies.[5] In *Woman, Native, Other: Writing Postcoloniality and Feminism*,[6] Trinh Minh-ha invokes Cha's work as an exemplary textual instance of postcolonial displacement. A volume of critical essays devoted solely to *Dictée*, edited by Norma Alarcón and Elaine Kim, appeared in 1994.[7] Norma Alarcón, along with colleagues such as Barbara Christian, collaborated with Third Woman Press to bring the text back in print in 1997. Yet another "rescue mission" is underway at the UC Berkeley Art Museum, where the curatorial staff has been engaged in an extended project of organizing the Theresa Hak Kyung Cha Archive, featuring her artwork, films, videos, pencil-scribbled journals, and a website. The curious inbalance effected by intense critical attention in certain areas and little public awareness in others raises questions about the critical excavations of "marginalized, ethnic" writers, projects that academia tends to see as reversing the history of neglect, as well as enabling a process of proper cultural remembering (the museum archive of Cha's work being the most vivid materialization of this act of memorialization).

While *Writing Self Writing Nation*, Alarcón and Kim's critical collection, has certainly broadened the notion of identity in *Dictée*—featuring pioneering analysis into Cha's political negotiations, examining the difference and multiplicity that exist on the levels of self, nation, and gender—what remains unexplored is the fundamental principle of *identification* that went into structuring those categories in the first place *and* whose processes haunt the very form of Cha's récit. Although, and perhaps precisely because, *Dictée* is not interested in identities, it is profoundly interested in the processes of *identification*. It seems complacent to label this increasingly prominent text as representative of the "multicultural, immigrant, feminist, postcolonial, and ethnic" subject when its enunciation operates through *de*contextualization and resists identification even on the simplest level.

As an autobiographical document, *Dictée* is anything *but* self-evident. It offers up bits of re-collected narratives that stand in the text as melancholic objects: half-buried, half-revived. In *Dictée*, acts of *recollection* (in the sense of memory recall) are frequently indistinguishable from acts of *collection* (in the sense of gathering up). There are sections, for instance, where personal memories reveal themselves to be borrowed lines from other texts. The process of memory within this text is difficult and recalcitrant, to say the least, effecting a double movement of retrieval and interment. How do we read its political intention when we can hardly locate a political subject? How do we construct a political subject when that "subject's" very voice, *along with its boundaries*, is always in oscillation? How does this apparently post-modern, seemingly ahistorical, and dislocated récit come to effect its intense, localized critique of cultural history and its reconstructions?

The difficulty of reading *Dictée* derives not only from its narrative opacity but also from the larger, critical problem of negotiating cultural studies and poststructuralism, especially in the field of minority literature. With its insistence on interdisciplinary studies and sociohistorical context, cultural studies has productively challenged the textualist approach of an earlier formalism. The formalist, we are told, tends to "enclose" the text, to isolate it and herself from the vicissitudes of ideology, of history and social life.

The urgency of reading *Dictee*'s "difficulty" comes precisely from its struggles with this critical divergence between material history and aesthetic formalism. Cha's récit offers an instance where formalism might be as responsive to local specificities of history and culture as it is attuned to abiding and transhistorical structures of thoughts—to questions of voice and genre, to philosophical, psychoanalytic, and other nonlocal modes of analysis. Indeed, *Dictée* raises the challenge that form and aesthetic (specifically, the style of the fragment) poses for the claims of cultural studies.

Intending to contribute to the range of analysis collected in *Writing Self Writing Nation*, this chapter seeks to study the specific, formal ways in which Cha's apparent postmodern aesthetic enacts her political project. I will read the novel as a critique of the desire for documentation. I also aim to complicate and add to the idea of "difference-as-intervention" so foregrounded in Alarcón and Kim's collection by introducing the concept of fantasy and mimesis as the two other logics equally at work in Cha's text. Before designating *Dictée*'s representative value as a piece of cultural evidence, a reader has to confront first the text's resistance toward it own visibility: the oblique relation it takes toward itself as an object of revelation. Clearly the text is preoccupied with history, specifically Korean national history and the contemporary legacy of that history in relations to the West. Fragments of the text, in the forms of calligraphy, narrative, newsprint, and personal letters, allude to Korea's history of foreign invasions: the repeated forays into Korea made by the Japanese and the Manchurians as early as the thirteenth and fourteenth centuries; the "spiritual" colonization of Korea by the French missionaries in the seventeenth century; and, starting with the Russo-Japanese War at the turn of the century, the invasions by Russia, Japan, Manchuria, and the United States. Yet Cha's book not only refuses to thematize or narrate that history in full but works hard to truncate that history. This so-called postcolonial autobiography displays, rather than resolves, the tension between public and private records. I suggest that the very *form* of *Dictée* effects a historical and cultural reconstruction that enacts, simultaneously, a critique of that reconstruction.

Resuscitation

How does that paradox work?

We need to step back and look at the desire for history, especially in minority literature. The desire to know and to bear witness as some kind of "redemptive" act has fueled many of the recent academic moves to recognize and understand the various histories and forms of colonization—a desire, in other words, for the documentary.[8] This desire becomes compounded when it comes to ethnic autobiographies in that, often in the service of producing a body of representative literature, such as Asian American letters, both writer and reader embark on a journey in search of a "whole" narrative—something along the lines of a package deal, ready for consumption. The documentary impulse as a mode of knowledge also carries certain pedagogical assumptions that reinforce the academic tendency to conduct "corrective re-readings" or to enable what Catherine Gallagher would call "the narrative of undoing."[9]

At first glance, *Dictée* would seem to possess all the signs of documentary desires. It is constructed almost like an archive itself, full of grainy black-and-white photographs, images, handwritten letters, historical chronologies. These pieces of "evidence" loosely cohere around the life of a Korean American woman immigrant, while providing contextual bits of information about familial and sociopolitical backgrounds. *Dictée* would thus seem a likely candidate to satisfy not only the academic will-to-knowledge but also the requirements of the traditional ethnic memoir. Yet, as already noted, *Dictée* hardly offers itself as a comprehensive or reliable source of information. Cha gives her readers evidences that are conspicuously lacking in proper documentation. None of the images are captioned or footnoted; the same may be said of the clearly plagiarized textual citations. We find, for example, dislocated in the text an unidentified, grainy black-and-white photograph of a mass protest (122). We want to know that photo's referent. Cha's private notes tell us that the photo documents the 1919 Korean Independence Movement demonstration, where over two hundred students demonstrated for democracy and protested against the Japanese-installed Korean government. The protest was crushed, and the Korean government subsequently declared to the world that the protest was part of a communist uprising. Images like these were used by the South Korean cold war dictatorship to justify itself. (Indeed, the Korean government used the same image in another student uprising against the government and subsequent massacre in the early eighties.)

We are, however, still left with the problem of how to read this image stranded in the text, how to read it as decontextualization. I want to suggest that rather than advocating some form of abstract universality, Cha's

use of the fragment/truncated image is intimately bound up with the particular history of modern Korea and its significance for Cha as a subject in
relation to those national memories. If the desire for redemption underlies
recent academic interest in marginalized histories, then the form of Cha's
text offers a critique of that documentary desire. Not only does this conjunction of immigrant and postcolonial autobiography—full of borrowed
and homeless voices—fail to privilege (or even account for) identity over
difference, but it fundamentally challenges what it means to be invested in
those terms ("identity," "difference"), and what it means to try to bear representative witness to a "lost" or "suppressed" history.

Cha's refusal to supply the available referent speaks to her suspicion of
the over-circulated image. Earlier in the text she writes about the image:

> The image. To appeal to the masses to congeal the information. . . . The
> response is pre-coded to perform predictably however passively possible.
> First examine neutralized to achieve the no-response, to submit to the
> uni-directional correspondence. (32–3)[10]

To Cha, the photograph can often offer a visual and facile mask of identification and sympathy. By refusing a unidirectional correspondence between
the image and the referent it supposedly guards, Cha resists photography's
easy promise to furnish evidence and to animate the desire to collect data.
Like all mass art forms, photography can often be what Susan Sontag in
On Photography calls a "social rite, a defense against anxiety, and a tool of
power."[11] As Trinh Minh-ha points out, the imperial gaze loves the image
of the "native" as a violated site.[12] And as critic Rey Chow demonstrates in
her recent article "Where Have All the Natives Gone?"[13] the liberal critic
does too. The gesture of redeeming these images has frequently served only
to re-violate them. Awareness of this contestation over the image, Dictée asks
how one represents history. When Cha writes about recording history—
especially traumatic history—one gets the sense of both the urgency and
the impossibility of the task:

> Unfathomable the words, the terminology: enemy, atrocities, conquest,
> betrayal, invasion, destruction. They exist only in the larger perception
> of History's recording. . . . Not physical enough. Not to the very flesh and
> bone, to the core, to the mark, to the point where it is necessary for this
> outcome, that does not cease to continue. (32)

The passage poses a double bind: the need to make history "real enough"
and the risks of reification presented by "making it real." Dictée's textual
solution to this dilemma suggests that modern Korea exists only as a history of found images—even, of dead images. The black-and-white photo of
that student demonstration and subsequent massacre is homeless because

that "original" event was homelessness itself, a story lost in the intervening publicity surrounding it. By giving us images without context, Cha does not advance a simplistic version of historical or aesthetic transcendence, such as the notion that the particular must be sacrificed to the universal. Instead, she is wary of identity for identity's sake, of the notion that the mere act of identification is sufficient for the restoration of past wrongs.

For Cha, the naming of history (and of marginalized people) only resurrects "unfathomable words." Specificity has been all too often deployed as containment, and the dream of a true or complete historical recuperation turns out finally to be untenable. Cha's use of the photo without context demonstrates that historical events cannot be recaptured in all their temporal and cultural specificities except as *a record*, with all the remembrance and the emptying-out of remembrance. It is not the historical event of the student protest that the reader is asked to interpret but rather its mediated representation. To confuse the two is to misunderstand Cha and the nature of history. The photo of the student protest is thus always already false, to the extent that it promises an impossible presence.

By challenging the documentary impulse underlying the ethnic or postcolonial *Bildung*, Cha disturbs the faith in either the "history lesson" or the narrative of redemption. This antidocumentary document takes apart traditional historic concepts of periodization, making it impossible to retrieve or recite historical atrocity as containable events.[14] This does not mean that Cha is proposing the sanctification/silencing of traumatic history.[15] On the contrary, the very form of *Dictée* suggests that the documentation of history must be recognzied as itself a process of pluralization and performative reiteration. It insists that retrieved history must be understood as an instance of dissimulated historicity with all the fantasmatic attachments inevitable in any act of reconstruction. To be given a piece of historical evidence is also to be given a history of its silence and revival. What we are given in *Dictée* is an afterimage of the event, *and* it is the afterimage that we have to deal with and that has been placed in constant and *uncanny* circulation. Cha's textual strategy distances and makes the overfamiliar (such as "news" and history) *un*familiar and thus *un*ownable.[16] Consequently, Cha's photo is own-able by neither the imperialist nor the liberal anthropologist. To see the photo is to hear—and witness the loss of—its melancholic call.

In this way the image effects, paradoxically, both attachment and detachment. Cha's words on the page opposite of the photograph read: "*Dead time. Hollow depression interred invalid to resurgence, resistant to memory. Waits. Apel. Apellation. Excavation*" (123). The presence of the image signals an equivalence between excavation and appellation: an Orphic narrative that collapses emergence with interment. *Dictée* deters us from reading the fragment as either reified value or pure disconnection. Rather Cha suggests that the collection and erasure that *is* the "fragment" may be the only kind of history that can memorialize without reappropriation. *Dictée* consequently problematizes the very nature of a "cultural rescue mission" and exposes that desire as an arena where epistemology and power are engaged in perpetual contestation.

In a chapter entitled "Melancholic Objects," Susan Sontag suggests in *On Photography* that photographs represent the melancholic objects of American nationalism. Explaining that since America, unlike European nations, has no antiques, no "real" historical objects, no "patina" (67) as she puts it, Sontag proposes that Americans love photography for replacing historical objects that they never had: "Photographs, which turn the past into a consumable object, are a short cut" (68). In Sontag's account, photographs are melancholic objects in the sense that they offer the screen through which America can mourn its lack of history by supplementing that lack with the photographic image. While the very possibility of possessing "real historical objects" must raise questions of its own (as someone like Cha would obviously suggest), Sontag does hit on something very provocative about the American relationship to the photograph (think of Edward Hopper, whose Americana harks back more to the photograph than its own painterly origins): Sontag has in essence proposed that the American love affair with the photograph is a love affair with the nation, that photographs make present the absence of history. Stocked up with photographic objects, America never has to deal with the questionability or lack of history.

But Sontag does not question the complications or the failures of such compensation. The melancholic logic that we have been exploring and Cha's usage of historic photographs both remind us that those photographic objects can finally never fully satisfy, nor can they supplant the lack of history, for they themselves embody such lacks. The image as a photograph is already itself homeless and decontextualized. Indeed, missing this melancholic insight also makes Sontag blind to certain misplaced (racial) origins buried in photography. That is, Sontag's book identifies the crisis and grief of American nationalism as a lack of history, but she herself is incapable of looking at how racial abjection has been used to compensate for that lack. Whenever Sontag treats the prurient nature of photography (which, for Sontag, includes still photography and film), whenever she looks into photography's "dark seamy corners" (57), she saw Asian or Asian Americans. Chinatown and the Chinese repeatedly pop up in her text as examples of the abject caught on film. Rather than analyzing how this abject, racialized presence might have enabled American camera-melancholy and hence the nostalgia for Americana itself, Sontag seems to criticize that so-called dark element for somehow catering to photographic "specularity." For example, Sontag cites Buster Keaton's 1928 silent film *The Cameraman* as an example of American fascination for violence. And yet the source of Keaton's visual melancholy derives from an accidental footage of a gang war in

Chinatown.[17] Sontag sees the American prurience for violence but misses what that violence says about the material, economic conditions of a racial community (inspite of heterogenous ethnic and national roots) squeezed into a segregated space, and how those economic conditions in turn serve the larger American economy. Sontag's unspoken distaste for these "dark seamy corners" verbalizes itself in the last chapter of *On Photography* where, in defense against the Chinese government's censorship of Antonioni's China documentary *Chung Kuo*, Sontag criticizes the simplicity of the "Chinese" understanding of photography: "it is characteristic visual taste of those at early stages of camera culture. . . . Presumably the Chinese will eventually make the same instrumental use of photography that we do . . ." (177). Yet the Chinese government's deployment of the photograph/image as national propaganda and pedagogy might in fact be doing exactly that: making instrumental use of photography. It is as though while Sontag can lament the image of the Chinese captured by the photographic frame, she cannot, however, imagine the Chinese *using* the camera. It is apparent that what Sontag's camera-eye of American nationalism frames but does not see is not the lack of historical objects, but the presence of denied historical subjects, the racial other.

Rather than suffering from the kind of national nostalgia for "real historical objects" that Sontag mentions, Cha's textual strategy (a collage of stranded objects) offers an alternative to historical records. Her textual strategy provides us with melancholic evidences—the kind of evidence that *registers loss, even as it recognizes the unrecognizability of the content of loss*. If the photograph is often used as a quotation, then Cha's refusal of the caption enacts a statement about refusing the deployment of photography as citable memory and thereby resisting the notion of memory as universal or collectively available/accessible for redemption. Cha's uncaptioned photographs effect, for the reader, a relation to the world that is melancholic: a trace of something lost that cannot be *named*.

Cha documents not "the native," but the making of "the native." Rey Chow helps us understand the dilemma surrounding the resuscitation of "the native":

> Is there a way of "finding" the native without simply ignoring the image, or substituting a "correct" image of the ethnic specimen for an "incorrect" one, or giving the native a "true" voice "behind" her "false" voice? (29)

Chow herself offers us some answers. She suggests that we recognize that (1) the image reflects above all the fantasies of the imperial gaze; (2) the severed image represents nothing more than just that, a record of severance; and (3) the "idealized native is, literally, topographically *nowhere*" (49).

What I called Cha's double strategy of attachment and detachment not only enacts the critical methods Chow called for but also implies that the no-whereness, the utopia, of the native is more than "a symptom (in the Lacanian sense) of the white man," as Chow points out; the native is, more crucially, a symptom of the so-called native herself.

As discussed in relatioin to Maxine Hong Kingston, the "native's" sense of her own nativism is always a mediated experience. Similarly, Cha's narrator gives us two scenes of homecoming. First we have a scene of her induction into U.S. citizenship:

> Documents, proof, evidence, photograph, signature. One day you raise the right hand and you are American . . . someone has taken my identity and replaced it with their photograph. . . . Their own image. (56)

Then we have a scene of her "homecoming" back in Korea:

> [Then] you return and you are not one of them. . . . They ask your identity. . . . Whether or not you are telling the truth or not about your nationality. They say you look other than you are. . . . You say who you are but you begin to doubt. . . . Why did you leave this country why are you returning. (57)

Both instances are tied in to the power of the image. If she were coerced by the image of American ideal citizenship, she is equally divorced from a "native" image of herself. These moments describe the construction of citizenship and how that process undermines any individual's autobiographical capability: the ability to place oneself in relation to history and community.

This relationship between self and community is not one of pedagogy but one of citation, with all its successful and unsuccessful imitations. For example, *Dictée* channels a host of women who embody, in various contexts, cultural mythologies: the Nine Muses, Korean nationalist martyr Yu Guan Soon, Saint Therese of Lisieux, and Joan of Arc. These figures exist as fragments in the text, alienated from the very cultural contexts that fantasized about them. Making their appearances through bits of letters, confessions, and images, these "heroines" confound rather than confirm their privileged status as "originals." The Nine Muses, for instance, appear as section headers, yet their constellation appears incomplete and divorced from their individual and proper jurisdiction. Parts of Saint Therese's confession, which may be said to be a forerunner of female confessionals, has been plagiarized as diegetic narration. Joan of Arc appears not as "herself" but as Maria Falconetti playing Carl Dreyer's film vision of Joan of Arc. The story of Korean nationalist Yu Guan Soon appears as a bare, true, but unrevealing biographical outline ("She is born of one mother and one father" [25]).

Rather than celebrating the performances of these figures, Cha reveals the performative nature of these models—or rather, the performativity that these figures have been solicited to enact. Judith Butler in *Bodies That Matter*[18] offers a succinct explanation of what is at stake in the difference between performance and performativity: "performativity must be understood not as singular or deliberate 'act,' but as the reiterative and citational practice by which discourse produces the effects that it names" (2). To recall our discussion of performance versus performativity in the figure of Linda Low in *Flower Drum Song*, the difference in these terms lies in the issue of agency. Whereas performance may imply volunteerism, performativity locates "power," not with the subject but with sociocultural citational practices.

Hence we understand a subject not as performing culture but as being performed by culture. In *Dictée*, figures such as Joan of Arc and Yu Guan Soon (both nationalist figures) stand in the text *as* cultural citations and redefine history as such citations. "Originality" gets exposed as citationality. These figures who are traditionally seen as originators of their own mythology—figures who may be said to have generated whole complexes of cultural and national fantasies—are here seen as instances of historical canonicity that operate to cover over their historicity. The production of the subject (as creator of her own myth and life story) is revealed as historically significant precisely as a consequence of cultural citations. We have been given not myths but the making of myths. The making of myth is the making of history. This helps us understand why Butler's formulation of performativity is also an insight about history: "[performativity's] apparent theatricality is produced to the extent that its historicity remains dissimulated (and, conversely, its theatricality gains a certain inevitability given the impossibility of a full disclosure of its historicity" (12–3). History serves as a narrative alibi for itself: it is the story that comes to cover over the gap between individual memory and communal imaginings. Once again, the relationship between story and self, between history and autobiography, is disturbed—not to mime postmodern aesthetics but to textualize the conjunction of political and ontological dispossession.

As much as Cha the exiled immigrant is defined by the traumatic history of her "heritage," she is dispossessed by that inheritance with equal vehemence. Cultural trauma as concept and phenomenon, like the photograph of the protest, recurs as a profoundly unlocatable event *and* threatens the discretion of the "I" precisely in that unlocatability, recalling Maurice Blanchot's meditation that

> [disaster] does not touch anyone in particular; "I" am not threatened by it, but spared, left aside. . . . We are on the edge of disaster without being able to situate it in the future; it is rather always already past, and

yet we are on the edge or under the threat. . . . To think the disaster (if this is possible, and it is not possible inasmuch as we suspect that the disaster is thought) is to have no longer any future in which to think it.[19]

A painful distance lies between memory and historical event. In hindsight, in history, it seems as if disasters never cease to speak: in papers, journals, histories. Yet one's "own" relationship to that disaster (one's ownership of that memory) can express itself *only in description*. Even "experience" cannot guarantee authenticity for the event. For no one can be at the center of an "event"; its "eventness" is its historicity and therefore at some level it is unavailable to personal experience or possession. There can be no simple memory and no simple identification, for either the first generation, such as the narrator's mother and women like Yu Guan Soon, or the next generation, who got to know such events via familial, cultural, and media mediation. In other words, the "I"'s relationship to historical trauma is always inherently journalistic.

Cha forces us to question the very idea of an original context in the first place and disturbs the reader's "historical" relation to history. She makes it impossible for us to remain in "[t]he illusion that the act of viewing is to make alteration of the visible" (79). We are allowed neither the complacency of spectatorship nor the consolation that bearing witness effects change. In reading *Dictée*, our instinct is to re-compose all the time, to "correct," to fact-check, to narrativize, to contextualize, to trace origins in this empire of signs. Our compositional desires are constantly evoked, exposed, and thwarted. Thus the deployment of photographs and other fragments in the text precludes imaginary identification and obscures collective memories. Although it can be said that the whole of twentieth-century literature, from Pound's first thirty cantos on, has been an assault on ideological narratives and the certitude of historical narration, what is astounding is that such awareness seems to almost wholly disappear when it comes to reading ethnic literature. What has been difficult to accept about Cha's *Dictée*, therefore, turns out to be not its lack of rhetorical coherence or even its narrative opacity, but rather the way it indicts our very desire to know and see the "other" through reading—implicates, in fact, our positions as private, historical, or literary witnesses of submerged histories.

Part II: For the Love of the Group

Genealogy and collective memory are central preoccupations and crises in Cha's autobiography. In a typically methodological yet elliptical fashion, *Dictée* presents us with what looks like a genealogy:

From A Far
What nationality
or what kindred and relation
what blood relation
what blood ties of blood
what ancestry
what race generation
what house clan tribe stock strain
what lineage extraction
what breed sect gender denomination caste
what stray ejection misplaced
Tertium Quid neither one thing nor the other
Tombes des nues de naturalized
what transplant to dispel upon (20)

This passage provides a dissection of classification, a genealogy of genealogy. We are being offered perhaps an alternative to Western social organization, a structure of communal organization based on bloodlines, perhaps
even an exposition of Confucian-Korean social codes. But even in those contexts, the passage hardly elucidates an origin but weaves a layering of spa-
tial and temporal relations.

To read the passage, one must see it as image rather than as a linear text.
The terms offered in each successive line are not sequential but almost identical in that they repeat a categorization with alternative, cross-disciplinary
vocabulary. Were we to repeat the passage's dissecting impulse and divide the
passage/stanza in half, we would see mirroring lines, both metonymic (returning to the same) and metaphoric (jumping over into another field;
metapherein, to transfer, to transport). Released from the teleological injunction of reading for progression, we would note, for example, a couplet
formed at the center: the line "what race generation" is not answered but,
rather, echoed by another equivalent inquiry "what house clan tribe stock
strain." Another mirrored couplet—once again a question that significantly
cannot be answered *except* by another act of interrogation—would be the
lines "what ancestry" and "what lineage extraction." Thus while the passage seems at first to offer a terminological breakdown, it in fact enacts echoes and proliferation. It exchanges sequentiality for seriality, and a particular seriality that self-reverses.[20] Beginning with distance ("From A Far"), the
passage concludes with a movement of relocation ("transplant") that is
equivalent to an act of dissipation ("to dispel upon"). We have gone from
distances . . . to distances.

Looking at Cha's peculiar version of this "family tree," how do we account for race's *positionality* in the middle of the passage? Let me answer
this question by taking an excursion through Freud's work on group psy-

chology, which may be read as a struggle over the problem of genealogy and in which Freud employs "race" as a tool of categorization. In Freud's series of essays published under the title *Group Psychology and the Analysis of the Ego* (1921), race makes a surprising guest appearance. This slim volume attempts to examine how an individual comes to "understand, think, feel and act in quite a different way from what would have been expected" when in a group.[21] Working from the assumption that group behavior and psychology differ from, and must be contrary to, individual behavior and psychology, Freud theorizes on what he calls the "group mind." It is at this point that Freud refers rather offhandedly, and startlingly, to what he calls "the racial unconscious." In the following excerpt, Freud first quotes Gustave Le Bon, the anti-Semitic French sociologist invested in the psychological attributes of race and author of *Psychologie des foules* (1895):

> "It is easy to prove how much the individual forming part of a group differs from the isolated individual, but it is less easy to discover the causes of this difference. . . . it is necessary in the first place to call to mind . . . the unconscious life. . . . Our conscious acts are the outcome of an unconscious substratum created in the mind mainly by hereditary influences. This substratum consists of the innumerable characteristics handed down from generation to generation, which constitute the *genius of a race*. . . ."

> Le Bon thinks that the particular acquirements of individuals become obliterated in a group, and that in this way their distinctiveness vanishes. *The racial unconscious emerges*; what is heterogeneous is submerged in what is homogeneous. As we should say, the mental superstructure, the development of which in individuals shows such dissimilarities, is removed, and the unconscious foundations, which are similar in everyone, stand exposed to view. (73–74; my emphasis)

In other words, for Le Bon, that which unites individuals in a group resides in the unconscious, which is here figured as race itself: the "racial unconscious." More than a mere metaphor, race *is* the trope of sameness: "a mental superstructure," a foundation "similar in everyone."

Freud will be invested in wrestling the idea of race away from the body—away from a biological, immutable pattern of development—into the realm of the psychological. He wants to reject Le Bon's finally biological view of race as "the innumerable common characteristics handed down from generation to generation, which constitutes the genius of a race." As Sander L. Gilman points out, Freud's work in group psychology is a barely disguised investigation of anti-Semitism.[22] For Le Bon, race stood in the "first rank" of those factors that help shape the underlying attitudes of the crowd. Racial character "possesses, as the result of the laws of heredity, such powers that its beliefs, institutions, and arts,—in a word, all the elements of its civilization—are merely outward expressions of its genius" (74).

Yet Freud remains attached to a notion of racial collectivity. Throughout his career Freud frequently employs race as analogy and metaphor. For example, in the essay "The Unconscious," he compares the unconscious with the preconscious by invoking the image of the "half-breed":

> We may compare them with individual of mixed races [*Mischlingen menschlicher Rassen*] who, taken all around, resemble whites, but who betray their color by some striking feature or other, and on that account are excluded from society and enjoy none of the privilege of white people.[23]

For Freud, the experience of repression and the inability to "pass" are analogous. More significantly, race becomes the tell-tale sign. The unconscious is like the passing Jew whose distinguishing Jewishness nonetheless resurfaces at inconvenient times. Hence in *Group Psychology*, we often get the strange feeling that Freud is repeating what he is taking Le Bon to task for.

Freud finally has an ethnopsychological view of the Jew. As Gilman points out, Freud believes in the uncanny (the return of a repressed, discarded old memory) nature of Jewish identity: to be haunted not by ancient religious tradition or even biological patterns but by "the suppressed discourse of anti-Semitism, expressed by Freud himself in the model of racial memory" (24). So the inheritance of racial memory is really a kind of *traumatic transmission* for Freud, where what is transmitted is not the event itself or the kernel but the trauma attached to the kernel. Thus, for Freud, in the case of Jewish history, cultural self-consciousness as the marginalized and the suppressed formed *the* factor justifying the continued collectivity of the Jewish people as a people. In his lecture on anxiety (1917) he argues that the "core" of "anxiety" is the repetition of some particular significant experience: "This experience could only be a very early impression of a very general nature, placed in the prehistory, not of the individual but of the species . . . or, one might add, in the prehistory of race."[24] This "affective state (anxiety) [is] constructed in the same way as a hysterical attack and, like it, would be *the precipitate of a reminiscence*" (394; my emphasis). Freud has replaced Le Bon's biologism with another kind of biologism, in this case, a biologism of traumatic memory.

Because Freud is invested in securing some form of Jewish genealogy—even if it is the inheritance of trauma—his work on group identification does not really entertain conflictual or failed identifications within any given group. In trying to imagine Korean genealogy, *Dictée* gives us a simplified map outline of Korean, divided by a bold black line, marked "DMZ" (78).

Clearly racial collectivity is intersected by other demands. That map of " a nation divided" reminds us of the multiple forces (national, imperial, economic, religious) that constitute group identities and allegiances. Unstated but implicit in the map are of course the ghostly yet very corporeal presences of other nations (China, Japan, Russia, and America) in Korea.

In speaking of the group, Freud has often been criticized for reproducing on the group level his model for subjectivity (the family romance) not to explore the mutual complicity of subject and group but to ensure the former's supremacy. (This insight, in fact, forms the basis of much of the shrewd reading of Freud conducted by Mikkel Borch-Jacobsen.)[25] I want to suggest that, in *Group Psychology*, Freud enlists "race" as a trope of communal assimilation in order to cover over precisely his elision of the possible gap between private and public fantasies. Identification and the group turn out to be two of the most troublesome terms in psychoanalysis. The former, though central to Freud's "structural theories" of the mind, nonetheless proves to be quite resistant to structural and theoretical assimilation. Identification can be "complete" or "partial," object-oriented (anaclitic) or not, with the father or with *the* father/Totem (and, at times, even the mother). At various stages (in works such as *The Ego and the Id*, "On Narcissism," and *Group Psychology and the Analysis of the Ego*), Freud introduces the idea of a primary identification as preobjective identification, but it takes on several guises: alternately chronological anteriority, elementary irreducibility, and phylogenetic memory. Secondary identification, on the other hand, receives fewer redefinitions while remaining equally unclear. A distinction might be that secondary identification presupposes an object-cathexis, inasmuch as it intervenes secondarily in the loss of the loved object. But object-relation opens yet another can of worms, since the division between object-relation and identification turns out to be another Freudian distinction that collapses in on itself and one that blurs the difference between primary and secondary identification.

What remains unaccounted for, by Freud and by us, is the question of how to understand racial identification in this maze of identificatory levels. Freud's work raises more questions than answers about this supposed substratum identification. Is race a concept born after generations of hereditary transmission or something that preconditions and predetermines that legacy? What is the temporal and teleological logic of Le Bon's "genius of a race" or Freud's emerging "racial unconscious"? In short, is race created or creative?

"Genius of a Race"

The answers to these questions remain unclear in Freud. But we can explore how Cha might answer them. The *American Heritage Dictionary* defines "genius" as "a natural inclination or talent" or "the prevailing spirit or character, as of a place, person, time, or group." This seeming contradiction between something inherent and something externally influenced, which continues to haunt the Freud essay, exemplifies a fundamental tension in the conceptualization of race. The passage from Cha, what I called Cha's genealogy of genealogy, textually demonstrates the terminological proliferation and breakdown surrounding the term "race." Her textual logic suggests that genealogical logic relies on progress and teleology while remaining inherently nonsequential. The logic of genealogy turns on self-referentialiality, each term offering support and alibi for the legitimacy of the others. Race, as at once a vehicle for *and* a trope of classification and identification, literally resides in this passage as the center that turns out to be hierarchically equivalent to the margins. What emerges is that race is not something that can be located on the inside or the outside, in the psychic or the social (the second opposition following so rapidly from the first) but is rather *something that transcends or refutes the dichotomy itself.*

It is this idea of race—not as the unconscious or prehistoric inheritance, but as the product of a relationship designed to bridge or naturalize the inherent gap between individual and collectivity—that renders racial *identification* such a political activity. In many ways, Freud prefers to romanticize the process of identification in group formation, but even as he does so, he runs into the question of power. I have already hinted that Freud in *Group Psychology* side-steps the potential tension between the individual and group identity. The distinction between individual and group, the starting point of the essay, begins to blur early on in the essay. Le Bon speaks of "contagion" and "suggestibility" (quoted by Freud; 7) as causes of group formation. Building on those concepts, Freud lays out a concept of hypnosis as the form of group seduction *and* identification. In the subsection entitled "Being in Love and Hypnosis" (43–53), Freud sets out to distinguish falling in love (where the object is introjected in the place of the ego) from the kind of identification that results from hypnosis (where the object is introjected in the place of the ego ideal, which is supposedly less libidinally charged).

Yet, for Freud, being in a group turns out to be not too different from being in love. In a self-qualifying and contradictory passage, Freud tells us:

> The hypnotic relation is the unlimited devotion of someone in love, but with sexual satisfaction excluded. . . . But on the other hand we may also say that the hypnotic relation is a group formation with two members. Hypnosis is not a good object for comparison with a group formation, because it is truer to say that it is identical with it. (115)

For Freud, the "group" is getting quite small. Here Freud opens the door, even if unintentionally, to the possibility of addressing race as an imaginarily structured identification. But here we run into a snag, because the uniting leader, for Freud, whether it be a group or an ideology or race, begins to look suspiciously like the Father. This is why in speaking of falling in love in the same essay, he fails to sustain the distinction he wanted to maintain between "identification" (where the object is introjected in the place of the ego ideal) and "falling in love/object-relation" (where the object is introjected in the place of the ego). For Freud, finally, falling in love is not far from falling into ideology (which is falling in love with the Father). Thus Freud starts out in the essay by distinguishing object-relations (a being-in-love that signals the over consumption of the object) from identification (which shows a lesser degree of sexual drive), but he fails to maintain the difference. When Freud adds to Le Bon's analysis by introducing the issue of the libido operating in the group—that being in a group is somehow like being in love—he collapses his own distinction. In other words, both identification *and* object-relation require, after all, a powerful fantasmatic and ideological investment on the part of the individual. Sexual satisfaction notwithstanding, we see that identification itself is also libidinally driven and certainly no less greedy. Indeed, both the act of falling in love (object-relations elsewhere for Freud) and group identification (hypnosis here) require and acquire powerful fantasmatic and ideological investment on the part of the individual. Moreover, Freud informs us that investment is conditioned by fear and, by extension, an identification with power:

> Hypnosis . . . contains an additional element of paralysis derived from the relation between someone with superior power and someone who is without power and helpless—which may afford a transition to the hypnosis of fright which occurs in animals. (47)

Hypnosis, and the identification derived from it, is structured by power. The individual, with what I call the deer-caught-in-the-headlights syndrome, is impressed into mirroring the group via fear, paralysis, and even love. Thus power facilitates identification: an identification that both is paralyzing and exhibits "the unlimited devotion of someone in love."

Freudian hypnosis, also known as love, describes the *power* of communal seduction, a seduction that operates specifically through the image. Louis Althusser will develop a version of this hypnotic love: ideology. In "Ideology and the State Ideological Apparatus," Althusser suggests that communal relations provide the individual an "image" with which to identify and represent him/herself. He writes, "Ideology is the system of the ideas and representations which dominate the mind of a man or a social group."[26] This terse sentence holds several implications for ideology's affinity for fantasy: first, ideology is representational; second, its hold is psychical; and third, it straddles both individual and communal properties. As precursor to the more recent critical examinations of ideology,[27] Althusser's work implicitly locates fantasy as a cornerstone of ideological operations. He distinguishes his own conceptualization of ideology from Marx precisely through the differentiating figure of Freud:

> Ideology is thus thought of as an imaginary construction whose status is exactly like the theoretical status of the dream among writers before Freud. . . .

> Ideology . . . is for Marx an imaginary assemblage [*bricolage*], a pure dream, empty and vain, constituted by the "day's residues" from the only full and positive reality, that of the concrete history of concrete material individuals materially producing their existence. (150–1)

Althusser retrieves ideology-*as*-fantasy out of its immaterial status and reconfigures it as a structural agency. For Althusser, ideology is not "mere fantasy" but *effects* "material reality." Or rather, material reality derives its realism, so to speak, from fantasmatic investments—fantasmatic because it is an "imaginary" construct that structures both the imagination and the material. As such, ideology provides the very foundation for an individual to conceive of him/herself in relation to a community.

But for Althusser, this imperative to imagine is firmly located in the prerogative of the social ideological apparatus. He continues:

> ([I]deology = illusion/allusion). . . . men represent their real conditions of existence to themselves in an imaginary form. . . . [and] it is the *imaginary nature of this relation* which underlies all the imaginary distortion that we can observe (if we do not live in its truth) in all ideology.

> . . . it is not their real conditions of existence, their real world, that "men" "represent to themselves" in ideology, but above all it is their relation to *those conditions of existence which is represented to them there.* (152; my emphasis)

We might infer that "men represent their real conditions of existence to themselves"—*and to each other*—in an "imaginary form." The individual fantasmatically invests in a representation of him/herself through communal relations, and it is that fantasy that confirms, retroactively, those relations.

Althusserian ideology thus offers an unexpected and crucial entry into the "imaginary" basis of social relations. It, however, cannot fully account for the complications that this imaginary basis brings for the concept of the subject. Althusser gestures towards a reconsideration of the role of fantasy in social relations, but insofar as ideological interpellation is a name Althusser gave to a process by which a human being is constituted as a subject through his or her relations to social, ideological practices, Althusser's main interests lie in the *securing* of the subject and assumes the homogenous results of its functioning. As Judith Butler's critique of Althusser in *The Psychic Life of Power* points out, there is a kind of a chicken-and-egg quality to Althusser's relefexive drama of call-and-answer: the subject is interpellated upon answering the call of the police/state, but what made the individual respond at all if the call has not already been installed within?[28] In what follows, I would like to pursue the power implications inhering in the notion of imaginary identification (that is, an identification secured through the image) and examine Cha's fable of dictation as a critique of hypnotic mirroring.

Echo and the Sound

Dictée focuses on the processes that enable group identification by dramatizing not only how "the voice within" comes into being as injunction from without, but also that the injunction without is always already an echo of something within. If the ego emerges from some state of infantile primary narcissism through the *imago*, a homomorphic identification, as Lacan would say, then Cha denaturalizes that *imago* and reminds us that what constitutes "the human" and the image of the human is very much socially and culturally dictated. The title *Dictée* serves as a metaphoric allusion to the dictaphonic structure of social and ontic interpellation, the former disguising itself as the latter. But how does a voice on the outside become a voice within, and what are the implications of recognizing that one's own fantasies of identity exist in relation to, or even echo, external social construction? In the rest of this chapter I argue that it is in the seemingly entrapping tautology of the mirror/circular dictation that Cha suggests a different kind of political resistance might be imagined.

Dictée offers us a series of parables, dramatizing the various forms of social interpellation as working precisely through echoing our desire for the echo—that is, our desire to repeat. The first prose section of the book opens with literally a record of a language lesson, where we are given the record of a French dictation in French and then the English translation that follows. What is obviously curious about the English translation is that it records all the commands of the dictation as well as the dictation itself, that is, the English translation spells out both the sentences being dictated *and* the punctuation commands. As critics Shelly Sunn Wong and Lisa Lowe have pointed out, this familiar and mundane scene of a grammar lesson resonates in the colonial context of Korea. The scene calls forth French missionaries' systematic colonization of Korea in the early twentieth century; it also reminds us of the central linguistic colonization to which Korea has been subjected, the dominant fact of modern Korean history: the Japanese occupation from 1910 to 1945. The language lesson is the sign of colonization.[29]

This coercive moment will be repeated in various forms throughout the text. We have already seen the moment when the narrator was naturalized as a United States citizen, another moment of mirroring, of authorization through an imagistic identification: "you are American . . . [in] . . . their own image" (56). Religious affiliation is also seen as such a moment of coercive mirroring:

Q: WHO MADE THEE?

A: *God made me.*

Q: GOD WHO HAS MADE YOU IN HIS OWN LIKENESS.

A: *God who has made me in his own likeness. In His Own Image in His Own Resemblance, in His Own Copy, In His Own Counterfeit Presentment, in His Duplicate, in His Own Reproduction, in His Cast, in His Carbon, His Image and his Mirror. Pleasure in the image pleasure in the copy pleasure in the projection of likeness pleasure in the repetition. Acquiesce, to the correspondence.* (17–8)

Cha's text suggests that these levels of interpellation—from infantile development to national to colonial to religious indoctrination—in fact mime each other, blurring the lines between ontic and social formation.

At the same time, these moments of seemingly complete compliance bespeak resistance as well. Perhaps resistance needs to be located not outside of a cultural relay (that is simply not possible, as we have seen through *Dictée*) but rather *within* that relay, that dictaphonic structure. In that opening language dictation (1), the subject not only recites poorly ("stutters, stops") but also translates poorly, verbatim (by refusing to heed the understood punctuation commands and by transliterating rather than making the required diacritical marks), and thereby exposes the disciplinary purposes of the dictation. One might say that the narrator of *Dictée* makes a poor scribe by being, in fact, too literal, too faithful. If authority calls for assimilation (to and of itself), then *Dictée* repeatedly exposes the necessary *imperfection* (incompletion) of that call—necessary because, as we have just seen, perfect identification with the Law can in fact only parody and expose that Big Other as an empty signifier, infinitely reproducible.

In the instance of Cha's version of the catechism, the narrator's parodic submission reveals the ironies of the demand in the first place for all to submit to the "One," the "Him." Furthermore, what Lacan would call the "subject-supposed-to-know" reveals itself as a source of clichés. Pushing the limits of Cha's aesthetics of repetition, one arrives at the inimitable as anything but that. Quite the contrary, the inimitable has the potential to initiate nothing but imitation, nothing but reproduction—a promiscuity of "the word made flesh." If dictation as form signals a model of conversion that transfers the individual into a subject of discourse through the repetition of form, a regulated reproduction, then *Dictée* provides the countermodel by which one sees the *in*discrimination of such regulation.

In a short video piece entitled "Re Dis Appearing" (1977), Cha uses a formal device to explore this strategy of translation-as-subversion. The video shows word cards while the narrating voice doubles itself in what seems like a translation: each French word is followed by its English translation. But as the video progresses, the voices overlap and the translation reverses, again and again, effecting a crisscross effect whereby one cannot tell which language is translating which. The temporal sequence of the narrative is also disturbed, creating almost a playback effect. The actual content also circles back on itself, ending where the video begun: "Commence. Begin. Fin. End." In other words, order and teleology are being made irrelevant, confounding our faith in the presence normally promised by the visual and in the temporality normally secured by the narrative.

Cha's aesthetics thus insist as much on the principle of sameness as on the principle of difference. Sameness can be at once fascistic *and* a strategy of intervention (that is, correspondences that enact *unauthorized* forms of reproduction). By not allowing for the mobility and complacency of translation, Cha suggests that it is precisely the radical contingency of terms such as "alien" and "original"—the mobility of their signification—that forms the basis for and finally offers a critique of both colonial *and* nationalist discourses of origin. Thus in a passage such as the "catechism" just cited, Cha disrupts patriarchal and colonial discourse by miming the very principles of mimesis initiated by the discourse of power.

With these scenarios of interpellation, we are clearly not far from the Freudian territory of identity as power, paralysis, and love. Even as Cha exposes power's paralyzing sameness ("Acquiesce to the correspondence"), she also acknowledges its hypnotic pleasures. As shown in my discussion of hypnosis, power facilitates identification, which makes community possible. Cha's passages bring our attention to another issue raised by the Freud essay: What of the libidinal (if not sexual) love and satisfaction in the act of group identification? In cruder terms, what of the pleasure of that paralysis? It is the production as well as the prohibition inhering in Cha's two scenarios that I now want to pursue. As Lowe writes, in Alarcón and Kim's anthology, "[i]maginary identification furnishes the effects of pleasure that may be exploited by a state apparatus to enlist subjects in its operations" (61). Yet Cha's work also suggests that "the effects of pleasure" may not be easily dismissable as "bad" pleasure, nor could we ignore the possibility that *all* acts of identification might function this way, might furnish pleasure. That is, all identification might be produced through imagistic repetition *and* be pleasurable ("pleasure in the image pleasure in the copy"), however coercive.

What does it mean to claim pleasure in that coercion, in that moment (as Freud describes it) of almost self-annihilating fright? In *The Freudian Subject*, Mikkel Borch-Jacobsen juxtaposes the *mise en scène* of identity with that identity's *mise en abîme*:

> [I]dentity, as such, is not susceptible to identification; *it does not identify itself*. . . .
>
> For to say *what* I am is relatively easy—that is even how I assure myself beyond all possible doubt: to paraphrase Descartes, I am what I think, wish, fantasize, feel, and so on. But to say *who* I am—who thinks, who wishes, who fantasizes in me—is no longer in *my* power. That question immediately draws me beyond myself, beyond my representations, towards a point . . . "the point of otherness" . . . where I am another, the other who gives me my identity.[30]

Since the "I" can only exist, rigorously speaking, as an unconscious certitude, it can only enjoy itself through a detour—a detour that is afforded by mimesis: "I am another, the other who gives me my identity." The political implications of this statement are more than a little startling, for if one enjoys one's identity as an other, then cultural dictation must be part and parcel of cultural enjoyment.

If *that* is the case, then our understanding of the concepts of cultural assimilation and commensurability would need to accommodate the seduction and necessity of social injunctions. This element of enjoyment and of necessity (of the other) has been critically missing from analyses of the marginalized or colonized subject. Denial or negation of those injunctions will not sufficiently address the patterns of cultural and political subjectivation. Indeed, both the "hypochondriacal" lessons of Maxine Hong Kingston in *The Woman Warrior* and Song's calls to himself at the end of David Henry Hwang's *M. Butterfly* show the impossibility of detaching social injunctions from ontological demands; the voice within has always already anticipated the voice without. Rather than denying the circularity of this autobiographical dictation or positing a subject outside of it, Cha locates the critique of identity within, not outside of, identity's mimetic functions.

The opening pages of *Dictée* demonstrate the emergence of the speaking subject *as an echo*:

> She mimicks [*sic*] the speaking. That might resemble speech. (Anything at all.) Bared noise, groan, bits torn from words . . . she resorts to mimicking the gestures with the mouth. The entire lower lip would lift upwards then sink back to its original place. She would then gather both lips and protrude them in a pout taking in the breath that might utter something. (One thing. Just one.) But the breath falls away. With a slight

tilting of her head backwards, she would gather the strength in her shoulders and remain in this position. (3)[31]

This Beckettian, infantlike creature coming to speech dramatizes the beginning of speech as imitation. Since listening remains one of the only physical activities of the human body that occurs simultaneously inside and outside the body, we might understand listening here to be *initiating* a boundary contestation. The sound that penetrates the infant is also the sound after which the infant fashions him/herself; the moment of shattering retroactively constitutes the possibility of boundary not experienced before. The infant mimes the sound he/she hears and, in that act of mimicry, experiences him/herself as at once possible and other—what Lacan calls the loss of self to self. Coming to listening and then speech condition coming-to-being. The speaking subject serves as, and is conditioned by, the dictaphonic structure, a voice-relay: "She allows others. In place of her . . . [t]he others each occupying her" (3). So there is no speaking subject as such that is not already an echo.

This speech lesson clearly recalls the French lesson already discussed. Cha clearly wants to imply that such a linguistic invasion can occur at a more ontological level. The point is not, however, to read these two sections as a reduction or universalization of the political to the ontological, that the colonial language merely exposes fundamental linguistic appropriations. Rather, the point is to understand the constitution of the subject as always already political. There is no subject without "the others in place of her." Consequently, the reader is not allowed to sentimentalize a prior, "original, native" voice. We have not been allowed, in other words, to imagine we might know a time before dictation. Here then we have the central political conceit of the text: the dictaphonic structure of linguistic interpellation: that language *is* occupation, *and* it is coercive.

The source of the speech injunction in that vocal mouthing scene is deliberately unlocatable because Cha is suggesting that injunction may be a condition of speech itself. It is with the echo itself that the echo identifies. Origin and any identification with it are seen as infinitely regressive, infinitely displaying others-in-place-of-the-self. *Dictée* offers an autobiography in the form of cultural dictation, but a dictation whose source is significantly, mournfully, *and* strategically unlocatable.

There can be no primary identification that is not already a secondary identification. We are seeing in this passage something more elementary than the Lacanian mirror-stage of misrecognition and subsequent identification: that is, more primal in that we are seeing an identification that is based on mimesis *alone*. The voice is not aspiring to some imaginary even if unrecognized whole, but the act of echo itself confirms the speaking subject. What Borch-Jacobsen had begun to tease out and what Cha demonstrates explicitly here is the possibility that mimesis might in fact *precondi-*

tion any identificatory possibilities. (Imagine the infant making a sound like "ma"; the sound is an instinctual source of pleasure to the child, and the parents' pleasure intensifies the pleasure for the child.) This suggestion would, for instance, resolve a seeming contradiction between Judith Butler and Borch-Jacobsen on the priorities of identification versus libidinal experiences. In a footnote in *Bodies That Matter*, Judith Butler writes that "whereas Borch-Jacobsen offers an interesting theory of how identification precedes and forms the ego, he tends to assert the priority of identification to any libidinal experience, where I would insist that identification is itself a passionate or libidinal assimilation" (246). I would suggest, however, that the two positions need not be mutually exclusive if we understand that Borch-Jacobsen has situated mimesis as preceding identification and the libidinal experience as simultaneous with it. In other words, the "passionate or libidinal *assimilation*" (my emphasis) that *is* identification for Butler also carries with it assimilative and mimetic impulses.

This is of course the very idea that threatens the logic of Freud's project in *Group Psychology*. The concept (that identification is always a libidinal experience, be it identification with group or "love") was embodied in his essay, but he could not afford to state it explicitly because of his attachment to separating identification from libidinal cathexis (as part of his efforts to keep eros distinct from politics). Consequently, we may return to Freud and draw the conclusion he resisted: in the formation of a group identity, it is not that "individual dissimilarities" are removed by some kind of collective unconscious such as a "racial unconscious" but rather that the promise of a "group" is precisely an image that offers itself as a mirror of similitude, as an image and promise of such collectivity. Hypnosis—with all its connotations of power, fright, and identification in his essay—does not bring out the racial unconscious. It *is* the racial unconscious.

The Promise

> It is the dream with which I identify myself
> —Lacoue-Labarthe

Freud's struggles with identifying identification at the nexus of the individual and the group is profoundly symptomatic of the problem of *reading* race even today. One of the central contradictions of Freud's essay was the fact that on the one hand, race is seen as instinctual, deeply embedded in the unconscious: interior, homogenizing, foundational, indifferent to individual differences. On the other hand, race is that which emerges from the outside, exerts influence to the extent of coercion. In this sense, we are seeing a theoretical specificity about racial identification that is different from gender identification: not that gender identification does not involve the group, but that it is structured through an exchange with, rather than the consolidation of, collective identity; whereas racial identification presents itself as always already a question of collective allegiance. This collectivity then promises to confer on the individual his or her individuality, his or her personhood.

The term that has been missing from the apparent dichotomy of identification and object relations is fantasy: the role fantasy (understood precisely as the *absence* of the object) plays in identification. As Freud himself suggests, certain aspects of the identificatory mechanism operate, as in melancholia, to annihilate the object. He writes: "[Identification] behaves like the derivative of the first, *oral* phase of the organization of the libido, in which the object *we long for and prize is being assimilated* by eating and is in that way annihilated as such" (37; my emphasis). In a way, we again encountering the correlation between cultural and psychoanalytic "assimilation": the object of imitation is introjected and then replaced by the "imagined" (in both Lacanian and Althusserian senses) relation of subject to itself. Out of the death of the object, fantasy is born. It is precisely that move of replacement— *from object-relation to an imagined relation to one's self*—that gives identification, personal or social, its hold. That momentarily emptied space is the space of the subject. Identification is completely object-driven in the sense that the self is the promised object, the fantasy of personhood. In the landscape of identification, the sublime object of ideology (that surplus value, that body-within-body) turns out to be nothing less than the promise of the self.

Kaja Silverman accounts for a version of this guarantee-of-the self in her exposition on what she calls "the dominant fiction," of which race may be considered an example, although, as I will demonstrate later, the dominant fiction of race demands a rereading of a paradox in Silverman's account. But first I will begin with what Silverman means by the term. She argues in *Male Subjectivity at the Margins* that "ideological belief . . . occurs at the moment when an image which the subject consciously knows to be culturally fabricated nevertheless succeeds in being recognized or acknowledged as a 'pure, naked perception of reality.'"[32] Dominant fictions thus work through a kind of fetishistic denial: *I know that is not so, but . . .* Silverman goes on to elaborate on this blind faith: "within every society, hegemony is keyed to certain privileged terms, around which there is a kind of doubling up of belief" creating what Silverman calls "ideological stress points" (17). It makes sense to think about race as a dominant fiction, as powerful as gender is in affecting and organizing individual subjectivity, and it makes even more sense to examine racial identification as an ideological stress point.

For Silverman, the dominant fiction consists of two kinds of mutually coercive identifications: the "imaginary" that is specular and forms the "moi" and the "symbolic" that is structural and operates at the level of the fantasmatic:

In other words, the fantasmatic . . . helps the moi "recognize" itself by eroticizing those images which are commensurate with its representational imperatives. Conversely, a particularly imaginary identification might conform to unconscious desires, but brings with it values capable of shifting the ideological significance of the fantasmatic. (7)

We might do well to question the very distinction between symbolic and imaginary identifications, for the fantasmatic by definition operates on both levels. The seemingly secondary processes of identifications in our lives in fact function at a very primary level.[33] But it should be noted that "dominant fiction" for Silverman has the specific content of "the ideological 'reality' [which] solicits our faith above all else in the unity of the family, and the adequacy of the male subject" (8); and that for Silverman, sexual difference is *the* primary dominant fiction. Consequently, even as she points out the inability to distinguish secondary identification from primary (22), a few pages later she distinguishes the secondary as "social" (28). In order to protect the integrity of sexual difference and the Oedipal complex, Silverman has to maintain the conceptual division she demythifies, resulting in a simultaneous deconstruction and affirmation of the presence of secondary identification.

The aspect of Silverman's argument that I find most instructive is the structure of "doubling" that undergirds psychic faith. This "doubling" effect helps us understand the hold that a synthetic concept such as race nonetheless exerts: the ideology of race so often enjoys a double status as an (inside) drive and an (outside) object. Race thus demands to be experienced as *at once, contradictorily,* intensely private/subjective and public/objective, a doubling. I suggest that, for Cha, *race is one of those particular fictions of identification that identifies identification.* It offers a parable of the parable, a myth of the myth. In speaking of the formation of a German nationalism through the Nazi myth, Lacoue-Labarthe offers a reading of the power of myth that proves to be relevant to this discussion. Specifically, he speaks of the myth of racial identification as a means of uniting a group of people by furnishing "an *image* with which one can identify oneself."[34] He focuses on the *in*visible, non-empirical aspect of racial identification:

[A]bove all, [the Nazi myth] designates this identity as the identity of something which is not given, neither as fact, nor as discourse, but which is *dreamed.* . . . that a race is above all the principle and the locus of a mythical power. If the Nazi myth was initially determined as the myth of the "race," it is because it is the myth of Myth, or the myth of creative power of myth in general. *As if* races were themselves, above all, the *dreamed types.* (305–7; my emphasis)

The key words "as if" signal the mechanisms of (re)presentation through which race as an ideology *enters* like a dream already there: what Lacoue-

Labarthe gives us is the logic of identification as simultaneously original and originating, that is, a process by which an external construct at once originates *and* historicizes itself: constructing, in effect, the event *and* the alibi.[35]

In a section named "Clio/History," Cha meditates on the construction of history itself as such a process of myth-making and type-casting:

> She makes complete her duration. As others have made complete theirs: rendered incessant, obsessive myth, rendered immortal their acts without the leisure to examine whether the parts false . . . according to History's revision.
>
> *Truth embraces with it all other abstentions other than itself.*
> *Outside Time. Outside Space. Parallels other durations . . . Oblivious to*
> *itself. . . .*
>
> She calls the name Jeanne d'Arc three times.
> She calls the name Ah Joong Kun five times.
>
> There is no people without a nation, no people without ancestry. (28)

History poses itself as transcendent of time ("outside time") but also always in time ("parallels other durations.") The ritualistic naming of heroic figures (Joan of Arc and the narrator's mother) enacts the call for female progenitors, both biological and cultural. Characteristic of Cha, this longing for foremothers is immediately qualified by a consciousness of the negative implications of such myth-making as well: "no people without a nation, no people without ancestry." Cha reminds us here that classification is also how nations and families organize and mobilize themselves to productive and inhibiting ends. This is why it is insufficient to say that Cha deconstructs social identities such as race and nationhood, for she is painfully aware of the inseparability of construction from deconstruction.

One of the most persistent "obsessive myths" of history then, I propose, is the idea of race itself. Lacoue-Labarthe offers us a way to think about racial identification *as* that myth that structures or that works to collapse but needs to maintain some kind of temporal division between "present" versus "prior" or more "primal" identification. Borrowing Lacoue-Labarthe's insights into Nazism as paradigmatic group formation through/as identification, we see the *idea* of race as that which must be experienced as *at once* and *contradictorily* the most private/subjective and the most public/objective. Earlier I wrote that what Freud uncovered was not the racial unconscious but an idea of race created retrospectively through the seduction and promise of collectivity. We can add yet another nuance to this hypnotic mirror: it is above all a mirror that reassures with its guarantee of history—

or, for Freud, prehistory. In *Group Psychology*, Freud does not uncover but has in essence *created* the racial unconscious. It is in Freud's confusion about the levels of identification and his inability to neatly account for his own metaphor's dual status of being an [inside] drive and an [outside] object that we can locate breakdown between individual and the group. There, too, we can begin to see that racial unconsciousness may not exist as a bedrock or foundation but rather as a technology. Moreover, it is a technology that must be disguised as nontechnical and internal.

One might say that the power of the race-myth rests within its *givenness*, its self-evidence. In Michael Omi and Howard Winant's *Racial Formation of the United States: From the 1960s to the 1980s*, the authors propose racial consciousness as ideology par excellence, the fulfillment of the logic of an idea by which the movement of history is explained as one consistent process. To say that race is fantasy is not to deny the material and political conditions that exist. (After all, the vicissitudes attending the theories of race that Omi and Winant recount demonstrate precisely that race is a changing concept responding to social and political demands.) On the contrary, only by recognizing race-as-fantasy can we begin to contest particular sets of assumptions. Omi and Winant point the way toward reconceptualizing race as an arena of contestation. Although their discussions remain devoid of psychoanalytic vocabulary, they come close to identifying fantasy as the structuring principle of racial formation. Their argument is worth retrieving at some length here:

> An approach based on the concept of racial formation should treat race in the United States as a fundamental *organizing principle* of social relations. . . .

> At the micro level, race is a matter of individuality, of the formation of *identity* . . . the ways in which we understand ourselves and interact with others, the *structuring* of our practical activity. . . . At the macro level, race is a matter of collectivity, of the formation of social structures. . . .

> The racial order is organized and enforced by continuity and reciprocity between these two "levels" of social relations. The micro- and macro-levels, however, are *only analytically distinct*. In our lived experience, in politics, in culture, in economic life, they are continuous and reciprocal.

> The theory of racial formation then suggests that racial phenomenons penetrate and link the two "levels" of social relationships. (my emphasis)[36]

First, Omi and Winant's thesis hinges on a conceptualization of race as akin to a fantasmatic, organizing principle, which traverses both public and private experiences. The psychoanalytic concept of the fantasmatic, which I defined in the previous chapter as the structuring principle that breaks down the division between what is "real and material" and what is "dreamed and illusory," proves to be particularly useful in helping to understand Omi and Winant's project to situate racial ideology as neither "essence" nor "illusion." Omi and Winant warn: "there is the continuous temptation to think of race as essence . . . and there is also an opposite temptation to see it as mere illusion, which an ideal social order would eliminate" (69). Second, Omi and Winant's formulation of race as operating on mutually reinforcing macro- and microlevels speaks to, albeit from different coordinates, the very problem of primary versus secondary processes that I have been discussing. "Racial phenomena penetrate and link the two 'levels' of social relationships" insofar as those two levels reinforce one another. They *mime* one another. But we must remember that mimesis is an act that implies both sameness and a preconditioning distance.

From afar, we have returned to distances. The narrator journeys "home" to Korea eighteen years later to find community in the form of memory: "My brother. You are all the rest all the others are you. . . . The stone pavement stained where you fell still remains dark. Eighteen years passed . . . Mother . . . We left here in this memory still fresh, still new. I speak another tongue . . . This is how distant I am" (85). *We left here in this memory*: departure and return form a circle of desire, and it is within the chase toward both past and future that "origin" can be conceived. As poet Robert Hass once wrote, "Longing, we say, because desire is full / of endless distances."[37] The loss of origin in *Dictée*—simultaneously racial, familial, national, and ontological—speaks of desire and a critique of that desire. The immigrant and the "post"-colonial subject share a similar problem: they are subjects constituted at the site of displacement. And by speaking of the problem of origin, I do not at all mean the difficulty of retrieving a proper origin but rather the impossibility of origin as an empty sign that is always set up as something devoutly to be wished for. Racial "identity," as one of the most powerful forms of collective fantasy, secured at the conjunction of the macro and micro (in Omi and Winant's terms), fails—indeed, cannot afford—to recognize the conditions of its own inception, its own fantasmatic beginnings.

DIFFICULT LOVES

Anna Deavere Smith and the Politics of Grief

Could politics ever be an expression of love?

—Ralph Ellison

Although race studies holds much intellectual capital in academic research today, the history of racial grief in America—
along with its accompanying burdens of conscience, consciousness, guilt,
and *ressentiment*—has made our capacity to communicate our thoughts
and feelings about these dark inheritances far from adequate. There is still
tremendous confusion in contemporary American society about how to approach the task of racial healing; indeed, at times, it seems as if race relations in America is doomed to play out a tragedy of endless retribution.

In a powerful dramatization of contemporary racial trauma in America,
playwright and performance artist Anna Deavere Smith records in her
docudrama *Twilight: Los Angeles, 1992* the aftermath of one such cycle of
retribution: three days of burning, looting, and killing in east Los Angeles
in response to the Rodney King verdict. From its inception, the King case
was mired in the history of black–white antagonism, and the ensuing riots
advanced that antagonism to encompass Korean Americans in the neighborhood under siege. This incident tells not just of racial rage but also of
grief—and the impossibility of taking on that grief when who is mourning
and what is being mourned for are contingent and conflicted. Through the
words of Mrs. Young-Soon Han, a former liquor store owner, Smith gives
us a sense of how binding and how insupportable it is to be caught between
grief and grievance; the ensuing monologue, based on transcribed interviews, is called "Swallowing the Bitterness":

[African Americans] finally found that justice exists in this society. . . . And I wonder if that is really justice . . . to get their rights in this way. . . . I waseh [*sic*] swallowing the bitternesseh, sitting here alone and watching them . . . and in a way I was happy for them and I felt glad for them. At leasteh [*sic*] they got something back, you know. Just let's forget Korean victims or other victims who are destroyed by them. They have fought for their rights . . . over two centuries . . . and I have a lot of sympathy and understanding for them, because of their effort and sacrificing, other minorities, like Hispanic or Asians. maybe we have to suffer more by mainstream. you know, that's why I understand, and then I like to be part of their 'joyment. but . . . I had mixed feeling as soon as I heard the verdict.

I wish I could live together with eh [*sic*] Blacks. but after the riots there were too much differences. the fire is still there.[1]

In the splintering landscape of grief, identification and sympathy are at once imperative and fraught. For whom do you grieve, and how do you do so, in this world of layered victimizations, violence, and enmity? In many ways the question of race, what Gunnar Myrdal called the American dilemma in 1944, continues to present today the central site of national grief today. The task of integrating a history of fierce difference, social damage, and psychical injury into one nation remains one of the focal tasks of American nation-making. And the work of American healing needs to be examined, not only from the perspective of dominant culture, but also from the vantage points of those who have been made into objects of national guilt. On Smith's multiethnic stage, it is precisely the ethical question of point of view that is being explored and, ironically, that is being criticized by critics in relation to the work.

I begin by describing Smith's theatrical method. Having interviewed over two hundred people with varying degrees of connections to the incident, Smith selects about fifty representatives from her collection of transcripts. She then, onstage, recites verbatim excerpts from those interviews while mimicking the interviewees' physical presence, including accents, slips of speech, and stammering. These selected and edited speeches come from men and women of a wide range of age, race, and class differences: from bystanders to principals in the events, from the police to the street gang, from the academic to the housewife.[2] The resulting overall structure provides a series of monologues in which people of different racial and economic backgrounds "have their say."

Smith's theater has been heralded by the media as a celebratory bringing-together of unheard voices, as a kind of multiculturalism in action. Literary and drama critics have also construed Smith's art as a form of racial healing. Both Ann Pellegrini and Peggy Phelan, for instance, have described

Smith's theater as a "talking cure," with Pellegrini characterizing Smith's work as "literally enact[ing] the possibility of recognizing the other in the self and the self in the other."[3] Yet, contrary to these interpretations, Smith's drama seems intent on highlighting the impossibility of finding such a cure. Smith herself writes in her introduction to the printed version of *Twilight*: "sometimes there is the expectation that inasmuch as I am doing 'social drama,' I am looking for *solutions* to social problems. In fact, though, I am looking at the *processes* of the problems" (xxiv). When we turn to the performance itself, the assembly of impassioned, conflictual testimonies repeatedly reminds the audience that there may never be enough expressions of individual or national justice, reparation, guilt, pain, or anger to make up for the racial wounds cleaved into the American psyche—remembered by both the dominant and the marginalized alike as inconsolability itself.

Smith opens her docudrama with a testimony from Rudy Salas, a Mexican American sculptor and painter whose words dramatize a difference between grievance and grief. In Smith's recitation of Salas's monologue, we hear first a strong voice of grievance. Smith-as-Salas recounts with precision the abuse perpetrated on him by the white police when he was a young man and earlier on by his white teachers in grammar school. (Salas's speech is recorded in the published version of the playscript with Smith's annotations of gestures.)

> [F]irst grade, they started telling me I was inferior because I was a Mexican and that's where (*He hits the table several times, taps, twenty-three taps until the line "the enemy" and then on "nice white teachers" his hand sweeps the table*) I realized I had an enemy and that enemy was those nice white teachers. (2)

Salas encounters "whiteness" as denigrating authority. For Salas, however, it is much easier to name racist acts than to process racism psychically. Salas's narrative begins to veer into a curiously abstract and self-pathologizing language when it tries to describe the emotional repercussions of those confrontations:

> It's not an enemy I hated. It's not a hate thing, the insanity that I carried with me started when I took the beating from the police. Okay, that's where the insanity came in. . . . one night the cop really tore me up bad. . . . They took me to a room and they locked the door behind me and there was four guys, four cops there kicking me in the head. . . . So from that day on I, I had a hate in me, even now. I don't like to hate, never do . . . and I still get things like that. . . . I still have that prejudice against whites. I'm not a racist! . . . [My son] Stephen was in Stanford! Came home one weekend to sing with the band. One night cop pulled a gun at his head. . . . How you think a father feels, stuff that happened to me fifty

years ago happened to my son? Man! They didn't tell me right away because it would make me sick, it would make me sick . . . and my oldest
son, Rudy, Didn't they, Margaret [his wife], insult him one time and they
pulled you over. . . . the Alhambra cops, they pulled you over and aww,
man. . . . My enemy. (1–7)

Alongside the exactness of his grievances, there is a strain of sorrow in this
speech that resists clarity, that expresses itself through contradictions and
aporia. The emotional impact and aftereffects of those racist encounters
become reduced to "it," "madness," "insanity," "this thing that came in."
This articulate man vigilantly recalls his history of being discriminated
against, but when it comes to the affective consequences of that discrimination, he is at a loss for appropriate words, stunned by "the thing" that "gets
in his head and makes him sick" (1–7). Thus, even as Salas understands the
injustice of racism, he still internalizes—indeed, pathologizes—his reactions
to it.

By opening her performance with the figure of Rudy Salas, Smith immediately both breaks down the understanding of the Los Angeles race riots
as a black-versus-white conflict and undermines the hope that grievance,
like rage, can adequately do the work of mourning.[4] Since there is no external structure to house the painful effects of racism, its complex legacies of
anger, shame, and guilt can only be internalized: the "thing" that "gets inside." (Anyone who has encountered racism face to face recognizes those
wordless and complicated feelings of humiliation—all the more so for knowing all the while, on a rational level, that it is the perpetrator who should be
feeling shamed. Yet the "self" takes on the shadow of that hatred. The elegiac strain of Salas's words testifies to that reflection.) These formative
moments of racialization and subjection at the hands of the law can hardly
be addressed by law. Even if the discriminated person could access that
arena, there stands another barrier: the legal sphere presents a distinctly
rational and institutional space. Within that world, which speaks the language of the rational and has no room for the nonrational, grief can express
itself only as a kind of irrationality: Salas's self-diagnosed "insanity."

This opening monologue initiates the theme of enmity throughout the
docudrama but also engraves in relief against that horizon the figure of grief.
Grief is the thing left over after grievance has had its say. The play's simple
structure, its "lineup" of plaintiffs, rather than resolving the issues at stake,
instead chisels out pockets of darkness around each "speaker's" testimony,
negative images left by each speaker that cast shadows on the speeches to
follow. Smith herself in her introduction calls *Twilight* an attempt to explore
"shades" of loss (xxi). Her technical fluency in the rapid transition from
character to character throughout the play may suggest facile displacement,
but the content of the performance belies that ease. The audience is made

to sustain the testimonies and their cumulative layers of unresolved grief; they cannot "move on" to the next "speaker" without carrying the shadows of those that came before—just as Smith's own body carries the memories of all these figures. In this way, Smith's docudrama enacts a form of melancholia, by opening the audience up to a series of multiple "presences" that flicker and vanish but do not wholly depart. Smith's work demonstrates that there is no simple "moving on," no complete shedding of the afterlife of these affidavits even after they have fallen into silence.

Smith herself points towards this notion of the residue later in the performance when she repeats the report of the county coroner, who, after the riot, speaks of the all-too-material, "disarticulated" (193) human remains that resist both bureaucratic classification and social rituals of mourning and resolution. Smith-as-Dean Gilmour tries to account for his findings:

> Human remains? Human remains is what we . . . you and I leave behind. . . . You also, after the fact, have animal activity. Dogs and . . . the other critters come along and will disarticulate bodies. Uh, rats, uh, all kinds of, uh, varmints and stuff. . . . Oh, here we go. Forty-one gunshot wounds. These are the races. Okay, but these are not official. Some of these are not. Twenty-six black, eighteen Hispanic, ten Caucasian, two Asian. . . . Gunshot wounds were forty, uh, traffics were six. Four assaults, Four arsons and four others. Sex were fifty-one males and seven females. (193–5)

The list does not make sense or add up, so to speak, because the categorization (be it racial, gender, or mathematical) itself highlights the unintelligibility of what is being confronted. These remains, made meaningless by the coroner's proliferation of medical and ethnic categories of body parts, stand as poignant metaphors for the stubborn remnants of grief. By the end of Smith's performance, key words that are meant to address grief—words such as "justice" and "reparation"—begin to take on peculiar and unstable meanings: a crisis not of no meaning but of too much meaning.

The difference—indeed, perhaps even incommensurability—between grief and grievance is very much the topic of Smith's theater. The emotional impact of testimonies such as that of Rudy Salas accrues throughout the performance and remains unresolved long after the curtains close. We are reminded that grievance, which has the guise of agency, in fact does not guarantee political action. Smith's docudrama raises the question of what it would take to sufficiently recognize a historically disenfranchised person in a democratic body politic that has not lived up to its own promise of equal rights and equal protection. Indeed, the philosophical and moral implications of conferring legal recognition have long been a standing problem in American history, especially at the site of race. American nationalism, galvanized by the dream of multiculturalism, is simultaneously founded on and split by racial differences. In his treatise *Multiculturalism: Examining the Politics of Recognition*, Charles Taylor suggests that multiculturalism itself embodies an inherent paradox of "recognition." According to him, the fundamental democratic premise of equality extends a philosophical promise of recognition. This recognition, however, is built on two competing terms: universalism on the one hand (the assumption of equality and sameness of all citizens) and incommensurable difference on the other (the belief that everyone must be recognized for his or her unique differences and cannot be compared to anyone else). I suggest that the competition between racial difference and racial allegiance in America creates multiple, even contradictory layers of meaning within what it means to recognize someone else and what it means to be recognized by someone. As a theater of meta-representation (a literalization of giving-voice-to), Smith's docudrama acts out these complications surrounding notions of recognition, representation, and their limits.

A traditional method of intervention in the history of racism has indeed been the demand for public recognition. This often takes the form of transforming the marginalized, racialized person from being an object bearing *grief* to being a subject speaking *grievance*. This move is thought to be a procedure by which a culturally disenfranchised individual or group of people come to occupy a place of speech and agency. This process, however, raises several related issues. First, the promise of acquiring public recognition, while not without its potentials, cannot really grant subjecthood to the disenfranchised since, strictly speaking, to be "recognized" is still to occupy an object position. To be recognized means that there has to be a recognizing agent, authority and dominant culture in this case. Second, adopting the position of the plaintiff may reverse the political value of alienating difference, but it does not address American culture's underlying ambivalence toward difference. Hence while grievance can be calculated and named, the underlying structure of differentiation continues to generate its history of abjection and coercions.

Third, the move from agencylessness to agency is not a mere matter of reversal; for instance, grievance for those socially not allowed to grieve is a different matter, with different implications, than grievance for those who have always been given access to voicing such grief. In the maelstrom of racial melancholia, the Freudian melancholic characteristic of being the complainer is a privilege not allowed the melancholic "object," who must live with unallowable and inexpressible grief. To put it in another way, public grievance is a social forum and luxury to which the racially melancholic minorities have little or no access. If the move from grief to grievance, for example, aims to provide previously denied agency, then it stands as a double-edged solution, since to play the plaintiff is to cultivate, for many critics, a cult of victimization.[5] So the gesture of granting agency through grievance confers agency on the one hand and rescinds it on the other. As a result, for many concerned with improving the conditions of marginalized peoples, the focus on psychical injury and its griefs is strategically harmful and to be studiously avoided. But this also means that we are so worried about depriving disenfranchised people of their agency that we risk depriving them of the time and space to grieve. A final problem is that since justice based on grievance and compensation tends to rely on the logic of commensurability and quantifiability, it is ill-equipped to confront that which is incommensurable and unquantifiable. (In this way we have not progressed far beyond the issues ignited by *Brown v. Board*, where the legal desire for provable and quantifiable social claims provoked uneasiness even for those proffering that proof.)[6] In short, we as a society are at ease with the discourse of grievance but terribly ill at ease in the face of grief.

Rudy Salas's speech incorporates the inarticulable loss that *is* the injury inflicted by racism ("It's not a hate thing, the insanity that I carried with me started when I took the beating from the police" [2]). It reminds us once again that, for the racial minority, the "object" that has been lost is the myth of an integral, inviolable self. The racially melancholic minority is doubly versed in the art of losing. The racially denigrated person has to forfeit the full security of his/her imaginary integrity (a process that, in psychoanalytic terms, is arguably necessary for anyone entering the symbolic) but then is forced to take in (rather than project that lack to another) and reidentify with that loss: a double loss. These layered losses for the racialized subject are then sanctioned, both legally and culturally.

The project of mediating among forgiveness, remembrance, and progress is a difficult but urgent one, and central to starting this effort is the distinction of grief from grievance. The confusion of grievance with grief on the part of the aggrieved racialized person, Smith demonstrates, only generates perverse versions of justice. In a chilling testimony from the chairperson of the "Free the LA Four Plus Defense Committee," Smith-as-Paul Parker rehearses the historical grievances of African Americans, insisting that America must confront the ways in which the effects of slavery are far from over and are in fact active in the ongoing process of racializing African Americans. Unlike Rudy Salas, whose lapses into wordlessness dramatize his incorporation of loss, Parker seems to have mastered his melancholic loss by asserting the subjective agency historically denied to him. But upon closer examination, this solution raises perturbing specters about what it means for the voiceless to acquire voice *within* the existing system of power.

It becomes clear that Parker's call for solidarity in the name of grievance operates through a disturbing logic of comparison. Beginning with a call for an authentic and loyal black identity that insists that "there can be no sympathy for the white man . . . not from real brothers and sisters," Smith-as-Parker concludes by slipping into a voice of discrimination: "we did not burn down our own neighborhood, we burned down these Koreans . . . the Koreans was like the Jew in the day and we put them in check. We got rid of all these Korean stores over here" (175). What underlies Parker's notion of fairness is a logic of commensurability ("an eye for an eye") displaced onto Korean immigrants that justifies violence. Here we see a person who, having himself been discriminated against, is now demanding racial allegiance in equally absolute terms and does not seem to see the irony or horror provoked by his echoing bigotry.

Parker's version of justice, however, is disturbing in more profound ways as well; it portrays a logic of identification in relation to authority that forces us to rethink the very possibility of autonomy or agency within such a reified power structure. In order for Parker to transform himself from an object of denigration to a speaking subject of grievance, he has chosen to assume the voice of denigration. This process suggests that political agency for those already operating within a deficit is likely to mean the assumption of oppressive authority—a visceral, "real-life" demonstration of what was happening in that bathroom in *The Woman Warrior*. If, in Fanon's words, "the black man *is* comparison"[7] (that is, a figure suffering from injunctive comparison to and rejection by the implicit standard of whiteness), then Paul Parker is repeating that same logic of comparison and rejection, with different players in position. He has created an other other, "the Koreans," in order to repeat the violent form of that othering from which he suffers. Parker consolidates his blackness the way that whiteness has historically consolidated itself: in counterdistinction to a racialized other. With Parker's testimony, we see a particularly vivid example of the insidious logic of identity, where a person who suffered from unbearable discrimination can say with no apparent self-reflection that he is "putting a race of people on notice." As Diana Fuss succinctly states, "racial identity and racist practice alike are forged through the bonds of identification"(14).[8]

But what exactly do we mean by identification? Before we go any further, we need to address this word and its loaded history. As the subjective corollary—indeed, the *vehicle*—for interpersonal negotiation, "identification" is pivotal to discussions of racial identity and dynamics. In its technical and psychoanalytic origins, the term denotes the elaborate, mediating process that relates self to other, subject to object, inside to outside. It is also a term that gets frequently and loosely invoked to refer to a range of responses in theatrical and cinematic analyses. In Smith's work these different uses of the concept come to the fore because "identification" is at issue on so many levels. There is the character's internal identification (such as when I speak of Paul Parker's identification with oppressive authority); there is the performer's identification with her character (What does it mean that

Smith is "acting like" someone else?) and then there is the audience's identification with the character and/or the performer. These "levels" of identification are distinct, even at times conflicting, but they are also in dialogue
with one another—hence the complexity and power of Smith's work and
what it has to say about racial identification. In what follows I hope to provide a relevant, though by no means complete, analysis of the notion of identification as it develops out of psychoanalytic thinking; how it might eluci-
date the web of sympathies and antipathies informing this drama; and what
it tells us about the links among identity, grief, and politics.

Identification is most often taken either at its most transparent or at
its most byzantine incarnation. In theatrical contexts, identification is
frequently used by reviewers to refer to a phenomenological, vernacular
notion of spectatorial empathy always raised in discussions of theatrical
reception. Audience empathy or "audience identification" implies a cognition, even momentarily, of sameness: "I identify with what I see on stage
because I feel the same or can imagine feeling the same."

Identification as a psychoanalytic concept, on the other hand, denotes
an intricate psychical process underlying subject formation. (According to
the Oxford English Dictionary, the term "identification" in the modern sense
of a psychological process does not appear until the nineteenth century with
the advent of psychoanalysis.) Identification is crucially *not* the same as
identity, although it is what secures for the latter its mythology of integrity.
Identification organizes and instantiates identity. It is a fluid and repetitive
process that in a sense completely opposes the certitude of identity, providing an origin of identity that identity would just as soon forget in order to
maintain its own immediacy and wholeness.[9] Yet as the mechanism that
subtends the possibility and the limit of any given identity, identification
serves as the vehicle for interpersonal negotiation. In this sense, to specify
a "social identity" is redundant, since all identification is social in nature.[10]

Interestingly enough, this apparatus for interpersonal navigation has its
origins in conceptualizations of grief. It is in speaking of melancholia that
Freud first solidifies the notion of identification:

> First there existed an object-choice, the libido had attached itself to a
> certain person; then, owing to a real injury or disappointment concerned
> with the loved person, this object-relationship was undermined . . . but
> the free libido was withdrawn into the ego and not directed to another
> object. It did not find application there, however, in any one of several
> possible ways, but served simply to establish an *identification* of the ego
> with the abandoned object.[11]

Here Freud explains melancholic incorporation as a procedure whereby the
bereft recuperates and "takes in" the lost object by "identifying" with it.

Identification is thus a form of cannibalism and/or duplication. A fundamental relationship has been set up between identification and the compensation of loss. As such, identification may in fact be said to be, literally, an *expression* of grief.

This duality of identification as a compensation for and expression of grief creates several paradoxes within this process of consolation. First, it initiates a procedure of fulfillment that concurrently reinscribes loss: a substitution that is also a gravestone. Second, it explains the contradictory impulses that the melancholic griever exhibits toward the lost-object-now-me. For one of the curious aspects of melancholia—really, its pathos—is the fact that the incorporation of the lost object offers but a self-punishing pleasure. The recathexis with the lost object achieved through identification yields at best a tenuous, ghostly connection. Hence the bereft's relationship to the incorporated object is sustained as much by anger and denial as by love. The subsequent denigration of the object, now installed inside, acts out precisely this idiosyncratic dynamic of love and rejection.

This complex relationship to loss, furthermore, turns out *not* to remain within the sole custody of pathology. Critics such as Diana Fuss, Judith Butler, and Elin Diamond have all pointed out that in developing the role of melancholic identification Freud was in fact laying the groundwork for what he came to believe was a fundamental process of ego formation.[12] In *Identification Papers*, Diana Fuss calls identification "an embarrassingly ordinary process, a routine, habitual compensation for everyday loss of our love-objects" and suggests that our psychic landscape is in fact populated by a host of "phantoms" (1, 3) called up by identifications. Judith Butler also makes explicit links among identification, melancholia, and ego inception. In *The Psychic Life of Power*, Butler points out that "the account of melancholia is an account of how psychic and social domains are produced in relation to each other":

> [I]t is unclear that [the] ego can exist prior to its melancholia. The "turn" that marks the melancholic response to loss appears to initiate the redoubling of the ego as an object; only by turning back on itself does the ego acquire the status of a perceptual object. . . . Not only is the attachment said to go from love to hate as it moves from object to ego, but the ego itself is produced as a *psychic object*; in fact, the very articulation of this psychic space, sometimes figured as "internal," depends on this melancholic turn. (168–9)

We might say that the ego comes into consciousness, so to speak (becomes a "perceptual object," acquires its ontological effect), *through* melancholia. Melancholic response to loss may be therefore be not just a characteristic of a sick ego but rather constitutive of the ego as such. Butler locates in Freud's 1917 essay a radical centralization of melancholia in ego formation:

Thus, in melancholia not only does the ego substitute for the object, but this act of substitution *institutes* the ego as a necessary response to or "defense" against loss. To the extent that the ego is 'the precipitate of its abandoned object-cathexis,' it is the congealment of a history of loss, the sedimentation of relations of substitution over time, the resolution of a tropological function into the ontological effect of the self. (167–98)

In her essay "The Violence of 'We': Politicizing Identification," Elin Diamond locates "Mourning and Melancholia" as the foundational essay in which Freud begins to map the topography of the psyche, which he will more fully develop in *Group Psychology and the Analysis of the Ego* (1921) and *The Ego and the Id* (1923). Diamond posits the activity of melancholic identification as a fundamental process of daily life, which in fact constitutes the history of a subject: "it would be impossible to conceptualize a subject in the process of identification who would not be engaged, however unconsciously, with the history of her identifications, which is at least partly the history of her psychic life with others" (396). Identification with all its melancholic origins has become a *constitutive* element of psychic life.

This condensed history of the origins and development of identification in psychoanalytic thinking holds several implications for how we understand *racial* melancholia and for how we read Smith's theatrical evocation of the concept. To begin with, if melancholic identification is "routine" (Fuss) or "constitutive" (Butler) to psychic development, then racial melancholia—a melancholic structure of identification played out in the sociohistorical realm of race relations—complicates practically all of the explicit and implicit terms of that routine: compensation and loss, love and its inverse, subject and object, incorporation and rejection. Indeed, when these terms get played out as sociohistorical relations, then they leave devastating, material effects on the lost or denied "object," the racial other.

Here in Smith's docudrama, with the character of Rudy Salas, we see an instance of the racially melancholic object pathologizing his racial grief as "insanity." Paul Parker provides another version of power's insidious impact on the psychical constitution of the "melancholic object": he incorporates power's identity, if not its abjection; he defies authority by identifying with it. We, however, have also seen how the acknowledgment of melancholic incorporation (a process of double loss for the racialized person) also embodies a critique of and even a strategy for dismantling authority: Linda Low's transgressive joy in *Flower Drum Song*; Kingston's imagined community built on morbidity; Ellison's strategy of reflecting incorporated loss onto the master; and Cha's deployment of devastated historical and personal fragments as unsentimental records.

For Smith, melancholic incorporation may be said to be the very form of her theater and the very strategy of her critique of power. Usually reticent about the political significance of her art (often calling herself "just a re-peater"), Smith does in a rare article discuss the political implications of mimicry as a performance technique. In a commentary published in the *New York Times*, Smith examines the art of impersonation as a specific study of authority:

> Authority likes to see itself imitated, followed. But impersonation is not
> the same as a mirror image or a videotape. For the health of a society, it
> should not be; it should, in fact, be authority turned upside down. Mim-
> ics study authority while standing on their hands.[13]

Authority likes to see itself imitated and followed, but, as is shown by the narrating scribe in Theresa Hak Kyung Cha's *Dicteé*, too faithful an imita-tion can end up unraveling authority's originality. Here in Smith's work, the very *medium* of imitation dismantles social and personal authority.

More than offering a theoretical critique of power, Smith's art traces the intangible residues of grief left over from the conflicts of racialization. The affective residue of a hostile racial exchange cannot be quantified materi-ally (What, after all, is the measure of sorrow?) even as that grief is aggra-vated, institutionalized, and confirmed through material-legal-cultural con-ditions. As an expression of grief playing itself out between the narratives of multiplicity and impoverishment, identification therefore presents a drama of intrasubjectivity that speaks the language of intersubjectivity. As Fuss writes, identification "invokes phantoms" (1). In other words, it is a group act taking place on a single stage/body. Smith's work takes the form of this process almost literally, raising complications for the act of "recog-nizing" someone. Yes, identification is a psychical mechanism that produces self-recognition, but it produces a very peculiar form of recognition: a rec-ognition borne out of a drama of otherness. Since multiculturalism is rooted in identity, and identity is a fiction of ontological integrity organized by identification (already a process of ceaselessly reproducing sameness and otherness), then we start to perceive that the problem of recognition in multiculturalism is being reflected through Smith's art and exposed as a structural, not just semantic, problem. And so before we can talk about justice or political recognition, we have to confront the psychical paradox inherent in the act of identification. The redemptive possibility of recogniz-ing the self in the other and vice versa (Pellegrini) proves to be difficult, if not impossible, since recognition as a vernacular euphemism for identifi-cation is contradictory in its inner workings.

The seemingly more mundane or superficial phenomenon of "audience identification" is not immune to identification's structural paradox. If the logic of identification is revealed in Parker's speech as an activity of psychi-cal consolidation and political solidarity that operates through repetitive othering, then Smith also demonstrates that the audience's identificatory relationship with the dramatic character can trace its own maps of attraction and rejection. Smith's monologues at once encourage and discourage audience identification with the character on stage. In dramatizing a dynamic of identification as a vicious circle of othering through the character of Paul Parker, Smith magnifies the problem of identification between viewer and the viewed that attends any specular performance. That is, in viewing the Parker testimony's harrowing logic of repetitive prejudice and exclusion, the audience is more likely than not to feel uncomfortable. With Parker as well as other characters, there is invariably a point in Smith's performance when the audience is shaken out of its specular, formal identification with the speaking character. The audience is made aware of its *position* as witnesses and how such positionality may itself hold political implications. The points of discomfort may be different for different people (for me, one such point of discomfort was the reminder that racial solidarity often speaks through the voice of discrimination), but it is impossible to sit through a Smith performance without experiencing the discomfort of either complicity or antagonism. Smith reminds us that there is no such a thing as "merely" watching.

The audience is propelled to an intense awareness of the specificities of what Elin Diamond calls the "historical contradictions" inhering in viewer responses. In her essay "The Violence of 'We,'" Diamond posits that it is impossible to conceive of "one audience," since each viewer carries his or her own heterogenous histories as a sociocultural being. By dismantling the phenomenological universals of subjects-of-viewing and the coherence of a spectatorial "we," Diamond politicizes the notion of "audience identification." She first points out that a traditionally conceived psychoanalytic perception of identification as mimetic, imperialistic, and narcissistic has led to a critical projection of an authoritative audience. She then suggests that there is another kind of identification, inherent in the development of the conceptualization of the term within psychoanalysis, that in fact problematizes the annihilation of difference.[14] Diamond argues for attention to the kind of identification between viewer and character that destabilizes, rather than confirms, the critical or spectatorial *we*, one that provokes rather than disguises the historical contradictions within a social status quo implied by a homogeneous notion of the audience-as-one.

This notion of historical contradiction (as an external corollary to identification's contradictory inner processes) proves useful in thinking about the critical reception of Smith's work. The contention over the potential partisanship of Smith's theater (for example, the complaint that she has, for example, expressed more sympathy for one character over another) itself signals the inevitable presence of sociohistorical context for the critic—a context that underlies his/her very affinity for a particular sympathy or identification. An example comes from Tania Modelski's analysis of Smith's earlier docudrama *Fires in the Mirror*. In one of the few critically sustained pieces focused solely on Smith's theatrical art, Modleski begins her essay by taking to task critics who read Smith's work as a "purely mimetic art," musing that "its postmodernism notwithstanding, there is something about the work that induces even sophisticated poststructuralist critics to lapse into older critical vocabularies in analyzing it."[15] The essay goes on to disentangle Smith's mimetic strategy from a transparent reading of representation:

> Part of the unsettling effect of [Smith's] performances is that although some of the figures Smith mimics are familiar to us (if only from their media representations), in many cases we are acutely aware of watching imitations without knowing the originals. Giving priority, as it were, to the copy over the original, Smith radically and viscerally contests ideals of authenticity, in effect "deterritorializing" her characters and getting them to act on a new common ground—the stage. (68–9)

Modleski's cogent appraisal of mimicry's critique of authenticity, however, turns back on itself, for we find that the ideals of authenticity have been replaced by an ideal of commonality ("getting them to act on a common ground"). As already discussed, from the vantage points of both the characters and the audience's receptions of these monologues, "a new common ground" cannot be a given—not even when we consider that common ground to be Smith's body. For Smith's own gendered and racial relations to each character create various effects. Moreover, each "representation" is necessarily fractured through both its own and the audiences' sociocultural, racial, and gender histories, what Diamond calls "historical contradictions." Thus for Modleski what begins as critical severance of mimicry from a notion of authentic representation and hence an implicit critique of the ideal of representation-as-recognition turns back into a commemoration of just such an idealization.

With such a retraction, Modleski's essay inevitably retreats into what she herself calls "older critical vocabularies" about representation. Returning to the familiar tenets of liberal multicultural identity politics, Modleski concludes her investigation with a criticism of Smith's failure to represent white women in a positive light. Finding Smith's portraits of white women in her performance to be "ridiculous" and "unhabilitated" (71), Modleski announces her disappointment: "If Smith was not prepared to acknowledge my oppression as a woman, I felt, I would not recognize hers as an African American" (70). Thus the very critic who applauds Smith's "deterritorialization" ends up taking Smith to task for being territorial; the critic who most effectively disconnected the shortcut between identity and representation ends up demonstrating the seduction of that alliance. In short, Modleski believes that Smith's authorial selection has undermined the power of her performance.

If we extend Modleski's critical insights into Smith's method rather than content, we can see that the activity of mimesis and its translations upsets the hierarchical assumptions traditionally upholding the binarism of the "original" and the "imitation."[16] Smith's "act" does not substantiate, either through a difference in imitation or through perfect replication, her characters' authentic ontology. Instead it highlights the element of performance in any individualistic moment of self-definition. As if to underscore this insight, Smith often thematizes the very notion of performance in acts of racial assertion. I return to Paul Parker's piece because it provides such a rich example of the kind of layered performances that Smith gives. In the character of Parker she offers a double performance: that of Smith performing Parker and that of Parker performing his racial-cultural "roots." Smith ends Parker's monologue with the following litany: "This is for Kunta. This is for Kizzy. This is for Chicken George" (176). Parker borrows from another's genealogy to authenticate his racial origin, history, and identity. The "self," and by extension "identity," cannot substantiate itself, make itself be known, except through an act of performed identification. Smith's performance of this performance exposes the intimacy between representation and parody, revealing "personality" as the type that it may always have been. (This aspect of Smith's dramatic method that denaturalizes rather than enacts authenticity is also why some interviewees, initially gratified by Smith's attention, ended up resenting Smith's portrayal, such as the more public denunciation of Smith by the woman called Rosa in *Fires in the Mirror*.) It is not necessarily that Smith has caricatured the people she imitates, but that often in seeing an echo of oneself, one begins to see those aspects of oneself, long naturalized and dearly held as particular claims of authenticity, as the performance that they really are.

In the same *New York Times* commentary, Smith argues that impersonation has the specific function of exposing power, of "turning authority upside down." Responding to the dangers of stereotyping in any act of impersonation, this essay locates the crux of this concern in *the performer's own positionality*, the assumptions and limitations offered by that position. By meditating on the positionality of other mimics, Smith offers an implicit contemplation of her own positionality, her own "historical contradictions" (in Elin Diamond's words), as the performer:

> So what *is* more dangerous: the possibility of giving offense or the refusal to look and to see? Eddie Murphy has done an impression of Jesse Jackson in which the mimicry is technically brilliant. As Mr. Jackson, he stops speaking and continues his thought in a soul tune with a three-men backup group. Would a white comic get away with combining these two

motifs—a powerful black political figure and Motown? Or would this be
considered racial stereotyping? Would some consider Mr. Murphy himself to have crossed over the line of what is acceptable? (20)

Smith's analysis of Eddie Murphy clearly raises questions about her own
work: what does it mean for a black woman to perform what she is not,
across gender and racial lines? Or, perhaps, what is it about being a black
woman that allows her to do so?[17]

While Smith insists on the necessary burdens of "turning authority upside down," she also acknowledges that not all racial bodies are created
equal, not because of any essential or moral reasons but because all racial
bodies exist within (indeed, are defined by) the history of power. Racial bodies embody racial histories. Because of the social history of black denigration and the theatrical history of minstrelsy, black bodies can occupy certain parodic spaces unimaginable for whites today, at least in progressive
circles. Hence Eddie Murphy can parody aspects of his "own" racial community with very different results from a white man. (And who can forget
Eddie Murphy's white-face routine on *Saturday Night Live?*) As we have already noted throughout this study, the stereotype signals, above all, a question of history, positionality, power, and powerlessness.

Moreover, Smith suggests that self-recognition in fact always navigates
between the type and the stereotype, between important symbolic acts of
cognition and false projections.[18] In *Twilight*, Paul Parker draws from Alex
Haley's genealogy to authenticate his own. Smith also uses other cultural
stereotypes, such as gender stereotypes, to emphasize unexpected affiliations
among characters. I am thinking of the portrayal of Elaine Young, the white
real estate agent whose feminine theatrics and racial ignorance Modleski
has found "extremely caricatured" and "unhabilitated." Self-nominated
"victim of silicone," Young offers a ridiculous and grotesque representation
of white femininity when she tells the story of her plight. After undergoing
a series of plastic surgeries following the explosion of silicone implants in
her cheeks, Young became an activist in the war against silicone implants.
For many reviewers, this character represents the stereotypical privileged
white woman living in the appearance-obsessed City of Angels; she embodies the unpleasant reminder that activism is often a form of self-interest. Yet
this woman's desperate quest to incorporate and embody cultural ideals of
feminine beauty and her subsequent literal internal implosion under the
weight of those ideals surely tells us something about the contemporary
sexual milieu for women. Young's "superficiality" also expresses the power
of sexual oppression.

Viewing the Young piece in the context of Smith's performance as a whole,
we can see other lines of connections. In a piece called "To Look Like Girls
from Little," Smith gives us the voice and words of Elvira Evers, a pregnant

Panamanian woman shot in the belly during the riots. Both mother and daughter survive, the baby-in-utero having taken the bullet in her elbow. Smith excerpts Evers's account to include the following detail:

> Jessica [an older daughter], bring the baby. . . . Yes yes. We don't like to keep the girls without earrings. We like the little girls to look like little girls from little. I pierce hers. When I get out on Monday, by Wednesday I did it, so by Monday she was five days, she was seven days, and I pierced her ears. (122)

A mother's decision to pierce her infant daughter's ears certainly cannot be equated with a piercing bullet from a race riot. Yet, in juxtaposition, the echo is surely difficult not to hear. The girl infant is doubly "pierced" by gender and racial inscriptions. In this light, Elaine Young appears as a tragic, potential fulfillment of the desire "to look like little girls from little."

Smith's theater thus creates this nexus of antagonisms and affinities, her own position as a woman of color generating its own sociohistorical contradictions. Her gender difference from Paul Parker, for example, stresses that character's misogyny. According to Parker, "to be a strong black man" is to adopt the pose of "Baby get me some" and to voice threats such as "we acted in a way that was just. . . . It might not be you but it might be your daughter" (176–8). The projection of violence onto the bodies of nonblack female subjects, while playing up white paranoia and stereotypes of black masculinity, also rubs up uneasily against Parker's own historic reminder, "you kidnapped us, raped our women." The alignment of racial and masculine violence renders the possessiveness of "our" women as uncomfortable as the threats against "their" women. Since the African American female subject has historically been "the target of rape" and the topic of "externalized acts of torture and prostration that we imagine as the peculiar province of male brutality,"[19] Parker's speech reclaims his racial integrity through a male brutality that disturbingly aligns him with white racist manhood.

Made aware of the mediating body in Parker's monologue, the viewer has to wonder about the place of the black woman in a scenario such as Parker's. Although Smith's mimicry of Parker's words offers no apparent commentary on its content, her editorial choices do: Smith performs Parker in the original context of their interview, when he was "living in the home of his girlfriend in Westwood" and "wearing IVY League clothing." His monologue directly follows the monologue of Maxine Waters, congresswoman, Thirty-fifth District, the prototype of a strong, outspoken black woman. Through this juxtaposition, Smith subtly reminds us of the kind of female figure excluded by Parker's worldview. As one listens to Parker, moreover, one cannot help but hear traces of Waters's speech, about young men in urban neighborhoods who possess nothing but anger and despair and who, having "dropped off of everyone's agenda," "live from grandmama to girlfriend"(168). Waters's piece situates Parker's broad, racial-historical claims within the context of contemporary, urban, racial-economic conditions. As a black woman, Smith's performance as Parker further highlights the gender conflict provoked by his words.

This leads us to the crucial question of Smith's own authority in this project. There are, after all, two "speaking" subjects on stage at any given time: the character and Smith. If, as I am suggesting, Smith disturbs the narcissism of authenticity central to any subjective experience, then what about Smith's own "subjectivity" in the process of her performance? Although this question seems in some ways presumptuous and unanswerable by a critic, it is the question that repeatedly comes up (in mundane and sophisticated versions of "with whom is she *really* identifying") in analysis of her work, whether it be in the mainstream media or academic treatises. In fact, I suggest that what grips critical attention about Smith's performance, usually expressed as a concern about her "subjectivity," really grows out of issues of ethics. The anxiety about her art derives from an uncertainty about the ethical and political implications of her work, which expresses itself in questions such as: Does mimicking people in crisis imply that their experiences have been invaded or co-opted; does Smith's own act of "incorporation" effect sympathy or parody?

Yet surely there are more productive questions to ask about Smith's art. It is revealing how receptions of her performance tend to bypass basic theatrical conventions, such as the difference between the external imitation of gestures versus the assumption of another's feelings. That theoretical distance becomes very abbreviated and threatened whenever we are in the realm of racial performance. The only aspect of Smith's subjectivity available for critical inspection must finally come from the editorial choices she makes as a writer and performer, rather than her sincerity. Indeed, strictly speaking, Smith does not identify with her characters; she *acts out* identifications. This is a subtle but crucial difference, one that is often overlooked, which explains why critical debates tend to center on her politics, rather than what she is saying about the politics of representation. The question of with whom is the performer identifying—that is, "Whose side is she on, anyway?"—is misdirected, for that line of inquiry disguises the more crucial questions of the ethical and political dimensions (and these may not be the same, as I argue later) of "stepping into" someone else's shoes. In short, in the war and necessity of racial representation, we need to ask what it means, ethically, politically, and psychically, to speak as someone else.

It is clear that what I would call the war of recognition is linked in complicated ways to interlocking notions of sympathy and identification. The ethics of sympathy has always circled around a misgiving about the comparison between the self and other and the implications of that comparison. The vernacular distinction between sympathy and empathy, for instance, attempts to quantify (how much or how deep) the extent of identification, but it is finally a poor distinction because it fails to address the following ethical issue: Is one's distanced-sympathy (from, say, a homeless person) a sign of respect or privilege? Similarly, is empathy a true gesture of understanding or only another form of narcissism? The sympathy–empathy dyad cannot accommodate the full complexity behind the processes of identification. The difference between sympathy and empathy, when we really come down to it, lies in self-positioning and the certitude of one's own identity positioned in relation to the other, but identity is itself an illusion of integrity and stability. So the same question still remains: What distinguishes privileged separation from a nonincorporative identification? Is it finally a matter of intentions?[20] And what would determine "intention" in this case?

Before we can talk about justice and adequate compensatory recognition, we have to talk about the role that identification plays in *de*stabilizing the groundwork of recognition. To return to Charles Taylor's explanation of the inherent paradox of "recognition" in multiculturalism, Taylor's paradox of how do we "give acknowledgement and status to something that is not universally shared" assumes that there is a universal standard against which comparisons can be made and that the condition for recognition is sameness or at least some form of commensurability. To put it crudely, for Taylor, it is difficult to recognize someone else precisely because he or she *is* someone else. Now it would seem that the solution is to dislodge sameness as the precondition for recognition, to find a form of identification that is not appropriative or self-confirming. Critics from different disciplines have taken up precisely this task of formulating an ethical recognition or ethical identification. I am thinking of Jessica Benjamin's clinical notion of intersubjectivity, which attempts to replace the subject–object relation with a subject–subject relation as the paradigm for patient–analyst dynamics; Drucilla Cornell's reworking of "mimesis" as a nonviolent ethical relation to the other; and Kaja Silverman's vision of "heteropathic identification."[21] All these meditations are theoretically engaging and politically seductive but cannot tell us how to enact or locate this ethical recognition, beyond turning to intentionality or discretion.

This dilemma owes much to the nature of identification itself, which is a process that is multiple, unmanageable, contradictorily incorporating, incorporated, ensnaring, and distancing. Trying to isolate an ethical identification is a bit like trying to discipline desire. It is the age-old problem of trying to find the "political" in a concept that seems in some ways inherently apolitical. There can be no solution to this predicament unless we begin to reconsider the nature of the political. And this is where Smith's work has been instructive for me. Rather than trying to judge her agency or intention in relation to her mimetic performance (which usually leads to debates about how authentic or parodic her acts are), I am more inclined to trace the distances and proximities created by her mimetic art and to think about what those shifting intervals tell us about making presence present, about identifying identity, about the dynamics of embodiment and loss inherent in representation.

What I want to think through, via Smith, is the possibility that the answer to the political dilemma of identification may not rest in trying to wrestle out a space of distance between self and other, subject and object, but to go instead for the opposite, to undertake the difficult task of immersion. By this new term "immersion" I hope to bypass the dead end of locating an "ethical identification." I think that ethics comes *after* identification and complicity—that is, after immersion has already taken place.

Immersion of course can be said to be the very method of Smith's theatrical technique, and its results demonstrate how that immersion, *in all its successes and failures*, might be the only way to confront this world of corrosive difference. Smith's submergence into the hosts of personalities is at once entrancing and estranging, a paradox reflected in the curious effect of her "presence" on stage. Compared to videotaped versions of her performance, Smith in person and on stage more successfully conveys the "real" presences of the characters, and yet at the same time, the audience is also made more aware of *her*, of the editorialization and craft that mediate such achievement. That is, even as one gets drawn into the pressing, authentic urgencies of these individuated voices, one is increasingly conscious of her mediation: the selection of monologues, their juxtaposition, the resulting echoes and contrasts, the choices of beginnings and endings. The virtuosity of her very bodily performance relies precisely on the embodiment of the other through a self-erasure that nonetheless insists on the materiality of the medium of the body.

Smith *reveals* presence as liminality. Her theater demands that we address the confluence of those contradictions inherent in any identificatory position. Smith dramatizes Diamond's insight that "the borders of identity, the wholeness and consistency of identity, is transgressed by the very act of identification" (396). The fact that this paradox must, however, be covered over by the very process of identification itself (that is, the Borch-Jacobson insight that identity can never, strictly speaking, know itself as identity)[22] is made all the more clear by the discomfort of being made to witness the simultaneity of identity and identification, the very activity of self-definition through inclusion and exclusion. In addition to the conflicted views being presented it is disturbing to witness how those views occupy one stage, indeed, one body. Anyone who has witnessed Smith's performances understands the discomfort of being made to watch the fine lines separating speaking *for*, speaking *as*, and speaking *against*. Critics have read her complicity with various opposing characters as constituting a kind of community, but her complicity with everyone also marks her distance from them. Her work speaks simultaneously to a desire for and a failure of community. It delineates boundaries even as it breaks them.

Smith's evocation of boundary as a question often provokes public discomfort. In an early performance of *Twilight*, Smith had chosen to perform a character in Korean, through memorized phonetics. The English-speaking audience and reviewers next day were noticeably upset by being excluded in this way and by Smith's perceived side-taking.[23] This incident tells us more about the audience and *its* community than about Smith's artistic choice. The use of Korean excludes only those who do not speak Korean. The incident demonstrates all too clearly that there is no place of speech that is not position-creating and that the address to one community is, by definition, the exclusion of another.

To occupy on a subjective level that space between inclusion and exclusion, boundary and boundarilessness, is indeed unbearable. Smith locates this voice in the words of Mrs. Young-Soon Han, whose speech I quoted at the beginning of this chapter. We are reminded of the impossibility yet urgency of sympathy in this world of layered alliances, victimization, violence, and enmity. Mrs. Han can empathize with the African American rioters because she is herself a racialized other, yet she cannot sympathize because she is also other to the other. If identification and sympathy go back to an old notion of "walking in the other's shoes," then we need to refine what that "walk" means. Peggy Phelan writes in her book *Unmarked*:

> *It is in the attempt to walk (and live) on the rickety bridge between the self and other—and not the attempt to arrive at one or the other—that we discover real hope.* That work is our always suspended performance—in the classroom, in the political field, in relation to one another and ourselves.[24]

Similarly, Smith understands sympathy not as some kind of self-less identification but rather as a kind of crisis of unbridgeability, a crisis of the awareness of boundary. However, this suspended performance represents for Smith, unlike Phelan, not a question of hope but really a kind of knowing, in the fullest and most present sense of knowledge, that the distance between self and other is neither measurable nor stable and that there are more than two sides to this negotiation. To watch Smith's performance is thus to confront the conditions for and the limits of comparison.

The discomfort of Smith's art is being made to watch conflicted views and to view them as all occupying one space: one stage and one body. We are witnessing the impossibility of "Many in One": Smith's body allegorizing the impossibility of the democratic body politics. Many people have called her work "healing"; I would say it is the opposite. Smith's art reveals all that cannot be healed, all that cannot be made commensurate, all that must remain complicit yet disunited.

Smith shows that it is in fact difficult to identify with someone of a different race, background, and opinion, especially if the differences at stake are material, economic, and historical privileges. But she also insists on how urgent it is to put oneself on that rickety bridge. Her drama suggests that the project of intersubjective negotiations might be retemporalized and respatialized as an in-between place, the middle ground that is not a cop-out but a crucial, strategic position in a divided world. This docudrama, after all, is named for such a middle ground: twilight. "Twilight" is thematized and theorized in two monologues in the docudrama: Smith as postcolonial theorist Homi Bhabha and Smith as L.A. gang member Twilight Bey. In a segment called "Twilight #1," Smith gives us the "voice" of Homi Bhabha:

> This twilight moment is an in-between moment. It's the moment of dusk. It's the moment of ambivalence and ambiguity. . . . It's exactly the moment when the L.A. uprisings could be something else than it was seen to be. . . . That fuzziness of twilight allows us to see the intersections of the event with a number of other things that daylight obscures for us . . . we have to interpret more in twilight, we have to make ourselves part of the act, we have to interpret, we have to project more. (232–3)

In another piece, called "Limbo/Twilight #2," Smith gives us the voice of Twilight Bey, organizer of the gang truce, who explains his name and his vision for his devastated community:

> I was twelve and thirteen, I stayed out until, they say, until the sun come up. Every night, you know. . . . I was a watch dog. . . . I stayed up in the neighborhood, make sure we wasn't being rolled on and everything . . . a lot of people said, "Well, Twilight . . . you have a lot more wisdom than those twice your age". . . .

> [A]nd it came ta me: "Twi," abbreviation of the word "twice" . . . "Light" is a word that symbolizes knowledge, knowing. . . . So twilight is that time between day and night. Limbo. I call it limbo. . . .

> So a lot of times when I've brought up ideas to my homeboys, they say, "Twilight, that's before your time, that's something you can't do now." When I talked about the truce back in 1988, that was something they considered before its time, yet in 1992 we made it realistic. So to me it's like I'm stuck in limbo, like the sun is stuck between night and day in the twilight hours. (253–4)

The world of the Oxford-educated, postcolonial philosopher conspicuously differs from the world of the American street youth who orchestrated the gang truce in east Los Angeles. Yet Smith culls this notion of "twilight" and the middle-space from these two speakers, making an implicit but direct link between intellectuality and the life of political action. While academic figures in Smith's performances generally appear pedantic and thus comic in their abstraction and solipsism, the connection between Bhabha and Twilight Bey separates intellectuality from pedantry. Both figures, in their own ways, relocate the question of an ethical identification away from nameable or quantifiable positions and to the interstices between identities and political stances.

For Homi Bhabha, twilight offers a temporal metaphor for posttraumatic reflection, as the moment when one can glimpse the intersections between peoples that have been obscured by the "hard edges" of stubborn opposition. In a rather lyrical distillation of much of what he has written in *The Location of Culture* and elsewhere, Bhabha in his interview by Smith urges us to rethink the compulsions of ideological certitude: "This twilight moment is an in-between moment. . . . It's the moment of ambivalence and ambiguity" (232). The nowhere of twilight releases us from the constraints of our given locations and cultural contexts, a shadow that allows us to see. In a sense, Bhabha is talking about ethics *in the face of*, not in spite of, unremitting conflicts. Bhabha's "intersection" offers a version of what I earlier called "immersion": the responsibility to enter the space of unlikely affinity. More than that, the principle of seeing through the "intersection" or the task of "immersion" is an acknowledgment of having always already entered the space of the other *and* to know the limits of that ingress, whether it be invasion or sympathy.

In a sense, we are talking about transforming, not domesticating, the vexing dynamics of identification into an ethical paradigm. That is, identification itself as an unruly psychical activity cannot be wrested into political or ethical values, but once we have accepted that psychical paradigm as the precondition for social relations, then comes the task of formulating an ethical response. Ethics, as I have claimed, comes after identification, not instead of it. Rather than denying identification's structural propensity for projection and incorporation, Bhabha for one recommends the *obligation* of such interpretation, incorporation, and projection, as well as an understanding of how they continue to shape, create, and re-create new "locales" of identity: "we have to make ourselves part of the act, we have to interpret, we have to project more." And is this not what Smith's theatrical method effects? Through the dramatic, Smith explores the possibility here urged by Bhabha, of sustaining an awareness of many conflictual claims that, in effect, shorts out the restrictions of one-on-one identification. Her theater *is* the imaginative movement from a dramatic to an ethical space. "Twilight: Los Angeles" is, indeed, the hour when you witness the crossidentifications being woven and unwoven on stage.

The other voice in the performance also concerned with ethics in a time of war comes from a very different location: the gang member Twilight Bey whose monologue closes the show. For Twilight Bey, known as the architect of the peace truce, "twilight" also poses a critical time of reflection, a temporal timeout from the constraints of partisanship and racial allegiances. Bey sees this timeout not as a retreat from but as an intense engagement with sociopolitical repercussion. Smith-as-Twilight draws a direct link between knowledge and action, proffered from within the lived ramifications of social reality and affective grief. This mourner walking the city without sleep in melancholic limbo embodies *both* action and inaction; the peace truce is, after all, the very symbol of active inaction.

And I wonder if this figure does not offer the most persuasive expression of what might be the potential inhering in "melancholic subversion," by which I mean not cure or some complacent satisfaction in "knowing better," but subversion in the sense of a *perceptual shift*, of individuals readjusting and realigning their entrenched relationships to one another. In the world of this young man, patrolling his embattled neighborhood at night, going up to "baseheads" to insist that they think about "what [they] are doing," we have a powerful argument for intellectual understanding, not as academic quietism but as a practice toward transformation. Perhaps to some this one man's efforts at shaking people out of their illusions of inviolate identities and accompanying, intractable positions might appear modest in comparison to the kind of urban war taking place in the inner cities. Yet it is precisely because we are talking about a landscape savaged by trenchant divides and unyielding enmity that these shifts of perceptions are far from insignificant. Immersed in the landscape he patrols, like some contemporary incarnation of Ellison's invisible man, Bey stands as a powerful dramatization of melancholic ambivalence not as the lack of position but as the sustainment of multiple conflictual positions. Bey spells out his ethical obligation, "I cannot forever dwell in darkness, I cannot forever dwell in the idea, of just identifying with people like me and understanding me and mine" (255).[25] This in-between state that Smith is forging and thematizing through these two monologues comes closest to what I imagine is the strategy of melancholia. Smith's exploration of a "twilight" way of seeing offers one of the strongest statements about the project of culling political insights from a system of pain and grief.

The ethical space of unlikely affinity grants, in many ways, the ideal answer to the tribal politics of racial conflict. It is, after all, the hypothetical space of citizenship. The tolerance for difference provides the theoretical basis for the political ideal on which polity is constructed. The city as political construction, from its roots in the *polis*, was invented as an alternative to the unending imperative of the tribal feud.[26] The project of the *polis* was to transform grief into ethics in the interest of the community, while grievance with its demand for retribution could only lead to the repetition of tribal allegiance and hence division. The ability to occupy that space of unlikely affinity is in fact the heart of the democratic ideal. The problem, however, comes from that ideal's resemblance to its corrupt form: the imperialistic occupation of the other. We come full circle back to the paradox in the melancholic heart of American democracy that I examined in chapter 1: the American desire to distinguish its democracy from its European imperialistic roots has always been contaminated by its own similar practices. When we turn to the lyrical roots of American imagining, we find the same tension and struggle. In Walt Whitman's "Crossing Brooklyn Ferry" (also known as "Sun-Down Poem") we see another twilight passage, where the poet faces the multitudes of different crowds and tries to construct imaginatively a relation to them, and we hear the very call of melancholia:

> We receive you with free sense at last, and are insatiate henceforward,
> Not you anymore shall be able to foil us, or withhold yourselves from us,
> We use you, and do not cast you aside—we plant you permanently within us,
> We fathom you not—we love you—there is perfection in you also,
> You furnish your parts towards eternity,
> Great or small, you furnish your parts toward the soul.[27]

"Crossing Brooklyn Ferry" is a disturbing text in relation to ethics in the face of difference because it seems to embrace a fundamental assumption that the maintaining of the prevailing condition of *not seeing* the other ("We fathom you not") is necessary for an imaginative fusion ("we love you"), suggesting that such melancholic incorporation is a prerequisite for assuming a social role.

Traditionally read as either a celebration of multiculturalism or as a utopian, narcissistic economy that fluidly and imperialistically absorbs the other, this poem in fact highlights the notion that the place of the self is always tainted by its inverse, that the disinterested other is at once fundamental to yet corrupted by democratic polity. In his seminal study of difference in Whitman (though he is talking about gender difference), Michael Moon points out that the poet's gaze in this poem (what he calls the "long view" of the poem), aimed at bridging the poet and the reader, and poet and the object of his gaze, are more tentative and projective than secure or triumphant:

> I prefer to take the speaker's omission to "face" his fellows directly . . . as a sign of the intensity of Whitman's attention to exploring certain difficult questions of desire. . . . "Sun-Down Poem" does not construct a bridge between the points it represents; rather, it circulates the reader back and forth between the points of desirously gazing and of being gazed at desirously, exploring as it does so *the contradictions that make one long*

to be looked at by the beloved from the place where one looks at the beloved—
even as one knows one can never be. (My emphasis)[28]

Moon reads the desire in the poem to be Oedipalized desire, but his reading holds insights into a melancholic economy as well. In examining the desires circulating around racial ideality, I have repeatedly shown how desire must be crossed (lost, unfaced) in order to constitute itself in a melancholic nation. Love must look away in order not to look away. The other that is "unfathomable" is as much subjected to this imaginary and impossible circuit of desire as the devouring "we." Thus melancholia, both living with the ghost of the alien other within and living as the ghost in the gaze of another, may be the precondition—and the limit—for the act of imagination that enables the political as such.

NEITHER WHITMAN'S NOR SMITH'S VISIONS OF UNLIKELY AFFINITY promises healing. (As Moon concludes, the last call in "Crossing Brooklyn Ferry" is not totalizing but "peculiar, partial, liminal"[110]). Instead, Smith and Whitman reveal from two historical vantages the fundamental history of loss and retention that finds and continues to sustain America. Smith's concluding urban vision, embodied by the figure of Twilight Bey, delineates a momentary negotiation, rather than erasure, of the past and future ravages of racial antipathy. In a world defined by sides, where everyone speaks in the vocabulary of "them" versus "us," not to take a side means to exist in an insistent, resistant middle ground that is also nowhere. The perspective that sees beyond the self is also the perspective that takes on the view of the other, which is also an impossible perspective. Smith's reenactment of Twilight Bey includes his acknowledgement, "You know, I'm in an area where not many people exist" (255). To hold that vision of knowledge, reserve, contemplation, vigilance, and multiplicity is also to remain homeless. The gesture of moving beyond "identifying with one's own," while ethically crucial, thrusts one out of time and space: "I'm . . . like the sun stuck between night and day" (Twilight Bey, 255). The resolution of Bey's monologue thus demonstrates that understanding may mean understanding the limits of understanding.

The same may be said of the political space that Smith occupies. We can think of Smith's art as delineating ethics rather than politics; perhaps Smith's work may even dramatize the incompatibility between the two. It could be that the provinces of affective history, psychical identification, and their griefs belong necessarily to the realm of ethics rather than to politics, which must speak the language of materiality, identity, and grievance. At the same time, I also believe that this theater is intensely focused on what is *political* about intersubjective dynamics. It is a theater that traces the distances between subjects and insists that these intervals ought to be the places of political reexamination. It is not that we do not know where to be in this kaleidoscope of often contradictory positions[29] but that Smith reminds us that we *do* have to occupy—at times unwillingly, at times only too willingly—these conflictual stances. Watching Smith's theater is to be called to occupy a place where you either do not want to be or cannot remain even if you want to. It is impossible, indeed unethical, to try to be "objective" or immune.

For Smith, the passage between self and the other is not just the "rickety bridge" Peggy Phelan describes but also the knowledge of the ravine underneath, the disorienting immersion that is the condition for any act of identification. The "no place" that is nonetheless an imperative: this is the difference between ethics and politics—or, at least, racial politics as we know it today, which operates on certitude, tribal allegiance, and prescription. This distinction may finally feed into the difference between grief and grievance, with grief belonging to the realm of thinking and living with loss, while grievance belongs to the realm of accountability. But the frequent conflation of grief and grievance underscores how important it is also to imagine a relationship between ethics and politics. And perhaps this is finally also the core of the difference between psychoanalytically informed thinking and the social realm of political language—the former laboring to carve out in space and time a subjective state vis-à-vis a racial geography not allowable by political categories and exigencies. At ease with neither hope nor nihilism, Smith's work struggles to redefine that negotiation as *the* ethical moment, and it is the transition from ethics to politics that will prove to be our most persistent challenge and the path of our most difficult loves.

NOTES

Preface

1. Quoted in Richard Kluger, *Simple Justice*, 318.
2. *Briggs v. Elliot*, 342 U.S. 350 (1952). Also quoted in Richard Kluger, ibid., 320.

Chapter 1. The Melancholy of Race

1. *Brown v. Board of Education*, 347 U.S. 484 (1954) and *Brown v. Board of Education*, 149 U.S. 294 (1955).
2. Social science research was first urged upon an American court early this century by Louis Brandeis in another landmark case dealing with the constitutionality of social welfare legislation (*Muller v. Oregon*, 1908). The "Brandeis briefs" set off a debate about the use of social science as "legal fact" that has lasted to today. See Kenneth Culp Davis, "An Approach to Problems of Evidence in the Administrative Process" and John Monohan and Laurens Walker, *Social Science in Law*.
3. Richard Kluger, *Simple Justice*, 316.
4. A copy of the "Social Science Statement" can be found in Philip B. Kurkland and Gerhard Casper, eds., *Landmark Briefs and Arguments of the Supreme Court of the United States: Constitutional Law*, 49:43–61.
The writing of the statement is itself a fascinating story, involving a range of issues: the competing claims of politics and science, of science and interpretation, of academia and social engineering. See Stephen L. Carter, "The Trap of Scientism"; Kenneth B. Clark, "The Social Scientists, the Brown Decision, and Contemporary Confusion"; Mark Chestler, Joseph Sanders, and Debora Kalmuss, *Social Science in Court*; Herbert Hovenkamp, "Social Science and Segregation before *Brown*"; John P. Jackson, Jr., "The Transformation of Social Science into Modern Authority in *Brown v. Board of Education*"; Richard Kluger, *Simple Justice*; John Monohan and Laurens Walker, *Social Science in Law*.
5. Appellees' Brief (1952), in Kurkland and Casper, *Landmark Briefs and Arguments*, 49:153.
In South Carolina, John W. Davis, lawyer for the state of South Carolina in the *Briggs* case, called the social scientific testimony "fluff." People who objected

to the psychological evidence included Bruno Bettelheim, who, in spite of his own works on the effect of Nazi concentration camps on their inmates, in a review of Kenneth Clark's book *Prejudice and Your Child*, stated publicly that there is no scientific evidence that racial segregation damages human personality; and Ernest van den Haag of the New School of Social Research who claimed one cannot assess personality damages associated with social stigma. (Bettelheim, "Discrimination and Science"; Ernest Van den Haag and Ralph Ross, *The Fabric of Society*.

6. "Opinion of the Court," *Landmark Briefs and Arguments*, 49:172–4. My emphasis.

7. My thanks to Robert Post for his conversation about this case as well as for introducing me to the fascinating world of constitutional history.

8. *Stell v. Savannah-Chatham County Board of Education* 220 F. Supp. 667 (1963), 669.

9. Little attention, for instance, has been paid to that aspect of Clark's work that stresses "damage" as the result of social environment rather than inherent disability or to Clark's emphasis that the white child also suffers detrimental psychological effects from witnessing the practice of racism. See Clark, *Prejudice and Your Child* and "The Social Scientists, the Brown Decision, and Contemporary Confusion" in *Appellants' Argument*. In his *Blackface, White Noise*, Michael Rogin will give examples in post–World War II American cinema of how popular culture continues to hystericize and naturalize the black body in pain.

10. Austin Sarat, *Race, Law, and Culture*, 5. A tremendous amount of scholarship has been generated in legal studies and in social science over the status of psychology as social or material evidence: authors include Anthony C. Amsterdam, Stephen L. Carter, Mark Chestler and Debora Kalmuss, Herbert Hovenkamp, and John Monohan and Laurens Walker, to name a few.

11. Contemporary criticism of affirmative action along with the development of black nationalism have also come to challenge, if not undermine, integration as an ideal in the dream of racial progress.

12. Subsequent research in the sixties confirmed the Clarks' experiment, which posits a direct correlation between oppression and self-esteem (Ralph Mason Dreger and Kent S. Miller, "Comparative Psychological Studies of Negroes and Whites in the United States"; Harold Proshansky and Peggy Newton, "The Nature and Meaning of Negro Self-Identity"). Research in the seventies failed to find consistent differences in self-esteem between the races (Morris Rosenberg and Roberta G. Simmons, "Black and White Self-Esteem"; Gloria Powell and Marielle Fuller, "Black Monday's Children"). This change in results, as argued by Roberta G. Simmons, "Blacks and High Self-Esteem," reflects the changing ideologies of the researchers. According to Simmons: "More recently, the champions of the oppressed emphasize the resiliency of minority group members and often view discussions of 'impairment' in family structure and in personality functioning as racist. Blacks are encouraged to internalize the 'Black Is Beautiful' credo and to fight actively against discrimination rather than to permit degradation of the self" (54). What is missing from this debate are: (1) a sustained analysis of what it means to have "internalized" an image and what it means to "replace" that interior image; and (2) a reexamination of the binaristic assumption dividing complete oppression on the one

hand and complete agency on the other. As this chapter goes on to discuss, the problem of minority status and self-perception continue to haunt researchers in the nineties.

13. Claude M. Steele, "Thin Ice: 'Stereotype Threat' and Black College Students."

14. Leonard Greene, "Brouhaha over Barbie Doll far from Being Just Kids' Stuff."

15. In 1951 we could easily find Dr. Fred Palmer's New Double-Strength Skin Whitening Cream ubiquitously advertising in the Harlem weekly *Amsterdam News*: "Be Lighter! Be Lovelier! Be Loved!" Today we can still find the same products advertised in African American and Asian American magazines, but the contemporary advertising strategy is more sanitized, slanted toward "health" issues such as sun damage or the unevenness of skin tones. Since its inception in the 1940s, *Ebony* magazine, for example, has been running multiple advertisements per issue for various brands of skin lightening creams (*New York Amsterdam News*, 1951).

16. See Walter Goodman, "Brown v. Board of Education: Uneven Results 30 Years Later," *New York Times*, May 17, 1984, B18:1.

17. Christopher Lasch, *The Culture of Narcissism*, xviii.

18. Sigmund Freud, "Mourning and Melancholia" (1917), *SE*, 14: 239–260. Cited hereafter in this chapter as *MM*.

Prior to Freud, melancholia of course enjoyed a long literary history, both as theme and as literary persona. Both European and Asian traditions have expressed a relationship among melancholia, aesthetics, and culture. Rey Chow, *Woman and Chinese Modernity*, talks about the connection between melancholia and the genre of the melodrama as conjoined regulators of social mores and ethics in the realm of aesthetic production. Ross Chambers, *The Writing of Melancholy*, offers a summary of western melancholia, concluding with its classical roots: "Melancholy was thought to result from the rising up of lower forces from within that people sought to suppress, as they would a vomiting of gall" (26). Already we see in the traditional view of melancholy the seeds of melancholia as the conflictual negotiation *within* the self and the subsequent activities of rejection, retention, and projection. While Chambers focuses on the aspects of melancholy that are "immobile" and "evanescent," I want to shift our notion of *melancholia* away from a precious vagueness to the specificity of a psychodynamic structure. Freud's reworking of melancholia presents one of the first treatises that examines the structure, rather than affect, of melancholia.

See also Robert Burton, *Anatomy of Melancholy*; Julia Kristeva, *Soleil noir*; Wolf Lepenies, *Melancholy and Society*; Max Pensky, *Melancholy Dialectics*; and Naomi Schor, *One Hundred Years of Melancholy*.

19. In developing his analysis of melancholia, Freud is uncharacteristically open to losses beyond those of erotic frustrations. According to this essay, the "object of loss" can range from "a loved person" to ideas such as "fatherland, liberty, ideal, and so forth" (*MM*, 164). Similarly, the nature of "loss" ranges from the actual death of the loved person or ideal to imagined disappointments.

20. Indeed, as critics have pointed out, there are indications that this melancholic ego formation may not be restricted to pathological exceptions but may in fact be fundamental to the formation of the ego itself. See Judith Butler,

The Psychic Life of Power; Elin Diamond, "The Violence of 'We'"; Diana Fuss, *Identification Papers*. See, too, chapter 6 of this study, where I analyze, in the context of performance artist Anna Deavere Smith, these critics' proposals about Freudian melancholia as a fundamental process of psychical formation and the implications that this assertion holds for understanding the entangled politics of identification and loss.

21. See Butler, "Psychic Inceptions," in *The Psychic Life of Power*, for a fascinating reading of the courtroom drama of Freudian melancholia.

22. Thomas Mann, *The Magic Mountain*, 596. Mann's comment highlights a particular aspect of melancholia that Freud does not talk about: the subject's relationship to the object beyond the internal drama. It is as if, for Freud, the "object" has, for all practical purposes, disappeared into the melancholic's psychical interiority. In short, one is led to ask, what happens if the object were to return—would the melancholic stop being melancholic? That scenario would seem to make sense except that, since Freud has posited melancholia as a constitutive element of the ego, the return of the object demanding to be a person of its own would surely now be devastating. Indeed, the return of the object may not be as blessed an event as one might imagine.

23. In psychoanalytic theory, incorporation and introjection have for the most part been understood as similar processes, and here I am using the terms interchangeably. There are, however, theorists (such as Nicolas Abraham and Maria Torok) who have argued for a differentiation between the terms. I examine this proposition and its implications in chapter 3 where I take a closer look at the relationship between psychoanalytic incorporation and cultural assimilation in relation to Maxine Hong Kingston's work.

24. Psychoanalytic melancholia has mostly been read in relation to gender identities in the works of Judith Butler on heterosexual melancholia in *Bodies That Matter*; Kaja Silverman on femininity and the melancholic nature of the negative oedipal complex in *The Acoustic Mirror*; and Juliana Schiesari, *The Gendering of Melancholia*.

Butler theorizes specifically about "drag" as a melancholic incorporation fantasy, whereby gender performance allegorizes a loss it cannot grieve but must act out. For Butler, homosexuality is the ungrieved loss for heterosexuality, the melancholia at the heart of heterosexuality: "Heterosexual melancholia is the melancholy by which a masculine gender is formed from the refusal to grieve the masculine as a possibility of love" (235). Heterosexuality is thus constantly resurrecting and burying the gay figure . . . hence the guilt about homosexuality. Heterosexuality is the "lost, proper" identity that represents the melancholia of homosexuality—a loss that can only be acted out as the desire for "straightness."

Silverman's chapter "Disembodying the Female Voice" in *The Acoustic Mirror* conducts an especially close reading of Freud and points out that the Freudian definition of female-gendering is essentially melancholic: the Oedipal complex by which a "girl becomes a girl," when she is asked to repudiate and disidentify with the mother even as she suffers from continual cultural pressures to identify with the mother, creates a melancholic condition of ungrieved loss and self-denial/denigration. Silverman works to revalue a sustained identification with the mother.

Frantz Fanon in *Black Skin, White Masks* is the first to gesture toward the conceptualization of race as melancholic, even though he never talks specifically about melancholia. In his discussion of "narcissism" he refers to the "black body" as "distorted, recolored, clad in mourning" (112). See my discussion in chapter 1 of *Flower Drum Song* for more detailed discussions of Fanon in relation to narcissism, beauty, and melancholia.

25. Michael Rogin, "The Two Declarations of American Independence." In *Race and Representation: Affirmative Action*, edited by Robert Post and Michael Rogin, 75–6. In an essay in the *Washington Post* Roger Wilkins proposes that there has been a price for the Declaration's doubleness: "by the time Thomas Jefferson wrote into the Declaration of Independence the sweeping egalitarian claim that underlies our myth of classlessness, the colonies had nurtured a slave culture and the psychic distortions required to sustain it for more than a century. A decade later, the Founding Fathers wrote slavery and its attendant racism into the Constitution, thus giving our racist ideology a legal standing that our egalitarian aspirations—set forth in our nonbinding Declaration—did not have. Racism was thus lathered into the foundations of our nation, and nothing—not the Civil War, not Reconstruction, not the Civil Rights revolution—has been able to blast it out of our culture and our psyches." "White Racism is Still the Problem," *Washington Post*, December 5, 1990, final edition, A25.

26. Michael Rogin, *Blackface, White Noice*, 24.

27. Abraham Kardiner and Lionel Ovesey wrote over fifty years ago in their treatise *The Mark of Oppression* that the lack of apparent signs of contrition does not mean that there is no awareness or a conscience ill at ease; indeed, the continual effort on the part of white supremacists to justify slavery and other forms of racism should signal to us that the refusal of guilt can often be the denial of such guilt and the further degradation and hatred of the other. Kardiner and Ovesey write: "Once you denigrated someone that way, the sense of guilt makes it imperative to degrade the object further to justify the entire procedure" (379). The denigration of an excluded object enacts a melancholic gesture of denial.

28. Toni Morrison, *Playing in the Dark*, 17.

Both in court and in writing, Kenneth Clark emphasizes the deleterious effects of segregation and discrimination on the psychological and moral development of black and white children. Clark and his colleagues write in "The Effects of Segregation and the Consequences of Desegregation: A Social Science Statement," Appendix to Appellants' Brief: "segregation, prejudices and discrimination, and their social concomitant potentially damage the personality of all children—the children of the majority group in a somewhat different way than the more obviously damaged children of the minority group" (in *Landmark Briefs and Arguments of the Supreme Court of the United States*, 143). They go on to say: "The report [the Mid-century White House Conference on Children and Youth, 1950] indicates further that confusion, conflict, moral cynicism, and disrespect for authority may arise in majority group children as the consequence of being taught the moral, religious and democratic principles of the brotherhood of man and the importance of justice . . . by the same persons and institutions who, in their support of racial segregation and related practices, seem to be acting in a prejudiced and discriminatory manner" (145). They also write: "The available scientific evidence indicates that much, perhaps all, of the observable differences among various racial and national groups may be adequately explained in terms of environmental differences" (148).

29. Paul Gilroy, *The Black Atlantic*, 129. Cited in the text hereafter.

30. Toni Morrison, *Unspeakable Things Unspoken*, 11.

31. I am thinking of Richard Dyer's work on film in the essay "Whiteness," which I discuss more fully in chapter 2 in relation to the construction of whiteness and beauty in Hollywood. See also Eric Sundquist, *To Wake the Nations*.

32. Frantz Fanon, *Black Skin, White Mask*, 8.

33. Michael Rogin, *Blackface, White Noise*, 15.

34. Julia A. Stern, *The Plight of Feeling*, 2.

35. Ibid., 2.

36. David Palumbo-Liu, *Asian/American*, 2. In examining the Asian American figure as the introjected "foreigner" within American polity, Palumbo-Liu's study expands the internal racial hauntings of American nationality beyond the black and white dyad to include Asian Americans as one of the central categories of constitutive loss in American imaginings.

37. Sollors, for example, quotes Justice Joseph Story in 1818 speaking about American Indians: "By a law of nature, they seem destined to a slow, but sure distinction. Everywhere, at the approach of the white man, they fade away. We hear the rustling of their footsteps, like that of withered leaves of autumn, and they are gone forever. They pass mournfully by us, and they return no more." *Beyond Ethnicity*, 115–30.

38. Richard Wright, *White Man Listen!* 79.

39. See Daryl Michael Scott's critique of the discourse of racial damage in *Contempt and Pity*.

40. My attempt to relocate discussions of racial injury away from a discourse of grievance is therefore not a rehearsal of Orlando Patterson's argument in *The Ordeal of Integration*, which contends that "the bizarre cult of the victim" has elided the history of progress since the civil rights era, effectively excluding African Americans from "the value of autonomy" that is "pivotal to American civic life." The problem lies not with voicing an agenda of grievance but with how that language of grievance has come to displace other terms in debates about racial injury. We have much to gain by a sustained investigation of the psychical and affective realities of racial discrimination. We need a new discourse about racial discrimination that does not automatically or solely resort to a vocabulary of victimization with its accompanying vicious cycles of blame, guilt, and denigration binding both the privileged and marginalized. (*The Ordeal of Integration*; see especially pp. 1–13 and 83–111.)

41. Years after the case, Kenneth Clark writes of the concerns that he and his colleagues continued to have about the possibilities of "social engineering." Sociologist John P. Jackson, Jr., points out that the social psychologists recruited by Thurgood Marshall, wary of what Kenneth Clark called social engineering, were themselves constantly aware of the tension between "objectivity" and "advocacy" (Jackson, "Creating a Consensus"). According to Jackson's documentation of the arduous writing process that went into the by-now-well-known "Social Science Statement," Brief to the Appellant, "a constant theme in the debates among the social scientists themselves was the separation of opinions

and interpretations from the 'facts' in the materials they represented to the court." In other words, these men were dealing with what is essentially a *literary* question: a question of narrative presentation and hermeneutics.

42. Ellison, *Invisible Man*, 4–5.

43. *Invisible Man* gives us a series of such white melancholic formation. The novel dramatizes this insight in the paint factory scene, for example, when the narrator learns that it takes a drop of black paint to make "true" whiteness. Another memorable example is the figure of Mr. Norton who is the white, liberal patron of the southern Negro college attended by the narrator. As a sponsor of Negro education, Norton builds a monument to the "progress of history as a mounting saga of triumphs" on the ghostly bodies of young black men (Ellison, 36). This man can be seen rhapsodizing about his visions for the Negro College and monumentalizing the black race even as he forgets the presence of the African American man driving him. Norton cannot see the young black man driving him but sees in the latter his own "destiny" (35). This is also the same man who manages to enjoy vicariously through the life of a poor black sharecropper the fulfillment of his own incestuous desires. See, too, Richard Dyer, "Whiteness."

44. Morrison, *The Bluest Eye*, 48.

45. Ibid., 22–3.

46. Ibid.

47. Richard Kluger, *Simple Justice*, 667. Gender was an elided issue in the original Clark experiment in several ways. First, a figure who has often been erased in the history of the experiment is the person who initiated this research, Mamie Clark, scientific partner and wife of Kenneth Clark. Second, the experiment included boys and girls as its subjects but did not distinguish or register possible gender differences in the responses. Third, the experiment read the racial implications of the dolls but not their potential implications as gendered objects.

48. Elizabeth Abel, "Bathroom Doors and Drinking Fountains," 436. Abel goes on to demonstrate how Jim Crow signs on bathroom doors and drinking fountains constitute a racial symbolic that while appropriating sexual difference ends up also destablizing that structure of difference. See, too, her perspicacious reading of "bathrooms" in Lacan, where she demonstrates that the language of racial segregation underwrites the Lacanian metaphor of sexual law.

49. See Paul Gilroy (*The Black Atlantic*), Ralph Ellison (*Shadow and Act*), and W. E. B. Du Bois (*The Souls of Black Folk*), on music and jazz.

50. W. E. B. Du Bois, *The Souls of Black Folk*, 181–91.

51. Saidiya Hartman, *Scenes of Subjection*, 35–6.

52. For the definitive history of Asian immigrants in America in the nineteenth and twentieth centuries, see Ronald Takaki, *Strangers from a Different Shore*.

53. The two "race books" that received the most publicity in 1997 both conceive of race in America as exclusively black and white: Stephen and Abigail Thernstrom, *America in Black and White*, and David A. Shiplers, *A Country of Strangers*.

54. *Li Sing v. U.S., 180 U.S. 486* (1901) and *Chin Bak Kan v. U.S., 186 U.S. 193*. See also Palumbo-Liu, *Asian /American*, especially pp. 17–42.

55. *Gong Lum v. Rice*, 275 US 78(1929). By the end of the century, as white-ness became increasingly significant as a kind of safety net, providing a baseline of eligibility to rights, opportunities, and minimal social position, many immigrants came quickly to understand the material advantages of being declared white. See also Adolph Reed, Jr., "Skin Deep: The Fiction of Race," *Village Voice*, September 24, 1996: "No one with an alternative would have wanted to attend Mississippi's schools for black people, which were never intended to provide anything like a decent education. A group of Chinese in Jackson therefore sought to exploit the ambiguity of their colored designation to escape that fate. The Chinese petitioners argued all the way to the Supreme Court . . . that as an intermediate group they were in crucial ways racially and culturally nearer to whites and therefore should be permitted to attend white schools." They lost the case.

56. *Korematsu v. U.S.*, 323 U.S. 244 (1944).

57. Lisa Lowe, *Immigrant Acts*, 5.

58. The contradictory evocations of Asian Americans as alternately victims of, beneficiaries of, or simply uninvolved in the contemporary debate over af-firmative action provides another example of the ghostly projections placed upon this unevenly raced body. Precisely as such a spectral display, Asian Americans as a group serve as a crucial barometer of the contemporary racial climate. See Michael Omi and Dana Takagi, "Situating Asian Americans in the Political Discourse on Affirmative Action," in *Race and Representation*, edited by Robert Post and Michael Rogin, 271–80.

59. Henry Louis Gates, "Authority, (White) Power and the (Black) Critic; It's All Greek To Me" and Barbara Christian, "The Race for Theory," both in *Critical Inquiry*. Henry Louis Gates, "A Debate on Activism in Black Studies: A Plea That Scholars Act Upon, Not Just Interpret, Events," and Manning Marable, "A Call to Protect Academic Integrity from Politics," *New York Times* April 4, 1998, A13, A15.

60. Lisa Lowe, "Heterogeneity, Hybridity, Multiplicity: Asian American Difference," in *Immigrant Acts*, 60–84. Originally appeared as "Heterogeneity, Hybridity, Multiplicity: Marking Asian American Difference," *Diaspora* (spring 1991): 24–44. Citations from this article come from the reprint version in *Immigrant Acts* and are in the text.

61. See Jacqueline Rose, *States of Fantasy*. In her introduction, Rose offers a critical model of psychoanalysis that posits an entrenched relationship between the asocial and the public, the subjective and the political. Rose argues that an examination of fantasy, for example, is crucial to political critique. For Rose, fantasy—far from being asocial or antagonistic to public being—plays a central, constitutive role in the modern world of states and nations. For her, this place of analysis is the only answer to escaping identity politics, "which challenges the dominant but without changing the rhetorical or psychic rules . . . and reproduces the stability of a counter-identification," on the one hand, and a sense of overly positivistic diasporic freedom that "cannot be a solu-tion since diaspora is the source of the problem" of modern statehood, on the other.

62. Hortense Spillers, "'The Permanent Obliquity of an In(pha)llibly Straight': In the Time of the Daughters and the Fathers," in *Changing Our Own Words*, edited by Cheryl A. Wall.

63. Some of the most compelling work in African American studies comes from critics working at the conjunction between psychoanalysis and feminism (Elizabeth Abel, bell hooks, Barbara Johnson, Kobena Mercer, Hortense Spillers, Claudia Tate.) Several of them acknowledge the difficulties of engaging psychoanalysis with race. hooks notes in *Black Looks* that while "courageous individual critical thinkers are increasingly using psychoanalysis in discussions of race, it is equally clear that there is a continued resistance on the part of many race scholars" (129). Mercer makes a similar point in "Fear of a Black Penis": "Psychoanalytic concepts now float freely in debates on cultural politics, but there is still a stubborn resistance to the recognition of unconscious phantasy as a structuring principle of our social, emotional, and political life" (80–83).

64. In *Psychoanalysis and the Black Novel*, Claudia Tate argues for psychoanalysis as a viable tool for reading black texts because it pays attention to "private" or "unsocialized desires" (7) not allowable by the political expediencies surrounding a black text, what she calls the "protocols of race." However, by posing "public, explicit, collective racial discourse" and the "implicit, private, psychological effects of narrative subjectivity" as antithetical to one another, Tate's argument retreats into an old dichotomy that consigns psychoanalysis to a "surplus" realm outside of sociomaterial concerns. I am interested in psychoanalysis precisely as a critical theory about the social, and about the inseparability between the social and the personal.

65. Joan Copjec, *Supposing the Subject*, vii–xiii.

66. The question of history in psychoanalysis is most easily, though not exclusively, located in the theorization of trauma. In writing about trauma, Cathy Caruth proposes in *Unclaimed Experience* that "through trauma, we can understand that a rethinking of reference is aimed not at eliminating history but at resuscitating it in our understanding, that is, at precisely permitting *history* to arise where *immediate understanding* may not" (19). In *The Location of Culture*, Homi Bhabha sees an explicit connection between history and psychoanalysis: "Psychoanalytic temporality . . . invests the utterance of the 'present'—its displaced times, its affective intensities—with cultural and political value. Placed in the scenario of the unconscious, the 'present' is neither the mimetic sign of historical contemporaneity (the immediacy of experience), nor is it the visible terminus of the historicl past (the teleology of tradition)" (215). Bhabha also makes explicit the connection between history and the psychoanalytic notion of trauma: "a historical *intermediacy*, familiar to the psychoanalytic concept of *Nachtraglichkeit* (deferred action) . . . [in which] the past is discovered in the present, so that the future becomes (one again) an *open question*, instead of being specified by the fixity of the past . . . makes available to marginalized or minority individuals a mode of performative agency" (219).

Chapter 2. Beauty and Ideal Citizenship

1. I place the term "Asian American" within quotations here for two reasons. I wish to denote the ambiguity that exists within this usually hyphenated term, since it is precisely the ambiguity between Asian *or* American that the term often provokes and, more important, that this film is anxiously negotiating. The term is also somewhat anachronistic for the late fifties world de-

picted in *Flower Drum Song*. The term "Asian American," strictly speaking, is a relatively recent formation, reflecting not a denotative category but a highly contested sign borne out of and bearing witness to the historical struggle for identity on the part of Americans with Asian descent. (See Lemuel F. Ignacio, *Asian Americans and Pacific Islanders* (*Is There Such an Ethnic Group?*) and Sau-ling Cynthia Wong, introduction to *Reading Asian American Literature*.) It is also worth remembering that in common parlance, Asians in America were initially known as "Celestial Beings" and later, when they became threats to white immigrant labor forces, the "Yellow Peril." The subsequent change in the sixties of the "Yellow Peril" to "Model Minority" will be further discussed later in this chapter.

2. C. Y. Lee, *Flower Drum Song*.

3. In subsequent years a number of Asians applied for naturalization, and a few succeeded, only to have their citizenship later declared null. As Sau-ling Cynthia Wong notes, after the Naturalization Act of 1790 limiting citizenship to "free whites" was challenged on behalf of blacks after the Civil War, "Asian immigrants became the most significant 'other' in terms of citizenship eligibility" (Wong, *Reading Asian American Literature*, 5, quoting Jeff Lesser, "'Always Outsiders': Asians, Naturalization, and the Supreme Court," *Amerasia Journal* 12:1, 83–110). See also Herbert R. Barringer, *Asians and Pacific Islanders in the United States*; Bill Ong Hing, *Making and Remaking Asian America through Immigration Policy, 1850–1990*; Lisa Lowe, *Immigrant Acts: On Asian American Cultural Politics*; Michael Omi and Howard Winant, *Racial Formation in the United States*; David Palumbo-Liu, *Asian/American: Historical Crossings of a Racial Frontier*.

4. See Norimitsu Onishi, "Merging Identity" in the *New York Times*, May 30, 1996.

5. As Lisa Lowe points out, the history of legalized exclusion and immigration discipline exercised on the Asian American body is also a history of gendering/masculinizing both the American and the Asian American national subjects. For her analysis of the intersecting lines of gender and race in the legal making of an "Asian American" immigration policy, see *Immigrant Acts*.

For historical and sociological information on and surrounding the period of bachelor societies, see: Thomas W. Chinn, *Bridging the Pacific*; Winston Elstob, *Chinatown*; Samuel D. Lee, *San Francisco's Chinatown*; Shirley Sun, *Three Generations of Chinese*; Chin-Yéu Chen, *San Francisco's Chinatown*; Judy Yung, *Unbound Feet*.

6. See Gina Marchetti, *Romance and the 'Yellow Peril'*.

7. *Flower Drum Song*, for example, makes a ghostly guest appearance in Wayne Wang's acclaimed *Chan Is Missing* (1982). *Chan* has been heralded as the first authentic Asian American film to enjoy crossover success and seems about as thematically, filmically, politically, and historically distant from *Flower Drum Song* as can be. Yet in the concluding sequence, where we see view of a realistic and desolate Chinatown, we also hear on the music track Linda Low's number "Grant Avenue, San Francisco, California, U.S.A." Disappeared from sight but lingering as music, Linda-as-citation fills the evacuated screen space, not as irony but as memory: rough and grainy, her Chinatown rings out in the film with all the deliberation of a *record*, a piece of music that denaturalizes itself as soundtrack, reenactment, and history.

8. For a reading of the Broadway musical and its propensity for abject elation, see D. A. Miller's *Place for Us*. Drawing from Miller's insights into the genre, this study argues that the musical's embarrassingly un-self-conscious penchant for exuberance offers not only a congenial home for gender melancholia but also the manic expression of racial and national dysphoria, a peculiarly American amalgamation of delight and repugnance.

9. Rich Long, "China Syndrome," *National Review*, March 24, 1997, 38–40. For responses from the Asian American community, see Frank H. Wu, "Every Picture Tells a Story," *Asianweek*, April 4, 1997, 11, and Emil Guillermo, "Isn't That Hysterical: Why A Racist Magazine Cover Isn't All Bad," *Asianweek*, April 4, 1997, 5.

This *National Review* cartoon is also horrifying in its reference to a whole tradition of anti-Chinese political and editorial cartoons widely published in mainstream American newspapers and magazines in the period between 1869 to 1900, when anti-Chinese sentiment and paranoia ran rampant in response to white labor anxiety. In addition to insulting or demonizing messages that accompany these nationally circulated images, the "Chinese" is invariably portrayed with squinting eyes, buck teeth, and coolie hat. See the pictorial collection Philip P. Choy, Lorraine Dong, and Marlon K. Hom, eds., *Coming Man*.

10. Homi Bhabha, "The Other Question—The Stereotype and Colonial Discourse," in *The Location of Culture*, 71. For an elucidation of the problem of conducting image analysis (on the level of whether it is a "good" or "bad" image), see Robert Stanley and Louise Spence, "Colonialism, Racism, and Representation," introduction to *Screen* 24:2, special issue (March–April 1983), 2–20.

11. The neglect of this question has undermined much of the work being done on the question of the stereotype. I do think, for example, that it is not merely a problem of rhetorical density, but rather a symptom, that the subject and object of authorial discourse often blur in Homi Bhabha's works on authority and the stereotype. In "Of Mimicry and Man," in *The Location or Culture*, Bhabha locates ambivalence on the part of the colonizer and thereby disturbs that authority; yet what remains untreated is the relationship between the object of ambivalent discourse and that ambivalence. This critique will be treated more thoroughly in the following chapters.

12. Hall's ethnic though ethnically indeterminate looks have provided Hollywood with an easy screen onto which to project race itself. The racialized subject par excellence, Hall enjoyed a career in film and on stage playing characters of various races, including everything from Asian (as here in *Flower Drum Song*) to African American (*Paradise in Harlem*, 1939) to Pacific Islander (*South Pacific*, 1958).

13. I take the term "recursive" from Barbara Johnson, "Is Female to Male as Ground to Figure?" in *Feminism and Psychoanalysis*, edited by Richard Feldstein and Judith Root, 255–68. Johnson dismantles the gendered, metaphoric hierarchy implicit in the relations between notions of foreground and background (or tenor and vehicle), by calling forth the idea of the "recursive" as it appears in drawing vocabulary. The "recursive" is designed to refer to a mutually constitutive relationship between positive and negative space, hence altering the fundamental hierarchical connotations conferred by those terms.

14. *San Francisco Chinatown on Parade: In Picture and Story*, a pamphlet published and distributed by the Chinese Chamber of Commerce, 1961.

15. C. Y. Lee, introduction to *San Francisco Chinatown on Parade: In Picture and Story*, 8.

16. Bhabha, "The Other Question," 66.

17. In Ethan A. Mordan's comprehensive introduction to Rodgers and Hammerstein's oeuvre, *Rodgers & Hammerstein*, Mordan argues that *Flower Drum Song* represents a choreographic setback from the innovations of other Rodgers and Hammerstein masterpieces such as *Oklahoma!* and *Carousel*. He cites, for example, *Flower Drum Song*'s use of an old style: the discrete "time-out" dream-ballet.

18. Or, at least, the only trace of the "East" in the lyrics comes from a fantasmatic allusion to Hiroshima and the Cold War anxiety over nuclear weaponry. See Bruce A. McConachie, "The 'Oriental' Musicals of Rodgers and Hammerstein and the U. S. War in Southeast Asia," in *Staging Difference*, edited by Marc Maufort (57–74). McConachie makes the argument that Rodgers and Hammerstein's three Orientalist musicals help to establish a legitimate basis for the American war against the people of Southeast Asia in the 1960s. My argument on *Flower Drum Song* suggests that Rodgers and Hammerstein are also formulating a very specifically *domestic* policy about American citizenship and the racial immigrant therein.

19. Ralph Ellison, *Shadow and Act*, 53–54.

20. Sollors, *Beyond Ethnicity*, 67–9, 172–3, 182–3. (Noted in Rogin, *Blackface, White Noise*, 72.)

21. Rogin, *Blackface, White Noise*, 69–70. For analysis of music's relationship to the melting pot, see: Ralph Ellison, *Shadow and Act*; Robert Hass, *Twentieth-Century Pleasures*; John Gennari, "'A Weapon for Integration': Frank Marshall Davis and the Politics of Jazz"; Tom McIntosh, "Reflections on Jazz and the Politics of Race"; John S. Otto and Augustus M. Burns, "Black and White Cultural Interaction in the Early Twentieth Century South: Race and Hillbilly Music"; Cecilia L. Ridgeway and John M. Roberts, "Urban Popular Music and Interaction: A Semantic Relationship"; Paul Rinzler, "Preliminary Thoughts on Analyzing Musical Integration among Jazz Performers"; Philip Tagg, "Open Letter: 'Black Music,' 'Afro-American Music,' and 'European Music.'"

22. Consider the following (in chronological order): *The Melting Pot* (1915), *The Singing Fool* 91928), *Road to Singapore* (1940), *Meet Me in St. Louis*, (1944), *The Al Jolson Story* (1946), *Jolson Sings Again* (1949), *Pagan Love Song* (1950), *West Side Story* (1957), *South Pacific* (1958), *Funny Girl* (1964), *Hair* (1967), *Fiddler on the Roof* (1971), *Saturday Night Fever* (1977), *Fame* (1980), *La Bamba* (1987). Although it may be argued that the musical, for all its celebration, has always been ambivalent about the ideology of the melting pot (for example, the tragic ending of *West Side Story*), it is still a remarkably faithful popular culture instrument in the expression of that ideal.

23. The shift in public representations of Asian Americans from "Yellow Peril" to "Model Minority" in the sixties marks the deployment of model minority as a form of containment on the one hand and a reprimand against other minorities on the other. This historical shift plays out precisely the collapse of the pathological into the euphoric that this chapter demonstrates. Furthermore, as I will shortly show, the weight of this swinging pendulum of alternate

pathologization and idealization is being absorbed mostly by the *female* Asian American subject, as is here the case of Mei Li.

24. In speaking about ideology and the formation of subjecthood, Althusser coins the term "interpellation" to refer to the splicing of an individual into a subject position. He gives the simple example of being hailed on the streets, and when one turns to answer the call, one is interpellated. A film example cited by Slavoj Zizek in *The Sublime Object of Ideology* is Hitchcock's *North by North-west*: when the Gary Grant character answers a call not meant for him, he is spliced into that other man's identity and life.

25. David Gutierrez, *Walls and Mirrors*.

26. Consider another citation closer to home that is being echoed here: the conclusion of *Oklahoma*, when illegality was evoked as an agent for American confirmation.

27. In contrast to Mei Li's public exposure, Linda Low, although a morally "exposed" character, is nonetheless finally redeemed through marriage and the status of her national identity, which has been literally naturalized: Sammy Fong happily tells his mother, "[Linda] is OK. She entered this country the *normal* way: through her mother!" (my emphasis).

28. Much of what has been written about beauty relates to femininity and feminism, which mostly speak—with or without self-consciousness—to and from a fundamental paradigm of the middle-class white point of view (De Beauvoir, Murdoch, Hall, Lambert, Wolf, Grieco, Cropper, Scarry).

For more on the question of feminine beauty and its relation to race, both through exposition and elision, see: Natasha B. Barnes, "Face of the Nation: Race, Nationalism and identities in Jamaican Beauty Pageants"; Wendy Chapkis, *Beauty Secrets: Women and the Politics of Appearance*; Kim F. Hall, "Beauty and the Beast of Whiteness: Teaching Race and Gender"; Véronique Nahoum-Grappe, "The Beautiful Woman," trans. Arthur Goldhammer, in *A History of Women: Renaissance and Enlightenment Paradoxes*, edited by Natalie Zeman Davis and Arlette Farge; Naomi Wolf, *The Beauty Myth: How Images of Beauty Are Used Against Women*.

29. Richard Dyer, "Whiteness," 42–8. See also Dyer's work on Marilyn Monroe as a cinematic apotheosis of whiteness and ideal femininity, in *Heavenly Bodies*.

30. D. W. Griffith's *Broken Blossom* (1919) established the stylistic use of white actors in yellow face to fill Asian roles. Some of the more "classic" yellow face performers included: Warner Oland and Boris Karloff, both of whom played Fu Manchu for four successive decades; Peter Sellers, who revived the character in 1980; Warner Oland also as Charlie Chan, a role later assumed by Sidney Toler and Roland Winters and in 1980 by Peter Ustinov.

31. I would argue that it is this demand for a critical mass of Asian performers, even more so than its racial stereotypes, that prevents *Flower Drum Song* from being revived as persistently as, say, *The King and I*, which for all its flagrant Orientalism not only is one of the longest running Broadway musicals but also recently won the Tony.

Flower Drum Song was most recently revived by the Peninsula Civic Light Opera in San Mateo, California, in 1996. Not surprisingly, in the press kit released by the company, the artistic director Rosemary Hood tells us that such a revival was "timely" (in spite of the piece's more blatant political problems) because of the Bay Area's strong Asian community (what she calls "local interest") *and* of the talent pool, the new generation of performers who are Asian. We may assume that with increasing opportunities for Asian Americans in theatrical performances we might begin to see the revival of *Flower Drum Song*. Indeed, playwright David Henry Hwang is writing a "suitable" new version of *Flower Drum Song* for a Broadway revival.

32. For a reading of "beauty" in relation to monstrosity in the context of feminist (not racial) readings, see Jane Gallop, "The Monster in the Mirror: The Feminist Critic's Psychoanalysis," in Feldstein and Root, *Feminism and Psychoanalysis*, 13–24.

33. Elaine Scarry, "Beauty and Its Relation to Justice," talk given at the "Aesthetics and Difference" Conference at University of California, Riverside, October 22, 1998. Drawing from Simone de Beauvoir, Simone Weil, and Iris Murdoch, Scarry argues that beauty encourages, rather than distracts from, justice by effecting a kind of "unselfing" on the part of the spectator. See Scarry, *On Beauty and Being Just*.

34. Nancy Kwan, the actress, is in fact Eurasian, born to a Chinese father and a British mother. Her biracial presence with its complicated signification is one of the reasons I find the movie version of *Flower Drum Song* fascinating. But even if Nancy Kwan were not biracial by birth, the coding of Linda's whiteness operates, as I point out, on several levels.

This fantasmatic whiteness on the part of Linda Low was much less pronounced in the Broadway version, where the role was played by Pat Suzuki. Suzuki offered a contrast to the Mei Li character (also played by Umeki in the Broadway version), not so much through a difference in body type, as through her brash sensuality. Only in the film version do we discern the fantasmatic interracial threat that articulates the unspoken national and racial anxiety submerged in the plot.

35. Lest the reader find my association of "long legs" with whiteness capricious or arbitrary, let me point out that the question of "long legs" versus "bowlegs" has historically haunted the Asian female body. Léopold Sédar Senghor, one of the founders of the Negritude movement, in a poetic meditation on Manhattan as *the* apotheosis of what is American, associates New York with the beauty of a leggy blond: "*New York! D'abord j'ai été confondu par ta beauté, ces grandes filles d'or aux jambes longues*" (*Oeuvre poétique*, 113–114). Low's "long legs" further and specifically mark her Westernness within the context of the history of stereotypes surrounding Asian body types. Critic Gordon H. Chang records the difficulties of Asian American performers in finding employment precisely because of their perceived body types: "Hollywood and the stageshow circuit usually wanted Asian Americans only as curiosities or for the annual Chinese New Year's Act, hardly enough work to sustain oneself. They were told: "Chinese dance? They don't have any rhythm,' besides, 'they've got terrible legs . . . they're bowlegged" ("Forbidden Fruits," 182). The term "bowlegged" came from the Cary Grant character in the 1931 film *Singapore Sue* but is in fact an echo of a conceptualization of Asian physical characteristics rooted as far back as the European Enlightenment. In the mid–eighteenth century, Immanuel Kant noted in his anthropological writings that a defining feature

of the so-called "Oriental" is "short legs with fat calves . . . although they all make themselves more beautiful on occasion" (quoted by Emmanuel Chukwudi, Eze, *Race and the Enlightenment*, 62).

In *Flower Drum Song*'s Celestial Garden and its real-life historical model, a nightclub called Forbidden City in San Francisco in the forties and fifties, Asian performers made themselves over to be more appetizing to white audiences—indeed, "make themselves more beautiful on occasion"—as a combination of Oriental exotica and some gestures of aesthetic comfort. For example, the real Forbidden City (filmically documented by Arthur Dong in *Forbidden City, U.S.A.*) flourished and drew a strong white clientele by featuring "Oriental" singers performing Cole Porter and playing the Big Band sound, publicizing the talents of a "Chinese Sophie Tucker" or a "Chinese Frank Sinatra," creating a form of American music in yellow face. See article and photo layout in "Life Goes to the 'Forbidden City'," *Life*, December 9, 1940; Gordon H. Chang, "Forbidden Fruits," 181–6.

It is therefore no coincidence that Linda Low the "long-legged dame" finds work and enjoys star billing in this "all-Chinese" show. The antidote to the historically imagined Chinese "symptom" of nonbeauty—and the most appetizing Chinese body in the world of this film—turns out to be the most *Western* Asian body that one can imagine.

36. This scene of female narcissism has enjoyed a long tradition in the musical. Think, for instance, of Bernstein's "I Feel Pretty" in *West Side Story*. These scenes of female self-celebration, however, are never without their gender troubles and pathos. See D. A. Miller, *Place for Us*. The lyrics and *mis en scène* of "I Enjoy Being a Girl," within the contestation of national, domestic borders being played out in *Flower Drum Song*, most visibly highlight the racial troubles inhering in these moments of self-celebration.

37. In *An American Dilemma*, Gunnar Myrdal specifically ties the rhetoric of "purity" to American thinking about segregation. He links the anxiety over "social equality" directly to an anxiety about miscegenation: "The kernel of the popular theory of 'no social equality' . . . will be presented as a firm determination . . . to preserve 'the purity of the white race.' . . . Important in this identification is the notion of 'the absolute and unchangeable superiority of the white race.' . . . It is further found that . . . sex becomes in this popular theory the principle around which the whole structure of segregation of the Negroes . . . is organized."

Here, curiously, the Chinese man is not taking the place of the other minority, the black man, in this movie. Rather, the "purity" and "superiority" of Wang Chi Yang's fatherly will, fulfilled by the end of the movie, suggests that a fantasmatic identification has been established between Chinese patriarchy and white patriarchy, except this identification has the added task of protecting white patriarchy in turn. The realization of the father's will in the movie secures the containment of Chinatown.

38. I have already discussed how the figure of Mei Li disturbs boundaries. Now we can refine the argument and see that she poses a national border threat, but not a racial threat, since she is a Chinese woman stealing into Chinatown. Indeed, we can say that, between the figures of Mei Li and Madame Liang, the ethnic containment of Chinatown within the United States works to confirm national boundaries even while alleviating the threat of racial mixing posed by a national identity blind to race and ethnicity.

39. There is yet another transgression being marked here. This robbery is also a chastisement of Chi Yang for having listened to his assimilated children and sister-in-law who talked him into depositing money in a bank in the first place. In short, Chi Yang, without ever setting his feet outside of Chinatown, was already being punished for participating in American capitalism.

40. Gunnar Myrdal, *An American Dilemma*.

41. Mei Li's etherealness is continually punctuated by humiliating, corporeal reminders: for example, scenes where prospective in-laws check her teeth and muscle tone, where her "social grace" reveals itself to be slavish labor, and so on. If the general American viewer of the early sixties were to accept her beauty as ethereal Eastern grace itself—and many did—then we have to also understand *that* understanding as itself already symptomatic of Western ideals about Eastern beauty/femininity.

42. Kwan remains to this day an ambivalent and vexing cultural icon for Asian American women. As recently as 1991, one can find in the self-proclaimed progressive Asian American journal *A. Magazine* a protracted meditation on Nancy Kwan: Therese On, "'Strictly a Female Female': Growing Up with Nancy Kwan." The article is not surprisingly a vexed combination of criticism of and tribute to Kwan as the emblem of Asian American femininity.

43. Considering Linda Low's pleasure at "the whistle," a better example of analogous interpellation might be the opening sequence of Hitchcock's *Birds*, where the Tippi Hedren character also hears a whistle: from a bird.

44. Sigmund Freud, "On Narcissism: An Introduction" (1914), *SE*, 14:88–89. Cited in text hereafter.

45. Jacques Lacan, "The Mirror Stage as Formative of the Function of the I as Revealed in the Psychoanalytic Experience," in *Écrits*, 1–7.

46. Frantz Fanon, *Black Skin, White Masks*, 113. Cited in text hereafter.

47. By now Fanon is as famous for what he *didn't* say about women of color as for what he did say about black men. Of the "woman of color," he writes, "I know nothing about her" (180). See Mary Ann Doane, "Dark Continents: Epistemologies of Racial and Sexual Difference in Psychoanalysis and the Cinema," in *Femmes Fatales* and Diana Fuss, "Interior Colonies: Frantz Fanon and the Politics of Identification," in *Identification Papers*.

48. Kaja Silverman, *The Threshold of the Visible World*, 33.

49. For an insightful discussion of the interplay among the fetish, the substitute, and nostalgia, see Joseph Roach, *Cities of the Dead*.

50. The other echo one might hear is, of course, "I enjoy being a girl who enjoys having a girl," but I emphasize Low's male identification because her lyrical joy in her own objectness derives precisely from, and to the extent that she can appropriate, the male gaze, whether it be, I would argue, a heterosexual or homosexual one.

For an analysis on the relationship between the figures of the gay impresario and the female star, see Alexander Doty, "The Queer Aesthete, the Diva, and *The Red Shoes*," in *Out Takes*, 46–71.

51. Judith Butler, *Bodies That Matter: On the Discursive Limits of Sex*, 12–3.

52. In the novel version of *Flower Drum Song*, Helen was not an option because her face was pockmarked. She was not only not beautiful but also seemed to physically embody the sickly conditions of Chinatown itself. In the movie version, Helen does not suffer such a physical or visual handicap, but

as I argue here, the character of Helen is still stigmatized and marked as the wrong choice within the national parable embedded within the movie.

Chapter 3. A Fable of Exquisite Corpses

1. Maxine Hong Kingston, *The Woman Warrior*, 182. Cited in text hereafter.

2. My detection of hypochondria on the part of the narrator does not come from an assumption that an Asian American ought to feel at home in Chinatown; rather, this chapter is interested in analyzing why the narrator herself makes this psychical connection between health and geography and the ways in which she assigns illness to the literal place of her familial and cultural origin.

3. Wong, *Reading Asian American Literature*, 118–66.

4. David Wong Louie, *Pangs of Love*, 209; Jessica Hagedorn, *Dogeaters*, 14; Hisaye Yamamoto, "Wiltshire Boulebard," in *Seventeen Syllaboes and Other Stories*, 20–33.

5. One of the leading psychologists in the field of Asian American mental health, Stanley Sue, points out precisely this fact in the book he cowrote with James K. Morishima, *The Mental Health of Asian Americans*. Sue and Morishima point out that the term "Asian/Pacific Americans" itself implies a homogeneity that is lacking among these peoples, whose divergent languages and cultures render the term highly inadequate. At the same time, they agree that the term is useful because it suggests some common issues for investigation. Sue's work emphasizes the importance of further research in the field of Asian American mental health and points out how little clinical and theoretical study has been done on the "psychopathology of Asian Americans" (46).

6. Although "hypochondria" as a term has been around for hundreds of years, theories of it are still as vague as the condition they denote. For centuries this condition attracted the attention of great doctors and philosophers who believed the disorder stemmed from a physiological imbalance and tried every drug and therapeutic regime at their command to control this common misery. By the mid–eighteenth century, with George Cheyne's *The English Malady*, the disorder began to reveal a split not only between body and mind, but also between philosophy and medicine. By the nineteenth century, hypochondria came to be associated with emotional rather than physical problems and, once identified as a mental disease, quickly acquired pejorative connotations and got parceled out among the psychoses and neuroses. From that point on, hypochondria acquired its modern characteristic as an emotional illness involving morbid preoccupation.

On the medical front little attention has been given to the disease in this century. The term itself dropped from national and international registers of recognized disorders. What recent literature exists on hypochondria comes from the field of psychology and continues to engage in a struggle to garner legitimacy for the somatic manifestation of the disease.

In literature, hypochondria, often accompanied by expressions of melancholia, has enjoyed a lively presence: in the writings of Montaigne, Chateaubriand, Proust, Mann, Kierkegaard, Dürer, Kafka, Benjamin, Adorno, Tolstoy, Tennyson, Darwin, Austen, just to name a few. As I argue in this chapter, "hypochondria" is surfacing with regularity among Asian American writers in this century. Little, if any, critical attention has been paid to the notion of hypochondria as a complex, conjoined textual expression of affective *and* sociological crisis at the site of racism and assimilation.

7. Michael Rogin, *Blackface, White Noise*.

8. The other community most noted for their "threatening" capacity for assimilation is of course Jewish Americans. For comparative discussions about mass culture's perceptions about Asian American and African American processes of assimilation, see Michael Rogin, "Making America Home—Racial Masquerade and Ethnic Assimilation in the Transition to American History" (reprinted in another version as "Racial Masquerade and Ethnic Assimilation in the Transition to Talking Pictures," in *Blackface, White Noise*).

When it comes to Asian Americans, the paradoxical anxiety about the assimilation of this "ideal minority" usually tends to express itself as an anxiety about economic and educational competition. American misgiving about these assimilating "ideal immigrants" can be sighted from the recent debates over affirmative action in university admittance policy to the barely displaced fear of the Asian "buying up" of America. For a detailed history of anti-Asian sentiment in America, from the initial fears that Asians will never assimilate to the fears that Asians have assimilated too much, see Bill Ong Hing, *Making and Remaking Asian America through Immigration Policy, 1850–1990*.

Another resurfacing of this anxiety about assimilation can be seen in popular culture in the increasing tendency in recent blockbuster science fiction movies to give hostile alien races, already an established trope, the evil and threatening characteristics of assimilation: for example, the lethal Borgs in *Star Trek: First Contact* (Paramount, 1996) who "are capable of assimilating all life, everywhere"(Lisa Schwarzbaum, "Space Jammin,'" *Entertainment Weekly*, November 29, 1996, 72); and the following year, the menace of adaptive imitation in *Mimic* (Dimension Films, 1997).

9. Bette Bao Lord, "Walking in Lucky Shoes," *Newsweek*, July 6, 1992, 18–9.

10. In the last couple of years the *New York Times* has featured annual stories on the status and implications of "hyphenated" citizenship in the United States: Jim Sleeper, "Hyphenated and Americans," *New York Times*, April 27, 1997, late edition sec. 7, p. 37; Celia W. Dugger, "Hyphenated and American," *New York Times*, March 21, 1998, late edition, A-1.

11. As dramatized by Jennie Livingston's 's 1991 documentary film on drag balls in New York City, *Paris Is Burning*, the standard of "realness" straddles faith and artifice—hence the pathos behind Venus Extravaganza's exclamation, "This is how I feel real!" For a discussion of *Paris Is Burning* and of drag as the simultaneous denaturalization and reidealization of hyperbolic heterosexual gender norms, see Judith Butler's "Gender Is Burning," in *Bodies That Matter*, 121–40.

12. Michel Serres, *The Parasite*, 197.

13. One may think of hypochondria as designed specifically to confound that difference. This boundary confusion in turn shares a certain logic with melancholia and subtends the etymological connection between melancholia and hypochondria. Judith Butler comes at this point from another direction. In *Bodies That Matter*, she offers the thesis and pun that while of course there is such a thing as a real body, what gives that body signification and meaning, what makes matter matter, however, is precisely its ideological and imaginative preconditions.

14. In *Melancholy and Society*, Wolf Lepenies calls melancholia a utopian dream.

15. Being ill when you are a child or growing up can always be seen as an enchanted interlude, with the outside world a safe, distant murmur. But this particular escape, as I will show, is tied in to the outside world as specific intrusions of racial and gender injunctions. It is also an interlude that follows on the heels of (and is a direct response to) a violent exchange with another child.

16. Louis Althusser, "Ideology and the State Ideological Apparatus," in *Lenin and Philosophy and Other Essays*.

17. One dramatization of the harrowing aspect of interpellation would be Hitchcock's *North by Northwest*, where the plot runs on a case of mistaken identity, a case of inescapable interpellation when the protagonist answers a wrong telephone call. See the chapter "'*Che Vuoi?*'" in Slavoj Zizek, *The Sublime Object of Ideology*.

18. Melanie Klein, "Infantile Anxiety Situations Reflected in a Work of Art and in the Creative Impulse," (84–94) (citations in text hereafter) and "Symbol Formation in Ego Development" (95–111) in *Selected Melanie Klein*. See Jacque Lacan's argument with Klein in "The Topic of the Imaginary" (73–88) and "Discourse Analysis and Ego Analysis," (63–69) in *The Seminars of Jacques Lacan*, book 1. See also Mary Jacobus's reading of Lacan's debate with Klein in "'Tea Daddy': Poor Mrs. Klein and the Pencil Shavings," in *Reading Melanie Klein*, 91–112.

19. Sigmund Freud, "On Narcissism: An Introduction" (1914), *SE*, 14:85.

20. My thanks to Judith Butler for pointing out to me the connection between *Versagung* and speech, and for her always inspiring analysis of the Freudian ego in a melancholic landscape. See *The Psychic Life of Power*.

21. The view that assimilation is an act of impoverishment and betrayal reductively assumes an exhaustive limit on the subjective resources of an individual. This view is particularly favored by racialist and nationalist discourses, which have orchestrated political relationships in such a fashion as to render certain identities to be mutually exclusive: that is, to be American comes at the price of being Asian.

22. Homi K. Bhabha, "Of Mimicry and Man: The Ambivalence of Colonial Discourse," in *The Location of Culture*, 86. Cited in text hereafter. Originally appeared in *October* 28 (Spring 1984): 125–133.

23. This is why the very notion of a "role model" when imposed on a minority subject often implies a paradox, because it means that someone has both attained and "given in" to dominant, normative ideals.

24. Social psychologists have isolated one aspect of this "vigilant worry" as the "stereotype threat": the anxiety for the racialized minority of being viewed through the lens of a negative stereotype, or the fear of doing something that would inadvertently confirm that stereotype. See Claude Steele, "Thin Ice." But my argument here is that the haunting notion of self-comparison can be evoked by an ideal as by a negative image—the point is that a psychical mechanism of measurement gets installed and operates somewhat as self-sabotage, even as it might spur the subject to compete. (This oversight of this fundamental mechanism of measurement, against ideals as well as denigration, is why the Steele research excluded "Asian minorities" from its analysis, since presumably "Asian minorities" do not suffer from the negative stereotype in an academic context.

The experiment overlooks the fact that "Asian minorities" are far from being immune to what Steele herself calls the "vigilant worry" of performance.)

25. Frantz Fanon, *Black Skin, White Masks*.

26. David Lloyd, "Race under Representation," 76: "The process of assimilation requires that which defines the difference between the elements to remain over as a residue." In assimilation, however, that difference is always attributed to the side of the one assimilating rather than seen as a mutually produced difference.

27. This, by the way, gives us a more immediate understanding of why the critical discourse in search of a "whole" subject in minority studies is problematic, because it merely duplicates the subjective drama already taking place at the level of the individual: the conscientious and exacting maintenance of a sense of self as "whole" and "integrated" bespeaks both the necessities of ontological survival and the socioracial ingredients that threaten the security of such an enterprise.

28. This is one aspect of what Fanon calls the "third person consciousness" of the raced subject in *Black Skin, White Masks* (110). In a sense, Fanon is writing obsessively about his version of the "doll test." See fn. 15 in *Black Skin, White Masks* (152–3) in which Fanon tells the story of the different identifications of "the young Negro" watching Tarzan movies in the Antilles versus in European theaters. Fanon asserts that in the Antilles, the black viewer identifies with Tarzan, while in European theaters, he identifies with the apes because that is how he suspects he is being seen.

29. Sau-Ling Cynthia Wong, "Autobiography as Guided Chinatown Tour? Maxine Hong Kingston's *The Woman Warrior* and the Chinese-American Autobiographical Controversy," in *Multi-cultural Autobiography and American Lives*, edited by James Payne, 248–79.

30. The attachment to authenticity has always been a part of the traditional fantasy shaping the reading of minority literature. See Sau-Ling Cynthia Wong, See also Henry Louis Gates, "Authority, (White) Power and the (Black) Critic; It's All Greek to Me," and Barbara Christian, "The Race for Theory."

Rey Chow points out in her discussion of the politics of reading between the East and the West that "the ideological division between 'West' and the non-West" is duplicated in the ways the two are institutionally examined: the former, through painstaking *refined* methodologies whose point is the absolute fragmentation of the human self (or the basic unit for social participation); the latter, through cathexes of *wholesomeness* that manifest themselves in moralistically 'correct' representations of 'Third World' collective resistances and/ or traditions" (*Woman and Chinese Modernity*, xiv). One does not need to go beyond American literature to see such a division; one does not need to leave the "First World" to witness Edward Said's Orientalism or Frederick Jameson's "Third World phenomenology."

When it comes to Asian American literature, this ideological division needs to be recast as the very conflict that *conditions* the identificatory double bind inhering in the category "Asian American." The Asian American text as a problematically "native" text cannot help but reopen this question of origin and the performance of this ideological/critical division. When Kingston asserts in an interview that her "books are much more American than Chinese," what is revealed is a desire to claim "home" over the gap/*Unheimlichkeit* of an identity that can neither experience itself as "truly" Chinese or as "completely" American (Interview with Paula Rabinowitz, *Michigan Quarterly Review* 26:1 (winter 1987): 177–87).

31. Nicholas Abraham and Maria Torok, "The Lost Object—Me," in *The Shell and the Kernel*, 140; cited in the text hereafter. The notion of endocryptic identification may be related to Laplanche's recent work on the "enigmatic signifiers"that a child receives from the parents and that he speculates might constitute the beginning of the unconscious in *Seduction, Translation, and Drives*.

32. Peggy Kamuf elaborates: "[By] that negative imperative phrase . . . the reader is already at fault before the law, before the law which comes *before* or *already*; by reading the command, he or she ignores it; but ignoring the command (by not reading it) does not rectify things, does not equal obedience to a command that also demands to be read, that is, to be acknowledged as command in order to have the force of command" (*A Derrida Reader*, xiv). An interesting racial analog for the sign whose law cannot be read because it must already be read is the Jim Crow signs. See Elizabeth Abel's reading of Jim Crow signs in "Bathroom Doors and Drinking Fountains."

33. Kaja Silverman, *The Acoustic Mirror*. See the chapter "Disembodying the Female Voice," where Silverman explicates the connection between melancholia and female subjectivity and goes on to revalue the negative oedipal complex as a way for female subjects to retain a productive (not castrating) identification with the mother, which in turn intervenes the injunctions of the Oedipal complex.

34. One can never really *know* the effects of immigrant trauma, since that is what assimilation is designed to safeguard against and since it is simply impossible to live in a state of constant, unremitting, social incommensurability.

35. King-Kok Cheung, *Articulate Silences*, 88.

36. Victor Burgin, "Diderot, Barthes, *Vertigo*," in *Formations of Fantasy*, edited by Burgin, 103.

37. Claire Kahane, "Dark Mirrors: A Feminist Reflection on Holocaust Narrative and the Maternal Metaphor." Work in progress, presented at the Object Relations Group, Berkeley, California, May 1999. Kahane examines the double bind of universalism and sentimentality surrounding the trope of the mother in discourses of trauma.

38. The narrator calls her own style of narration "twisted," an uneven branching that not only recalls the notion of a twisted family tree but also offers a visualization of the kind of identification that a bicultural subject may have with maternal origins.

39. Freud, "The Common Neurotic State," in *SE*, 16:391.

40. There is also a wealth of literature from wide-ranging disciplines (sociology, medicine, psychology, and anthropology, to name only a few) that focuses on the larger question of social memory in relation to private memory. See Paul Connerton, *How Societies Remember*; Pierre Bourdieu, "Social Space and Symbolic Power"; Elaine Scarry, *The Body in Pain*; Arthur and Joan Kleinman, "How Bodies Remember."

41. See also Robert Burton, *The Anatomy of Melancholy*, 44; Carla Cantor with Brian Fallon, *Phantom Illness: Shattering the Myth of Hypochondria*.

42. Jane Austen, "Sanditon," in *Minor Works: The Oxford Illustrated Jane Austen*, 409. Cited in text hereafter.

43. I am indebted to D. A. Miller for pointing out the relationship between health and the social as figured in *Sanditon*. Miller's essay "The Late Jane Austen" makes an explicit connection between the social world of the Austen novel and what Miller calls "a culture of morbidity." For a reading of the racialization of Miss Lambe as encoding Austen's increasing preoccupation with her own illness, see pp. 75–6.

44. *Publishers Weekly*, August 9, 1976.

45. *New York Times Book Review*, November 7, 1986.

46. Paul Gray, "Book of Changes," *Time*, December 6, 1976; Diane Johnson, *New York Review of Books*, February 3, 1977.

47. Estelle C. Jelinek, ed., *Women's Autobiography*; Sidonie Smith, *A Poetics of Women's Autobiography*; Lee Quinby, "The Subject of Memoirs"; Sidonie Smith and Julia Watson, eds., *De/Colonizing the Subject*.
Let us take for our example the last article. While appearing in a volume that specifically proclaims its intentions of "de/colonizing the Subject," the article ironically reinscribes *The Woman Warrior* back into the very values that the essay claims the text has escaped: the reading remains indebted to an ideology of authenticity and the whole Subject. Quinby first argues that Kingston "constructs a new form of subjectivity . . . an *ideographic selfhood*," which "refuses the particular forms of selfhood, knowledge, and artistry that the systems of power of the modern era (including the discourse of autobiography) have made dominant" ("The Subject of Memoirs," 306–7). However, she goes on to produce just such a *Bildung*: "Kingston constructs a subjectivity through a form of writing that forces the American script of her text to reveal its intricacies in the way the Chinese ideographs do. . . . Each of [Kingston's stories within the text] adds a stroke to her ideographic selfhood, and each stroke is a form of resistance to the deployment of power that would either constrain women's sexuality or hystericize it." Quinby's rhetoric undermines her thesis. The conceit of an "ideographic selfhood" reveals an exotic investment not far from the kind of critique that focuses on "prose delicate and precise as porcelain." Even more problematically, the concept of an ideographic selfhood almost literally reinscribes the subject right back into a language at once inaccessible and oppressive. She neglects the possibility that the "intricacies" of the Chinese first person pronoun "I" can bind with their own history of oppression and that as much as "the strokes can flow" they can just as easily be inscriptions written into body, as is dramatized by the scene where the Woman Warrior has Chinese ideographs carved onto her bare back. In her eagerness to secure the narrator's liberation from the oppressive condition of possessing a failed and unauthentic "American selfhood," Quinby falls back on Kingston's supposed access to another kind of cultural authority (that intimate relationship to an "ideographic selfhood") and thereby fails to note that the narrator finds the Chinese ideographic "I" just as confounding as the simple three strokes of the American "I."

48. See Frank Chin, introduction to *The Big Aiiieeeee*. As is general knowledge by now, some critics have found the Kingston novel disturbingly fantastical, inaccurate, and reprehensible in its negative representation of the Asian American community. Kingston has been accused of being negligent in her "duty" to provide more accurate or "real" tales about the Asian American community.

49. J. Laplanche and J.-B. Pontalis, *The Language of Psycho-Analysis*, 211–2, 229–231.

50. Nicolas Abraham and Maria Torok, *The Shell and the Kernel*, vol. 1, 9, 13. All further citations are in the text. See especially the essays "The Illness of Mourning and the Fantasy of the Exquisite Corpse" (1968) and "Mourning or Melancholia: Introjection versus Incorporation" (1972).

51. In his introduction to *The Shell and the Kernel*, Nicholas Rand offers a summary of introjection that lends itself to a clear analogy for assimilation:

> The process of introjection [is] a constant process of acquisition and assimilation, the active expansion of our potential to accommodate our own emerging desires and feelings as well as the events and influences of the external world. Introjection is in fact the psychic counterpart of the child's development and its dependence on others.
>
> Introjection is the process of psychic nourishment, growth, and assimilation, encompassing our capacity to create through work, play, fantasy. . . . [It] represents our ability to survive shock, trauma, or loss; it is the psychic process that allows human beings to continue to live harmoniously in spite of instability, devastation, war, and upheaval.

Notable is the analogy that this definition of introjection must hold for the colloquial notion of cultural assimilation: the emphasis on a developmental coping mechanism as a defense against trauma; the conception of life as a series of transitions, voyages, translations; the attention to intrasubjective negotiations (how one processes the demands of a differing external world). In fact, Rand himself, in a footnote, briefly suggests that Abraham and Torok's notion of introjection can provide a psychoanalytic base for sociology and cultural studies: "For example, the investigation of introjection and its vicissitudes [which may include its absence] can shed light on the politics and emotional intricacies of colonization . . . a methodological complement to comparative analysis in ethnology and cultural anthropology" (15).

52. For Abraham and Torok, melancholia/incorporation, unlike the "good work" of introjection, creates a "psychic tomb." The notion of the "psychic tomb" was first developed by Abraham and Torok in *The Wolf Man's Magic Word* and expanded more fully in their essay "The Illness of Mourning and the Fantasy of the Exquisite Corpse," in *The Shell and the Kernel*. For Abraham and Torok, incorporation is but a nostalgia for introjection that failed to take place.

53. Guy de Maupassant, "At Sea," in *Pierre and Jean, Father and Son, Boitelle and Other Stories*, 2, cited in text hereafter.

54. Psychoanalysis remains intensely interested in theories of mourning. The history and development of mourning theories in psychoanalysis extend well beyond Freud to include Karl Abraham, Melanie Klein, D. W. Winnicott, Nicolas Abraham and Maria Torok, John Bowlby, Kimberly Leary and others. What has been surprising is the stubborn attachment to duplicating the Freudian structure of "healthy" versus "pathological" mourning. In all the variety of writings, there has been little written about mourning that does not turn to relinquishment as the necessary outcome of healthy mourning. We are witnessing the same phenomenon here with Abraham and Torok who while setting out to complicate Freud's notion of incorporation end up reproducing the

structure of health versus pathology by their differentiation of introjection from incorporation. Another vivid example of this attachment to relinquishment comes from the latest edition of the *Diagnostic and Statistical Manual of Mental Disorders*, Psychoanalytic Manual, 4th ed., 1994, which, driven by managed care and pharmaceutical economics, shrinks the period of "normal depression after the loss of a loved one" from six months, as prescribed in the first edition in 1940, to now "twenty-one" days.

55. Sander Gilman, "The Hottentot and the Prostitute: Toward an Iconography of Female Sexuality," in *Difference and Pathology*.

56. See also Adrienne Kennedy, *People Who Led to My Plays*, an example of this kind of cultural, familial, and subjective "confusion." This question from Kingston also asks us to reimagine the relationship between psychoanalysis and cultural difference: What relationship does your psychobiography bear to public history? It is because the theoretical relationship between ethnic identity and subject formation has not been either re-imagined or disturbed that an engagement between the social and the psychoanalytical has been so difficult to sustain. Hence the urgency of this project comes from the need to shift the questions of multiculturalism radically away from an identity-based thinking to inquiries that encompass the roles that public and private fantasies and desires play in historical formation of the "racial-ethnic subject."

57. Kingston's prose embodies the proposition I put forth in chapter 2, in the discussion of *Flower Drum Song*: that the birth of an Asian American citizen as a national category *and image* occurs, spectacularly and disturbingly, in the conjunction of public and private imaginations.

58. Benedict Anderson, *Imagined Communities*.

59. Hence, while the narrator's identification with the Woman Warrior has been taken as a parable for the novel's ethnic and feminist *Bildung*, that story is in fact told as much for its negation as for its promise. After telling the story of the Woman Warrior in an oddly unstable first person pronoun, the very first sentence that greets the reader is: "My American life has been such a disappointment" (45).

60. For an examination of anti-Japanese sentiment during World War II, see Ronald Takaki, *Strangers from a Different Shore*. For a dramatic demonstration of anti-Asian racial anxiety during World War II, see the following articles, which came out simultaneously the week after Pearl Harbor: "How To Tell Your Friends from the Japs," *Time*, December 22, 1941; "How To Tell Japs from the Chinese," *Life*, December 22, 1941. Both articles systematically offer photos as well as diagrams designed to help Americans distinguish the Japanese from the Chinese. The discourse seeks to separate allies from enemies, but the underlying assumption is of course the opposite. It reveals rather the racial paranoia that, in fact, one may *not* be able to "tell the Japs" from the "friendly" Chinese, thereby reinscribing the supposedly insidious nature of Asians as a whole and fueling the racial fear that the articles claimed to want to allay.

61. The fantasy of Fa Mu Lan not only offers a critique of American social integration but stands as a specific critique of the Communist revolution in mainland China, a revolution that gets deconstructed by this fabled retelling as a delusion of community. The narrator tells us: "It is confusing that my family was not the poor to be championed. They were executed like the barons in the stories, when they were not barons. It is confusing that birds tricked us"(51).

In the Fa Mu Lan legend, the birds guide the warrior from her mountain re-treat into war against the warlords on behalf of the people. The misleading birds in this second telling emblematize a failed socialist narrative, suggesting how grand social narratives can be deceptive. Thus the diegesis turns out to find this metadiegesis indigestible. Fa Mu Lan, far from a simple tale of success, has come to be a story of disillusionment on personal and national levels. The narrator's adolescent realization that "[f]ights are confusing as to who has won" (50) jars against the grand narratives of Communist revolution on the one hand and American socialization on the other.

62. This "community" that Kingston addresses is also quite specifically Cantonese American. Hence the nostalgic relation to mainland China is quite different from say, that of Taiwanese Americans, reminding us that "Chinese American" is a very inadequate and limited category and is really useful only in relation to the racialized world of American ethnicity, which has little room yet for thinking about other racial communities' own ethnic diversity.

63. Much of the history of Kingston criticism falls into two categories: constructivist readings of the text as a progressive ethnic and/or feminist *Bildungsroman*, where the narrator overcomes her destabilizing experiences of ethnic and gender discriminations to construct a positivist identity, or what might be called essentialist readings, which rest on issues of the text's cultural (in)authenticity. These two trends also often manifest themselves over the question of genre and autobiography, devolving into that stubborn, ongoing debate about fiction versus truth in autobiographical analysis.

Chapter 4. Fantasy's Repulsion and Investment

1. Sigmund Freud, "Mourning and Melancholia" (1917), *SE*, 14:228. Cited hereafter in this chapter as *MM*.

2. While development in mourning theories in psychoanalysis since Freud has advanced in several directions (Karl Abraham, John Bowlby, Melanie Klein, Kimberly Leary, Abraham and Torok), there remains a surprisingly stubborn attachment to the separation of "good" versus "bad" mourning. What remains most fascinating about Freud's work is precisely its internal slippage, which allows for a more mobile theorization on the relationship between mourning and melancholia.

3. Wendy Brown, *States of Injury*, 7.

4. Zora Neale Hurston, "How It Feels to be Colored Me," in *I Love Myself When I Am Laughing . . . And Then Again When I Am Looking Mean and Impressive*, 154.

5. Homi Bhabha, "Of Mimicry and Man: The Ambivalence of Colonial Discourse," in *The Location of Culture*, 86.

6. The contributions of Eric Lott, David Roediger, Michael Rogin, and Saidiya Hartman have shown that the formation of private fantasies and the performance of public illusions are intimately interwoven. The convoluted network of identification and crossidentification, for example, that can be found in a phenomenon like blackface minstrelsy (performed by whites and blacks) have made it impossible for us to view racial crossdressing as simply a past, historical phenomenon. Blackface is only the most visible and fragrant version of the various levels of racial performances that simultaneously straddle the

desire for incorporation and the need for denigration. For Lott and Rogin, these moments of crossings, whether it be a self-announced performance or more subtle forms of subjective maneuvers, announce longing and affinity as much as denigration and hostility.

7. These texts' investigations of the role that racial fantasy plays in the subjective *and* political formation of a racial identity, taken together, are especially significant when one considers how both mark pivotal moments in the mobilization of their respective racial communities as collective identities. That is, Ralph Ellison's meditation on fantasy and identity both gave impetus to and delimited the cultural nationalism that defined the political language of his time, just as *M. Butterfly* crystallizes a certain moment of Asian American aesthetic politics. *M. Butterfly* and *Invisible Man* both confront, through different responses, the uneasy collision between a politicized collective identity and fantasy's unpredictable effects.

8. While Ellison may be seen as one of the most prominent and originating male writers in the African American canon, Hwang may be seen as an equally inceptive figure for the Asian American letters. As such representative figures, it is no wonder that masculinity and race are the two projects at stake in their works. Furthermore, Ellison's novel is as theatrically invested as Hwang's drama in the *performance* of race.

9. Richard Fung, "Looking for My Penis."

10. In addition to Hwang's explicit investigation of Asian American invisibility in *M. Butterfly*, there has been a whole generation of male Asian American writers who have remained in dialogue with racialized male invisibility as laid out by Ellison. A clear example is Chang-Ray Lee's novel *Native Speaker*, for which *Invisible Man* serves as something of an intertext.

11. Morris Dickstein, "Ralph Ellison, Race, and American Culture" in *Raritan*.

12. Danny Kim, "Invisible Desires: Homoerotic Racism and Its Homophobic Critique in Ralph Ellison's *Invisible Man*," *Novel* (1997), 309–328. For Kim's discussion of Ellison's sense of racialized sexual humiliation in both *Invisible Man* and *Shadow and Act*, see especially pages 309–311 and 315–316.

13. David Henry Hwang, *M. Butterfly*. Hwang loosely based his play on a brief newspaper clipping accounting the strange tale of French diplomat Bernard Boursicot (Gallimard in the play), who travels to China in 1964 where he begins a two-decade long love affair with a female Chinese opera singer, Pei Pu (Song Liling in the play), who turns out to be a man.

14. David Eng, "In the Shadows of a Diva: Committing Homosexuality in David Henry Hwang's *M. Butterfly*." *Amerasia Journal* (1994); Marjorie Garber, *Vested Interests* (1992); Miriam Horn, "The Mesmerizing Power of Racial Myths," *U.S. News and World Report* (1998); Kathryn Remen, "The Theater of Punishment: David Henry Hwang's *M. Butterfly* and Michel Foucault's *Discipline and Punish*," *Modern Drama* (1994); Robert Skloot, "Breaking the Butterfly: The Politics of David Henry Hwang," *Modern Drama* (1990).

15. David Eng, "In the Shadow of a Diva: Committing Homosexuality in David Henry Hwang's *M. Butteerfly*," *American Journal* 20:1(1944), 94.

16. Joyce Waddler, *Liaison*, 51.

17. Philip P. Choy, Lorraine Dong, and Marlon K. Hom, *Coming Man: Nineteenth Century American Perceptions of the Chinese* (1994); Saikaku Ihara, *Com-*

rade Loves of the Samurai. There are also popular tour guides in the seventies to Asia which talks about how it is difficult to tell Asian men from women because of how "hairless" and "smooth" Asian men are.

18. Sander L. Gilman, "The Hottentot and the Prostitute: Toward an Iconography of Female Sexuality," *Difference and Pathology.*

19. See also D.A. Miller, "Secret Subjects, Open Secrets," *the Novel and the Police.*

This moment of audience reaction is also reminiscent of the moment in Hitchcock's *Vertigo* when the audience, along with Scotty, sees Madge's painting which superimposes her own face on top of a reproduction of Carlotta's portrait. The moment is funny for most of the audience, but for those whose humor was not untinged by Scotty's repulsion at the sight of this incongruous substitution, we recognize that it is a moment when the audience have come to occupy Scotty's melancholia, the melancholia that keeps him in necrophilia, that renders the sight of replacement and substitution horrifying.

20. This is a pleasure that can in no way be admissible. Since for centuries the writing of masculinity constitutes an elaborate denial of passivity and masochism, Gallimard could no more admit his masochistic pleasures than he could his homosexual desires. See Leo Bersani and Ulysse Dutoit in *Arts of Impoverishment* and Kaja Silverman in "Masochism and Subjectivity" on the conflation between masochism and sadism.

21. Jean Laplanche and J.-B. Pontalis. "Fantasy and the Origins of Sexuality," in *Formations of Fantasy,* edited by Victor Burgin; cited in text hereafter.

22. In his work on hysteria and traumatic structure, Freud had initially posited an original scene of parental seduction, the memory of which can be triggered by a later event. Halfway through his career, however, Freud abandoned the "original, real" scene of seduction for a scene of fantasized memory (that is, the child fantasized the seduction, which comes to acquire a psychical reality). It would seem that Freud has reached the heart of psychoanalysis: the existence of a fantasy so powerful as to achieve the paradox of "psychical reality." Yet Freud goes on to claim that the fantasized memory exists to mask the development of infantile sexuality.

Pointing out that Freud's claim implies that sexuality is endogenous, traumatic, and therefore needs masking, Laplanche and Pontalis draw the following conclusions: Freud still offers us a conceptual scheme that divides the external from the internal, the event from its constitution; and the description of a spontaneous infantile sexuality (which was disguised by the fantasy) is nonetheless basically endogenous in development, so that when Freud relegates the first/originary scene to fantasy, he has actually undermined the point of "psychical reality" because the move merely signals a return to biologism. Fantasy in fact serves as a "double disguise" for Freud (14). By claiming that the fantasy of seduction is a disguise for infantile sexuality, Freud is in fact returning to an old allegiance to "reality." This suggests the following paradox: at the very moment fantasy is discovered by Freud, it is also in danger of being obscured by endogenous reality. As Laplanche and Pontalis conclude, "We have indeed the fantasy, but we have lost the structure" (16). In short, Freud is stuck in a stubborn double bind whereby he wants to invest fantasy with its own place yet remains so attached to the idea of *some* truth that he went on to posit a "primary or original fantasy" that is phylogenetic and pre-historic. That is,

Freud is still trapped by needing to show what Laplanche and Pontalis called "what's under the counter" even though he has said that there is nothing— nothing "real," that is—under the counter. Similarly, I think what is seductive about *M. Butterfly* is its provocation for the audience to look underneath the costume even though there is nothing underneath that we do not already know is there.

23. Judith Butler, "The Force of Fantasy."

24. This is also why Eng's essay "In the Shadows of a Diva" falls into a slippage between what he calls Gallimard's "true homosexuality" and his "fantasmatic allegiance with the queer."

25. Kwame Anthony Appiah, *In My Father's House*, 45.

26. David Eng reads the last example as a rhetorical moment, where Song sees no point in asking because their homosexual relation was always a given and the tale spun about it a fiction, a fantasy ("In the Shadows of a Diva," 97). But there is another possibility, which is that Song cannot ask because to ask would reveal his own investment, which the play, I will demonstrate, wants to erase. In short, the play places a gag order on Song.

27. Nicolas Abraham and Maria Torok, *The Wolf Man's Magic Word*, pp. xv, xvii.

28. Ralph Ellison, *Invisible Man*, 143. Cited in text hereafter. For my discussion of Mr. Norton, see the introduction.

29. See Phillip Brian Harper, "'To Become One and Yet Many': Psychic Fragmentation and Aesthetic Synthesis in Ralph Ellison's *Invisible Man*," for an informative reading of the struggle of the invisible man as a continuous negotiation between the demands of individual versus communal voice.

30. It is outside the scope of this chapter to discuss it, but Ellison's meditation on subversive strategies in relations to the "master's tongue" can be placed very interestingly within the context of existing debates regarding the critical treatment of minority literature with respect to mainstream literary criticism. See, for instance, the debate between Barbara Christian and Henry Louis Gates: Barbara Christian, "The Race for Theory," and Henry Louis Gates, "Authority, (White) Power and the (Black) Critic; It's All Greek To Me."

31. There is a similar moment in *Black Skin, White Mask*, when the narrator saw himself through the eyes of a white boy on the street.

32. Richard Dyer, "Whiteness."

33. Daryl Michael Scott, *Contempt and Pity*, 49. For exceptions of critics who have noted Rinehart's potential for effective subversion, see Morris Dickstein, "Ralph Ellison, Race, and American Culture," 46; Philip Brain Harper, "'To Become One and Yet Many,'" 697–9; and Lawrence P. Jackson, "Ralph Ellison, Sharpies, Rinehart, and Politics in *Invisible Man*," 81–2.

34. For a similar dramatization, see Zora Neale Hurston, "How It Feels to be Colored Me," in *I Love Myself When I Am Laughing*, and Barbara Johnson's reading of that essay in *A World of Difference*.

35. Toni Morrison, *Playing in the Dark*, 16.

36. Another interesting network of connections can be among the following: Ellison's scene of counter-incorporation, the Maupassant story of the pestilential arm from chapter 3, the larger question of ethnic others as communal objects of mourning, and Jacques Derrida's work on "spectrality" in *Specters of Marx*. Derrida expands on a notion of radical contamination called "spectrality"

in Marx's writings, according to which an idea or spiritual form is incarnated or given a prosthetic body, which is then (mis)taken by the subject as his or her own corporeal body. The real subject's body thus becomes spectral when it incorporates this prosthetic body. This clearly echoes the melancholic racial structure I have ascribed to American nationalism at large, and bears resemblances to both Toni Morrison's theorization about the constitutive "things unspoken" in the body of American literature and what the Maupassant story "At Sea" says about communal unity in mourning. We might say that the communal body in "At Sea" is simultaneously incarnated and made spectral by its incorporation of the amputated subject, Javel, Jr., made into a synecdoche as the "prosthetic," severed arm.

37. Insofar as white racism can be seen as castrating and homosexuality as bearing the sign of castration, then this particular moment of masculine relinquishment in Ellison seems to me a crucial qualification of Danny Kim's reading of homophobia in the text of *Invisible Man*.

38. bell hooks, "Reflections on Race and Sex," in *Yearning*, 58.

39. Lee Edelman, "The Part for the (W)hole: Baldwin, Homophobia, and the Fantasmatics of 'Race,'" *Homographesis*, 45.

40. The crisis of authenticity can also be contextualized within a postmodern crisis of legitimacy. From Kant to Arendt, Christian to Gates, Kingston to Chin it is clear that the politics of liberalism can both appeal to and uncomfortably run up against the cultural investment in legitimacy.

41. Robert Bone, "Ralph Ellison and the Uses of the Imagination," in *Ralph Ellison*, edited by John Hersey, 110.

42. Irving Howe, *Selected Writings, 1950–1990*, 119.

Chapter 5. History in/against the Fragment

My thanks to Lawrence Rinder, Curator of the University Art Museum at UC Berkeley, and to his assistant Stephanie Cannizo for allowing me to study the archival material on Cha even as they are busy cataloguing the work. Although Cha's film and video work is outside the purview of this chapter, seeing Cha's work has greatly contributed to my understanding of the political-aesthetic at work in *Dictée*. (I have tried to refer in the notes to particularly evocative or relevant pieces that might be brought into dialogue with the issues raised in this chapter.)

1. Pusan, the second largest South Korean city and the principal seaport in the republic, was invaded by the Japanese in 1592; the port was opened to Japanese trade in 1876 and to general foreign commerce in 1883. After 1910, when Korea became a Japanese protectorate, the city was the center of a flourishing trade with Japan. During the Korean War, Pusan was a major port of entry and supply depot for United Nations forces, hence a target for the advancing Chinese and North Korean armies.

2. Collected in the UC Berkeley Art Museum, Theresa Hak Kyung Cha Archive.

3. Cha's one-person exhibition history includes: Union Gallery in San Francisco (1978); the San Francisco Art Institute (1979); The Queens Museum, New York (1981); Mills College Art Gallery, Oakland (1989); Whitney Museum of Contemporary Art, New York (1992); UC Berkeley Art Museum, Berkeley

(1992). Her work has also been included in group exhibitions, most recently "Difference: On Representation and Sexuality," the New Museum of Contemporary Art, New York, 1984; "Autobiography: In Her Own Image" (named after a line from *Dictée*), which traveled to Atlanta, Oakland, Florida, and Texas (1989); and "Korean Filmvideo," UC Berkeley Art Museum, Berkeley, California 1992.

4. The term "visionary films" is taken from P. Adam Sitney, *Modernist Montage*.

5. A shorter version of the first section of this chapter was presented as a talk, "History and Fragment: Theresa Hak Kyung Cha's *Dictée*," at the annual conference of the American Comparative Literature Association at Notre Dame University, April 1996, South Bend, Indiana and has appeared in *MELUS* 23:4 (winter 1998): 119–33.

6. Trinh Minh-ha, *Woman, Native, Other*.

7. Norma Alarcón and Elaine Kim, eds., *Writing Self Writing Nation*. This collection of essays addresses for the first time Cha's text as an act of political intervention produced at the intersecting (not isolated) sites of race, gender, and imperialism. The essays by Lisa Lowe and Shelley Wong in this volume are especially illuminating in articulating the nature of difference as political strategy.

8. In *The Culture of Redemption*, Leo Bersani examines many of our assumptions regarding the redemptive virtues of literature. I am suggesting that what Bersani calls the "corrective will," along with its accompanying documentary desire, strongly motivates minority and ethnographic discourse. Indeed, more than providing the motivation, such "will" often dictates the critical approaches to the ethnic text.

9. Catherine Gallagher has spoken of what she calls plots of "undoing" through which nations invested in progressive narratives seek to rewrite their own histories of behaving otherwise. "Undoing: Time Travel, Counter-factuals, and Affirmative Action," talk given at the School of Criticism and Theory Conference, UC Berkeley, April 29, 2000.

10. Theresa Hak Kyung Cha, *Dictée*. All further citations are from the 1992 Tanam Press edition and are in the text.

11. Susan Sontag, *On Photography*, 8. Cited in text hereafter.

12. Trinh Minh-ha, *When the Moon Waxes Red*.

13. Rey Chow, "Where Have All the Natives Gone?" in *Writing Diaspora*, 27–54.

14. For a treatise on the question of history in the genre of film documentaries, see Trinh Minh-ha, "Documentary Is/Not a Name."

15. The politics surrounding the representation of historical trauma have a well-developed history in relation to the Holocaust. In discussing the usage of the Holocaust as metaphor in Plath, Jacqueline Rose offers a pithy summary of the politics of Holocaust representation. Jacqueline Rose, *The Haunting of Sylvia Plath*. See especially Rose's discussion of Plath's poem "Daddy."

16. In his 1919 essay "The Uncanny," in *SE*, 17:217–256. Freud speaks of a type of anxiety that he designates *unheimlich* (which in German literally means "not homelike" or "not at home"). By tracing the linguistic ambivalence of the root *heimlich*, Freud notes that two opposing meanings reside in the word *heimlich*: both "at home" and "not at home." Hence, *unheimlich*/the

uncanny came to denote both "at homeness" and "not at home." That is to say, what is uncanny is not necessarily the unfamiliar or the stranger but the familiar and the known. The term *unheimlich* thus refers to that moment of doubleness when something reminiscent of "home" turns into something unfamiliar and disturbing.

17. I use "melancholy" here instead of "melancholia" to distinguish between melancholy as affect (which is how Sontag is using the term) and melancholia as a psychical structure.

18. Judith Butler, *Bodies That Matter*. Citations are in the text hereafter.

19. Maurice Blanchot, *The Writing of the Disaster*, 12.

20. For those interested in further study in the difference between sequentiality and seriality in postmodern American poetry, see Joseph Conte's *Unending Design*.

21. Sigmund Freud, "Group Psychology and the Analysis of the Ego" (1921), *SE*, 18:72. Cited in text hereafter.

22. Sander L. Gilman, *Freud, Race, and Gender*. Cited in text hereafter.

23. Sigmund Freud, "The Unconscious" (1915), *SE*, vol. 14, 190.

24. Sigmund Freud, "On Anxiety," *Introductory Lectures on Psychoanalysis*, *SE*, 15–16:392. Cited in the text hereafter.

25. See, for example, Mikkel Borch-Jacobson, *The Freudian Subject*.

26. Louis Althusser, "Ideology and Ideological State Apparatus," in *Lenin and Philosophy and Other Essays*, 149. Cited in the text hereafter.

27. I am thinking of the works of Ernesto Laclau, Slavoj Zizek, and more recently, Mladen Dolar.

28. Butler, *The Psychic Life of Power*, 5–6, 95–6.

29. Both Lisa Lowe and Shelley Sunn Wong have analyzed the "language lesson" in *Dictée* as a symbolic and critical repetition of national colonization. See Lisa Lowe's "Unfaithful to the Original: The Subject of *Dictée*" (35–72) and Shelley Sunn Wong's "Unnaming the Same: Theresa Hak Kyung Cha's *Dictée*" (103–142) in *Writing Self, Writing Nation*, edited by Elaine Kim and Norma Alarcon, cited in text hereafter. Another interesting text by Cha herself, which extends this exposition on language as a political tool, is the short prose piece "Temps Morte," in *Hotel*. In "Temps Morte," the act of conjugation takes on the tone of frantic approximation, a chase in and against time:

> take are taking took have been taken have been taking have had been taking had taken will take will have been taking will have taken will have had taken know are knowing have known have been knowing have had been knowing had known will know will have known will have had known . . .

It would also be interesting to analyze Cha's text alongside a Samuel Beckett piece such as *Ill Seen Ill Said*.

30. Mikkel Borche-Jacobsen, *The Freudian Subject*, 8–9.

31. In her video piece *Mouth to Mouth* (1978), Cha trains her camera on a mouth opening and closing, barely visible through heavy static. The mouth looks both as if it were trying to speak and drowning, the waves of static seeping into and flowing out of the mouth. The piece not only refers to Beckett's work in *Not I* but also graphically enacts the conflations taking place in Cha's

own memoirs: the confusions between subject and sociality, self and speech, interiority and exteriority.

32. Kaja Silverman, *Male Subjectivity at the Margins*, 17. Cited in text hereafter.

33. Borch-Jacobsen does not speak of the fantasmatic, but he arrives at a similar insight when he points out the mimetic function of identification as something that breaks down the difference between imaginary and symbolic identifications: "We shall have to connect desire with mimesis, instead of tying it first to interdiction, to the Imaginary instead of the Symbolic . . . except that in my view the distinction is no longer pertinent" (20).

34. Philippe Lacoue-Labarthe, "The Nazi Myth," 305; my emphasis. Cited in the text hereafter.

35. Anthony Appiah offers a reading of race as the illusory promise of both origin/home and memory/history in his chapter "Illusions of Race," in *My Father's House*.

36. Michael Omi and Howard Winant, *Racial Formation in the United States*, 66–68. Cited in the text hereafter.

37. Robert Hass, "Meditation at Lagunitas," in *Praise*, 4–5.

Chapter 6. *Difficult Loves*

1. Anna Deavere Smith, *Twilight: Los Angeles, 1992, On the Road: A Search for American Character*, 247–9. This book transcript records materials from versions of the play initially developed and performed in the Mark Taper Forum in Los Angeles in 1992 and then at the New York Shakespeare Festival in 1992. Smith has made changes and additions in later performances. In this chapter, I will make specific reference to some additions Smith inserted in a 1996 performance at the Marine Theater in San Francisco. But unless otherwise noted further citations are from this edition and are in the text. The transcript includes phonetic notes, grammar mistakes, and punctuation errors.

2. Smith edits the transcripts in length only; that is, she determines where a monologue begins and ends, but she does not edit the text within those limits, so that each speech may maintain as much as possible within such an edit its integrity in terms of movement, logic, and content.

3. Ann Pellegrini, *Performance Anxieties*, 71. See, too, Peggy Phelan, "Performing Talking Cure."

4. The Los Angeles riots are all the more disturbing when one recalls, as do a couple of characters within this play, that the Watts riots in the sixties also generated just as much media attention and as many proclaimed political resolutions.

5. Consider, for example, critics such as Orlando Patterson, or those who criticize Kenneth Clark and other social scientists whose work was crucial to the dismantling of desegregation in America for having done so through the tool of black victimization, leaving what these critics feel is an irascible legacy of psychical damage.

6. Herbert Hovenkamp, "Social Science and Segregation before *Brown*," and John P. Jackson, Jr., "Creating a Consensus."

7. Fanon writes in *Black Skin, White Masks*: "[N]ot only must the black man be black; he must be black in relation to the white man. . . . Negroes *are* comparison" (9, 211). For expanded discussions of the black man as a figure of comparison and relationality, see Diane Fuss' chapter "Interior Colonies: Frantz

Fanon and the Politics of Identification," in *Identification Papers*, 141–65; see also Natalie Melas, "Versions of Incommensurability," 275–80.

8. Revisiting his figure of the black man as comparison and relationality, Diana Fuss points out Fanon's implicit proposition that colonialism may inflict its greatest psychical violence precisely by attempting to exclude blacks from the very self-other dynamics that makes subjectivity possible. But here we see that the victim can appropriate yet another in order to exercise this self-other dynamic. Diana Fuss, *Identification Papers*, 141–65.

9. I am claiming here that identity tries to keep identification at a distance in order to maintain the certitude of its integrity. In *Identification Papers*, Diana Fuss formulates a similar account of this uneasy, symbiotic relationship from the reverse position, asserting that it is identification doing the distancing: "Identification is a process that keeps identity at a distance, that prevents identity from ever approximating the status of an ontological given, even as it makes possible the formation of an *illusion* of identity as immediate, secure, and totalizable" (2).

10. Even a child's identification with an inanimate object in early childhood may be said to be a *social* relation. For a dramatic demonstration of that sociality, see Melanie Klein's discussion of a child's identification with furniture and animals in "Infantile Anxiety Situations Reflected in a Work of Art and in the Creative Impulse," in *Selected Melanie Klein*, edited by Juliet Mitchell.

11. In "Mourning and Melancholia"Freud equates identification specifically with melancholic incorporation, an equation that will remain relatively constant in psychoanalytic thinking (see Jean Laplanche and J.-B. Pontalis, *The Language of Psycho-Analysis*), with modifications from theorists such as Abraham and Torok, who, as discussed earlier, have nuanced the notion of incorporation by distinguishing it from introjection.

12. Diana Fuss, *Identification Papers*; Judith Butler, "Psychic Inceptions: Melancholy, Ambivalence, Rage," in *The Psychic Life of Power*; Elin Diamond, "The Violence of 'We': Politicizing Identification," in *Critical Theory and Performance*, 390–8. All are cited in the text hereafter.

13. Anna Deavere Smith, "Inside the Political Mimic's Fun-House Mirror," *New York Times*, August 16, 1992, late edition, 20.

14. Diamond offers an intriguing exposition on why Freudian identification, for all its confusions, permits more "material specificity" in political critique than Lacanian identification (395–6). Arguing that identification in Lacan is narcissistic in nature and occludes difference and contradiction, Diamond suggests that Freud's notion of identification, as a history of one's "psychic life with others," implies that the ego is literally built out of a series of "historical contradictions." She points out that the ego, according to Freud, who also uses the term interchangeably with "self," is permeable and constantly in the process of transformation. Hence Freudian identification, for Diamond, structurally embodies temporality and the specificities of history.

15. Tania Modleski, "Doing Justice to the Subjects," in *Female Subjects in Black and White*, 58. Cited in text hereafter. Modelski calls this Smith's diasporic consciousness, borrowing from Daniel Boyarins. Modleski also addresses the issue of competitive trauma or subaltern experiences (for example, the argument that slavery is far worse than the Holocaust and vice versa, as one character did in *Fires in the Mirror*.).

16. See Walter Benjamin, "Art of Translation," in *Illuminations*.

17. My thanks to Zita Nunes for inspiring this meditation on the particularity of the relationship between Smith's raced, gendered body and the "impersonal," purely formal art of imitation. Tania Modelski in the essay quoted earlier would suggest that Smith can "get away" with this kind of mimicry because the black female body has historically served as a nurturing stage, a screen for projection, from Plato's cave on. I would add that we should also pay attention to those moments when Smith's raced and gendered body inflect negatively or fail to fully accommodate the "other" bodies it is enacting, which truly highlights the raced and gendered relations within notions of performance and stereotype.

18. In *Difference and Pathology*, Sander L. Gilman makes the argument that stereotypes are fundamental to individuation and subject-formation. Suggesting that the bipolar nature of the stereotype that reflects our Manichean perception of the world as "good" or "bad" has its roots in infantile development, Gilman sees the continuous deployment of the stereotype in adult life as a defensive mechanism, arising "when self-integration is threatened" (18). His argument is thus that stereotypes and the "Other" are necessary, even if undesirable, structures for individual and social formations. Covering Jewish madness, the figure of the Hottentot, and more, Gilman's work unpacks the uses of and desire for the stereotypical other in art, theory, culture, and nationhood.

My argument shifts the emphasis away from the Manichean effect of the stereotype in order to emphasize two other points. First, reductive or simplified symbolic images often function to help us identify ourselves, not only through the differentiation and projection of the negative other, as Gilman demonstrates, but also through the commonality of recognition and shared signs, shorthand signposts of cultural similarity. I would say not that identity is structured not on the psychical differentiation of "me-good" versus "you-bad" but instead on the active and constant negotiation between the two.

Second, I want to decompose the bipolar structure of domination and denigration implied in discussions of the stereotype, which duplicates the good–bad Manichean assumptions behind the stereotype (that is, the usual alignment between a dominant subject with the one doing the stereotyping/othering and the minority as the object of such a projection, which Gilman's work does not disturb). In addition to examining how dominant cultures and subjects have used the stereotypical other for measures of self-individuation, we must be prepared to examine also the relationship between the stereotype and the one being stereotyped. What kinds of subjective negotiations must go on there, and what are the implications for critiques of power to recognize that everyone at some point draws from the reservoir of stereotypes about others and about themselves?

19. Hortense Spillers, "Mama's Baby, Papa's Maybe," 66.

20. An example of the limitations of judging by intentionality would be Richard Schechner's treatment of Smith. His essay "Anna Deavere Smith: Acting as Incorporation" judges that Smith's mimicry cannot be appropriative because it is "sincere" and "deep."

21. Jessica Benjamin, *Like Subjects, Love Objects*; Drucilla Cornell, *Beyond Accommodation*; Kaja Silverman, *The Threshold of the Visible World*.

22. Mikkel Borch-Jacobsen, *The Freudian Subject*.

23. In an early performance of the piece, when it first appeared at the Mark Taper Forum, Smith spoke one monologue entirely in English and one in Span-

ish, with translations in supertitles. Theater critic John Lahr for the *New Yorker* responds, "the emphasis is more on sociological clarity than on the speaker's idiosyncratic poetry. . . . The show's opening speech, in Korean, gets the evening off on a symbolically correct but theatrically wrong foot" ("Ark Angels," *New Yorker*, April 4, 1994, 96; quoted by Shannon Jackson, "Iterating Subjects, Privileged Speech: Infelicities in Anna Deavere Smith's *Twilight*," essay in progress).

24. Peggy Phelan, *Unmarked*, 174.

25. Let me offer a "real-life" dramatization of the kind of mind-shift that Smith's work enacts. In the Spring of 1995, Smith performed *Twilight* at the Marine Theater in San Francisco. On a Wednesday matinee, the audience was an unlikely combination: elderly white theater ladies and a crowd of mostly African American children between the ages of twelve and fourteen. It turned out that the performance that day coincided with the teachers' strike in the Oakland School District, and out of desperation the administrators packed the students off to this show across the bay. The youngsters talked, joked, blew bubblegum, and threw wrappers at one another—not so much out of rudeness as out of unfamiliarity with "theater etiquette." When the curtains rose and during the opening moments of the performance, they giggled, pointed, and talked with one another, entertained by Smith's virtuosity in impersonation. But half an hour later into the performance, a gradual silence settled into the audience. The smaller heads in front of me leaned forward, grew still, intense. A frown gathered on the profile of the young boy two heads over, and the girl to his right bit her lips anxiously. The youths were placed in the unusual and uncomfortable position of being reminded of their own communal interests and the interests of those unlike themselves. The effects of seeing this multiple perspective on these young viewers, themselves dropping through the holes of city politics, were very moving to me.

26. Think, for example, of the resolution of the Oresteia of Aeschylus. It seems appropriate here to return to a classic definition of the *polis* as a philosophical root of modern democracy, especially since the racial conflicts in this country have created a cycle of vengeance and tribal politics.

27. Walt Whitman, "Crossing Brooklyn Ferry," *Norton Anthology of Poetry*, 3rd ed., 767.

28. Michael Moon, *Disseminating Whitman*, 107, 110. Cited in the text hereafter.

29. See, for example, Sandra L. Richards, "Caught in the Act of Social Definition."

WORKS CITED

Abel, Elizabeth. "Bathroom Doors and Drinking Fountains: Jim Crow's Racial Symbolic." *Critical Inquiry* 25 (1999): 435–81.

Abel, Elizabeth, Barbara Christian, and Helene Moglen, eds. *Female Subjects in Black and White: Race, Psychoanalysis, Feminism.* Berkeley: University of California Press, 1997.

Abraham, Nicolas, and Maria Torok. *The Shell and the Kernel.* Trans. Nicholas T. Rand. Chicago: University of Chicago Press, 1994.

———. *The Wolf Man's Magic Word: A Cryptonymy.* Trans. Nicholas Rand. Minneapolis: University of Minnesota Press, 1986.

Adam, B. D. "Inferiorization and 'Self Esteem.'" *Social Psychology* 41(1978): 47–53.

Aeschylus. *The Oresteia Trilogy.* Mineola, N.Y.: Dover, 1996.

Alarcón, Norma, and Elaine Kim, eds. *Writing Self Writing Nation: Essays on Theresa Hak Kyung Cha's DICTEE.* Berkeley, Calif.: Third Woman Press, 1994.

Alsbrook, James E. "Minority Report: Students Fare Equally When No Problems." *The Ethnic Newswatch. Los Angeles Sentinel* 61: 52(March 28, 1996). A7.

Althusser, Louis. *Lenin and Philosophy and Other Essays.* Trans. Ben Brewster. London: Monthly Review Press, 1971.

———. *Philosophy and the Spontaneous Philosophy of Scientists and Other Essays.* Trans. Ben Brewster et al. London: Verso, 1990.

Amsterdam, Anthony C. "Thurgood Marshall's Image of the Blue-Eyed Child in Brown v. Board of Education." *New York University Law Review* 68, 2(May 1993): 226–36.

Anderson, Benedict. *Imagined Communities: Reflections on the Origins and Spread of Nationalism.* London: Verso, 1983.

Appiah, Kwame Anthony. *In My Father's House: Africa in the Philosophy of Culture.* New York: Oxford University Press, 1992.

———. "The Uncompleted Argument: DuBois and the Illusion of Race." In *Race Writing and Difference,* ed. Henry Louis Gates. Chicago: University of Chicago Press, 1986.

Argument: The Oral Argument before the Supreme Court in Brown v. Board of Education of Topeka, 1925–55. Ed. Leon Friedman. New York: Chelsea House, 1969.

Ashmore, H. S. *The Negro and the Schools.* Chapel Hill: University of North Carolina Press, 1954.

Austen, Jane. "Sanditon." In *Minor Works: The Illustrated Jane Austen.* Oxford: Oxford University Press, 1954.

Bad Object Choice, ed. *How Do I Look? Queer Film and Videos.* Seattle: Bay Press, 1991.

Baker, Houston. *Afro-American Literary Study in the 1990s.* Chicago: University of Chicago Press, 1989.

———. "To Move without Moving: An Analysis of the Creativity and Commerce in Ralph Ellison's Trueblood Episode." In *Speaking for You: The Vision of Ralph Ellison,* ed. Kimberly W. Benston. Washington: Howard University Press, 1987.

Balibar, Etienne, and Immanuel Wallerstein. *Race, Nation, Class: Ambiguous Identities.* Trans. Chris Turner. London: Verso, 1891.

Barnes, Natasha B. "Face of the Nation: Race, Nationalism, and Identities in Jamaican Beauty Pageants." *Massachusetts Review* 35, 3(fall–winter 1994): 471–92.

Barringer, Herbert R. *Asians and Pacific Islanders in the United States.* New York: Russell Sage Foundation, 1993.

Benjamin, Jessica. *Like Subjects, Love Objects: Essays on Recognition and Sexual Difference.* New Haven: Yale University Press, 1995.

Benjamin, Walter. *Illuminations: Essays and Reflections.* Trans. Harry Zohn. New York: Schoken Books, 1968.

Berlant, Lauren. *Anatomy of National Fantasy: Hawthorn, Utopia, and Everyday Life.* Chicago: University of Chicago Press, 1991.

Bersani, Leo. *The Culture of Redemption.* Cambridge: Harvard University Press, 1990.

Bersani, Leo, and Ulysse Dutoit. *Arts of Impoverishment: Beckett, Rothko, Resnais.* Cambridge: Harvard University Press, 1993.

———. *Caravaggio's Secrets.* Cambridge: MIT Press, 1998.

Bettelheim, Bruno. "Discrimination and Science." Review of Kenneth B. Clark's *Prejudice and Your Child. Commentary* (April 1956): 384–386.

———. *Surviving and Other Essays.* New York: Knopf, 1979.

Bhabha, Homi. *The Location of Culture.* New York: Routledge, 1994.

———. "Postcolonial Authority and Postmodern Guilt." In *Cultural Studies,* ed. Lawrence Grossberg, Cary Nelson, and Paula A. Treichler. New York: Routledge, 1992.

———. ed. *Nation and Narration.* New York: Routledge, 1990.

Blanchot, Maurice. *The Writing of the Disaster.* Trans. Ann Smock. Lincoln: University of Nebraska Press, 1986.

Bone, Robert. "Ralph Ellison and the Uses of the Imagination." *Ralph Ellison: A Collection of Critical Essays,* ed. John Hersey. New Jersey: Prentice-Hall, 1974.

Borch-Jacobsen, Mikkel. *The Emotional Ties: Psychoanalysis, Mimesis, and Affect.* Trans. Douglas Brick et al. Stanford: Stanford University Press, 1992.

———. *The Freudian Subject.* Trans. Catherine Porter. Stanford: Stanford University Press, 1988.

Bourdieu, Pierre. "Social Space and Symbolic Power." In *Outline of a Theory of Practice*. Trans. Richard Nice. Cambridge, U.K.: Cambridge University Press, 1977.

Boyarin, Daniel. *Unheroic Conduct: The Rise of Heterosexuality and the Invention of the Jewish Man*. Berkeley: University of California Press, 1997.

Boyarin, Daniel and Jonathan Boyarin. *Jews and Other Differences*. Minneapolis: University of Minnesota Press, 1997.

Breitweiser, Mitchell Robert. *American Puritanism and the Defense of Mourning: Religion, Grief, and Ethnology in Mary White Rowlandson's Captivity Narrative*. Madison: University of Wisconsin Press, 1990.

Briggs v. Elliot, 342 U.S. 350 (1952).

Brodzki, Bella, and Celeste Schenck, eds. *Life/Lines: Theorizing Women's Autobiography*. Ithaca, N.Y.: Cornell University Press, 1988.

Brown v. Board of Education, 347 U.S. 484 (1954).

Brown v. Board of Education, 149 U.S. 294 (1955).

Brown, Wendy. *States of Injury: Power and Freedom in Late Modernity*. Princeton: Princeton University Press, 1995.

Burgin, Victor, ed. *Formations of Fantasy*. New York: Routledge, 1986.

Burton, Robert. *The Anatomy of Melancholy*. London: G. Bell, 1923.

Butler, Judith. *Bodies That Matter: On the Discursive Limits of "Sex."* New York: Routledge, 1993.

———. "Burning Acts: Injurious Speech." In *Deconstruction is/in America: A New Sense of the Political*, ed. Anselm Haverkamp. New York: New York University Press, 1993.

———. *Excitable Speech: A Politics of the Performative*. New York: Routledge, 1997.

———. "The Force of Fantasy: Feminism, Mapplethorpe, and Discursive Excess." *Differences* 2(summer 1990): 105–125.

———. *Gender Trouble: Feminism and the Subversion of Identity*. New York: Routledge, 1990.

———. *The Psychic Life of Power: Theories in Subjection*. Palo Alto: Stanford University Press, 1997.

Butler, Judith, and Joan W. Scott, eds. *Feminists Theorizing the Political*. New York: Routledge, 1992.

Cadava, Eduardo, Peter Connor, and Jean-Luc Nancy, eds. *Who Comes after the Subject?* New York: Routledge, 1991.

Callahan, John F. "Reflections Out of Season on Race, Identity, and Art: 'American Culture is of a Whole. From the Letters of Ralph Ellison." *New Republic* (March 1991): 34–49.

Cantor, Carla, with Brian Fallon. *Phantom Illness: Shattering the Myth of Hypochondria*. Boston: Houghton Mifflin, 1996.

Carter, Stephen L. "The Trap of Scientism." *American Enterprise* 9:5(September–October 1998): 60–2.

Caruth, Cathy. *Trauma: Explorations in Memory*. Baltimore: Johns Hopkins University Press, 1995.

———. *Unclaimed Experience: Trauma, Narrative, and History*. Baltimore: Johns Hopkins University Press, 1996.

Cha, Theresa Hak Kyung. *Dictée*. New York: Tanam Press, 1982.

———. "Temps Morte." In *Hotel*. New York: Tanam Press, 1980.

Chambers, Ross. *The Writing of Melancholy: Modes of Opposition in Early French Modernism*. Trans. Mary Seidman Trouille. Chicago: University of Chicago Press, 1993.

Chang, Gordon H. "Forbidden Fruits." *Amerasia* 17, 1(1991): 182.

Chapkis, Wendy. *Beauty Secrets: Women and the Politics of Appearance*. Boston: South End Press, 1986.

Cheah, Pheng. "Mattering." *Diacritics* (spring 1996): 108–39.

Chen, Chin-Yéu. "San Francisco's Chinatown: A Socio-Economic and Cultural History, 1850–1882." Ph.D. diss., University of Michigan, 1992.

Cheng, Anne. "The Melancholy of Race." *Kenyon Review* 44, 1(winter 1997): 47–70.

———. "Memory and Anti-Documentary Desire in Theresa Hak Kyung Cha's *Dictée*." MELUS 32, 4(winter 1998): 119–33.

———. "Race and Fantasy in Modern America: Racial Assimilation/Subjective Dissimulation in *M. Butterfly* and *Invisible Man*." In *Literary Studies East and West*. Vol. 10. *Multiculturalism and Representation*, ed. John Reider and Larry E. Smith. Honolulu: University of Hawaii Press, 1996.

Chestler, Mark, Joseph Sanders, and Debora Kalmuss. *Social Science in Court: Mobilizing Experts in the School Desegregation Cases*. Madison: University of Wisconsin Press, 1988.

Cheung, King-Kok. *Articulate Silences: Hisaye Yamamoto, Maxine Hong Kingston, Joy Kogawa*. Ithaca, N.Y.: Cornell University Press, 1993.

Cheyne, George. *The English Malady*. London: G. Strahan, 1733.

Chin, Frank, Jeffrey Paul Chan, Lawson Fusao Inada, and Shawn Wong, eds. *The Big Aiiieeeee: An Anthology of Asian-American Writers*. Garden City, N.Y.: Anchor, 1975.

Chinn, Thomas W. *Bridging the Pacific: San Francisco Chinatown and Its People*. San Francisco: Chinese Historical Society of America, 1989.

Chiu, Jeannie. "Specularity and Identity in *Invisible Man*." *Critical Sense* (spring 1996): 104–28.

———. "Uncanny Doubles: Nationalism and Repression in Frank Chin's 'Railroad Standard Time.'" *Critical Mass* 1, 1(fall 1993): 93–107.

Chow, Rey. *Woman and Chinese Modernity: The Politics of Reading between West and East*. Minnesota: University of Minnesota Press, 1991.

———. *Writing Diaspora: Tactics of Intervention in Contemporary Cultural Studies*. Bloomington: Indiana University Press, 1993.

Choy, Philip P., Lorraine Dong, and Marlon K. Hom. *Coming Man: Nineteenth Century American Perceptions of the Chinese*. Seattle: University of Washington Press, 1994.

Christian, Barbara. "The Race for Theory." *Cultural Critique* (spring 1987): 51–63.

Chu, Patricia. "The Invisible World the Emigrants Built: Cultural Self-Inscription and the Anti-romantic Plots of *The Woman Warrior*." *Diaspora* 2, 1(spring 1992): 95–115.

Clark, Kenneth B. Appendix to Appellant's Brief. "The Effects of Segregation and the Consequences of Desegregation—A Social Science Statement." In *Landmark Briefs and Arguments of the Supreme Court of the United States: Constitutional Law*, ed. P. B. Kurland and G. Caspar. Arlington, Va: University Publications of America, 1975.

———. *Prejudice and Your Child*. Boston: Beacon Press, 1955.

————. "The Social Scientists, The Brown Decision, and Contemporary Confusion." In *Appellant Argument: The Oral Argument Before the Supreme Court
in Brown v. Board of Education of Topeka, 1952–55*, ed. Oliver Brown. New
York: Chelsea House, 1969.

Clark, Kenneth B., and M. P. Clark. "Development of Consciousness of Self and
the Emergence of Racial Identification in Negro Preschool Children." *Journal of Social Psychology* 10(1939): 591.

————. "Emotional Factors in Racial Identification and Preference in Negro
Children." In *Readings in Social Psychology*, ed. T. M. Newcomb and E. L.
Hartley. New York: Holt, 1947.

————. Summary and Integration of Discussion and Conclusions of the July
23, 1954 Conference of Social Scientists. (n.d.). Box 65, folder: "Reargu-
ment, 2nd Social Science Memoranda re. Question IV, April 1955, Conference of Social Scientists to the Legal Division of the NAACP, 23 July 1954."
Kenneth B. Clark Papers, Manuscript Division of the Library of Congress,
Washington, D.C.

Clifford, James. *The Predicament of Culture: Twentieth-Century Ethnography, Literature and Art*. Cambridge: Harvard University Press, 1988.

Cody, Gabrielle. "David Henry Hwang's *M. Butterfly*: Perpetuating the Misogynist Myth." *Theater* 20(spring 1989): 24–7.

Connerton, Paul. *How Societies Remember*. Cambridge, U.K.: Cambridge University Press, 1989.

Conte, Joseph M. *Unending Design: The Forms of Postmodern Poetry*. Ithaca, N.Y.:
Cornell University Press, 1991.

Copjec, Joan. ed. *Supposing the Subject*. New York: Verso, 1994.

Cornell, Drucilla. *Beyond Accommodation: Ethical Feminism, Deconstruction, and
the Law*. New York: Routledge, 1991.

Davis, Kenneth Culp. "An Approach to the Problems of Evidence in the Administrative Process." *Harvard Law Review* 55(1942): 364–425.

De Beauvoir, Simone. *Le Deuxieme Sexe*. Paris: Gallimard, 1949.

De Certeau, Michel. *Heterologies: Discourse on the Other*. Trans. Brian Massumi.
Minneapolis: University of Minnesota Press, 1986.

De Lauretis, Teresa. *The Practice of Love: Lesbian Sexuality and Perverse Desire*.
Bloomington: Indiana University Press, 1994.

————. *Technologies of Gender: Essays on Theory, Film, and Fiction*. Bloomington:
Indiana University Press, 1989.

De Man, Paul. *The Rhetoric of Romanticism*. New York: Columbia University
Press, 1984.

De Maupassant, Guy. *Pierre and Jean, Father and Son, Boitelle and Other Stories*.
New York: Collier, 1911.

De Vos, George A. "Adaptive Strategies in U. S. Minorities." In *Minority Mental
Health*, ed. Enrico Jones and Sheldon Korchin. New York: Praeger, 1982.

De Vries, Hent, and Samuel Weber, eds. *Violence, Identity, and Self-Determination*. Stanford: Stanford University Press, 1997.

Deeney, John J. "Of Monkeys and Butterflies: Transformations in M. H.
Kingston's *Tripmaster Monkey* and D. H. Hwang's *M. Butterfly*." *MELUS* 18,
4(winter 1993): 21–39.

Derrida, Jacques. *The Specters of Marx: The State of Debt, the Work of Mourning
and the New International*. Trans. Peggy Kamuf. New York: Routledge, 1994.

Diagnostic and Statistical Manual of Mental Disorders. Psychoanalytic Manual. 4th ed. Washington, D.C.: American Psychiatric Association, 1994.

Diamond, Elin. "The Violence of 'We': Politicizing Identification." In *Critical Theory and Performance*, ed. Janelle G. Reinelt and Joseph R. Roach. Ann Arbor: University of Michigan Press, 1992.

Dickstein, Morris. "Ralph Ellison, Race, and American Culture." *Raritan* 18(spring 1999): 30–49.

Dietz, Mary. "Citizenship with a Feminist Face: The Problem with Maternal Thinking." *Political Theory* 13, 1(February 1985): 19–37.

Doane, Mary Ann. *Femmes Fatales: Feminism, Film Theory, and Psychoanalysis.* New York: Routledge, 1991.

Doland, Jill. "Geographies of Learning: Theatre Studies, Performance, and the 'Performative.'" *Theatre Journal* 45(1993): 417–41.

———. *Presence and Desire.* Ann Arbor: University of Michigan Press, 1993.

Dolar, Mladen. "Beyond Interpellation." *Qui Parle* 6, 2(spring/summer 1993): 75–96.

Doty, Alexander. "The Queer Aesthete, the Diva, and *The Red Shoes.*" In *Out Takes: Essays on Queer Theory and Film*, ed. Ellis Hanson. Durham, N.C.: Duke University Press, 1999.

Draft of Social Science Statement. (n.d.). Box 63, folder: "Appendix to Appellant's Brief: 'The Effect of Segregation and Consequences of Desegregation: A Social Scientist Statement.' September 22, 1952, Drafts 2/2." Kenneth B. Clark Papers, Manuscript Division of the Library of Congress, Washington, D.C.

Dreger, Ralph Mason, and Kent S. Miller. "Comparative Psychological Studies of Negroes and Whites in the United States." *Psychological Bulletin* 57 57(1960): 361–402.

Dreyer, Carl Theodor. *Four Screen Plays.* Bloomington: Indiana University Press, 1970.

DuBois, W. E. B. *The Souls of Black Folk.* New York: Bantam, 1989.

Dyer, Richard. *Heavenly Bodies.* London: Macmillan, 1986.

———. "Whiteness." *Screen* 29(August 1988): 44–64.

Edelman, Lee. *Homographesis: Essays in Gay Literary and Cultural Theory.* New York: Routledge, 1994.

Ellison, Ralph. *Invisible Man.* New York: Vintage, 1990.

———. *Shadow and Act.* New York: Vinatge, 1953.

Endo, Russell, Stanley Sue, and L. Nathaniel Wagner, eds. *Asian Americans: Social and Psychological Perspectives.* Vol. 2. New York: Science and Behavior Books, Inc. 1980.

Eng, David. "In the Shadows of a Diva: Committing Homosexuality in David Henry Hwang's *M. Butterfly.*" *Amerasia Journal* 20, 1(1994): 93–117.

———. "Managing Masculinity: Race and Psychoanalysis in Asian-American Literature." Ph.D. diss., University of California, Berkeley, 1995.

Eze, Emmanuel Chukwudi, ed. *Race and the Enlightenment: A Reader.* Cambridge, Mass.: Blackwell, 1997.

Fanon, Frantz. *Black Skin, White Masks.* New York: Grove Press, 1967.

Feldstein, Richard, and Judith Root, eds. *Feminism and Psychoanalysis.* Ithaca, N.Y.: Cornell University Press, 1984.

Foucault, Michel. *Technologies of the Self*. Cambridge: University of Massachusetts Press, 1988.

Frankiel, Rita V., ed. *Essential Papers on Object Loss*. New York: New York University Press, 1994.

Freud, Sigmund. *The Standard Edition of the Complete Psychological Works of Sigmund Freud* (SE). Trans. James Strachey. London: Hogarth Press, 1955.

Fung, Richard. "Looking for My Penis: The Exoticized Asian in Gay Video Porn." In *How Do I Look? Queer Film and Videos*, ed. Bad Object Choices. Seattle: Bay Press, 1991.

Fuss, Diana. *Identification Papers*. New York: Routledge, 1995.

Gallop, Jane. *The Daughter's Seduction: Feminism and Psychoanalysis*. New York: Cornell University Press, 1982.

Garber, Marjorie. *Vested Interests*. New York: Routledge, 1992.

Gates, Henry Louis. "Authority, (White) Power and the (Black) Critic: It's All Greek to Me." *Cultural Critique* (fall 1987): 19–46.

———. *Loose Canons: Notes on the Cultural Wars*. New York: Oxford University Press, 1992.

———. "On Authenticity." *New York Times Book Review*, November 24, 1991, section 7.

Geller, Jay. "The Aromatics of Jewish Difference: Benjamin's Allegory of Aura." In *Jews and Other Differences*, ed. Daniel Boyarin and Jonathan Boyarin. Minneapolis: University of Minnesota Press, 1997.

Gennari, John. "'A Weapon for Integration': Frank Marshall Davis and the Politics of Jazz." *Langston Hughes Review* 14(1996): 16–33.

Gilman, Sander L. *Difference and Pathology: Stereotypes of Sexuality, Race and Madness*. Ithaca, N.Y.: Cornell University Press, 1985

———. *Freud, Race, and Gender*. Princeton: Princeton University Press, 1993.

Gilroy, Paul. *The Black Atlantic: Modernity and Double Consciousness*. Cambridge: Harvard University Press, 1993.

Golden, Thelma. ed. *Black Male: Representations of Masculinity in Contemporary American Art*. New York: Whitney Museum of Modern Art, 1994.

Goodman, Walter. "Brown v. Board of Education: Uneven Results Thirty Years Later." *New York Times*. May 17, 1984. B18:1.

Greene, Leonard. "Brouhaha over Barbie Doll Far from Being Just Kids' Stuff." *Boston Herald*, December 20, 1995, 2nd ed.: 10.

Grosz, Elizabeth. *Volatile Bodies: Toward a Corporeal Feminism*. Bloomington: Indiana University Press, 1994.

Gutierrez, David. *Walls and Mirrors: Mexican American, Mexican Immigrants, and the Politics of Ethnicity*. Berkeley: University of California Press, 1995.

Hacker, Andrew. *Two Nations: Black and White, Separate, Hostile, Unequal*. New York: Ballantine Books, 1992.

Hagedorn, Jessica. *Dogeaters*. New York: Pantheon, 1990.

Hall, Kim F. "Beauty and the Beast of Whiteness: Teaching Race and Gender." *Shakespeare Quarterly* 47, 4(winter 1996): 461–75.

Hamacher, Werner. "One 2 Many Multiculturalisms." In *Violence, Identity, and Self-Determination*, ed. Hent De Vries and Samuel Weber. Stanford: Stanford University Press, 1997.

Harasym, Sarah, ed. *The Post-Colonial Critic: Interviews, Strategies, Dialogues.* New York: Routledge, 1990.

Harper, Phillip Brian. "'To Become One and Yet Many': Psychic Fragmentation and Aesthetic Synthesis in Ralph Ellison's *Invisible Man.*" *Black American Forum* 23, 4(winter 1989): 681–700.

Hartman, Saidiya. *Scenes of Subjection: Terror, Slavery, and Self-Making in Nineteenth-Century America.* New York: Oxford University Press, 1997.

Hass, Robert. *Praise.* New York: Ecco, 1979.

———. *Twentieth-Century Pleasures: Prose on Poetry.* New York: Ecco, 1997.

Hawks, Terence, ed. *Textual Practice.* London: Methuen, 1987.

Hing, Bill Ong. *Making and Remaking Asian America through Immigration Policy, 1850–1990.* Stanford: Stanford University Press, 1993.

hooks, bell. *Black Looks: Race and Representation.* Boston: South End Press, 1992.

———. *Yearning: Race, Gender, and Cultural Politics.* Boston: South End Press, 1990.

Horn, Miriam. "The Mesmerizing Power of Racial Myths." *U. S. News and World Report,* March 28, 1988: 52–3.

Hovenkamp, Herbert. "Social Science and Segregation before *Brown.*" *Duke Law Journal* 85(June–September 1985): 624–643.

Howe, Irving. "Black Boys and Native Sons." In *Selected Writings, 1950–1990.* San Diego: Harcourt Brace Jovanovich, 1990.

———. "A Negro in America." In *Celebrations and Attacks: Thirty Years of Literary and Cultural Criticism.* New York: Horizon Press, 1979.

Hurston, Zora Neale. *I Love Myself When I Am Laughing . . . And Then Again When I Am Looking Mean and Impressive.* New York: Feminist Press, 1979.

Hwang, David Henry. *M. Butterfly.* New York: Plume, 1989.

Ignacio, Lemuel F. *Asian Americans and Pacific Islanders (Is There Such an Ethnic Group?)* San Jose, Calif.: Filipino Development Associates, 1976.

Ihara, Saikaku. *Comrade Loves of the Samurai.* Trans. E. Powys Mathers. London: Tuttles, 1972.

Irigaray, Luce. *Ce sexe qui n'en pas un.* Paris: Editions de Minuit, 1977.

Jackson, John P., Jr. "Creating a Consensus: Psychologists, the Supreme Court, and School Desegregation, 1952–55." *Journal of Social Issues* 54, 1(spring 1998): 143–78.

———. "The Transformation of Social Science into Modern Authority in Brown v. Board of Education, 1945–1957." Ph.D. diss. University of Minnesota, 1997. University Microfilm no. 97-15292.

Jackson, Lawrence P. "Ralph Ellison, Sharpies, Rinehart, and Politics in *Invisible Man.*" *Massachusetts Review* (spring 1999): 71–95.

Jackson, Rosemary. *Fantasy: The Literature of Subversion.* London: Macmillan, 1981.

Jacobus, Mary. "'Tea Daddy': Poor Mrs. Klein and the Pencil Shavings." In *Reading Melanie Klein,* ed. Lindsey Stonebridge and John Phillips. London: Routledge, 1999.

Jameson, Frederic. "Third World Literature in the Era of Multinational Capital." *Social Text* 15(fall 1986): 65–88.

JanMohamed, Abdul R., and David Lloyd, eds. *The Nature and Context of Minority Discourse.* New York: Oxford University Press, 1990.

Jelinek, Estelle C., ed. *Women's Autobiography: Essays in Criticism*. Bloomington: Indiana University Press, 1980.

Johnson, Barbara. "'Aesthetic' and 'Rapport' in Toni Morrison's *Sula*." *Textual Practice* 7, 2(summer 1993): 165–72.

———. "No Short Cuts to Democracy." In *Fires in the Mirror: Essays and Teaching Strategies*, ed. Pamela Benson. Boston: WGBH Educational Print and Outreach, 1993.

———. "The Re(a)d and the Black." In *Richard Wright's Native Son*. New York: Chelsea House, 1988.

———. *A World of Difference*. Baltimore: Johns Hopkins University Press, 1987.

Jones, Enrico E., and Sheldon J. Korchin, eds. *Minority Mental Health*. New York: Praeger, 1982.

Jones, Leon. *From Brown to Boston: Desegregation in Education, 1954–1974*. Metuchen, N.J.: The Scarecrow Press, 1979.

Kahane, Claire. "Dark Mirrors: A Feminist Reflection on Holocaust Narrative and the Maternal Metaphor." Work-in-progress. Presented at the Object Relations Group, Berkeley, California, May 7, 1999.

Kamuf, Peggy, ed. *A Derrida Reader: Between Blinds*. New York: Columbia University Press, 1991.

Kardiner, Abraham, and Lionel Ovesey. *The Mark of Oppression: A Psychosocial Study of the American Negro*. New York: Norton, 1951. (Later editions 1961 and 1967, New York: Meridian Books, with subtitle *Explorations on the Personality of the American Negro*.)

Kehde, Suzanne. "Engendering the Imperial Subject: The (De)construction of (Western) Masculinity in David Henry Hwang's *M. Butterfly* and Graham Greene's *The Quiet American*." In *Fictions of Masculinity: Crossing Cultures, Crossing Sexualities*, ed. Pater F. Murphy. New York: New York University Press, 1994.

Kennedy, Adrienne. *People Who Led to My Plays*. New York: Theatre Communications Group, 1988.

Kim, Daniel. "Invisible Desires: Homoerotic Racism and Its Homophobic Critique in Ralph Ellison's *Invisible Man*." *Novel* 30, 3(spring 1997): 309–28.

Kim, Elaine H. "Defining Asian American Realities through Literature." *Cultural Critique* 6(spring 1987): 87–111.

———, ed. *Asian American Literature: An Introduction to the Writings and Their Social Context*. Philadelphia: Temple University Press, 1982.

Kingston, Maxine Hong. *The Woman Warrior: Memoirs of a Girlhood among Ghosts*. New York: Vintage Books, 1976.

Klein, Melanie. *Selected Melanie Klein*, ed. Juliet Mitchell. New York: Free Press, 1986.

Kleinman, Arthur, and Joan Kleinman. "How Bodies Remember: Social Memory and Bodily Experience of Criticism, Resistance and Deligitimation Following China's Cultural Revolution." Talk delivered to the Seminar Series on Remembering and Forgetting, Commonwealth Center for Literary and Cultural Change, University of Virginia, January 27, 1993.

Kluger, Richard. *Simple Justice: The History of Brown v. Board of Education and Black America's Struggle for Equality*. New York: Vintage Books, 1975.

Kristeva, Julia. *The Kristeva Reader*. Ed. Toril Moi. New York: Columbia University Press, 1986.

————. *Soleil noir: dépression et mélancolie.* Paris: Seuil, 1987.

Kurkland, Philip B., and Gerhard Casper, eds. *Landmark Briefs and Arguments of the Supreme Court of the United States: Constitutional Law.* Arlington, Va.: University Publications of America, 1975.

Lacan, Jacques. *The Four Fundamental Concepts of Psychoanalysis.* Trans. A. Sheridan. New York: Norton, 1981.

————. "The Mirror Stage as Formative of the Function of the I as Revealed in the Psychoanalytic Experience." In *Écrits: A Selection*, trans. Alan Sheridan. New York: Norton, 1977.

————. *The Seminars of Jacques Lacan.* Book 1. *Freud's Papers on Technique, 1953–1954.* Trans. John Forrester. New York: Norton, 1988.

————. *The Seminars of Jacques Lacan.* Book 2. *The Ego in Freud's Theory and in the Technique of Psychoanalysis, 1954–1955.* Trans. S. Tomaselli. New York: Norton, 1991.

Laclau, Ernesto. *Politics and Ideology in Marxist Theory: Capitalism, Fascism, Marxism.* London: NLB, 1977.

Lacoue-Labarthe, Philippe. "The Nazi Myth." Trans. Brian Holmes. *Critical Inquiry* 16(winter 1990): 291–312.

————. *Typography: Mimesis, Philosophy, Politics.* Cambridge: Harvard University Press, 1989.

Lambert, Ellen Zetzel. *The Face of Love: Feminism and the Beauty Question.* Boston: Beacon Press, 1995.

Laplanche, Jean. *Seduction, Translation, Drives.* Ed. John Fletcher. Trans. Martin Stanton. London: Institute of Contemporary Arts. 1992.

Laplanche, Jean, and J.-B. Pontalis. "Fantasy and the Origins of Sexuality." In *Formations of Fantasy*, ed. Victor Burgin. New York: Routledge, 1986.

————. *Jean Laplanche: Seduction, Translation, Drives.* Ed. John Fletcher and Martin Stanton. London: Institute of Contemporary Arts, 1992.

————. *The Language of Psycho-Analysis.* Trans. D. Nicholson-Smith. New York: Norton, 1973.

————. *Life and Death in Psychoanalysis.* Trans. J. Mehlman. Baltimore: Johns Hopkins University Press, 1976.

————. *New Foundations for Psychoanalysis* (1987). Trans. David Macey. London: Blackwell, 1989.

————. "To Situate Sublimation." *October* 28(spring 1984): 8–26.

Lasch, Christopher. *The Culture of Narcissism: American Life in an Age of Diminishing Expectations.* New York: Norton, 1979.

Lee, Chang-Rae. *Native Speaker.* New York: Riverhead Books, 1995.

Lee, C. Y. *Flower Drum Song.* New York: Farrar, Straus and Cudahy, 1957.

————. Introduction to *San Francisco Chinatown on Parade: In Picture and Story.* The Chinese Chamber of Commerce, San Francisco, 1966.

Lee, Samuel D. *San Francisco's Chinatown: History, Function, and Importance of Social Organization.* San Francisco: San Francisco Chamber of Commerce, 1951.

Lejeune, Philippe. *On Autobiography.* Minneapolis: University of Minneapolis Press, 1989.

Lepenies, Wolf. *Melancholy and Society.* Trans. Jeremy Gaines and Doris Jones. Cambridge: Harvard University Press, 1992.

Lewis, Barbara, "The Circle of Confusion: A Conversation with Anna Deavere Smith." *Kenyon Review* 15, 4(fall 1993): 54–64.

Lim, Shirley Geok Lin. "Immigration and Diaspora." In *An Inter-ethnic Companion to Asian American Literature*. Cambridge: Cambridge University Press, 1996.

Lloyd, David. "Race Under Representation." *Oxford Literary Review* 1, 2(1991): 28–39.

Lloyd, David, and Abdul JanMohamed. "Minority Literature—What's To Be Done?" *Cultural Critique* 7(fall 1987): 5–18.

Lott, Eric. *Love and Theft: Blackface Minstrelsy and the American Working Class*. New York: Oxford University Press, 1993.

Louie, David Wong. *Pangs of Love*. New York: Plume, 1992.

Lowe, Lisa. *Immigrant Acts: On Asian American Cultural Politics*. Durham, N.C.: Duke University Press, 1996.

Lye, Colleen. "*M. Butterfly* and the Rhetoric of Antiessentialism: Minority Discourse in an International Frame." In *The Ethnic Canon*, ed. David Palumbo-Liu. Minneapolis: University of Minnesota Press, 1995.

Lyons, Charles R., and James C. Lyons. "Anna Deavere Smith: Perspectives on her Performance within the Context of Critical Theory." *Journal of Dramatic Theory and Criticism* 9, 1(fall 1994): 43–66.

McAdoo, Harriette Pipes. "Racial Attitudes and Self-Concept of Young Black Children Over Time." In *Black Children: Social, Educational, and Parental Environment*, ed. Harriette Pipes McAdoo and John Lewis McAdoo. Los Angeles: Sage, 1975.

McIntosh, Tom. "Reflections on Jazz and the Politics of Race." *Boundary 2*, 22(1995): 25–35.

Mann, Thomas. *The Magic Mountain*. New York: Vintage, 1969.

Marchetti, Gina. *Romance and the "Yellow Peril": Race, Sex, and Discursive Strategies in Hollywood Fiction*. Berkeley: University of California Press, 1993.

Marks, Jonathan. "Black, White, Other: Racial Categories Are Cultural Constructs Masquerading as Biology." *Natural History* (December 1994): 33–5.

Martin, Carol. "Anna Deavere Smith: The Word Becomes You: An Interview." *TDR: The Drama Review* 37, 4(winter 1993): 45–62.

Martin, Stephen-Paul. "Theresa Cha: Creating a Feminine Voice." In *Open Form and the Feminine Imagination: The Politics of Reading in Twentieth-Century Innovative Writing*. Washington, D.C.: Maisonneuve Press, 1988.

Maufort, Marc, ed. *Staging Difference: Cultural Pluralism in American Theater and Drama*. New York: Peter Lang, 1995.

Melas, Natalie. "Versions of Incommensurability." *World Literature Today* (spring 1995): 275–80.

Mercer, Kobena. "Fear of a Black Penis." *Artforum* 32, 8(April 1994): 80–3.

Miller, D. A. *Place for Us: Essay on the Broadway Musical*. Cambridge: Harvard University Press, 1998.

———. "The Late Jane Austen." *Raritan* (spring 1990): 55–79.

Mitchell, Juliet. *Psychoanalysis and Feminism: Freud, Reich, Laing and Women*. New York: Vintage, 1974.

Modleski, Tania. "Doing Justice to the Subjects: Mimetic Art in a Multicultural Society: The Work of Anna Deavere Smith." In *Female Subjects in Black and White: Race, Psychoanalysis, Feminism*, ed. Elizabeth Abel, Barbara Christian, and Helene Moglen. Berkeley: University of California Press, 1997.

———. *Loving with a Vengeance: Mass-Produced Fantasies for Women*. New York: Methuen, 1982.

Mohanty, Chandra Talpade, Anne Russo, and Lourdes Torres. *Third World Women and the Politics of Feminism*. Indianapolis: Indiana University Press, 1991.

Monohan, John, and Laurens Walker. *Social Science in Law: Cases and Materials*. Mineola, N.Y.: Foundation Press, 1985.

———. "Social Science Research in Law: A New Paradigm." *American Psychologist* (June 1988): 456–72.

Moon, Michael. *Disseminating Whitman: Revision and Corporeality in* Leaves of Grass. Cambridge: Harvard University Press, 1991.

Mordan, Ethan A. *Rodgers and Hammerstein*. New York: Abrams, 1992.

Morishima, James K. *The Mental Health of Asian Americans*. San Francisco: Jossey-Bass, 1982.

Morrison, Toni. *The Bluest Eye*. New York: Plume, 1994.

———. *Playing in the Dark: Whiteness and the Literary Imagination*. Cambridge: Harvard University Press, 1992.

Moy, James. "Asian American Visibility: Touring Fierce Racial Geographies." In *Staging Difference: Cultural Pluralism in American Theater and Drama*, ed. Marc Maufort. New York: Peter Lang, 1995.

———. *Marginal Sights: Staging the Chinese in America*. Iowa City: University of Iowa Press, 1993.

Muller v. Oregon, 208 U.S. 412 (1908).

Mulvey, Laura. "Visual Pleasure and Narrative Cinema." In *Feminism: An Anthology of Literary Theory and Criticism*, ed. Robyn R. Warhol. New Brunswick, N.J.: Rutgers University Press, 1997.

Murdoch, Iris. *The Soreignty of Good Over Other Concepts: The Leslie Stephen Lecture*. Cambridge, U.K.: Cambridge University Press, 1967).

Murray, Timothy. *Drama Trauma: Specters of Race and Sexuality in Performance, Video and Art*. New York: Routledge, 1997.

Myrdal, Gunnar. *An American Dilemma: The Negro Problem and Modern Democracy*. New York: Harper and Row, 1962.

Nahoun-Grappe, Veronique. "The Beautiful Woman." Trans. Arthur Goldhammer. In *A History of Women: Renaissance and Enlightenment Paradoxes*, ed. Natalie Zeman Davis and Arlette Farges. Cambridge: Harvard University Press, 1993.

Olney, James. ed. *Autobiography: Essays Theoretical and Critical*. Princeton: Princeton University Press, 1980.

Omi, Michael, and Howard Winant. *Racial Formation in the United States: From 1960–1980*. New York: Routledge and Kegan Paul, 1986.

On, Therese. "'Strictly a Female Female': Growing Up with Nancy Kwan." *A. Magazine* 1, 1 (April 30, 1991): 50.

Onishi, Norimitsu. "Merging Identity—A Special Report: New Sense of Race Arises Among Asian Americans." *New York Times*, May 30, 1996. A1:1.

Otto, John S., and Augustus M. Burns. "Black and White Cultural Interaction in the Early Twentieth Century South: Race and Hillbilly Music." *Phylon* 35(1994): 407–17.

Palumbo-Liu, David. *Asian/American: Historical Crossings of a Racial Frontier*. Stanford: Stanford University Press, 1999.

———, ed. *The Ethnic Canon: Histories, Institutions, and Interventions*. Minneapolis: University of Minnesota Press, 1995.

Patterson, Orlando. *The Ordeal of Integration: Progress and Resentment in America's "Racial" Crisis*. New York: Civitas, 1997.

Pellegrini, Ann. *Performance Anxieties: Staging Psychoanalysis, Staging Race*. New York: Routledge, 1997.

Pensky, Max. *Melancholy Dialectics: Walter Benjamin and the Play of Mourning*. Amherst: University of Massachusetts Press, 1993.

Phelan, Peggy. "Performing Talking Cure: Theatre, Lies, and Audiotape." In *Language Machines*, ed. English Institute. New York: Routledge, 1993.

———. *Unmarked: The Politics of Performance*. London: Routledge, 1993.

Porter, Judith R., and Robert E. Washington. "Black Identity and Self-Esteem: A Review of Studies of Black Self-Concept, 1968–1978." *Annual Review of Sociology* 5(1979): 53–74.

Post, Robert, and Michael Rogin, eds. *Race and Representation: Affirmative Action*. New York: Zone Books, 1998.

Powell, Gloria, and Marielle Fuller. "Black Monday's Children: A Study of the Effect of School Desegregation on Self-Concepts of Southern Children." New York: Appleton-Century-Crofts, 1973.

Proshansky, Harold, and Peggy Newton. "The Nature and Meaning of Negro Self-Identity." In *Social Class, Race, and Psychological Development*, ed. Martin Deutsche, Irwin Katz, and Arthur R. Jensen. New York: Holt, Rinehart, and Winston, 1968.

Quinby, Lee. "The Subject of Memoirs: *The Woman Warrior*'s Technology of Ideographic Selfhood." In *De/Colonizing the Subject: The Politics of Gender in Women's Autobiography*, ed. Sidonie Smith and Julia Watson. Minneapolis: University of Minnesota Press, 1992.

Reinelt, Janelle, and Joseph Roach, eds. *Critical Theory and Performance*. Ann Arbor: University of Michigan Press, 1992.

Remen, Kathryn. "The Theatre of Punishment: David Henry Hwang's *M. Butterfly* and Michel Foucault's *Discipline and Punishment*." *Modern Drama* 37(1994): 391–400.

Richards, Sandra L. "Caught in the Act of Social Definition: *On the Road* with Anna Deavere Smith." In *Acting Out: Feminist Performances*, ed. Lynda Hart and Peggy Phelan. Ann Arbor: University of Michigan Press, 1996.

Ridgeway, Cecilia L., and John M. Roberts. "Urban Popular Music and Interaction: A Semantic Relationship." *Ethnomusicology* 20(1976): 233–51.

Rinder, Lawrence R. "The Theme of Displacement in the Art of Theresa Hak Kyung Cha and a Catalogue of the Artist's *Oeuvre*." Master's thesis, Hunter College, City University of New York, 1990.

Rinzler, Paul. "Preliminary Thoughts on Analyzing Musical Integration among Jazz Performers." *Annual Review of Jazz Studies* 4(1988): 153–60.

Roach, Joseph. *Cities of the Dead: Circum-Atlantic Performance*. New York: Columbia University Press, 1996.

Roediger, David R. *The Wages of Whiteness: Race and the Making of the American Working Class*. New York: Verso, 1991.

Rogin, Michael. *Blackface, White Noise: Jewish Immigrants in the Hollywood Melting Pot*. Berkeley: University of California Press, 1996.

———. "Making America Home—Racial Masquerade and Ethnic Assimilation in the Transition to American History." *Journal of American History* 79, 3(December 1992): 1050–1077.

———. "The Two Declarations of American Independence." *Race and Representation*, ed. Robert Post and Michael Rogin. Berkeley: University of California Press, 1999.

Rose, Jacqueline. *The Haunting of Sylvia Plath*. Cambridge: Harvard University Press, 1992.

———. *States of Fantasy*. Oxford: Clarendon Press, 1996.

Ross, Chambers. *The Writing of Melancholy: Modes of Opposition in Early French Modernism*. Chicago: University of Chicago Press, 1993.

Rosenberg, Morris, and Roberta G. Simmons. "Black and White Self-Esteem: The Urban School Child." Washington, D.C.: American Sociological Association, 1972.

Said, Edward. *Orientalism*. New York: Pantheon Books, 1978.

San Francisco Chinatown on Parade: In Picture and Story. San Francisco: The Chinese Chamber of Commerce, San Francisco, 1966.

Santner, Eric L. *Stranded Objects: Mourning, Memory, and Film in Postwar Germany*. Ithaca, N.Y.: Cornell University Press, 1990.

Sarat, Austin. *Race, Law, and Culture: Reflections on Brown v. Board of Education*. New York: Oxford University Press, 1997.

Scarry, Elaine. "Beauty and Its Relation to Justice." Talk given at the Aesthetics and Difference" Conference, University of California, Riverside, October 22, 1998.

———. *The Body in Pain: The Making and Unmaking of the World*. New York: Oxford University Press, 1985.

———. *On Beauty and Being Just*. Princeton: Princeton University Press, 1999.

Schechner, Richard. "Anna Deavare Smith: Acting as Incorporation." *TDR: The Drama Review* 37, 4(winter 1993): 63–64.

Schiesari, Juliana. *The Gendering of Melancholia: Feminism, Psychoanalysis, and the Symbolics of Loss in Renaissance Literature*. Ithaca, N.Y.: Cornell University Press, 1992.

Schor, Naomi. *One Hundred Years of Melancholy*. Oxford: Clarendon Press, 1996.

Scott, Daryl Michael. *Contempt and Pity: Social Policy and the Image of the Damaged Black Psyche, 1880–1996*. Chapel Hill: University of North Carolina Press, 1997.

Scott, Nathan A., Jr. "Ellison's Vision of *Communitas*." *Carleton Miscellany* 18, 3(winter 1980): 41–50.

Senghor, Léopold Sédar. *Oeuvre poétique*. Paris: Seuil, 1964.

Serres, Michel. *The Parasite*. Trans. by Lawrence R. Schehr. Baltimore: Johns Hopkins University Press, 1982.

Shimakawa, Karen. "'Who's to Say?' Or, Making Space for Gender and Ethnicity in *M. Butterfly*." *Theatre Journal* 45, 3(October 1993): 349–62.

Shipler, David A. *A Country of Strangers: Black and White in America*. New York: Knopf, 1997.

Silverman, Kaja. *The Acoustic Mirror: The Female Voice in Psycho-analysis and Cinema*. Bloomington: Indiana University Press, 1988.

———. *Male Subjectivity at the Margins*. New York: Routledge, 1992.

———. "Masochism and Subjectivity." *Framework* 12(1996): 2–9.

———. *The Threshold of the Visible World*. New York: Routledge, 1996.

Simmons, Roberta G. "Blacks and High Self-Esteem: A Puzzle." *Social Psychology* 41(1978): 54–7.

Sitney, P. Adam. *Modernist Montage: The Obscurity of Vision in Cinema and Literature.* New York: Columbia University Press, 1990.

Skloot, Robert. "Breaking the Butterfly: The Politics of David Henry Hwang." *Modern Drama* 33(1990): 59–66.

Smith, Anna Deavere Smith. "Cultural Views: Inside the Political Mimic's Fun-House Mirror." *New York Times*, August 16, 1992, late ed., 2:20.

———. "Defining Identity: Four Voices (George C. Wolf, Angela Davis, Robert Sherman, Ntozake Shange)." *New York Times*, May 24, 1992, late ed., 4:11.

———. *Fires in the Mirror: Crown Heights, Brooklyn and Other Identities.* New York: Anchor Doubleday, 1993.

———, writer and sole performer. (Visual.) *Fires in the Mirror: Crown Heights, Brooklyn and Other Identities.* Dir. George C. Wolf. American Playhouse. Public Broadcasting System. April 28, 1993.

———. Interview by Thulani Davis. *Bomb* 41(fall 1992): 40–3.

———. "Not So Special Vehicles." Speech transcript. *Performing Arts Journal* 50–51(May–September 1995): 77.

———. *Twilight: Los Angeles, 1992. On the Road in Search of an American Character.* New York: Anchor Books, 1994.

———, writer and sole performer. (Visual.) *Twilight: Los Angeles, 1992.* Dir. San Francisco Marines Memorial Theater, April 28, 1993.

Smith, Sidonie, and Julia Watson, eds. *De/Colonizing the Subject: Politics and Gender in Women's Autobiography.* Minneapolis: University of Minnesota Press, 1992.

Social Scientific Argument against Segregation in the Schools. (n.d.), Box 61, folder: "NAACP General Correspondence, 1951–52, 1/6." Kenneth B. Clark Papers, Manuscript Division of the Library of Congress, Washington, D.C.

Sollors, Werner. *Beyond Ethnicity: Consent and Descent in American Culture.* New York: Oxford University Press, 1986.

Sontag, Susan. *On Photography.* Farrar, Straus, Giroux, 1977.

Spencer, M. B., Geraldine K. Brookins, and Walter R. Allen, eds. *Beginnings: The Social and Affective Development of Black Children.* Hillsdale, N.J.: Erlbaum, 1985.

Spillers, Hortense. "Mama's Baby, Papa's Maybe: An American Grammar Book." *Diacritics* 17, 2(summer 1987): 65–81.

———. "'The Permanent Obliquity of an In(pha)llibly Straight': In the Time of the Daughters and the Fathers." In *Changing Our Own Words: Essays on Criticism, Theory, and Writing by Black Women,* ed. Cheryl A. Wall. New Brunswick, N.J.: Rutgers University Press, 1989.

Spivak, Gayatri Chakravorty. *In Other Worlds: Essays in Cultural Politics.* New York: Methuen, 1987.

Stang, Joanne. "Rodgers and Hammerstein's Brand on the Musicals." *New York Times Magazine,* November 30, 1958: 16–8.

Stanley, Robert, and Louise Spence. "Colonialism, Racism, and Representation." Introduction to *Screen* 24, 2(March–April 1983): 2–20.

Steele, Claude M. "Thin Ice: 'Stereotype Threat' and Black College Students." *Atlantic Monthly* 284, 2(August 1999): 44–54.

Stell v. Savannah-Chatham County Board of Education. 220 F Supp. 677 (1963).

Stephens, Michael. *The Dramaturgy of Style: Voice in Short Fiction.* Carbondale: Southern Illinois University Press, 1986.

Stern, Julia A. *The Plight of Feeling: Sympathy and Dissent in the Early American Novel*. Chicago: University of Chicago Press, 1997.

Stewart, Susan. *On Longing: Narratives of the Miniature, the Gigantic, the Souvenir, the Collection*. Durham, N.C.: Duke University Press, 1998.

Sue, Stanley, and James K. Morishima. *The Mental Health of Asian Americans: Contemporary Issues in Identifying and Treating Mental Problems*. San Francisco: Jossey-Bass. 1982.

Sun, Shirley. *Three Generations of Chinese*. Exhibition catalogue. Oakland, Calif.: Oakland Museum, 1973.

Sundquist, Eric. *To Wake the Natioins: Race in the Making of American Literature*. Cambridge: Balknap Press of Harvard University Press, 1993.

Swain v. Charlotte-Mecklenburg Board of Education 402 US 1 (1970).

Tagg, Philip. "Open Letter: 'Black Music,' 'Afro-American Music,' and 'European Music.'" *Popular Music* 8(1989): 285–98.

Takaki, Ronald. *Strangers from a Different Shore: A History of Asian Americans*. New York: Penguin, 1989.

Tate, Claudia. *Psychoanalysis and Black Novels: Desire and the Protocols of Race*. New York: Oxford University Press, 1998.

Taylor, Charles. *Multiculturalism: Examining the Politics of Recognition*. Princeton: Princeton University Press, 1994.

Thernstrom, Stephen, and Abigail Thernstrom. *America in Black and White: One Nation, Indivisible*. New York: Simon and Schuster, 1997.

Trillin. Calvin. "Black or White." *New Yorker*. (April 14, 1986): 62–78.

Trinh, T. Minh-ha. *When the Moon Waxes Red: Representation, Gender, and Cultural Politics*. New York: Routledge, 1991.

———. *Woman, Native, Other: Writing Postcoloniality and Feminism*. Bloomington: Indiana University Press, 1989.

———. "Documentray Is/Not a Name." *October* 52(spring 1990): 76–100.

Tushnet, Mark V. *Making Civil Rights Law: Thurgood Marshall and the Supreme Court, 1936–1961*. New York: Oxford University Press, 1994.

TuSmith, Bonnie. "Literary Trickerism: Maxine Hong Kingston's *The Woman Warrior*." *Literature* 2, 4(1991): 249–59.

van den Haag, Ernest, and Ralph Ross. *The Fabric of Society: An Introduction to the Social Sciences*. New York: Harcourt, 1957.

Waddler, Joyce. *Liaison: The Real Story of the Affair that Inspired M. Butterfly*. New York: Penguin, 1993.

Wald, Priscilla. *Constituting Americans: Cultural Anxiety and Narrative Form*. Durham, N.C.: Duke University Press, 1995.

Walters, Barbara. "'The Strangest Love Story of All': The Real M. Butterfly." ABC 20/20, August 12, 1994. Interview transcript no. 1432-2.

Weber, Sam. "'Between a Human Life and a Word': Benjamin's Excitable Gestures." Paper presented at University of California Humanities Research Institute Conference, University of California, Santa Barbara, April 14, 1997.

Weil, Simone. *Waiting for God*. Trans. Emma Graufurd. New York: Harper and Row, 1951.

Wellman, David. *Portraits of White Racism*. Cambridge, U.K.: Cambridge University Press, 1977.

West, Cornel. *Race Matters*. New York: Vintage Books, 1994.

Whitman, Walt. "Crossing Brooklyn Ferry." In *Norton Anthology of Poetry*, ed. Alexander W. Allison, Herbert Barrows, Caesar R. Blake, Arthur J. Carr, Arthur M. Eastman, and Hubert M. English, Jr. 3rd ed. New York: Norton, 1970.

Wicker, Tom. "In the Nation: The Hard Job Remains." *New York Times*, December 28, 1984. late city final ed., A-1, A-31.

Wilkins, Roger. "White Racism Is Still the Problem." *Washington Post*, December 5, 1990, final ed.

Williams, Patricia. *The Alchemy of Race and Rights: Diary of a Law Professor*. Cambridge: Harvard University Press, 1991.

Winnicott, D. W. *Playing and Reality*. New York: Routledge, 1971.

Wolf, Naomi. *The Beauty Myth: How Images of Beauty Are Used against Women*. New York: Doubleday, 1991.

Wong, Sau-Ling Cynthia. "Autobiography as Guided Chinatown Tour? Maxine Hong Kingston's *The Woman Warrior* and the Chinese-American Autobiographical Controversy." In *Multicultural Autobiography and American Lives*, ed. James Payne. Knoxville: University of Tennessee Press, 1992.

———. *Reading Asian American Literature: From Necessity to Extravagance*. Princeton: Princeton University Press, 1993.

Wong, Shelley Sunn. "Unnaming the Same." In *Writing Self Writing Nation*, ed. Norma Alarcón and Elaine Kim. Berkeley, Calif.: Third Woman Press, 1994.

Wright, Richard. *White Man Listen!* New York: Anchor Books, 1964.

Yamamoto, Hisaye. *Seventeen Syllables and Other Stories*. Latham, N.Y.: Kitchen Table: Women of Color Press, 1988.

Yung, Judy. *Unbound Feet*. Berkeley: University of California Press, 1995.

Zizek, Slavoj. *The Sublime Object of Ideology*. London: Verso, 1989.

———. *The Plague of Fantasies*. London: Verso, 1997.

ACKNOWLEDGMENTS

I am indebted to many for the help they gave as I was writing this book. I would like to thank the University of California for providing an intellectual home for this project and for the series of grants that enabled me to finish this book, including fellowships at the Townsend Center for the Humanities and the Center for the Teaching and Study of American Cultures. My work on the concept of racial melancholia has been refined through exchanges with colleagues and students at the Legacies of Freud Conference sponsored by the Society for the Humanities at Cornell University, the UC Humanities Research Institute, the Race and Psychoanalysis Forum at the Modern Language Association, the Association for the Psychoanalysis of Culture and Society, and the Object Relations Study Group sponsored by the Townsend Center. Excerpts from earlier versions of this book have previously appeared in *The Kenyon Review*, *MELUS*, and the volume *Multiculturalism and Representation*.

My archival research owes a great deal to the expertise of Corliss Lee and Oliver Heyer at the UC Berkeley Library, Stephanie Cannizzo at the UC Berkeley Art Museum, and Barbara Hall and Faye Thompson at the Academy of Motion Picture Arts and Sciences. I also thank Kathleen Croghan, Becky Hsu, Shawna Ryan, and Catherine Sprechter for their invaluable research assistance and their friendships.

At various stages of writing this book, I have relied on the wisdom and kindness of several individuals. Conversations with Leo Bersani, Gregory Blatman, Judith Butler, Ron Choy, Troy Duster, Emory Elliot, Jason Friedman, Catherine Gallagher, Stephen Greenblatt, Saidiya Hartman, Lewis Hyde, Shannon Jackson, Arlene Keizer, Valentina Vavasis, Bill Worthen, and the late William Nestrick have fueled my thinking as well as my imagination. The comments of Ann Banfield, Mitchell Breitwieser, Lee Edelman, and Natalie Melas were crucial in helping me formulate several important revisions. I am especially thankful for the attentive re-readings and steady support of Elizabeth Abel, Robert Hass, Sharon Marcus, and Katherine Snyder. They have been generous with their hearts as well as their ideas. More than anyone, David Miller understood the personal investments underlying my intellectual queries and gave me the courage to welcome the risks in that connection. His capacity to see the world anew has kept my mind fresh through the years of writing this book. I am continuously grateful to him for a regard that has never looked away.

Everyone who has written a book knows the cost of such a process for the person who shares the author's life. I wish to thank my husband Marc Freedman, who was finishing his own book at the time, for his love and patience. He has filled up a space in my life that was not empty until he appeared.

Finally, this book is dedicated to my parents, whose immigrant experience I consider to be part of the origin of this project. Through times when life could not have been easy, they always managed to create a haven for me. They have continued to inspire me with their capacity for change and for joy. I thank my father for reading every word of this manuscript even though its language is outside of his professional expertise, and I am grateful for my mother who understands everything about me that I am still learning.

INDEX

Page references in italics denote illustrations.

interpellation (*continued*)
  definition of, 209n24
  levels of, 159–160
  pleasure and, 52
introjection
  definition of, 219n51
  in ego formation, 75–76
  vs. incorporation, 99, 200n23
  in mourning, 95–97
invalidism, 93
invisibility, 15–17, 127–128, 130
  as disembodiment, 136
  vs. exclusion, 130
  internalization of, 17
Invisible Man (Ellison), 107–108,
    127–137
  on castration, 134, 135
  on freedom, 136–137
  on homophobia, 108
  on incorporation, 179
  on racial invisibility, 15–16, 17
  on sexuality, 127–137, 128–
    129, 136
  on white melancholy, 203n43

Jackson, Jesse, 183
Japanese Americans. *See* Asian
    Americans
Jefferson, Thomas, 11
Jewish Americans, 10, 153,
    214n8
Joan of Arc, 148
Johnson, Barbara, 205n63,
    207n13
Jones, Leon, 5
justice, 210n33

Kamuf, Peggy, 217n31
Kardiner, Abraham, 201n27
Keaton, Buster, 146–147
Kelly, Gene, 31
Kim, Danny, 108, 129
Kim, Elaine, 141, 142, 160
The King and I, 32
King, Rodney, 169

Kingston, Maxine Hong
  on authenticity, 84, 218n47
  The Woman Warrior, 26–27,
    65–102, 161
  bathroom scene, vii–viii,
    18–19, 75–76, 78, 176
  on community, 99–101
  Fa Mu Lan myth, 101, 220–
    221n61
  ghost-free country of, 66–
    67, 82, 88, 94
  on incorporation, 179
  on internalization, 73–74
Kjar, Ruth, 76
Klein, Melanie, 75–76
Kluger, Richard, 19
Korea, history of, 41, 50, 125,
    143, 158–159
Korematsu v. U.S., 22
Koster, Henry, 31
Kuntzel, Theirry, 139
Kwan, Nancy, 32, 39, 56–59,
    210n34, 212n42
  life of, 50–51, 210n34
  photographs of, 47, 48, 49,
    57

Lacan, Jacques, 28, 53, 159, 162
Lacoue-Labarthe, Philippe, 163,
    165–166
language
  Abraham on, 91
  coercion and, 162
  exclusion and, 189
  of grief, ix
Laplanche, Jean, 119–120, 121,
    122, 217n31, 223n22
Larsen, Nella, 105
Lasch, Christopher, 7
Lawrence, D. H., 13
Le Bon, Gustave, 105, 152–153
Lee, C. Y., 31, 34, 38–39
legal recognition, 173–174
liberty, 105
libido, 156, 163